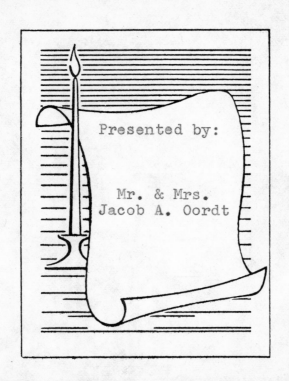

Presented by:

Mr. & Mrs.
Jacob A. Oordt

THE MISSISSIPPI VALLEY FRONTIER

ALSO BY JOHN ANTHONY CARUSO

The Liberators of Mexico
The Appalachian Frontier
The Great Lakes Frontier
The Southern Frontier

THE MISSISSIPPI VALLEY FRONTIER

The Age of French Exploration and Settlement

JOHN ANTHONY CARUSO

Author of the American Frontier Series

Maps by
Neil E. Bolyard

THE BOBBS-MERRILL COMPANY, INC.

A SUBSIDIARY OF HOWARD W. SAMS & CO., INC.

PUBLISHERS · INDIANAPOLIS · NEW YORK · KANSAS CITY

For my wife, Marie

Preface

THIS is the fourth volume of my projected narrative history of the American Frontier. Like the other volumes of this series, it is complete in itself. It is the first of two volumes on the frontier history of the Mississippi Valley; its principal theme is clearly stated in its subtitle: *The Age of French Exploration and Settlement.* The volume develops a feeling for the physical setting as part of the malleable whole by beginning with a description of the Mississippi River. The next six chapters, which furnish the volume with a secondary theme, describe the customs and manners of the principal Indian tribes living on the west bank of the river in frontier times. I have endeavored to describe the Indians as they actually were—human beings with distinct cultures of their own, not as irresponsible and blood-thirsty savages, as they are usually depicted. The ensuing chapters on the explorations of the Mississippi and Missouri valleys are based on primary sources and selected secondary works. Wherever necessary, I have re-evaluated and authenticated my material in accordance with the most recent findings of the best scholars. The concluding chapters of this volume contain accounts of early settlements in present Missouri and a description of Creole society.

Originally I intended to cover the entire frontier history of the Mississippi Valley in a single large volume. But I discovered early in my research that I would need another sizeable volume to give adequate treatment to the magnificent American period. The next volume, based on considerable manuscript material and frontier newspapers and subtitled *The American Territories,* will begin with a background chapter including Anglo-American voyages in the Mississippi Valley during the colonial period and will proceed with chapters on the Louisiana Purchase, Lewis and Clark, Zebulon Pike, the fur companies, and the social, economic, and political development of Orleans, Louisiana, Missouri, Arkansas, Iowa, and Minnesota territories.

The frontier provided the main substance of American history for nearly three centuries. In a very real sense, here is the true history of the American people. The frontier has naturally attracted the attention of many able writers. Nearly all of its aspects and its sections have been described in a seemingly endless stream of books. Yet no single writer has attempted a detailed narrative of the entire American frontier. The textbooks are generally excellent, but they cannot provide space for the details which endow history with life. Theodore Roosevelt's vividly written *The Winning of the West,* published about seventy-five years ago, covers only one of the frontier regions and a part of another. Furthermore, it is badly organized, full of inaccuracies and misinterpretations, sometimes mixed with fiction or legend, and pervaded by an ultra-patriotism fashionable in the nineteenth century but seemingly silly in our sophisticated age. I decided to try to fill a large gap in American history with a series on the frontier from the earliest times to the statehood movements. Though a statehood movement does not necessarily signify the end of frontier conditions, it is for the narrative historian as good a stopping place as any.

The aim of this series is simply to make the American frontier come alive, to try to achieve with history what Joseph Conrad set as his goal for fiction: "My task which I am trying to achieve is, by the power of the written word to make you hear, to make you feel—it is, before all, to make you *see.* That—and no more, and it is everything." Because I seek immediate experience, not intellectual analysis, I naturally use narrative to tell an ordered story and to preserve the color, action, and humanity of history. Not that I eschew analysis, which is often necessary for evaluation of historical events and for clear understanding of their significance or importance. But in this series analysis is either interwoven with event or immediately follows event; it does not stem from a preconceived general theory or hypothesis which tries to provide a scientific explanation for a historical period. Theories of history may be clever or adroit, but I doubt that any of them can comprehend the variables of history to bring us closer to the truth about the past and to help us understand ourselves and our fellow men, as some technical historians claim. History, indeed, is quite wonderful in itself. It can function very well on its own manifold powers; it needs neither a scientific crutch to strengthen it nor pseudo-science to lend it an air of profundity. A work of history is intrinsically profound when it speaks clearly to all mankind; when, as the late George M. Trevelyan said, it makes its appeal to scholar and general reader alike. Technical history, on the contrary, has little or no relevance for mankind. Therefore, it is hailed in one year only to be repudiated in another. The Buckles and Beards go by the board. The Parkmans and Prescotts remain.

The sources of history contain many of the elements found in drama or fiction: narrative, action, color, description, characterization, psychology, and the interplay of human relationships. The neglect of any of these elements really constitutes an inaccuracy. In this respect, Lord Macaulay was quite right in stating that a historical work may be accurate in all of its facts and yet be entirely false in its presentation of a historical age. Even anecdotes, if they are authentic, are remarkably effective in creating interest and in capturing the atmosphere of an age in a way no amount of theory can do. The faithful reconstruction of any phase of the past requires unfaltering dexterity of language. The notion that history must be dull in order to prove its accuracy is nowadays recognized as an academic superstition. History is so rich in every element of life that none of it need be invented. Nevertheless, as one of the humanities, it requires the imaginative appeal of any other form of literature. It can be valuable to mankind only when it helps to solve human problems, when it projects common goals; when, in brief, it serves as a moral force. It can best exemplify these attributes when it is literature or art.

The present volume, like the others in this series, was made possible by the experience, knowledge, and patience of many persons. For many kinds of help I am grateful to Agnes Patton, Virginia Perry, Ethel Gaston, Lorice Boger, Clifford Hamrick, Stokely B. Gribble, Mildred I. Moyers, Elizabeth J. Douglas, Charles Patterson, and Wayne Barrett of the National Geographic Society. I am again endebted to Dr. Robert F. Munn, Director of Libraries, West Virginia University, for his unfailing and generous encouragement, and to Dr. Ruel E. Foster, Professor of English, West Virginia University, for reading some chapters of this book and offering me valuable suggestions. I am grateful to Dr. William T. Doherty, Chairman of the Department of History, West Virginia

University, for reducing my teaching load so that I could devote mornings to my writing, and to Dean Quintus C. Wilson, School of Journalism, West Virginia University, for placing his fine collection of Minnesota books at my disposal.

I herewith offer thanks to the following publishers for permission to reproduce copyrighted material: the Institute of Jesuit History, Loyola University, for quotations from Jean Delanglez, *Hennepin's Description of Louisiana,* and Jean Delanglez, trans. and ed., *The Journal of Jean Cavelier;* the Missouri Historical Society for a quotation from Charles van Ravenswaay, "Arts and Crafts of Upper Louisiana," in its *Bulletin* for April, 1956; Appleton-Century for short quotations from Grace Lee Nute, *The Voyageur,* and Grace Lee Nute, *Caesars of the Wilderness;* Ross & Haines for quotations from A. T. Adams, ed., *The Explorations of Radisson;* the Johns Hopkins Press for a quotation from Edmund Robert Murphy, *Henry de Tonty: Fur Trader of the Mississippi;* the Macmillan Company for selections from Charles Hamilton, ed., *Cry of the Thunderbird;* the University of Oklahoma Press for quotations from Seymour Feiler's translation of Jean-Bernard Bossu, *Travels in the Interior of North America,* John Joseph Mathews, *Wah'-Kon-Tah,* and John Joseph Mathews, *The Osages;* Holt, Rinehart, and Winston for a quotation from Walter Havighurst, *Upper Mississippi* and a quotation from Hodding Carter, *Lower Mississippi;* Corinth Press for a quotation from Henri Joutel, *A Journal of La Salle's Last Voyage;* and E. P. Dutton for songs from J. Murray Gibbon, *Canadian Folk Songs Old and New;* Cornell University Press for quotations from Nellis M. Crouse, *Le Moyne d'Iberville,* and Nellis M. Crouse, *La Vérendrye;* Houghton Mifflin Company for a quotation from Bernard De Voto, *The Course of Empire;* and the Champlain Society of Toronto for quotations from Lawrence J. Burpee, ed., *Journals and Letters of Pierre Gaultier de Varennes de la Vérendrye and His Sons.*

I am grateful to my wife and children for their patience and forbearance while this book was being written. Last but not least I want to thank Lawrence Grow of the Bobbs-Merrill editorial staff for his unfailing kindness, wise counsel, and perspicacious literary guidance in getting this book ready for publication.

JOHN ANTHONY CARUSO

Morgantown, West Virginia

Contents

THE MISSISSIPPI VALLEY FRONTIER

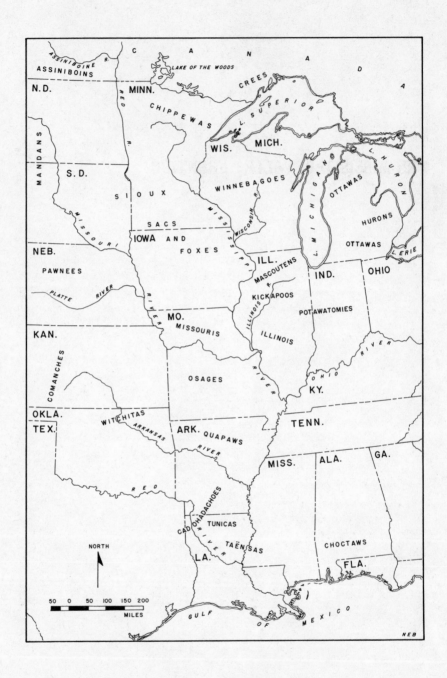

1

The Father of Waters

In THE GLACIER COUNTRY OF NORTHERN MINNESOTA, AMID GROVES OF PINE, swamps of tamarack, and swales of wild celery and wild rice, flutters a timid little stream. Some four inches deep and about ten feet across, it foretells nothing of its significance in the development of a great nation, nothing of its eminence among the rivers of the world. Undeterminedly, almost imperceptibly, it moves from the north end of clear and pine-rimmed Lake Itasca. The American explorer and folklorist Henry Rowe Schoolcraft discovered the lake in 1832 and he named it by coining a word from the last four letters of *veritas,* meaning true, and the first two letters of *caput,* meaning head.[1]

The stream meanders through pine forest and marshland, where the Sioux and the Chippewas roamed in frontier days. For sixty miles it flows northward with increasing speed through pine forests interspersed with birch, balsam, and tamarack. Then it reaches Lake Bemidji, where its broadening course turns eastward toward Lake Superior. But eventually it glides through Lake Cass and Lake Winnibigoshish and bends southward across cutover timberlands. It narrows in rock-bound channels, broadens in swales of wild rice, and drops gradually as it hurries past Grand Rapids and Brainerd. Beyond this town the river meets the Crow Wing from the west, almost doubles its size, and leaps over a series of falls and rapids which suggests the names of such towns as Little Falls and Sauk Rapids and which once culminated in the Falls of St. Anthony at present Minneapolis. Today, walls of concrete restrain its pristine grandeur. By this time the river has dropped nearly nine hundred feet from its source six hundred miles away. Yet its journey has

1

scarcely begun, though it has already flowed a hundred miles farther than the entire length of the Seine and three times as far as the entire length of the Jordan.[2]

The Ojibways or Chippewas called its headwaters Mechesebe, from *meche,* meaning great, and *sebe,* meaning river. French traders and missionaries imaginatively translated this name as Father of Waters and applied it to more of the river. The Indian tribes along the lower river called it Chacaqua, Tamalisieu, Tapatu, or Mico. Hernando de Soto called it Rio Grande de Florida; later, his compatriots called it Escondido, from its numerous bayous, cut-offs, and wandering channels that made it difficult to follow, and Palisado, from the trees and branches that they saw floating in the stream near its mouth. The French called it St. Louis, for the patron saint of Louis XIV; Conception, for the Immaculate Conception of the Blessed Virgin; Baude, for the family name of Governor Frontenac; and Colbert, for the great French statesman.[3] But the most American of all these names is, of course, Mississippi, as we spell it. Despite its sand-barred s's and p's, it is a name which only a great nation can afford. It is a name which, with its meandering syllables, suggests the mighty stream as it flows nearly twenty-five hundred miles from its unpretentious source at Lake Itasca to its awesome mouth at the Gulf of Mexico.

The Upper Valley is rich in legend. Here roamed Manabozho or Winnebojo, the great spirit man of Indian mythology, whom Grace Lee Nute called "the combined Messiah, Puck, Prometheus and Loki of the Chippewa."[4] Like most mythical heroes, his origin and parentage are obscure; he lived with his grandmother, who was a daughter of the moon; and he grew to manhood with such anomalous and contradictory powers of body and mind, of humanity and divinity, that he became the savior of his people. He was a friend of the animals, the protector and legislator of the Chippewas, and the great model or ideal of all their ceremonies, customs, and habits. Henry Wadsworth Longfellow fashioned Hiawatha, the Iroquois hero, in the image of Manabozho and endowed him with some of the powers of his prototype:

> *Skilled in all the crafts of hunters,*
> *Learned in all the lore of old men,*

2

In all youthful sports and pastimes,
In all manly arts and labors.
    Swift of foot was Hiawatha;
He could shoot an arrow from him,
And run forward with such fleetness,
That the arrow fell behind him!
Strong of arm was Hiawatha;
He could shoot ten arrows upward,
Shoot them with such strength and swiftness,
That the tenth had left the bow-string
Ere the first to earth had fallen!

He always adjusted his miraculous powers to circumstances and exerted them in accordance with Indian maxims and means. Swallowed, canoe and all, by Nahma, a great sturgeon, in a story reminiscent of the Biblical Jonah, Manabozho or Hiawatha enlisted the assistance of the squirrel to drag the canoe crossways

Lest from out the jaws of Nahma,
In the turmoil and confusion,
Forth he might be hurled and perish.

Then he killed the sturgeon while his bird friends

Toiled with beak and claws together
Made the rifts and openings wider
In the mighty ribs of Nahma,
And from peril and from prison,
From the body of the sturgeon,
From the perils of the water,
They released my Hiawatha.

Manabozho cleared the earth of monsters and giants and removed all obstacles to the navigation of rivers. This he did by way of miracles performed with the assistance of his animal friends. When he planned to destroy the great serpents, he changed himself into an old tree and stood on the beach until they came out of the water to sun themselves.

3

Once the Great Evil Spirit or water lynx flooded the earth in retaliation for an injury he had sustained at the hands of Manabozho. The hero rescued himself and his grandmother by climbing a great pine on a high headland. When the water began to recede he sent the muskrat and other animals to find the earth. All of them failed except the beaver, which finally succeeded in bringing up some grains of soil on its paws. This enabled Manabozho to restore the earth to its inhabitants. With the assistance of the kingfisher, which had instructed him in the art of camouflage, Manabozho killed the Great Evil Spirit and rewarded his feathered friend by painting him in bright colors.[5]

The Chippewas associated every rock, every field, every stream with some wondrous exploit of their mythical hero. Schoolcraft observed that they made frequent allusions to Manabozho when they traveled in company with each other or with white persons who possessed their confidence. One of Schoolcraft's guides once showed him fragments of rock broken under Manabozho's blows. At another time a young Chippewa, pointing to some huge boulders of greenstone, told him that they were pieces of rock broken off in Manabozho's combat with his father. At still another time, a Chippewa hunter and trapper indicated to him a small island in the Mississippi. "Under that island," he said, "Manabozho lost a beaver."[6]

From the Falls of St. Anthony the Father of Waters flows southward for nearly nine hundred miles through what may be called its Middle Valley to the mouth of the Ohio at Cairo, Illinois. This is a region of towering bluffs, such as Maiden Rock from which the tragic Winona plunged to her death in Lake Pepin; Trempealeau, a conical mountain amid a number of delightful little islands, whose romantic character resembles the Rhine Valley between Bingen and Coblenz; and Piasa, a perpendicular pillar which reminded Giacomo Beltrami, the Italian explorer of Minnesota, so much of the palaces of Pompey and Domitian in the Villa Barberini on Lake Albano that he imagined himself in their midst.[7] The incomparable Mark Twain, who since boyhood knew and loved the magnificent beauty of the region, paid homage to it in some of his most poetic sentences:

The majestic bluffs that overlook the river, along through this region, charm one with the grace and variety of their forms, and the soft beauty

4

of their adornment. The steep, verdant slope, whose base is at the water's edge, is topped by a lofty rampart of broken, turreted rocks, which are exquisitely rich and mellow in color—mainly browns and dull greens, but splashed with other tints. And then you have the shining river, winding here and there and yonder, its sweep interrupted at intervals by clusters of wooded islands threaded by silver channels; and you have glimpses of distant villages, asleep upon capes; and of stealthy rafts slipping along in the shade of the forest walls; and of white steamers vanishing around remote points. And it is all as tranquil and reposeful as dreamland, and has nothing this-worldly about it—nothing to hang a fret or a worry upon.[8]

The river, bearing mute evidence of millions of years of geological development, broadens and narrows, narrows and broadens, and encompasses more than five hundred islands of many sizes. Some are covered with dense cottonwood, maple, and oak forest, some run like links in a chain and are bordered with lotus beds, and some are matted with willow thickets whose lower branches of drifted dead leaves attest to the high water mark of the previous spring. Nourished by many sizeable rivers—including the St. Croix, the Chippewa, the Black, the Root, the Upper Iowa, the Turkey, the Maquoketa, the Wapsipinicon, the Rock, the Cedar-Iowa, and the Skunk—the Mississippi in its Middle Valley is wider, though not deeper, than it is in its Lower Valley. It flows past such busy towns as Red Wing, Winona, La Crosse, Dubuque, Clinton, Davenport, Muscatine, Burlington, Keokuk, Quincy, and Hannibal. Then eighteen miles above St. Louis, the Father of Waters receives the tumultuous Missouri which bears huge masses of driftwood and mud from a thousand prairies as far away as the Rockies. At Cairo it receives the Ohio with its water from twenty-three states and a province of Canada. As Walter Havighurst picturesquely says, the Mississippi "draws the snows from the Big Horns and the Alleghenies into the vast midland valley, until the spring that quenched a Pennsylvania farmer's thirst mingles with the sluice that washed a miner's gravel in Montana."[9] And yet the Middle Mississippi contributes only about two-thirds as much water to the Lower Mississippi as does the Upper Mississippi.[10]

In frontier days settlers from the eastern states, standing on the decks of steamers taking them to their new land of promise, marveled at the beauty of the region and compared its high bluffs to the palisades of

the Hudson. Then came the Germanic immigrants who likened much
of the Middle Valley to the valley of the Rhine. It is a region rich in
history. It moulded the proud destinies of Marquette and Jolliet, Robert
de la Salle, Nicolas Perrot, Pierre Charles Le Sueur, and other explorers
—each of whom we shall meet in his proper time and place. And it was
the region, too, of the Sacs and Foxes and, south of them, of the Osages
who, in defense of their villages, colored the Father of Waters with
their blood.

The Lower Valley of the Father of Waters, which is said to begin at
the mouth of the Ohio and to end at the Gulf of Mexico, has its own
distinct characteristics. Here the Mississippi is a turbid stream of immense volume, well deserving its nicknames of Old Man River, Old
Devil River, and Old Big Strong. For more than a thousand miles it
pursues its devious course, destroying banks and islands at one locality,
reconstructing them at another, and absorbing tributary after tributary
without visible increase in girth, until it is itself absorbed in the Gulf
of Mexico. This is a region of swamps, bayous, and lakes generally
oozing a mass of mud which rests on blue clay from twenty to forty
feet below. On its fertile hummocks grows an endless variety of trees
and flowers. This is the land of the umbrella-shaped cypress, which
thrives on alluvial ground and which raises a straight trunk of from
sixty to eighty feet without a limb before throwing out innumerable
branches with short, fine, tufted leaves of so deep a green that they
appear almost brown. This is the land of the palmetto whose buds often
sustained starving Spanish conquerors and French explorers, and whose
generous leaves roofed the primitive huts of such regional tribes as the
Quapaws, the Caddoes, and the Taënsas. This is the land of the live
oak with its tall, long branches and its luxurious foliage rivaling that of
the northern elm. And this is the land of the magnolia: tall, sensitive, and
graceful, with showy and fragrant pink and white blossoms, bark as
light as that of the beech, and glossy leaves like those of the orange.
Mississippi, on whose alluvial bottoms it thrives, has chosen the magnolia as her state flower.

In its Lower Valley the Mississippi flows with a gradient of only a
few inches a mile through a flood plain ranging from fifty to a hundred

miles wide. Every year it carries down and empties into the Gulf of Mexico about four hundred million tons of mud. To transport it by rail would require five hundred trains, each of fifty cars hauling fifty tons in each car every day for a full year. Here the river is only a little more than half of what its width is above Cairo, though it is much deeper and more turbid. Cutting like a rapier into its banks, it creates loops or "oxbows" and horseshoe curves "so deep," wrote Mark Twain, "that in some places if you were to get ashore at one extremity of the horseshoe and walk across the neck, half or three-quarters of a mile, you could sit down and rest a couple of hours while your steamer was coming around the long elbow at a speed of ten miles an hour to take you on board again."[11] During high flood the river may jump through one of the oxbows, creating crescent-shaped lakes or bayous and straightening itself by as much as thirty miles. Twain observed that these "cut-offs," as they are often called,

> have had curious effects: they have thrown several river towns out into the rural districts, and built up sand-bars and forests in front of them. The town of Delta used to be three miles below Vicksburg; a recent cut-off has radically changed the position, and Delta is now *two miles above* Vicksburg.[12]

Twain describes how the Father of Waters had, on a number of occasions in frontier days, shortened itself considerably by what he called "this ditching business":

> Once there was a neck opposite Port Hudson, Louisiana, which was only half a mile across its narrowest place. You could walk across there in fifteen minutes; but if you made the journey around the cape on a raft, you traveled thirty-five miles to accomplish the same thing. In 1722 the river darted through that neck, deserted its old bed, and thus shortened itself thirty-five miles. In the same way it shortened itself twenty-five miles at Black Hawk Point in 1699. Below Red River Landing, Raccouri cut-off was made (forty or fifty years ago, I think). This shortened the river twenty-eight miles. In our day, if you travel by river from the southernmost of these three cut-offs to the northernmost, you go only seventy miles. To do the same thing a hundred and seventy-six years ago, one had to go a hundred and fifty-eight miles—a shortening of eighty-eight miles in that

7

trifling distance. At some forgotten time in the past, cut-offs were made above Vidalia, Louisiana, at Island 92, at Island 84, and at Hale's Point. These shortened the river, in the aggregate, seventy-seven miles.[13]

He computed that the river in the Lower Valley had been twelve hundred and fifteen miles long in 1699, eleven hundred and eighty in 1722, and one thousand and forty miles in the middle of the nineteenth century. On the basis of these computations, he facetiously observed that, in the distant future, the Lower Mississippi would shorten itself out of existence:

> In the space of one hundred and seventy-six years the Lower Mississippi has shortened itself two hundred and forty-two miles. This is an average of a trifle over one mile and a third per year. Therefore, any calm person, who is not blind or idiotic, can see that in the Old Oölitic Silurian Period, just a million years ago next November, the Lower Mississippi was upward of one million three hundred thousand miles long, and stuck out over the Gulf of Mexico like a fishing-rod. And by the same token any person can see that seven hundred and forty-two years from now the Lower Mississippi will be only a mile and three-quarters long, and Cairo and New Orleans will have joined their streets together, and be plodding comfortably along under a single mayor and a mutual board of aldermen. There is something fascinating about science. One gets such wholesale returns of conjecture out of such a trifling investment of fact.[14]

Hodding Carter, who has written beautifully of the Lower Mississippi, states that its charm is not readily discernible to the casual observer, who is aware only of its swift current, its mud, which gives it an unpleasant color, and its occasional bluffs which, together with its concrete mattresses and emergency spillways, restrain its seasonal rampages. Its monotonous expanse of tangled flatness has inspired no epic poem. Carter, who has spent most of his life on or near the river, believes that the Lower Valley appeals to the geographer, historian, and engineer, rather than to the poet. To the people of the Lower Valley, he writes, the river has brought identification and meaning, though their cultures are too diversified and complex to allow it to give them uniformity. But it has beauty, though this is revealed only to those who know the Lower Valley well and have caught its every mood:

8

Some say that beauty ends where the blueness of the Ohio is drowned at Cairo in the green and yellow and brown of its merging. But have they seen the Mississippi at Natchez, tawny in the sunset, its river sky of crimson and indigo and gold plummeting from the bluffs to the flat green land beyond its western banks? Have they watched from the levee the lights of barge and showboat, so yellow in the thick, whispering night? In the fury of a storm in the South Pass, the whitecaps rise so high that you cannot see the reedy rim of land across the river; only angry water and a grey sky from which the heron and pelican have vanished. And there is humbling beauty in this unity of wild water and wild heaven. In the fall we hunt the deer in the swampy forests between the river and the levees. Go quietly at dawn into those brakes of cypress and cane and cottonwood and water oak. Paddle beside the banks of the Lower Mississippi's bayous and false lakes which once were part of its channel. You will find something of what the Spaniard, the Frenchman, and the Englishman swore and marveled at: the disordered lavishness of a wilderness sprung from the earth droppings of a river's uncounted years.[15]

2

Sioux Manners and Customs

THE FIRST WHITE MEN IN THE UPPER VALLEY FOUND TWO LEADING INDIAN tribes: the Sioux and the Chippewas. The Sioux, who called themselves the Dakotas, were a tall, sturdy, proud, fierce, and warlike people. Four of their seven tribes or "council fires" lived in present Minnesota, which in their language meant "the land of the sky-blue waters." At one time they made their homes on either bank of the Mississippi, but they were destined to give them up to the Chippewas, a short, stocky, and strong tribe of Algonkian stock who invaded Minnesota from the country north of Lake Superior. Availing themselves of the superior arms they had obtained from French traders, the Chippewas pushed the Sioux back to Sandy, Leech, and Red lakes. A hundred years later, about the middle of the eighteenth century, the Chippewas drove the Sioux out of their forest homes at Sandy Lake and Mille Lacs to the country west of the Mississippi and south of the Crow Wing rivers. So the Sioux became a prairie people, while the Chippewas won for themselves a wonderful country of lakes, rivers, and forests.[1]

American editors and authors of the East have subjected these tribes to a great many misconceptions. Walter S. Campbell categorized these in a brilliant essay. He stated that many white men, seeking assurance of their own superiority and, conversely, of the Indian's inability to govern himself, fashioned him in the image of Hiawatha. They saw him as a child of nature—a simple, guileless creature in close rapport with nature and wild animals. Like other misconceptions, this one held a few grains of truth, but it failed to explain how the Indian created his own culture and defended it heroically against overwhelming odds.[2]

11

A similar misconception, which Campbell called as old as the Garden of Eden, was that of the Indian as a noble savage. Overlapping the notion of the Indian as a child of nature, this one was more virile and sublime. It promised material benefits through alliance with him. It was popularized by classical poets of the Gilded Age and by Jean-Jacques Rousseau, François Chateaubriand, and James Fenimore Cooper. Inspired by man's conviction that the world was getting worse, it engendered much nostalgia for the good old days when the world was ruled by heroes and demi-gods.[3]

Quite different was the average frontiersman's conception of the Indian. Living apart from him and therefore knowing him only superficially, he pictured the Indian as a lazy beggar or a filthy drunkard who hung around white settlements, whining, wheedling, scheming, and lying for the purpose of gaining good will and support. Mark Twain entertained such a notion. Knowing only a few indigent Indians, he contemptuously dismissed Cooper's conception of the noble savage and believed, as did Will Rogers, that all he knew was what he read in the newspapers.[4]

Another fallacy was that the Indians were descendants of the lost tribe of Israel. Emanating from people who derived their only knowledge from the Bible, this theory might have been a great boon to the Indians. Unfortunately for them, it made little headway with the frontiersmen. Many of them were either too ignorant to know or not religious enough to care whether the Indians were chosen people or not.[5]

A more popular misconception among the whites was that of the Indians as a vanishing race. This flattered them into believing that God was removing the Indian from their path in order to prepare for their own eventual acquisition of the continent.[6]

To such writers of western themes as Ned Buntline and Buffalo Bill, the Indian was a kind of red devil of the plains. He was "a cruel and hideous monster, thirsting for the blood of innocent white men." This rationalization enabled the conquering race to justify their invasion of Indian lands. And it made possible the success of the dime novel with its unerring rifle, Old Hawk-Eye or Diamond Dick, and its Wild West Show. "A few honest souls," wrote Campbell, "openly admitted that they wanted the Indian lands and intended to take them for that reason."[7]

Yet the frontiersman owed much of his success to the Indian he conquered. Without the Indian the history of the United States, and indeed of the world, would have been quite different. The exploration and the occupation of the United States were everywhere facilitated by Indian guides who knew the trails, portages, and watercourses which their people had used for centuries. The pioneers marched westward on Indian trails, particularly those along the ridges and through mountain gaps. Frederick Jackson Turner paid tribute to the importance of buffalo trails:

> The buffalo trail became the Indian trail, and this became the trader's "trace"; the trails widened into roads, and the roads into turnpikes, and these in turn were transformed into railroads . . . . The trading posts reached by these trails were on the sites of Indian villages which had been placed in positions suggested by nature; and these trading posts, situated so as to command the water systems of the country, have grown into such cities as Albany, Pittsburgh, Detroit, Chicago, St. Louis, Council Bluffs, and Kansas City.[8]

The Indians made distinct contributions to American civilization in agriculture, sports, dress, and language. As they advanced toward civilization they discovered the advantages of controlling wild plants and of breeding them by seed selection. Along with this contribution the Indians passed on to the pioneers the sports of canoeing, tobogganing, snowshoeing, lacrosse, and the less strenuous diversion of reclining in hammocks. Important, too, were his ideas and devices for hunting and fishing, such as catching fish by torchlight and wires, calling moose, and the technique of trailing and capturing larger game and wild animals. Major Henry Hopkins Sibley may have derived his Sibley tent from the Chippewas. The sleeping bag may be derived from the war moss bag of the Athapascan. Leather pantaloons, hunting shirts, leggings, and deerskin moccasins were all part of pioneer attire. And all of these articles of clothing were eloquent of their indebtedness to the race they conquered. Many of our towns, cities, and states bear proud Indian names. And we have enriched our language with the daily usage of many Indian words or phrases: brave, firewater, Great White Father, Great Spirit, happy hunting ground, medicine man, paleface, squaw man, bury the hatchet, smoke the peace pipe, warpath, and war paint.[9]

13

Toward the middle of the seventeenth century the Sioux were living among the Winnebagoes west of Green Bay. But a little later they were reported to the missionaries as situated some eighteen days' journey north and west of Sault Ste. Marie. They were always warlike and fierce. The French explorer and fur trader Nicolas Perrot, who in 1686 built Fort St. Antoine near the present site of Trempealeau, Wisconsin, found them on the point of going to war against the Foxes around Green Bay. Realizing that such a conflict would disrupt the fur trade, he summoned the chiefs and tried to frighten them into remaining peaceful by telling them that the Miamis, Foxes, Illinois, Mascoutens, and Kickapoos had formed an army of four thousand men to fight against them. This torrent, he said, would sweep them away. Why not return to their families and hunt beavers for him? They replied haughtily that they had left their homes to fight their enemies and that they would not have to travel far to find them. Perrot then adopted another device in his determination to dissuade them from their avowed purpose. "I desire you to live," he told them, "but I am sure you will be defeated. . . . What I have told you is true, for I really have kept back the tribes, who have obeyed me. But now you are intending to advance against them; the road that you would take I close to you, my brothers, for I am not willing that it should be stained with blood. If you kill the [Foxes] or their allies, you cannot do so without first striking me; if they slay you, they likewise slay me; for I hold them under one of my arms, and you under the other. Can you then do them any wrong without doing it to me?" So saying, he presented them with the calumet they had once given him. They refused it.

This insult was more than he could bear. Flinging the peace pipe at their feet, he said: "It must be that I have accepted a calumet which dogs have sung to me, and that they no longer remember what they said to me. In singing it to me, they chose me as their chief, and promised me that they would never make any advance against their enemies when I presented it to them; and yet today they are trying to kill me." These words had the desired effect. The chief rose and assured him that he would command his men to lay down their weapons. He picked up the calumet and hung it on a pole toward the sun in an open place inside the fort. Then he obtained from his headmen a promise that they would make no hostile advance against the Foxes and their allies. Sending for

14

the peace pipe, he placed it before Perrot, one end in the earth and the other held upright by a small forked stick. He removed Perrot's shoes and replaced them with a pair of beautifully made moccasins. Finally, he presented him with a dish of dried grapes and placed some of them in his mouth. "I remember," he said, "all that these men promised to thee when they presented to thee this calumet; and now we listen to thee. Thou art depriving us of the prey that the Spirit had given us, and thou art giving life to our enemies. Now do for us what thou hast done for them, and prevent them from slaying us when we are dispersed to hunt for beaver, which we are going to do. The sun is our witness that we obey thee."[10] They kept their promise for several years.

The Sioux tempered their aggressiveness with common sense. Close observers of human nature, they quickly discerned the true character of their most casual acquaintances. They soon discovered the strong points of a white man with whom they were dealing, and they commonly knew a great deal more about him than he did of them. They were very sensitive to ridicule and dreaded to appear in a ludicrous light. They were sometimes displeased by visits from white men who asked impertinent questions and scanned their clothing and furniture too closely. They were courteous as long as the white men were present, but they spoke ill of them after they were gone. The men seldom talked to each other in loud, angry tones, even when they were angry. When deadly enemies met they often conversed as pleasantly as though they had been the warmest of friends. They uttered their threats, even when they intended to carry them out, in a low voice and in ambiguous terms, saying much less than they meant. Their loudest threats were intended to alarm white men and children.[11]

The women sometimes fought each other with their hands, pulling hair and tearing garments. But the men nearly always used deadly weapons in their quarrels. Angry scuffles and fisticuffs were hardly known among them. A sober Indian seldom struck his antagonist unless he intended to kill him. The men showed their anger only when they were greatly enraged. A salutary fear of the knife, which was always at hand, doubtless made them more respectful and courteous in their deportment toward each other than they would have been otherwise. Nevertheless, they did not always suppress their violent emotions, which

15

they often expressed with eloquence and gesticulation. The women fought with what has always been the most efficacious weapons of their sex, namely tears and tongue, which they knew how to use as well as any American virago.[12]

The Sioux lived in two kinds of homes: the bark-covered hut or lodge, and the skin-covered tipi. In summer they lived in their lodges. The side posts of a lodge were five or six feet long and one or two feet apart. These supported poles that ran to the ridgepole, which rested front and back on longer and forked posts securely tied with basswood bark. The lodge was covered with bark cut from standing green elm trees. Each piece of bark was five or six feet long and of varied width. The lodge had one or two doors, depending on its size. Running the full length of each side of the interior were benches that were about two feet high and about five or six feet wide. Covered with bark or with buffalo robes and mats, these benches served as chairs, tables, and beds.[13]

Most of the work on either a lodge or a tipi was done by women. E. D. Neill has given us a vivid picture of a Sioux woman building a tipi, in which her people lived in autumn and winter, when they were hunting:

> Arriving late in the afternoon at the appointed camping ground, she clears off the snow from the spot upon which she is to erect the [tipi]. She then, from the nearest marsh or grove, cuts down some poles about ten feet in length. With these she forms a frame work for the tent. Unstrapping her pack, she unfolds the tent cover, which is seven or eight buffalo skins stitched together, and brings the bottom part to the base of the frame. She now obtains a long pole, and fastening it to the skin covering, she raises it. The ends are drawn around the frame until they meet, and the edges of the covering are secured by wooden skewers or tent pins. The poles are then spread out on the ground, so as to make as large a circle inside as she desires. Then she or her children, proceed to draw the skins down so as to make them fit tightly. An opening is left where the poles meet at the top, to allow the smoke to escape.[14]

The tipi was built to face the morning sun, but it was so well ventilated that it remained comfortable all day long. It usually stood on elevated ground near a river or creek to protect it from heavy or prolonged rain or flash floods caused by rain higher in the valley.[15] On the ground in the

16

center of the tipi blazed a large fire around which from seven to fifteen persons could sleep through the winter night "with far more comfort than a child of luxury upon a bed of down."[16]

The Sioux lived largely by hunting and fishing. Occasionally they raised a small vegetable crop, usually corn, that barely sufficed to last them for a few days. The women performed most of the agricultural work. They chose a sizeable field where a steady growth of wild artichokes, which they called *panghai*, indicated rich and mellow ground. They covered it with conical little mounds. The presence of ripe strawberries announced to them the arrival of planting time. They soaked their seed corn until it sprouted. Then they planted it deep in the soil with their hands. As soon as it showed three or four leaves they loosened the earth around it with their fingers. When it was tall enough they hilled it up thoroughly with their wooden hoes. They usually planted a kind of small corn, though they were acquainted with a larger kind and could have raised good crops.[17] In each field stood a watchtower from which women and children scared off flocks of blackbirds or red-winged blackbirds. When they saw the birds approaching the watchers uttered a kind of cry until they succeeded in scaring the birds away.[18]

In times of great scarcity they relied heavily on the fruits and esculent roots which were indigenous to their region and which suited their uncultivated taste. They were especially fond of red plums which grew on small bushes here and there on the banks of many of the rivers. These were dried and laid up for the rough months ahead. Or they sought chokeberries, which grew on low bushes in great quantities along the shores of Minnesota's innumerable lakes.[19]

Among their favorite roots was the prairie turnip, which they called *teesenah* and which grew everywhere on the high plain. Collected in large quantities for winter use, it was eaten raw or boiled. Sometimes they dried and pulverized it into a tolerable substitute for flour. In any form, it supported life for several months in the absence of meat.[20] Another root was the *psinchincha*, which resembled and was half as large as a hen's egg. Still another root, the *psincha*, was spherical and about an inch in diameter. Both roots grew at the bottom of shallow lakes or marshy ground. The women, wading in water up to their waists, felt for the *psinchincha* with their feet, detaching it from the mud and gathering it eagerly when it rose to the surface. But the *psincha* did not

17

float. They had to raise it with their feet until they could reach it with their hands. This was a difficult operation which required much dexterity where the water rose to their arms. They also searched for the *mdo*, the root of a slender vine which coiled around weeds and which resembled our sweet potato. When it was ripe enough it was delicious, but it was not very plentiful.[21]

They hunted a great variety of animals. Among their prey were buffalo, elk, black-tail deer, white-tail deer, big-horn, antelope, wolves of several kinds, red and grey foxes, beaver, otter, grizzly bear, badger, skunk, porcupine, hare, rabbit, muskrat, and panther. The buffalo provided them with leggings, shirts and skirts, and moccasins. They used every part of the animal as food, save the horns, hoofs, and hair. Even the hide sustained them during trying occasions. They used the skin to roof their lodges and to make their clothes, the sinews for bow strings, and the horns to hold their powder. They fashioned the bones into dressing tools or pounded them up for their marrow. When the hair was seasonable, from the first of October to the first of March, they preserved it as they dressed the skins, which they wore themselves or exchanged with white traders for various necessities.[22]

The white men introduced them to a new and improved garb. The women began to wear coats of printed cotton cloth. The coat had a low neck, tight sleeves, and an open bottom. Its skirt, made of a single piece of blue broadcloth, was lapped and partly sewn together, supported a girdle at the waist, and had an outer and an inner fold of unequal lengths. It could be shortened or lengthened, as occasion required, by changing the length of the outer fold, which usually reached halfway between the knee and the ankle. The wearer shortened it when she walked in deep snow or through grass and bushes.[23]

The woman's leggings were usually made of red or blue broadcloth. This garment reached from the knee to the ankle, was fastened at the upper end with garters, and was tucked at the lower end into the moccasins.

Sioux women wore no headgear save the blanket. In winter some wore woolen coats, or more than one cotton coat. But both women and girls chopped wood in the coldest weather without mittens and with nothing on their arms and shoulders save for one thickness of cotton cloth. Blankets, however, were either fastened to their waists or lay

18

near by, ready to be wrapped around them as soon as they had chopped as much wood as they could carry.[24]

They showed good taste in selecting and wearing ornaments. When they wore many beads they arranged them in strings of different lengths so that they could cover their throats and breasts. They wore very little paint. Young girls put a little vermilion on the top of their heads, where their hair was parted, and painted a small red spot on each cheek with the end of their fingers.[25]

The men wore heavy coarse wool blankets. They were usually white, but some were green, red, or blue. For hunting they preferred white blankets, which, they believed, animals feared less than those of other colors.[26]

When they traveled in cold weather they wore buffalo skins. The old and feeble wore blankets of deerskin with the hair on because they were warmer than clothes and lighter than buffalo robes.[27]

In summer they preferred cotton shirts. In winter they wore blanket coats over these shirts. In the absence of buttons, the coats were fastened with a piece or two of reed or wire. Their winter buckskin leggings were nearly as long as their legs. The lower end of each legging fitted the top of the moccasin and fastened under it. The moccasins were often decorated with porcupine quills, beads, and ribbons. The breechcloth, which men wore over their loins, was made of blue wool. About a foot wide and three or four feet long, it passed between the legs and fell like an apron about a foot before and behind. The men cut off their hair across the forehead a little above their eyes, leaving the rest long. Some had naturally curly hair. The young men usually wore their hair in two braids and decorated them with small metal ornaments which sometimes hung down on each side of the face. They carried small mirrors, obtained from French traders, in which they admired themselves while they daubed their faces with paint. The girls were told that they would be ruined if they dared look in mirrors. They warded off such disaster by using other reflectors. The young men spent much time braiding their hair and painting their faces with various kinds of paints. The older men seldom braided their hair, which they kept confined with a band tied around their heads. Young men often wore such unseemly ornaments as skunk or fox skins around their ankles.[28]

Like other Indian tribes, the Sioux believed that the whites reared

19

their children unwisely. They thought that white children were coddled like pets or fragile toys, which made them the objects of competition, quarreling, restraint, bribing, and punishment. The children of such treatment could only grow up dependent, immature, irresponsible, and confused. The Indians were not surprised that white children harbored much resentment toward their parents and that, when they attained adult wills and appetites, they became potential enemies of society.[29]

The Sioux, therefore, refrained from overprotecting their children and from favoring any of them. In accordance with tribal custom, they provided each child with a second father and mother, who were usually friends or close relatives. The second mother taught a child never to shame its blood mother by displeasing her in any way. And the second father, selected for his excellence in hunting, fighting, horse-catching, and religious fervor, imparted to the boy the discipline, experience, and responsibility necessary for successful adult life. He also taught the boy how to walk behind his father, how to cling to the rawhide strings on his breechcloth, and how to mount a tame old horse by climbing up its foreleg as though it were a tree. After he was seven years old he never again addressed his blood mother or sister directly. Instead he spoke to her through a third person. The second father prepared him for manhood by escorting him to some far barren hill, stripping him to his breechcloth and moccasins, and leaving him there, under the scorching sun and in chilling darkness, without food and water. This ordeal purged the boy of all superficiality and mundane desire, and prepared him to dream of the Great Spirit. By the third or fourth day he dreamed. He was then brought down, gaunt and weak, from the hill, and gradually given food and drink until he was replete. Meanwhile the second father and holy men tried to interpret his dream or vision, which was to guide him for the rest of his life.[30]

Henceforth he performed his duty in conformity with the interpretation of his dream. He protected and defended his mother and father, his brothers and sisters, his hunting grounds; he helped with meat and with the increase and care of the horse herds; he brought no discredit to his good name. As he grew older his bow became larger and he no longer pointed his arrows at a stationary target. He killed muskrat, then deer, then bear, then buffalo. Before long he announced to his friends that he wished to marry. In accordance with custom, he requested them to

furnish him with a wedding suit. Then he obtained a wife, not by court-
ship but by purchase. The early settlers of Virginia purchased their wives
from the London Company, sometimes for as much as one hundred and
twenty or one hundred and fifty pounds of tobacco. A young Sioux paid a
higher price for his wife, perhaps as much as he paid for a horse or four
or five guns or six or eight blankets. To be bought as a wife was no disgrace. The higher the price paid for her the better was she pleased, for
this proved that she was considered valuable.[31]

The young man consulted with his wife-to-be, heeding her pref-
erences in making arrangements for their marriage. But sometimes her
parents compelled her to marry a man she disliked, employing the kind
of threats or arguments used by the whites. Since the Indians never
treated their children harshly, they saw the futility of trying to drive a
spirited girl to extremes. She might elope with one who was unable to
protect her; or, if she found no other way of escape, she might kill herself, as did Winona, who plunged into Lake Pepin because her father
forbade her to marry the man she loved and because she could not accept the man her father had chosen for her. Suicide happened often
enough to serve as a salutary warning to those who had young women
of marriageable age.[32]

Most young women of the tribe were willing to marry men with
whom they had little acquaintance, provided they liked them and knew
them to have good reputations. They really had little or nothing to do
with selecting their husbands, though their parents always complained
of their fickleness. Usually a brother gave his sister away in marriage.
If she had no brother or no brother of suitable age, her parents or other
relatives made the marriage contract. Though no Sioux ever paid so
much for his wife as Jacob paid for Rachel, he usually paid higher
prices than he could afford without the aid of his friends.[33]

The kind of property he offered for his wife usually included horses,
guns, cloth, and kettles. If he had no property of his own he solicited
contributions from his friends. Then he gathered and carried all this
property to the residence of the girl he wished to buy. If she accepted
what he had to offer she completed the bargain and married him without
further ceremony. If he were a young man he could not look his wife's
parents in the face, speak their names, or address them in conversation.
If he had something to communicate to them, he used the plural instead

of the singular form. If he spoke of them, he used the third instead of the second person. Parents and wives also observed this custom in speaking of their in-laws. Of course this whimsical prohibition resulted in better relations between mothers-in-law and sons-in-law than those existing in civilized countries; but unfortunately it extended to such a large circle of relatives that none of them would supply the name of another if he were asked to do so.[34]

Some of the influential or affluent Sioux had more than one wife. In view of woman's unneutral attitude toward those of her sex, no man was surprised at her constant feuding, especially when a man was involved. So any wise man who took more than one wife tried to marry sisters because they were less likely to quarrel than were women between whom no ties of blood existed. Only realization of the assistance that several wives could render each other during hunting expeditions reconciled the Sioux to the practice of polygamy. Husband and wife were never demonstrative of their affection, though they often were attached to one another. The attachment was sometimes short-lived. A husband would separate from his wife, only to return to her after a short absence. Sometimes a husband left his wife, not because he was dissatisfied with her, but because he disliked her relatives or because, if he belonged to a different village than she did, he became homesick.[35] They were strongly attached to their children. They had a saying among them that a mother was with her children whenever they thought of her, and that she felt a pain in her breast whenever anything serious happened to them.

The Sioux were pantheists. They believed that a spirit lived in every stick, every stone, every leaf, every shrub, and that the visible as well as the invisible world was an immense temple of spirits that played their torments upon mankind. Yet they were not idolators. For they worshiped, not the image itself but its spiritual essence. This system of giving a spiritual essence to every manifestation of nature, whether animate or inanimate, prevailed among all the Indians of both South and North America.[36]

The Sioux believed that most of their gods delighted in making them miserable or in destroying them. James W. Lynd described all their divinities, save Getci Munito or the Great Spirit, as doers of evil deeds and as workers in the night:

When the hail has destroyed all their crops and famine is upon them; when, in the deep snows of winter, the buffaloes, thick around their lodges, are seized with a sudden panic, and run for days with their noses in the wind, rendering it impossible to follow; when a whole camp is struck down by some epidemic, and fear and dread are in their midst: then it is that the Genii delight to torture and pursue, to pull, wrack, tear, and rend them with all sorts of tricks and inventions, till their wrath is appeased or the people can escape. The ubiquitous Unktomi tortures them in their hunger by bringing herds of buffaloes near the camp, which they no sooner start to pursue than he drives away by means of a black wolf and a white crow; Cantidan draws the hungry hunters to the depths of the wood by imitating the voices of the animals, or by the nefarious "cico! cico!" when he scares them out of their senses by showing himself to them; and the vindictive I'ya drives them back from the hunt to the desolation of their own lodges.[37]

The chief man god of the Sioux was Wakantanka. But he was a kind of heartless god who, having created the world, lost interest in it. He lapsed into a strange silence, as though he no longer cared for any of his creatures. And since he was deaf to his children and to their interests, they refrained from praying to him, making sacrifices to him, and dancing in his honor. When they called on the Great Spirit, as they often did in conversation with the whites, they meant the God of the White Man, not that of the Sioux. Their great active god and, therefore, the chief object of their worship, was Unkteri or Oontayhee. Unkteri manifested himself as an immense ox with eyes as big as the moon. His invisible powers resided in his horns and tail, which he could shorten or lengthen as he pleased. In the beginning he assembled in grand conclave all the water animals, ordered them to bring up dirt from beneath the water, and proclaimed death to the disobedient. The beaver and other animals forfeited their lives. But the muskrat bravely went beneath the water and after a long time appeared, nearly exhausted, with some dirt. From this Unkteri fashioned the earth into a large circular plain. Then he ground a deity, one of his own offspring, into powder, which he sprinkled on the earth, thereby producing worms. These matured into infants and, in time, into fully grown Sioux, which Unkteri collected and then distributed all over the world.[38]

Many Sioux discovered bones of the mammoth in their wanderings.

Though these bones were of enormous size, they resembled those of the buffalo or ox. Since the Sioux worshiped many other animals they naturally selected the largest of which they had knowledge as their chief active god. To his worship they dedicated most of their festivals. Since his bones had never been found on land, they deduced that he lived in water. They prized his bones highly for their magical powers.[39]

The Sioux supposed that thunder was the voice of Wakinyan, a bird which destroyed its enemies by striking them down with bolts of lightning. Many of them thought they had seen Wakinyan. With their staunch belief in Wakinyan's existence, their terrified imaginations often discovered this bird among the dark flying clouds of a thunderstorm.[40]

Another of their major gods was Taku-Shkan-Shkan, who was omnipresent as well as invisible. He was incarnate evil—full of revenge, exceedingly angry, very deceitful, and an inexorable searcher of hearts. He flew with the four winds and he traveled in the granite boulders on the plains of Minnesota. He was never so happy as when he saw scalps which were warm and reeking with blood. To the boulders in which he resided he gave the power of motion. Many Sioux believed they had seen them move some distance on level ground, leaving a track or furrow behind them. Though this could have been the work of some cunning rogue, it was more than likely that of Taku-Shkan-Shkan. So they worshiped him to appease his anger, revenge, and deceit as much as possible.[41]

Still another important god was Heyoka, who was also called Waziya because he had four persons. One was a small and tender man with two faces. Another was a little old man with a cocked hat and enormous ears. Another was a man with a flute hanging from his neck. And still another was a man as invisible, mysterious, and gentle as a zephyr which moves the grass and ripples the lakes and rivers. Heyoka was a paradox. He called bitter sweet and sweet bitter. He groaned when he was full of joy. He called black white and white black. He lied when he told truth. He went naked in winter and wrapped himself up in buffalo robes during summer. From his abode in the hills he inspired certain men and women to make the wind blow, the rain fall, and the grasses grow or wither.[42]

24

Half-dressed, heavily painted, and wearing long conical hats, the Sioux gathered at a feast in his honor. They filled a huge kettle with water and meat, built a fire under it, and watched it until it began to boil. Then they began to dance and sing excitedly while they plunged their hands into the boiling water and stuffed themselves with chunks of meat. They threw the scalding water over their backs and legs and complained, without wincing, that it was cold. The uninitiated were unaware that the celebrants had deadened their skins by rubbing them with a certain grass.[43]

To the Sioux their medicine men or *wakan* were just as holy as were the Druids to the ancient Britons. As demi-gods, they were the most influential and powerful members of the tribe. They asserted that their origin was miraculous. They claimed to have sprung from a seed which the breeze had wafted like that of a thistle to the dwelling of the gods, who had received them to intimate communion. The gods instructed them in the mysteries of the spirit world and sent them in every direction to study the character of all the tribes. They decided on a residence and entered the body of a girl who was about to become a mother and who ushered them into the world.[44]

Though they entertained confused and uncertain notions of life after death, they firmly believed in the immortality of the soul. They spoke of the dead as having gone to the land of ghosts or to the happy hunting grounds or to the country of the spirits. Like other people all over the world, they had an instinctive dread of death. They believed that when a thief died he carried whatever he had stolen into the next world, where it became an intolerable burden to him. They also believed that a person who hanged himself had to wear the cords around his neck forever in the country of the spirits.[45]

They called many doings or undertakings *wakan*, meaning sacred, dangerous, magical, or calamitous. They were as superstitious about performing certain things as are some Americans about beginning an important undertaking on Friday, walking under a ladder, or stepping in the path of a black cat. To declare a thing *wakan* was nothing more than a superstitious appeal against undertaking what was considered improper or dangerous. To say that a thing was *wakan* was to give sufficient reason why it should not be done. It was *wakan*, for example, to point

25

a gun at another person, even in sport; to throw gunpowder into the fire; to whittle or hack a stick while it burned; and to threaten to kill a relative, even in jest. One morning a young man asked his brother to go hunting with him, threatening to kill him if he refused. Their father, overhearing them, cried, "Stop, my son, that is *wakan.*" In his anger, however, the son made light of the admonition, saying that the gods, though many, could not hear him because he had spoken in a low voice. He went hunting without his brother, but that night, as he drew near his home, he accidentally killed him in attempting to shoot a bird.[46]

S. R. Riggs, who conducted missionary work among the Sioux in 1838, found that they were greatly disturbed by the eclipse of the sun. "The sun is sick," they said; "it will die." Riggs went to one of their villages with a smoked glass so that they might observe the eclipse more distinctly. Some of them said that everything looked strange, but they could not explain why. They asked Riggs whether that day was regarded as more sacred than another. The men and boys were eager to look through the glass, but the women refused. When he asked them why they were afraid of the mirror, they replied, "It is *wakan.*"[47] When the eclipse passed off they agreed that the sun was well again.

Riggs found that the women apostatized readily because, being practically slaves, they were easily led and influenced. But he learned that the men were proud and lordly; they regarded any abandonment of their ancestral religion as high treason against the Evil Spirit's empire. Though they allowed their wives and daughters to become Christians, they themselves refused to do so, carefully explaining that they never followed the example of their women. Riggs found that they were as persistent in observing their superstitions as are some American farmers in believing that turnips should not be sown or bushes cut at a certain time of the moon.[48]

They were pathetically mournful and reverent in their burial and mourning ceremonies. As soon as a person died, or even while he was dying, his relatives or friends dressed him in fancy clothes and embroidered moccasins. When he died they wound his body tightly in a blanket, blankets, or clothes. Then they burst into wailing. This consisted of singing or chanting a tune in a voice that was alternately mournful, wild, soft, and loud, as they called on their beloved departed. Each person lamented by himself, paying little attention to others, taking little pain to produce harmony. E. D. Neill has left us a pathetically beautiful example of a lament uttered by a woman who had lost her *choonkshe* or little daughter:

Me choonkshe, me choonkshe, alas! alas! My hope, my comfort has departed, my heart is very sad. My joy is turned into sorrow, and my song into wailing. Shall I never behold thy sunny smile? Shall I never more hear the music of thy voice? The Great Spirit has entered my lodge in anger, and taken thee from me, my first born and only child. I am comfortless and must wail out my grief. The pale faces repress their sorrow, but we children of nature must give vent to ours or die. *Me choonkshe, me choonkshe.*

The light of my eyes is extinguished; all, all is dark. I have cast from me all comfortable clothing and robed myself in comfortless skins, for no clothing, no fire, can warm thee, my daughter. Unwashed and uncombed, I will mourn for thee, whose long locks I can never more braid; and whose cheeks I can never again tinge with vermillion. I will cut off my dishevelled hair, for my grief is great, *me choonkshe, me choonkshe.* How can I survive thee? How can I be happy, and you a homeless wanderer to the spirit land? How can I eat if you are hungry? I will go to the grave with food for your spirit. Your bowl and spoon are placed in your coffin for use on the journey. The feast for your playmates has been made at the place of interment. Knowest thou of their presence? *Me choonkshe, me choonkshe.*

When Spring returns, the choicest of ducks shall be your portion. Sugar and berries also, shall be placed near your grave. Neither grass nor flowers shall be allowed to grow thereon. Affection for thee, will keep the little mound desolate, like the heart from which thou art torn. My daughter, I come, I come. I bring you parched corn. Oh, how long will you sleep? The wintry winds wail your requiem. The cold earth is your bed, and the colder snow thy covering. I would that they were mine. I will lie down by thy side. I will sleep once more with you. If no one discovers me, I shall soon be as cold as thou art, and together we will sleep that long, long sleep from which I cannot awake thee, *me choonkshe, me choonkshe.*[49]

Sometimes they buried their dead in coffins obtained from white men. Usually they placed their dead on trees or scaffolds. In the region of the Minnesota River they wrapped them in buffalo skins and fastened them among the branches of trees. They probably never used coffins before they became acquainted with white men. Living in a cold region

27

and having no implements with which to dig, save the crude hoes they made, they could not bury those who died in winter. They could preserve the bodies from wild animals only by hoisting or placing them on trees or scaffolds. Some historians have erroneously attributed this custom to Sioux laziness or indifference.[50]

They often had to carry their dead, as they carried their wounded, on crude litters for a considerable distance through deep snow. In summer, when they were in their villages, they usually buried their dead; but in autumn and winter, when they were away hunting furs or making sugar, they found burying a disagreeable undertaking. Some dying persons, influenced by man's natural dread of being buried, requested their friends to place their bodies on scaffolds. They deposited food, often choice meat, on the grave or beneath the scaffold, and left it there for several days. They believed it had a spiritual life which nourished the soul of the departed. Near the grave or scaffold they also placed such objects of affection as flowers and beads.[51]

Like other tribes, the Sioux believed that Getci Munito, or the Great Spirit, manifested himself to them in the rising smoke from what the French called the calumet or peace pipe. The mysterious, spirit-like nature of the smoke impressed them as *wakan* or sacred. They venerated it, together with the tobacco that made it possible, in their ceremonial rites and in their councils. They also worshiped the catlinite or soft red stone from which they carved with their primitive tools the bowls of the calumet. The hollowed stems were two or three feet long and were usually made from reeds of red willows. The Sioux obtained much of their pipestone from the county of the same name in southwestern Minnesota. The effigy mounds, shaped in the form of birds, buffaloes, bears, or snakes, have disappeared; but they recall the legend, described by Lynd, of how the quarry became sacred ground. One sultry evening the Sioux had gathered in the quarry to dig the stone when, just before sunset,

the heavens suddenly became overclouded, accompanied by heavy rumbling thunder, and every sign of an approaching storm, such as frequently arises on the prairie without much warning. Each one hurried to his lodge expecting a storm, when a vivid flash of lightening, followed immediately by a crashing peal of thunder, broke over them, and, looking towards the huge boulder beyond their camp, they saw a pillar or column of smoke standing upon it, which moved to and fro, and gradually settled down into the outline of a huge giant, seated upon the boulder, with one long arm extended to heaven and the other pointing down to his feet. Peal after peal of thunder, and flashes of lightening in quick succession followed, and this figure then suddenly disappeared. The next morning the Sioux went to this boulder, and found these figures and images upon it, where before there had been nothing; and ever since that time the place has been regarded as *wakan* or sacred.[52]

Here, says Longfellow, Getci Munito once summoned all the tribes of the world and admonished them to forget their animosities:

> *I am weary of your quarrels,*
> *Weary of your wars and bloodshed,*
> *Weary of your prayers for vengeance,*
> *Of your wranglings and dissensions;*
> *All your strength is in your union,*
> *All your danger is in discord;*
> *Therefore be at peace henceforward,*
> *And as brothers live together.*
>
> *Bathe now in the stream before you,*
> *Wash the war-paint from your faces,*
> *Wash the blood-stains from your fingers,*
> *Bury your war-clubs and your weapons,*
> *Break the red stone from this quarry,*
> *Mould and make it into Peace-Pipes,*
> *Take the reeds that grow beside you,*
> *Deck them with your brightest feathers,*
> *Smoke the calumet together,*
> *And as brothers live henceforward!*

By their veneration of the calumet the Sioux bound themselves to treaties and agreements, made friends of perfect strangers, assured other tribes safe passage through their country, and promoted peace.

But the most conspicuous feature of their environment was the buffalo. Though this animal was found in every part of the American frontier, its true home was in the tall and nutritious grasslands of the prairies over which it lumbered in search of a cool region in summer and a warm region in winter. Migrating in circles four or five hundred miles in diameter, each of the four or five great herds overlapped as they wintered on the gramas or on the seedier grasses that rose through the snow where another herd had grazed in the warmer months. Massive in size and gregarious in habit, the buffalo was a ponderous and rather stupid animal cursed with a slow gait, clumsy movement, relatively poor eyesight, and indifference to sound. Its sense of smell, though keen, was useless when it was approached from down the wind. Despite its physical shortcomings, it thrived and multiplied in unbelievable numbers, thanks to its immunity to serious disease and to its great recuperative powers, which were perhaps fostered by dry climate. Hornaday says that the leaves of the forest could have been counted more easily than the buffaloes on the Great Plains, even in the latter part of the nineteenth century.[53]

The buffalo not only determined the economic and the social pattern, but also the geographic distribution of the Sioux and other tribes. Its presence led them to pursue hunting and to neglect agriculture. Its tasty flesh and its useful hide attracted larger and larger numbers of Indian hunters as they retreated westward with the advance of the frontier: from the Appalachians to the Great Lakes, from the Great Lakes to the Mississippi, from the Mississippi to the Great Plains. There Indian and buffalo lived in constant interaction. There the Sioux thought and acted only as they were moved by their easy victims. In the horse they discovered a new means of conquering the buffalo, which was almost their sole subsistence—their shelter, clothing, and food. The buffalo also furnished them with most of their amusement and entertainment. It provided them with a test of strength and courage and character. It even became a part of their ethics and their religion. Often, after a successful hunt, they painted and embroidered their finest robe and took it to a high hill. There, in ceremonial offering, they gave thanks to the Great Spirit and to the buffalo they had killed that they might live. And since their lives depended on it they continued to use every cunning device to hunt it down. But they never succeeded, with their crude weapons, in lessening the great herds. Only the American frontiersman with his swift horse, his dextrous lariat, and his unerring rifle could overtake the buffalo and spell its doom. And even then, for a time, it continued to prosper and to show little fear. Perhaps in its innumerable fellows it found security against its own susceptibilities.[54]

The chief sport of the Sioux was the deer hunt, which usually lasted from October to April. Each hunter carried a bag made of animal skin which he had tanned without removing the hair, head, feet, or tail. The skin, usually that of some small animal such as skunk, mink, or fox, had been removed from the carcass through an opening at the throat. The opening served as the mouth of the bag, in which the hunter carried his pipe and tobacco, touch-wood, flint, and fire-steel. These indispensable articles assured him of smoking pleasure and, more importantly, fire in winter.[55]

Supplying themselves with clothing, guns, and ammunition, the various bands began to move into the hunting country. Sometimes the few horses they owned carried their heaviest burdens. More often they placed their supplies on frames attached to two poles which resembled the shafts of a wagon. The rear end dragged on the ground and the front end was strapped over the saddle and around the horse like an ordinary breast-collar. Sometimes they harnessed dogs in the same manner. Whenever they crossed a stream two of their strongest men would hold up the rear of the shaft.[56]

When they approached the hunting country they scattered in bands until they divided for the purpose covering a wider territory. Though they held the land in common, each band went to the part of the country most accessible from his summer village. Sometimes, perhaps every two or three years, they departed from their usual resort and hunted over the whole country. They carried little or no food and left behind them only those who were unable to walk and who had to take care of invalids. Few of them were willing to remain in the village, for the deer hunt, regardless of hardships, had strong attractions for young and old. The old men and women, if they could do nothing else, beguiled the long winter evenings with tales of their youth or of deeds of hunters and warriors of days gone by.[57]

They traveled only a short distance during the day, for they required considerable time to pitch their tents and prepare for the night. Those

31

who arrived first at the camping ground selected the best place for their tent and secured the nearest wood and tent poles. Thus the hardest labor often fell to those least able to perform it.[58]

The chief, or, in his absence, his chief man, regulated the movements of the hunting party. He appointed young men to build a fire. At this fire the hunters met about daybreak before departing together to the hunting ground. To give all of them an equal chance at the game, they appointed the place of hunting for each day and prescribed boundaries beyond which none might pass unless circumstances necessitated otherwise. All of them, save little children, had to wade streams.

They shared every deer they killed. The deer slayer gave notice of his kill to those with whom he hunted by giving a certain shout. He waited for a short time. Then, if nobody appeared, he cut up the deer and carried it home. But if somebody came he divided the flesh equally with him while he took the skin for himself. If two or three came, each had a right to a certain portion of the flesh, but if more than three came, only the first three to arrive had any claim to it. The man who killed the deer always kept the skin and wrapped his portion of flesh in it.[59]

The entrails were cleaned, cooked, and eaten on the spot of the killing. They laid the tripe on the coals until its inside layer peeled off as clean as though it had been soaked in water. But they were not as meticulous in cleaning the entrails. For these they used only their knives, believing that the deer ate nothing unclean and could not, therefore, poison them when they ate any part of it. Since they had eaten nothing for an entire day, their stomachs were not very fastidious, especially in cold weather. One branch of the Sioux tribe ate parts of the buffalo raw; another ate no raw meat, even when it was dried.[60]

When the hunters went out in the morning, the children began watching from camp for them to return with game. As soon as they saw a hunter bring in a deer they shouted, "Oo-koo-hoo! Oo-koo-hoo!" And when they ascertained which man had the skin they yelled his name so loud that the whole hunting party could hear it. They continued to watch and proclaim the names of the successful hunters until nightfall. They had a different shout for every kind of animal that was killed.[61] The admiration of the Sioux for their buffalo and deer hunters equaled that of the American public for their baseball heroes.

But they reserved their highest esteem for the braves who took the

32

largest number of scalps in war. When they returned home a feast was held at which those who had taken part in the campaign came forward and formally "counted" or announced the number of scalps they had taken. The famous scalp dance was danced in their honor. This was one of the very few dances in which both men and women participated. The latter did much of the dancing. The scalp dance was gravely decorous—devoid of any of the exultation one might expect to witness on such an occasion. The expression of triumph was rather in the singing. A woman, usually an elderly one, began the dance by seizing a staff to which a scalp had been attached. Meanwhile other women, clad in their best apparel and wrapped in blankets, formed a circle around her. They stood very straight, with sad countenances and downcast eyes. At a signal, they jumped simultaneously a few inches sideways. Keeping time to the music, they slowly danced around the circle. The men joined some stages of the dance, forming a separate line and facing the women as they danced back and forth and beat their drums. They sang the scalp song which included the words, "He stood pointing his gun, but missed fire, and I was not afraid." They repeated these words at intervals, while the women responded with short, shrill cries. They danced into the night. The reverberations of the drums, the loud, defiant song of the men, and the shrieks of the women—all combined with the darkness to provide the proper atmosphere for the gruesome business of dancing around a scalp of their dead foes.[62]

Samuel W. Pond, who spent several years among the Sioux as a missionary, stated that the dancing of the women was less distasteful than that of the men. To his pious eyes the whole dance was a disgusting performance. It furnished, he said, "a convenient opportunity for illicit intercourse between the sexes; for, in the excitement and confusion of the dance, some of the dancers might slip off into the darkness without being missed. The more thoughtful of the Indians complained of the demoralizing influence of the scalp dance when held in the night. Are any of our dances similarly demoralizing?"[63]

Perhaps the most important ceremony of the Sioux was the sun dance. It was a combination of ancient ceremonies which had been modified and adapted to their particular environment. It assumed many variations, depending on circumstances and the branch of the tribe performing it. It usually started in late June or early July as an offering to

33

the Great Spirit to bless them with many buffaloes during their annual hunt and to protect them against such prevalent and dreadful diseases as cholera, measles, smallpox, and tuberculosis. In some sun dances they shed their own blood, or, in their metaphoric words, "spread red carpets on the ground," to ward off a great drought, the approaching danger of a forest fire, a powerful force of attacking Indians, or the power of the white man to seize their favorite hunting grounds.[64]

The Sioux believed that the achievement of full adult life depended on successful participation in the sun dance. Its tortures were often painful and permanently injurious to the bodies of the dancers. These rigors were calculated to engender such cardinal virtues as bravery, integrity, and generosity. Though it had a basic pattern, the dance varied with the dream and medicine of its leader and with the purposes he desired to fulfill. It lasted from one to eight days with interludes of gyrations, ceremonies, and dancing. It began very early in the morning, when its participants, who numbered from five hundred to several thousand, traveled on horseback to the place chosen for the dance. They charged in every direction for an hour to frighten what ghosts and bad spirits might have gathered there. Then their leader, accompanied by virgins and children whose ears were to be pierced, set out to select a suitable cottonwood to serve as the sun-dance pole. They allowed nobody to approach it save those whom they had chosen to fell it. When it came down, they all dashed toward it, as though they were attacking an enemy, and carried it, branches and all, to the spot where the ceremony was to be performed. Again they charged in every direction to scare away ghosts and bad spirits. Then they cleaned off the branches of the tree to a foot or two below its forked top. They festooned the top with fetishes, red, white, and blue banners, fertility images of a man and a buffalo, and an image of the paradox god Heyoka.[65]

While drummers and singers marched and shouted around the tree, it was set up in the center of a ring. Composed of men and women, the ring was about five hundred yards in circumference. At this point the children entered the ring, where six old men pierced their ears with a knife and fastened earrings in them. Now a small group of men placed near the pole the skull of a buffalo, over which they cried as they gyrated madly. Then the virgins went up to the tree, touched it, raised their right hands to the sun, bowed to the skull, and retired from the ring.

They were warned previously that if any of them was unchaste, she would fall dead as soon as she touched the tree because the skull represented the animal which would carry her away to the spirit land.[66]

Missionary Riggs once witnessed a sun dance performed by the Teton branch of the Sioux. The dancers had been fasting for three days and nights and they were as "gaunt as greyhounds." Each had a whistle in his mouth and a banner with a long staff in his hands. Sixty men began a crashing roll on ten big drums, while the dancers danced as they whistled and gazed steadily at the sun. They continued this ceremony until morning, when seven of the dancers were fastened to the pole by rawhide thongs tied to the wooden skewers thrust in their breasts. Two of them danced toward the pole, made a short prayer, and ran backwards as fast as they could. They broke loose and fell on their backs. Another man succeeded, by a desperate struggle, in breaking loose not only from the pole but from a horse to which he had also been fastened by means of skewers thrust through the flesh of his arms. The other four men failed to break loose and paid the penalty of having to give away four of their horses. That evening, as the sun disappeared behind the clouds, the leader of the sun dance put the buffalo skull on his head and muttered a few words to his audience. Then, with a wave of his hand, he told them to go home. The torturous dance was over.[67]

3

Chippewa Society

THE OTHER IMPORTANT TRIBE OF THE UPPER VALLEY WAS THE CHIPPEWAS
or Ojibways. They lived in the deep, interminable forests abounding
with beautiful lakes and murmuring streams whose banks were rimmed
with sweet maples, birch, pine, spruce, tamarack, poplar, ash, elm, and
basswood. Their origin is one of the mysteries of unrecorded time.
William W. Warren thought that their original home was a rich country
in the west. He believed that they were either pushed eastward or
migrated voluntarily until they reached the Atlantic, where the white
men turned them again in the direction whence they came. The Chippewas believed that at about the time of Columbus their ancestors
gathered at the present town of La Pointe, on the west side of Madeline,
which is one of the Apostle Islands at the entrance of Chequamegon Bay.
There they encountered French traders, who persuaded them to trade
their skins, which they had obtained solely for their own use, for firearms, blankets, trinkets, and firewater. They never waged war against
their white friends; they preferred to acquire their civilization.[1]

The extravagant promises of the traders and the earnest solicitations
of the missionaries attracted them in increasing numbers to the Apostle
Islands, where they hunted until the game supply was exhausted. Then
the need of furs to trade with the French lured them to present northeastern Minnesota. They met and defeated the Sioux and pursued them
as far as the Mississippi River. Then, for a decade, they engaged the
Sioux in fierce guerrilla warfare between Lake Superior and the Mississippi River. Their superior arms enabled them to push westward
from Fond du Lac and the adjoining islands of the St. Louis River. After

1679, when Duluth established the first permanent trading post at Grand Portage, they poured into Minnesota from east and north. Again they attacked the Sioux, whom they drove farther and farther away from Lake Superior, from the region of Sandy Lake, in present Aitkin County, Minnesota, and eventually from Leech Lake. Then they dominated timbered country as far north as the Canadian border, as far west as the Red River of the North, and as far south as Little Falls, in present Morrison County, Minnesota, and between Leech Lake and the upper Minnesota River.[2]

The Chippewas were an attractive people with well-developed chests and frames which were more sinewy and lighter than those of many white men. They had the small and beautifully shaped hands of aristocrats. Joseph A. Gilfillan, who for many years served as a missionary among them, wrote admiringly of their noble bearing:

> The men have an erect, graceful, and easy carriage, and a beautiful springy step and motion in their native wilds, where they walk and look like the lords of creation. In their beauty of motion in walking the men far surpass our race; there is no swinging of the arms, or other awkward motions, but grace and a beautiful poise and carriage of the body.[3]

They were proud of their thick and strong hair which turned grey only when they were very old, and they could boast beyond middle age of their even, white teeth, though they neither cleaned them nor took care of them. The men became old before they became stout. Gilfillan attributed their slenderness to their meager diet and to their incessant spitting of tobacco.[4]

Quite different was the appearance of their women. They trudged along with heavy tread. Gilfillan surmised they had acquired this plodding step from their female ancestors, who for many centuries had carried heavy packs and burdens of as much as two hundred pounds wherever they went. A man rarely carried a pack. If his wife was with him, she carried it, unless they were forced to share it because of its weight. He strode magnificently in front, carrying only his gun, while she cheerfully bore her load in accordance with the custom of her tribe. Sometimes, when she carried a wigwam, her load was bulky. At its top perched her baby, securely tied to keep it from falling from its perilous

38

height. Mile after mile she sometimes carried over her head an eighty to one hundred pound canoe, which she could invert at will for passing over portages. She was usually expert with the ax and, indeed, with all kinds of heavy labor. By middle age she usually became stout and fleshy with a large waist. She often weighed more than a man.[5]

As a people who traveled chiefly by water, the Chippewas regarded the canoe as an article of great economic importance. They believed that their ancestors had learned the craft of canoe-making from Mana-bozho himself. It required such skill and experience that only veterans practiced it, though they permitted the assistance of young men. The Chippewas regarded it with great respect, for the welfare and safety of the tribe depended on it.

The average canoe measured about three double armspreads long and about three or four handspreads wide. It was covered with birch bark cut in early spring, when it was easily removed from large trees. Hiawatha sang of the joy of building a canoe from the light bark of the birch:

> *Give me of your bark, O Birch-tree!*
> *Of your yellow bark, O Birch-tree!*
> *Growing by the rushing river,*
> *Tall and stately in the valley!*
> *I a light canoe will build me,*
> *Build a swift Cheemaun for sailing,*
> *That shall float upon the river,*
> *Like a yellow leaf in Autumn,*
> *Like a yellow water-lily!*

The birch canoe could carry from six to ten adults, four of whom were needed as paddlers if they wished to travel rapidly. Its ribs, thwarts, and rim were made of cedar, and parts of it were sewn with split roots of either the tamarack or the spruce. A dextrous whittling of the ribs was necessary to assure the balance of the canoe and to keep it from upsetting. Chippewa standards in this endeavor were so high that only a few veterans were considered capable of achieving them.[6]

The process of canoe-making required exceptional patience and skill. The craftsman usually placed two pairs of short poles upright in

39

the ground as wide apart as he desired and laid on them a frame of flat boards. On this frame, which he now placed on the ground, he laid sheets of birch bark and weighted them down with stones. The edges of the bark were fastened to the cedar lining or rim of the canoe. Inside, next to the bark, were placed flat pieces of wood. On these were fastened the ribs, which were braced with narrow crossbars and which extended from rim to rim across the bottom of the canoe. Two or three women sewed together the pieces of bark whose edges, in turn, they sewed to the rim of the canoe. Before covering the seams with pitch they allowed the canoe to dry for three or four days while they carefully protected it from the sun. Thus, says Longfellow, the birch canoe was finished—

> *In the valley, by the river,*
> *In the bosom of the forest;*
> *And the forest's life was in it,*
> *All its mystery and its magic,*
> *All the lightness of the cedar,*
> *All the larch's supple sinews;*
> *And it floated on the river*
> *Like a yellow leaf in Autumn,*
> *Like a yellow water-lily.*

George Catlin thought that Chippewa bark canoes were perhaps "the most beautiful and light model of all the winter crafts that ever were invented." But they needed experienced handling to keep them from upsetting. Light as a cork, they glided over the water, gracefully swaying under the skillful balance of Indian paddlers. But, like anything wild, they were "timid and treacherous under the guidance of a white man; and if he be not an experienced equilibrist, he is sure to get two or three times soused, in his first endeavours at familiar acquaintance with them."[7]

In winter the Chippewas traveled by dog team, toboggan, or sled. Usually a team consisted of three dogs harnessed to a toboggan or sled by means of rawhide collars and straps. On such a vehicle the Chippewas could travel, one group after another, for from forty to fifty miles a day. The word toboggan was derived from the Chippewa *nobugidaban*.

40

The toboggan was especially adapted to travel through the woods because its load was close to the ground. It was made of hardwood from sapless trees. Its end piece was turned by exposing it either to the heat of a large fire or to boiling water. Its load was secured by means of cords that passed back and forth through cleats placed along the width and breadth of the toboggin. It was usually drawn by dogs which required only the width of a footpath. To its rear was fastened a strap which served as a brake. On descending a steep hill, the driver or his companion held the strap to keep it from running the dogs.[8]

The Chippewas lived in wigwams, in peaked lodges, in bark houses, and in tipis. In accordance with the Algonkian custom which extended from Canada to North Carolina, they applied the term wigwam, meaning "he dwells," to every type of dwelling. Like those of the Sioux, the wigwams were made of pole or saplings, bark, or hides, and bulrushes tied together with green basswood and basswood twine. A lodge, in which often lived two or three generations, had at least one entrance, a fire at each end, and a smoke hole over each fire. They had a custom that limited the youngest person to the center of the lodge, where they were obliged to pass their elders in entering or leaving. One of the mothers presided over a fire, where she prepared the food and cooked it. Then, sitting next to the door of the lodge, where she kept her utensils or small portions of food, she served the largest meal of the day, which usually began at sundown and lasted until late at night.[9]

The mother used pointed sticks to remove the meat from the kettle, if it was too hot to use her fingers. She gave a piece of it to the young men, each of whom cut off with his hunting knife what he wished to eat. The meal, served in shallow trays of unsplit bark or bowls made of hardwood, included such dishes as roasted or boiled corn on the cob, pumpkins and squash (cultivated in their own gardens), and maple sugar prepared in the form of "hard sugar," "gum sugar," or granulated sugar. This sugar was used as a seasoning and eaten as a delicacy.[10] They seasoned some of their dishes with wild ginger, bearberry, and mountain mint. They thickened and flavored their broth with corn silk and dried pumpkin blossoms. Sometimes an evening meal included white potatoes, boiled or roasted acorns, milkweed flowers, roots of a number of plants, basswood or aspen sap, white pine moss, and a sweetish substance they obtained behind the outer bark of the woodbine.

They boiled dried berries and seasoned them with maple sugar or combined them with moose fat or deer tallow. Sometimes they baked a bread called *legolet,* by mixing flour and salt with water and by kneading the dough into round, flat loaves. They were also very fond of fish, which they caught in seines, and of all the animals they trapped except marten. They considered beaver tail a great luxury because it was so fat. They often boiled their water and flavored it with the leaves of the wintergreen, raspberry, spruce, and snowberry, or the twigs of wild cherry.[11]

Their bedding consisted of blankets and of deer or bear hides tanned with the hair retained. Some members of the dwelling had pillows and thin beds made of hide or cloth and filled with feathers from the wild duck. Sometimes they spread cedar boughs on the ground and covered them with rush mats on which they placed their bedding at night. When they rose in the morning they rolled it up and used it as seats or placed it along the walls of the lodge.[12]

Nature provided them with most of their clothing. The soft deer-skins, tanned in an expert manner and colored a golden brown, made attractive coats for their women. The leaves of the burdock protected their heads from the broiling sun. The sinuous nettle provided them with thread, which they could twist fine or coarse as they desired. Rabbit skins lined the cradle boards, moccasins, and caps of their children and kept them warm while they slept. In early times, before the advent of the fur traders, the women dressed in a single garment made of two deerskins, one in back and one in front. These were fastened together at the shoulders and held in place by a belt. With the broadcloth that the fur traders brought them they made dresses for festive occasions, though they always wore buckskin when they were at work.[13] The simplest type of moccasin, worn by infants and old women, consisted of two pieces of deer or moose hide "with a plain seam extending the length of the sole and up the front and back of the foot." Another type of moccasin had a puckered seam up the front and a plain seam up the back. Some scholars surmise that this type of moccasin furnished the name of their tribe, Ojibway, or a variation of it, meaning "puckered."[14]

They were very fond of personal ornaments and gave much attention to the care and arrangement of their hair. Old men, more than women

42

and young men, wore earrings consisting of bunches of small, elongated metal cones suspended at the tip. Sometimes these were so numerous that they weighted down the wearer. The favorite ornament of dancers was a brooch woven of stiff moosehair which they wore in their hair. Young women reddened their cheeks with bloodroot, and men kept their faces smooth in wind and cold by greasing their faces with deer tallow. The young warriors mixed colored earth with powder and grease to make paint, which they applied in designs on the palms of their hands and then pressed on to their faces. Sometimes they applied paint directly to their faces and then removed as much of it as was necessary to leave a war design or pattern. Often on their faces they painted images of the bodies of men in patterns. When they went to war they mixed "medicine" with the paint they applied to their faces and bodies. Though they carefully plucked out their whiskers, they were very proud of their handsome hair. They kept it smooth by greasing it with bear grease or deer tallow. They cut it in a fringe across the forehead and put up the remainder in two braids. Sometimes they wore fillets of beads across their foreheads to keep their hair in place. Older men often wore a short braid at each temple and put up the rest of their hair in two braids, which they either left suspended or tied on the top of their heads. They believed that the source of their manly strength was in their hair. Once Mary Warren English, an American teacher, walked into a wigwam where a young woman was combing her brother's hair, and jestingly asked him for some of it. "No," replied the young man, seriously; "I would lose all my strength if I cut my hair." Men often dreamed that their hair shielded them from the Sioux, their bitterest enemies. Once a warrior dreamed that he was fighting the Sioux and that they could not see him because of the luster of his hair. But his friends saw him clearly just as soon as the fighting stopped.[15]

The average family included two or three children. By the firing of guns the father announced that his wife had given birth to a child during the night. Immediately the men in the father's family and the men in another family began a contest for possession of the child. They threw cold water and sometimes a mixture of flour on each other and fought and wrestled until, at the end of the contest, they were wringing wet. The leader of the victorious party carried the infant four times around a fire, while his friends sang a song which contained words meaning,

43

"We have caught the little bird." Then the mother secured her child by giving presents to the victorious party. She began to train it for a straight and vigorous life. She pinned it up tightly, confining all its body save possibly its hands and fingers, in cotton cloth and placed it in a red or blue cradle of birch bark softened by moss. Above its head was a hoop which supported a blanket to keep it warm in winter and a thin cloth to shield it from summer heat. Near the hoop was a leather strap which enabled the mother to carry her child on her back. On the hoop she flung two articles representing spiders to catch, as in a spider's web, all the evil things that come in contact with it.[16]

Many children derived their names or nicknames from allusions to incidences of birth, descriptions or characteristics of animals or persons, or fancied resemblances to places and things. One Chippewa bore the name of Little Money because his round face reminded his mother of a small silver coin. Little Cat was so named because in her childhood she scratched savagely. The name Stands Alone indicated that its bearer in his boyhood had been aloof and reserved. Without Teeth was a long time in teething. Stump received this name because of his short stature.[17]

The mother was always a close companion of her children. She was especially close to her daughters who learned many household tasks from watching or helping her. They early learned how to chop wood and how to carry it on their backs. As they grew older they carried larger and larger bundles of wood until they could carry into the wigwam one load big enough for the night's use. "You must not grow up to live outdoors and be made fun of because you do not know how to make a good wigwam." By this admonition the mother induced her daughter to make birch bark rolls like those which covered wigwams. She also learned how to make maple sugar, gather wild rice, and do all the chores the women of her tribe were expected to do. Her reputation as a quiet and industrious worker soon spread to other villages whose young men sought her hand in marriage.[18]

The most influential feature of Chippewa society was the *medewiwin*, a combination of medical and religious society. While its primary purpose was the preservation of knowledge of herbs for use in prolonging life, it found its highest conception in a deity called *mide manido*, meaning Grand Medicine Spirit. Subordinate to him were four *manido*, one residing at each of the cardinal points, and there was a multitude of

44

lesser *manido* who assumed the forms of bears or water animals. The *mide manido,* who looked like a man and who lived on the earth about a hundred years, went among wise men in the world and taught them the use of remedies that cured mental and physical illnesses. The ethics of the Grand Medicine Society was based on the principle that rectitude is rewarded with longevity and that evil is inevitably punished. Lying, stealing, and the use of alcoholic beverages were strongly condemned. Though the Grand Medicine Society usually tried to bring the sinful back to the path of righteousness by gentle admonition, it had the authority to put to death hardened sinners or heretics by administering subtle poisons.[19]

The Grand Medicine Society kept its records and teachings on rolls of heavy birch bark. The outside of a roll enumerated, by means of large circles, the "lodges" or degrees of the society. The inside of a roll contained records and teachings. The rolls may be compared to the trestle board of the Masonic Order, which is printed and published to provide the esoteric with lists of degrees and details of ceremonies without disclosing any of its secrets.

One of the most colorful activities of the Grand Medicine Society was its rite of beseeching the *mide manido* to grant it a request before it held a meeting. Its members repaired to what was known as a sweat lodge, which was a small framework of bent poles closely covered with blankets to keep any air from entering it. There their leader, usually a venerable old man, heated on a fire four stones which they regarded as their messengers to the *mide manido.* Dipping a bunch of grass in water, the leader sprinkled the largest stone while he said three times, "We-e-e, ho-ho-ho," and his companions replied, "Ho-ho-ho." Then the leader said in a clear, loud voice: "I desire this messenger to say to *mide manido* that we desire health and long life." After each of them had performed the same ceremony, they lifted the blankets from the lodge, wiped the sweat from their faces, drank a little water, and went to the meeting of the *medewiwin,* confident that the *mide manido* would grant their request.[20]

In summer the Grand Medicine Society held its rite of initiation. The members "shot" into the candidates spirit power from medicine bags made of weasel skin, mink skin, wildcat hide, or the skin of a rattlesnake.

In these bags they carried herbs and charms which they said they had learned to use from the four lesser gods who, with their faces painted the colors of dawn and with each holding a live otter, appeared in the eastern sky. The bags also contained *migis* or white shells which they "shot" into both the candidates and themselves. The candidates immediately lost consciousness and fell to the ground. When they awoke they were told that one of the shells had come out of their mouths and that, therefore, they had been accepted as members of the society.[21]

Most Chippewas were never accorded the distinction of belonging to the Grand Medicine Society, though it greatly influenced their lives. They found social contentment in other customs of their limited society. Their children, girls as well as boys, were avid participants in outdoor sports. They were expert swimmers. They jumped into the water without removing their clothes, which dried on them when they were finished swimming. The Chippewa boy was fond of strapping to his foot a strip of wood on which he coasted on the snow down the steepest hills to test his bravery and self-control. In another favorite game a group of children blindfolded one of their playmates. Before he chased them, the "it" child had to tap each playmate, ask a number of questions, and answer them himself:

"What do you want?"
"I want a fire."
"Who's with you?"
"My horse."
"How high is your horse?"
"As high as a pine tree."
"How far can your horse go?"
"As far as you can see."
"Try to catch your horse."

With these words the blindfolded child tried to catch each of his playmates.[22]

The Chippewas subjected both their daughters and their sons to an ordeal of purification to determine their fitness for full adult life. The mother made a wigwam for her daughter some distance from their home and left her there without food for four days and four nights. During her isolation she was permitted to scratch her hair or body only with a stick. At the end of her ordeal she was feasted, though she was forbidden to taste any fruit, or vegetable until she had performed the proper ceremony. Then her parents invited a member of the *medewiwin* and other persons to a feast of strawberries which the girl had picked. While the medicine man drummed and sang, he held a spoonful of berries to her lips; she moved as if to eat them, only to refuse them. She repeated this teasing ceremony with the medicine man four times before she accepted them and ate them. The other persons followed suit. Thus she showed the patience and discipline which underlies so many Indian customs. She repeated the ceremony with the medicine man with every fruit and vegetable, even with wild rice which they picked in the autumn.[23]

Adolescent boys, too, underwent the ordeal of purification. It differed from that of the Sioux only in some of its details. The father took his son, who had blackened his face, a considerable distance from their lodge and made a nest for him in a tree. There he left his son for three or four days without food. "When you sleep tonight," the father might say, "perhaps something will appear to you. If you get a good dream, it will be a good thing for you. Perhaps you will see a big town. That would be good luck and would mean that if a white man sees you he will like you." Sometimes the boy had to try as many as ten times before he could dream. After each attempt his father might ask, "Didn't you see anything?" And the boy might reply, "No." Eventually, he dreamed: a man came to him and told him that his name would be Bijiki, which in old Chippewa meant buffalo, and like a buffalo he must become— very strong and full of endurance, virtues which he must show for the rest of his life.[24]

Closely guarded by her parents, an unmarried girl was usually modest in her behavior with a young man. He first talked to her parents at the door of her lodge. If they approved of him, they permitted him to proceed to the middle of the lodge, which she occupied with her brothers and sisters. But the girl was not allowed to leave with him. If he called late in the evening her mother or grandmother stirred the fire to make it burn bright, filled her pipe, and sat up and smoked. Though he knew he was watched he remained in the lodge, playing his courting flute. If his intentions were honorable he indicated his ability to provide for his family by killing a deer or some other animal. He brought it to the girl's parents who invited him to share in the feast

47

if they approved of him. And they allowed him thereafter to come and go as he wished. In playing his courting flute he often sang a tender love song, one of which has been translated in this manner:

> *Awake! flower of the forest, sky-treading bird of the prairie. Awake! awake! wonderful fawn-eyed one. When you look upon me I am satisfied; as flowers that drink dew. The breath of your mouth is the fragrance of flowers in the morning, your breath is their fragrance at evening in the moon-of-fading-leaf. Do not the red streams of my veins run toward you as forest-streams to the sun in the moon of bright nights?*
>
> *When you are beside me my heart sings; a branch it is, dancing, dancing before the Wind-spirit in the moon of strawberries. When you frown upon me, beloved, my heart grows dark—a shining river the shadow of clouds darken, then with your smiles comes the sun and makes to look like gold furrows the cold wind drew in the water's face. Myself! behold me! blood of my beating heart. Earth smiles—the waters smile—even the sky-of-clouds smiles—but I, I lose the way of smiling when you are not near.*
>
> *Awake! awake! my beloved.*[25]

To which the young woman might reply in the following song:

> *My love is tall and graceful as the young pine waving on the hill, and as swift in his course as the noble, stately deer; his hair is flowing, and dark as the blackbird that floats through the air, and his eyes, like the eagle's both piercing and bright; his heart, it is fearless and great, and his arm is strong in the fight, as his bow made of ironwood which he easily bends. His aim is as sure in the fight and chase, as the hawk, which ne'er misses its prey. Ah, aid me, ye spirits! of water, of earth, and of sky, while I sing in his praise; and my voice shall be heard, it shall ring through the sky; and echo, repeating the same, shall cause it to swell in the breath of the wind; and his fame shall be spread throughout the land, and his name shall be known beyond the lakes.*[26]

They knew no marriage ceremony. They simply lived together, lessening their tokens of affection while strengthening those of attachment. They made their home either with her parents or in a lodge of their own. After living with his wife for some time, the man might take another wife or two and sit majestically among them, or he might

48

abandon them all without providing for them or for their children. In accordance with custom, he provided for his children only as long as he lived with them. He lost no respect whatever in failing to support them or even in deserting them.

In any case, he continued to love them tenderly, spending much time telling them stories which he had heard from his own parents or grandparents. He told them, perhaps, the story of the horned sturgeon, which has been translated loosely as follows:

> Once some people got into their canoes to look for sturgeons; some spears they had; far out at sea they went. And while looking down into the water, every now and then they beheld a sturgeon, whereupon they thrust a spear at the sturgeon. By and by a certain man was heard saying: "Oh, behold the form of this sturgeon! It has horns in the same manner as a moose!"
>
> Thereupon all came in canoes to see how the sturgeon looked. "Verily, it is horned!" they said. "That is a manitou sturgeon!"
>
> Accordingly they smoked, some tobacco too they put into the water. When they had finished smoking, they went away.
>
> Now, another canoe of people went thither, and they saw the sturgeon. Then, taking up his spear, one of the men thrust it into the sturgeon. And when they brought it up from the water, then they beheld a bald eagle clinging fast to the head of the sturgeon. Thereupon heartily did all the people laugh.[27]

Sometimes the Chippewas wove a fable derived from that of white men and adapted to please their native taste and understanding:

> Once on a time, while a fox was running about over the country, he killed a hare. Accordingly, when he had eaten one half of it, he left behind the other half. Again he went running hither and thither, but he did not kill another hare. Whereupon he remembered his cache where he had placed one-half of a hare.
>
> Once when the crow too was flying about, he saw where there was a hare. Greatly pleased was he, now that he was going to have some food to eat. And just as he was about to eat, he saw a fox coming along on a run. Whereupon he exclaimed: "Hawi, hawi, hawi!" And so, taking up the meat, he carried it away; upon a tree he alighted; very hungry at the time was the crow.

49

Now, the fox saw the crow alight. He went over to the place under-neath where the crow was perched, and this he said to him: "Crow, truly beautiful is the garment you have on. Very handsomely are you clad."

And so when the crow laughed, "Aᵃ, aᵃ, aᵃ, aᵃ!" too wide did he open his mouth as he laughed; whereupon, when he dropped the hare, it fell to the ground.

So the fox seized his hare; he laughed at the crow, "Hwaᵘ, hwaᵘ, hwaᵘ, hwaᵘ!" Whereupon he ate the hare. Now, the crow was angry, even though at the same time he laughed. "Aᵃ, Aᵃ, Aᵃ, Aᵃ!" And so with that he rose and flew away.

That is as far as the story goes.[28]

An old Chippewa named Odinigun regaled Frances Densmore with his version of the first world, which existed long before the birth of the supreme tribal god Manabozho, or Winibojo, as Odinigun pronounced the name. It was created by a small animal who brought up a bit of earth from the primal ocean.

The first earth was called Caca. It was in this part of the country. The people who lived there were not wise. They had no clothing, but they sat around and did nothing. Then the spirit of the creator sent a man to teach them. This man was called ockabewis [messenger]. Some of those early people lived in the south where they did not need any clothing. But the people around here were cold and began to worry about what they should do. The ockabewis saw the southern people naked and homeless and left them to themselves. He came farther north where the people were suffering and in need of his assistance. He said, "Why are you sitting here with no clothing on?" They replied, "Because we do not know what to do." The first thing he taught them was how to make a fire by means of a bow and stick and a bit of decayed wood. Then he taught them how to cook meat by the fire. They had no axes, but he took a pole and burned it in two over the fire. He taught them to boil meat in fresh birch bark. It was a long time before they had things as he wanted them, but after a while they were made comfortable by his help. They had no minds or ideas of their own, only to do as the ockabewis told them to do. This was long before Winibojo.

The ockabewis told them that they must fast and find out things by dreams and that if they paid attention to these dreams they would learn how to heal the sick. The people listened and fasted and found in dreams how to teach their children and do everything. The young men were taught that they must regulate their lives by dreams, they must live moral lives, be industrious, and be moderate in the use of tobacco when it should be given to them. They were especially taught that their minds would not be clear if they ate and drank too much. Tobacco and corn were given them, but it was the ockabewis who taught them how to use them. After a while Winibojo was born, but he had to do as the natives did.[29]

A Chippewa *adizoke* or fairy tale was often a combination of Hans Christian Andersen, *Uncle Tom's Cabin,* and fanciful ideas entirely foreign to Indian life. It naturally enjoyed great popularity, especially among the older Indians, because it was novel to them. Little Wolfe, a man proficient in story-telling, told Frances Densmore a fairy tale one cold night. The tale showed the influence of biblical teaching, current history, and the tales of travelers from across the sea. It told of a rich boy who was raised in the cellar of a large stone house with only a black-and-tan dog as his companion. He saw daylight only through a small window until, at the age of ten, he was allowed to come out on a platform to examine a boat built of gold and silver by one of his father's friends. Curious to see the rich man's son for the first time, civilians and soldiers gathered from miles around on the platform. They greeted him with hurrahs and booming of cannon when, escorted by his parents, he made his way with his dog to the boat. Suddenly the boat—

started and he did not know in which direction it was going. The boy and his dog were running from door to door, playing in the boat. The boy went to turn around and saw his shadow on the wall. He could see it go before him. He wished his boat to travel on the earth, and when he found it was running along the earth he looked ahead and saw a lake. He said, "I wish my boat to go safely to the lake." He kept on playing. He looked out and saw his shadow still running along beside him and he talked to his shadow. He saw something shining in the water ahead. The boy spoke to the boat again. "Go ahead. If that shining thing is a house, you must stop in front of it." The boat suddenly shook. The boat went in front of the house. The boy saw a door and rapped on it. The door opened and a man was there who was very glad to see him and said he was alone in the house as the boy was in the boat. The boy said, "Come in my boat and you shall be part owner." So the man locked the door and got on the boat with his new friend. Now there were three on the boat. The boat started and they began to play around again. The boy was so happy, playing from one corner of the boat to another. Suddenly the boy stopped, looked out, and noticed how fast they ran in the water. He said, "My boat, go back as you came." Then he went on playing. He looked out and the boat was on dry land. They played some more, then they looked out and saw some one sitting on the land.

The boy said to his friend, "Who is that?" The man said, "It is some one sitting there." The boy said to the boat, "You must go where those people are and stop near them." He forgot that he had told the boat to stop and did not notice until the boat shook and stopped. He opened the door. The dog jumped out before him. Both started to run toward the figures. The man went, too. They found some men sitting in a circle. They sat close together. Each man sat cross-legged with his left hand on his knee and his awl in his right hand which he held up as high as his head. All were looking at something on the ground. The boy said, "My friends, what are you doing with those awls?" The boy looked on the ground and it was all glistening with beautiful rings. They threw the awls to see which would hit the center of a ring. The boy said, "My friends, can I buy those rings? I will give the contents of my boat for them." They said, "Is that true?" "Yes; give me the rings and I will give you what is in my boat."[30]

Whereupon he took a ring and put it on his finger. The boy gave them all the money on the boat, which turned around and started for home. Meanwhile his father had been watching through spyglasses for his return to the city. One day his father saw approaching a speck as small as a mosquito and he knew that his son was returning. "Our son's boat looks light in the distance," said the father to his wife. Amid the booming of cannon the boy reached the city where, on landing, his father asked him, "Where are the goods?" The lonely boy replied he had exchanged them for a friend. And he and his friend and his dog went back to live in the cellar of his large stone house.

Sometime later the boy, the friend, and the dog started on another journey to a distant land. Its inhabitants were colored people warring with invading whites. The voyagers saw a Negro whipping a beautiful white girl who was the daughter of a high officer and who had been captured during the war. The boy bought the girl with the contents of his boat and returned with her to his home, where they lived again in the cellar. But the father took pity on the girl and ordered his son to take her back to her people in a vessel with two flags, two cannon, 10,000 men, eight officers, and five hundred sailors, in case he needed to fight the natives of the country.

The boy was delighted. It did not take long to make this great boat. The little boy's room was on one side of the boat and his friends were on the other side and there was a stairway in the middle. This was the first time the boy discovered that he was an officer. When the time came to start he was dressed in officer's clothes and got on the boat with his friend, the dog, and the girl.[31]

After they had been on the ocean for a long time, four of the eight officers grew envious of the boy's beautiful friend. They plotted against him and even won the other officers to their side. One day they threw the boy overboard. But a spirit bird rescued him and restored him to the girl, who now became his wife. The spirit bird was really the body of a dead man which the boy had bought on one of his journeys. The boy found that his wife had presented him with a son. The spirit bird ordered him to kill his son with his sword. He was about to do so when the spirit bird said, "Stop! Now I know you pity me, for you were willing to kill the child for me. Bring up this child. I see your pity. You bought my body after I had been killed. Although I had money—a trunkful—I believe you did it from pity. Now I am going to leave you."

As soon as the spirit bird disappeared the boy returned in triumph to his father, who received him with unbounded joy. And he and his wife and child lived in the cellar of the large stone house until he was one hundred years old.[32]

The tale was spun in accordance with many accepted literary standards and with an admirable degree of drama. The elements of unity and of interest lie in the voyages with their charming variations. The boat that moves without oars or paddles is a steamboat. And the sailor with a sword is an officer of the United States Navy. These things suggest the influence of the white man's civilization in the tale. Despite its medley of ideas, its construction remains intact. It has, also, an exciting cumulative thread: the boy, then the boy and his dog, then the boy, the dog, and the man; then the boy, the dog, the man, and the girl. The bird spirit gives the tale a kind of cohesion. And the sections, divided by the boy's return to the cellar between voyages, hold the listener's attention for a time, then let it relax, and then call it up again with increased fascination of plot.

4

The Sacs and Foxes

IRONICALLY, THE INDIANS WHO GAVE THEIR NAME TO THE STATE OF IOWA figured the least in its history. Like the Otos, the Missouris, and the Omahas, they were a Siouan people who had sprung and separated from the Winnebagoes. At the beginning of the eighteenth century Pierre Charles Le Sueur, learning that they were living near the mouth of the Blue Earth River in present Minnesota and hearing that they were good farmers, sent messengers to invite them to settle near the fort he was building; but they had already departed for the Missouri, where they fought with their allies, the Sioux, against the Sacs. They were then a very small tribe, though they had once been numerous and formidable. In 1804 Lewis and Clark found them occupying a single village of two hundred braves or eight hundred persons. Yet the tribe has won a nobler and more lasting fame than some of the larger ones, for its name graces one of our greatest agricultural states and two of her rivers, one of her counties, one of her cities, and several of her villages. And the name also honors a county in Wisconsin, villages in Kansas, California, Louisiana, and Texas, and parks and summer resorts in a number of other states.[1]

The most important tribes in Iowa were the Sacs and Foxes who, however, were not native to the region. Though they migrated westward from present Wisconsin, they figure so prominently in the frontier history of the Mississippi Valley that they deserve full treatment here. Both were of Algonkian stock. The Sacs or Sauks, who originally were not associated with the Foxes, believed they derived their name, which means People of the Yellow Earth, from Getci Munito who, on creating

55

the world, moulded in his hands some yellow clay in the image of a human being and made it come alive by blowing on it four times.[2] This man was undoubtedly the Adam of their tribe.

When the Sacs first met with white fur traders and missionaries from Canada they lived in the eastern peninsula of Michigan. In 1667 Father Claude Allouez described them as the most savage people he had ever known. Though they constituted a sizeable tribe, they had not yet accepted sedentary culture; they led the existence of wanderers and vagabonds in the forest. The missionary learned that they killed any Frenchman they found in an isolated place because they could not endure the sight of his whiskers. Yet he joyously reported, just two years later, that they were the first to receive religious instruction from him in one of their villages at the DePere Rapids, Wisconsin, where they had been driven by hostile Indians.[3] By the middle of the seventeenth century they had moved again, this time to the southern part of Green Bay, where they began to trade with the Foxes, who had formed a settlement of six hundred lodges about a hundred miles away.

The Foxes called themselves Musquakie or Meskwaki, meaning Red Earth, because they believed that Getci Munito had made them from red clay to distinguish them above all others as the first tribe he had created. In the Algonkian tongue they were known as Outagamies, meaning Foxes or, in French, Renards. The site of their earliest home is unknown, though tradition clearly indicates that they once resided along the waters of the St. Lawrence. Later they may have lived in present Rhode Island. Gradually they wandered or were driven westward until, in the middle of the seventeenth century, they reached Lake Michigan and the Green Bay region. They told missionaries that the first white people they saw were Englishmen and the second were Frenchmen, who were hostile toward them and who, by allying other tribes against them, eventually succeeded in driving them westward and across the lakes.[3]

The long and close association of the Sacs with the Foxes led the American government and many historians and journalists to regard them as one nation. Actually, they constituted two separate and distinct tribes. They had consolidated principally to strengthen their military chances against neighboring and hostile Indians. To this end each imposed on the other obligations which were maintained throughout their defensive alliance. Beyond military necessity, however, they had little common interest or feeling. Later in their history they acted in complete independence of each other in declaring war or in making peace either with the whites or with other Indian tribes. The confederacy, therefore, was not a new nation—not even in the meager sense of the word as it was understood among Indian tribes. Neither tribe denationalized the other. And they never amalgamated, though the American government often linked them together in treaties. No error could be more palpable than to believe, as did many writers and government officials, that they were "as one people."[4] To the present day each tribe has maintained its ancient clans and its perfect line of chieftainship.

Yet the Sacs and the Foxes resembled each other in language and in most of their manners and customs. Both were of Algonkian stock. Both owned the culture of the eastern Woodland People, though it was modified by practices adopted from Plains tribes. Both were physically and tastefully attired in breechclout and beaded moccasins. The men of each tribe treated their scalp locks with vermilion and yellow, streaked their faces with red, blue, and yellow, and hung a string of wampum or bear's claws around their necks with ear bobs to match. Their governments were similar. The civil chiefs were selected on the basis of heredity, and they exercised the authority of enforcing simple tribal rites. Though they interfered in all tribal matters, they were often greatly influenced by their braves or principal men in matters of peace or war. The prerogative of a chief was to direct; the duty of a brave or warrior was to fight. The amount of influence each chief commanded depended on his personality. If he were wise in council, he exerted great power among his people; if he were brave in war, he commanded their admiration and loyalty. If, on the contrary, he showed no such qualities, he found himself merely a faint voice in tribal affairs. Regardless of his own qualifications, he appreciated knowing the wishes of the tribal council which ultimately wielded the authority of the tribe.[5]

Despite political similarities each group displayed some striking differences in personality and character. The Foxes were braver or more reckless in battle than the Sacs, though they were much inferior to them in political administration. Since the Sacs were four times as numerous as the Foxes, they led them and therefore commanded a greater prestige among whites and Indians alike. The Foxes had the reputation of being stingy, arrogant, and inordinately fond of firewater. The Sacs, on the contrary, were generous and hospitable toward the whites, compassionate toward defeated enemies, and moderate in their use of alcoholic beverages.[6]

In this essentially military and agricultural society, the duties of men and women were necessarily sharply drawn. They lived in constant fear of attack, which might easily result in the death of their families, the destruction of their homes, and the loss of their identity as a tribe. Thus the men, whether in camp or on the march, always kept themselves in a state of readiness. Their duties, therefore, related largely to their perilous circumstances. They hunted, fished, and trapped—activities which in a pristine society were always toilsome, frequently dangerous, and sometimes fatal, especially in winter. They also made war, administered laws, formed treaties, and attended to the general regulation of tribal affairs. In such a society food was always a serious problem. No idle hands could be tolerated, and the women, with the assistance of their children and old men, were assigned to the tasks of realizing a subsistence. They skinned, stretched, and prepared for market the skins that were brought home. They cooked and made camp. They planted corn and vegetables in the spring, hoed them in the summer, and harvested them in the autumn. And yet they never neglected the more natural field of their labor, that of tending their homes and rearing their children. From these drudgeries they often found diversion in such important prerogatives as performing ceremonies and religious rites in tribal affairs. Their multitudinous activities led casual observers to believe erroneously that they were mere drudges or slaves of their indolent and pleasure-seeking husbands.[7]

The mothers seldom resorted to corporal punishment in correcting their children. A mother punished her recalcitrant child by blackening his face, depriving him of his meals, and sending him out of the lodge. He was not allowed to return home until he was ready to ask for forgiveness. Then his mother would wash off the black from his face and give him something to eat.[8]

When a boy was six or seven years old his mother placed a small bow into his hands and sent him out to hunt birds near the lodge or the village. When he was eleven or twelve his father bought him a shot gun, sent him out to hunt ducks and geese. At the same time the boy was taught how to approach a deer, elk, or buffalo and how to set a trap. Sometimes a boy's father took him on a hunting trip and showed him the tracks of different animals. The boy nearly always paid great attention to what his father taught him.[9]

The girls, as a matter of course, were under the direction of their mothers. They learned how to make moccasins, leggings, and mats. And they were kept continually employed to impress marriageable young men with their diligence.[10]

Most boys and girls of either the Sacs or the Foxes were married before they were out of their teens. A young man encountered no difficulty in finding a wife, particularly if he was an adroit hunter or had distinguished himself as a warrior. In seeking a wife a young man sometimes followed the custom of his tribe by striking up a friendship with a relative, often a brother, of the girl he desired to marry. To him he would disclose his intention, declaring that he was a good hunter and had taken part in a number of battles. He assured him that, if he could have the girl as his wife, he would serve her relatives faithfully until the birth of his first child. Then, in accordance with the custom of his tribe, he would take her away to his or her parents. On receiving this message, her parents either accepted or rejected the offer without consulting her.[11]

During the summer hunting excursion, when parental vigilance was relaxed, an occasional young man might carry off a girl to his wigwam. On returning to his village, he might approach the girl's parents, tell them that he meant to keep her as his wife, and, by way of gaining their approval, might offer them a part of his hunt, a horse, some goods, or a little whiskey. If her parents accepted his gifts they gave up their daughter without another word.[12]

A young man who saw a girl he wanted to marry would watch for an opportunity to speak to her. If she accepted his attentions, he would inform his parents. They would ask for presents or goods or horses if for some reason they were reluctant to give up their son. On the other hand, the parents of the girl might reject an offer of property and insist instead on a period of servitude. Then the young man would come and hunt for them for one, two, or three years, as they agreed, before they would relinquish their right to their daughter.[13]

The Sacs and Foxes could have as many wives as they could afford, though very few of them had more than five. Chief Keokuk told the missionary, Cutting Marsh, that he had five wives and seven children living, though "he had lost more than ten; he has also had a good many women whom he has put away."[14] A man could very easily get rid of his wife as soon as either he or she tired of each other. A wife, however, was his property. If she misbehaved, he could kill her without fear of revenge from her relatives. He could order her to return to him. Yet the Sacs and Foxes seldom maltreated their wives. The average husband would listen to his wife's rantings all day without being disturbed in any way. Marsh observed that wives often quarreled or fought among themselves over their husband's affection. The husband often witnessed these manifestations of jealousy, but never interfered with them. If one wife was driven off he made no ado about her "but either lets her go or else perhaps he may go to the lodge where she [lives] and keep company with her there. Indeed the man takes little or no interest apparently in the affairs of his wife or wives and but very few converse with their wives familiarly or treat them as equals."[15] Frequently, a man of fifty or sixty with two or three wives married a girl of sixteen. On her he showered all his attention as long as his energy or stamina permitted, but he continued to regard his first wife as head of his family.[16] The prevailing rule was to marry sisters, since they were less likely to quarrel among themselves.

Though the Sacs and Foxes were warlike tribes, they never declared war on their enemies. When a neighboring tribe provoked them and failed to redress grievances within a specified time, they simply took to the warpath without warning. Old warriors instilled their sons or grandsons with a love for war by feeding them a steady diet of military stories. They seized every opportunity to take to the warpath, sometimes even against tribes unknown to them. They prepared for war by fasting, praying, and dreaming of victory. Then, in improvised lodges which they raised outside of their village, they made belts of blue wampum, painted them vermilion, and invited young men to declare themselves for war by wearing them and by smoking. These young men were led against the enemy and taught the art of attacking when they neared enemy territory. They traveled slowly, hunting as they advanced and storing jerked beef for sustenance on their return. They carried medicine bags on their backs and their leader sang war songs to which his warriors responded with guttural cries while dancing around him.[17]

The man whom they chose to carry their kettles invariably served as their cook. As soon as they encamped they would bring him wood and water and furnish him with meat. They rewarded him for his services by allowing him to keep the best piece of meat for himself.

As long as they wore their vermilion belts of war the Sacs and Foxes fasted and abstained from cohabitation, which they regarded as a sacrilege during any military campaign. Before they made an attack they sent forward some of their cleverest young men to reconnoiter or spy on the enemy. As soon as the spies returned their comrades surprised the enemy by attacking him before daylight. If they were defeated they scattered, living on the jerked beef they had stored. If they were victorious, the first among them to kill an enemy was given the privilege of leading his comrades toward home. On the way they usually killed the elderly prisoners, whose spirits they sent to their deceased friends as an act of atonement. After dancing in triumph among the younger prisoners they generally adopted them and considered them representatives of their beloved dead. Some chiefs enslaved their prisoners or sold them to other chiefs, who often encouraged them to become warriors. These adopted warriors received new names and free status as soon as they killed an enemy. The owners of female slaves generally made them their concubines and considered any children borne by them as their legitimate offspring. Some female slaves became free women simply by marrying their owners.[18]

The Sacs and Foxes usually buried their dead. Customarily, a man who believed he was dying chose his own place of interment, which sometimes was as far as a hundred miles away. On the day he died his relatives put him in a crude bark coffin and, with much weeping and howling, carried him to a shallow grave. Before the burial one or two relatives called for attention by waving a *puccamawgun* (war club) while another said in an audible voice: "I have killed so many men in war, I give their spirits to my deceased friend, who lies here, to serve him as slaves in the other world." Then they filled the grave with earth and, on the following day, built over it a kind of cabin of split boards. If the deceased man had been a brave, they planted a vermilion post at the head of his grave. The scalps he had taken in war were enumerated on this post. On the same day the dead man's relatives received his property. This included clothing, ceremonial paraphernalia, and implements for cultivating the soil, preparing food, dressing skins, and making garments and tent covers. If he was married, his widow or widows returned to their nearest relatives. The younger widows were compelled to become the wives of his brother, if he wanted them. Sometimes the dead man's widows were his principal mourners. For months after their husband's death they appeared in rags and disheveled hair and with a black spot made with charcoal on their cheeks to denote their bereavement. Often they repaired to the woods where, out of hearing distance of any person, they cried aloud for a long time, then returned to their lodges quite composed. When, at the suggestion of their friends, they ceased their mourning, they washed themselves, put on their best clothes and ornaments, and painted stripes of red on their cheeks.[19]

The Foxes and Sacs believed that the spirit of a dead man hovered around his village for a few days and then departed to the land of repose. On its journey the spirit arrived at a large prairie, over which it saw a distant forest that looked like a blue cloud. The spirit had to float above the prairie to the edge of the forest near a deep and rapid stream. Then it would cross the stream on a pole. If the spirit was from a good person it would cross and find all the spirits of dead relatives. The woods abounded with all kinds of game and the spirit lived in everlasting happiness. On the contrary, the spirit of a bad person fell off the pole into the water. It was then carried by the current to the residence of the evil spirit, where it remained forever in indigence and extreme misery.[20]

The relatives of a dead person often visited his grave, hoed away the grass around it, swept it clean, and occasionally placed choice meats and tobacco near it. All Indians were very fond of their children. A sick man hated to leave the world if his children were young. If, on the contrary, they were grown up and married, he knew he was a burden to them and cared little whether he lived or died.[21]

62

From the hard realities of life the Sacs and Foxes found release by dancing, feasting, gaming, and story-telling. Most of the dances of the Sacs and Foxes were, like those of other tribes, ceremonial and religious. A few were purely social. In addition to their own dances they adopted some of those of other tribes. The main instruments in their ceremonial, pantomimic, or dramatic dances were the rattle and the drum.[22] Their great favorite was the buffalo dance. Putting on skins of buffalo heads with horns attached, they imitated that animal by throwing themselves into different postures, by mimicking its groans, and by attempting to horn each other. All the while they kept exact time to rattle and drum. The women often joined in the dance, remaining nearly in the same spot as they sang in shrill voices above those of the men.[23]

The Sacs and Foxes were also fond of gambling and playing games. They frequently would bet their horses, wampum, and whiskey. They were fond of horse racing and foot racing. They played lacrosse with great skill. In summer young men conducted sham battles which provided them with entertainment as well as with invaluable experience for warfare. This game was played by horsemen and footmen. The horsemen would attack a group of footmen who were escorting some of their friends to the village. The footmen would beat off the horsemen until, after many encounters, they succeeded in bringing their friends safely home. In these encounters some of the footmen were trampled by the mounts, but these mishaps never aroused their anger. When the game was over they all retired on the best of terms with one another, agreeing that anger was beneath the dignity of brave warriors.[24]

In war games as well as in peace ceremonies the Sacs and Foxes worshiped Wesahkah, their principal god. Resembling Noah of the Old Testament, Wesahkah created a new world after the old had been destroyed by a flood. At the beginning of time the Great Spirit addressed the gods of the earth in this manner:

Spirits of my breath, I have created you all to enjoy the earth and widespreading waters, and with you I shall now make a division of them. Wesahkah shall possess the dry land and Nahmepashe and Mahshekenapeck the waters. But Wesahkah shall be chief and you shall obey him in all things, for to him I have given my terrestrial sphere to make war and peace with whomsoever he will. At length he will become elated and say within himself, "I am the Great Spirit. Moreover, in memory of this eventful day I shall create a race of beings after my own likeness."

Wesahkah accordingly created man in his own image. And legions of spirits flew from the presence of the Great Spirit to their destined homes. They compensated man for his nakedness by giving him knowledge of fire, wild animals with hair and fur, and birds with feathers.[25]

Such was the world when mankind was under the protection of Wesahkah.

But these halcyon days soon faded. The Aiyamwoy, a race of terrible giants who were descendents of the gods of the sea, became so numerous that they overran the world. They filled Wesahkah's children with dread and threatened them with destruction. Wesahkah sent his brother, Nahpattay, to the gods of the sea to remonstrate against the depredations of the Aiyamwoy; but instead of listening to him, they slew him. His blood, however, ran from the sea into the land, and a drop of it became a body into which Nahpattay's spirit entered, giving him life again. He sought safety in flight, but the Aiyamwoy soon overtook him and devoured him, leaving not a drop of his blood. Wesahkah, hearing of his brother's fate, became enraged. He fasted for ten days, vowing destruction of the gods of the sea. Then he heard his brother's spirit crying for entrance at the Door of Life; but he answered, "Go to the land of spirit and there be chief of men who shall die like yourself."[26]

When Nahpattay's spirit had departed, Wesahkah armed himself with a great spear and went with the speed of an eagle to fight the Aiyamwoy, who had devoured his brother. He met and slew them. And the gods of the sea retaliated by waging war against Wesahkah, vowing to destroy him even at the risk of their own lives. They called a great council in which they agreed to flood the world. Hearing of their plans, Wesahkah fasted again for ten days. Then he prayed to the Great Spirit, who answered him and preserved mankind and the wild animals and birds. But when the flood began to overflow the plains, Wesahkah took his family and their possessions and fled to refuge on a high mountain. But the flood soon overtook them. Whereupon Wesahkah built a great raft on which he put a male and a female of every creature and floated it on the surface of the great waters. Soon Wesahkah repented of his wrath and once more fasted for ten days. Then he dreamed he saw dry land.

Awaking, he sent the tortoise to fetch him some clay. When the tortoise failed in this mission, he sent the muskrat, which brought up clay between its claws. From that clay Wesahkah formed dry land. Then he distributed all living creatures on the face of it. And they lived in peace and happiness because the flood had destroyed the Aiyamwoy and, indeed, all evil spirits.[27]

Wesahkah was now sole chief of the earth and all the creatures on it. In time they became so numerous that they could no longer dwell in one place. So their leaders, Sanke, Musquakie or Red Fox, and Ashekan, met at Wesahkah's dwelling, which was called Mixed Water, where they decided to separate the people into tribes and take them toward the south. Before the three fathers or leaders departed with their charges, Wesahkah gave each of them a *meshaum* or grand medicine bag. In each bag, the names and wars of ancient gods were recorded by knots on strings and by stones and hieroglyphics. The bag also contained the revelations which they supposed Wesahkah had delivered to their ancestors.[28]

The faithful Sacs and Foxes regarded the *meshaum* with profound veneration and observed its ordinances implicitly. It taught them to fast every morning in the winter season, to fast ten days in order to obtain signal revenge on their enemies, and to invoke Wesahkah and make a sacrifice to him when they killed a bear or some choice game. It forbade women to enter a religious lodge or to eat any cooked meat during their menstrual periods. It exhorted them to give away property to the poor for the good of their departed relatives. It taught that the Great Spirit gave them the wild beasts for their sustenance. It required them to forgive injuries inflicted on them by their families or tribe, but to revenge the wrongs inflicted on them by their enemies.[29]

The *meshaum* was considered so sacred an object that it was hung on the limbs of a tree to protect it from any unclean person, especially from any unclean woman. They decreed death to any white man who opened and examined it. A white man living near the Dubuque mines on the Mississippi once saw a *meshaum* hanging on a tree outside an Indian lodge. The father and mother had gone on a hunting expedition or to attend some chores, leaving their children in the lodge. Led by curiosity, the white man took down the *meshaum* and examined it. The children, seeing their father's *meshaum* profaned in such a manner,

65

began to cry. When the parents returned and learned what had happened, they formed parties to hunt the desecrator down. He had to leave the country to save his life.[30]

The Sacs and Foxes believed that if they fulfilled the requirements of the *meshaum,* they would go to Chepakmunk, meaning Happy Land, when they died. Chepakmunk was located "far in the west" and it abounded in game of all kinds and whatever was pleasing to the sight and taste. If, on the contrary, they died in wickedness, they would be attracted to Mahnasanoah, meaning The River of Death; but, unable to cross it, they would plunge into it. The river had no power over the good, who passed it safely, joined the legion of Nahpattay, and enjoyed everlasting happiness.[31]

No social event was more important to a devotee of the *meshaum* than that of making a feast, or invocation for the Great Spirit. He summoned the cooks, and the followers of the *meshaum.* With them he decided whether the invocation was to be a dog-feast, the most sacred of all, or merely a feast of venison. They selected the dog or the deer, scrubbed the kettles, and ascertained that the lodge in which the feast was to be given was carefully screened with heavy curtains. Then they gathered the singers who, as soon as the kettles were put on the fire, began chanting sacred songs. These songs consisted of only a few words repeated over and over. Meanwhile old women responded by emitting sounds through their noses that sounded like distress or derangement rather than devotion. "Go and you shall have two horns upon your forehead," ran the words of one of these sacred songs, "and when you return your horns shall be blue like the sky." This has been interpreted as meaning: "Go and be masters of the beasts of the fields and of the fowls of the air."[32]

Reverend Marsh was once invited by Chief Appenoore to witness an invocation. He accepted the invitation as a matter of civility. As he entered the lodge in which the feast was given he heard the chief repeat the requisitions of the *meshaum* in a brief speech. The chief then ordered the cook to serve the guests. Marsh observed that:

When they took the kettles from the fire a ladle full of the broth contained in them was taken out and one went round the fire pouring a little of it into the fire very carefully as he went round. And each portion was also

carried once round the fire before it was given to the individual. No one
began to eat until all were served, but each was engaged in taking off the
things with which the pieces of venison were tied together, or else in
stripping them to pieces as no knives or forks were permitted to be used.
When all were in readiness to eat, the kettles having been with much care
turned over at each end of the fire, each one, beginning at the head, uttered a few words, which were thanks to the [cooks], and then began to
eat. The same expression of thanks was given at the close. Some, I observed, were unable to eat their portion, such sent out and invited a friend
to come to their assistance as nothing must be left which could be eaten,
and the remainder viz:—the strings and bones were all collected and
burnt in the fire, together with some stuff taken from the [*meshaum*],
which was considered as a kind of incense. Then followed a long speech
or prayer by the chief speaker and he was followed by the chief with another. These speeches were said over in a solemn but hurried manner and
are used at every sacred feast. After all these and other ceremonies also
were performed it was announced that the feast was closed and as each
went out he went once round the fire; the whole occupying an hour and a
half or two hours.[33]

Marsh noticed that one Indian was remarkably scrupulous in performing
every ceremony and in requiring others to do as he did. He castigated
Marsh's interpreter as "a very bad man" because he had used a little
salt. Marsh recalled, however, that the Indian had been intoxicated the
day before. He observed that baseness of conduct or vileness of character did not disqualify them from participating in the *meshaum* which
was peculiarly suited to their habits and manners. It laid no restraint on
their unbridled appetites and passions and threatened no penalty for
skeptics and unbelievers. The drunkard, the dabauchee, or the glutton
could perform all of the requirements of the *meshaum* and, when he
died, still go to the Happy Land. Their prayers entailed no confession of
sin and, therefore, no atonement for it. Marsh found no word in their
language for sin and no idea of repentance in the evangelical sense. He
told them that atonement, renovation of heart, or spiritual cleansing was
necessary to make them acceptable in the sight of God. In response,
some of them laughed at him as a bearer of idle tales, while others replied that they did not believe in these ideas or that they had never heard
anything about them.[34]

5

The Little Ones

S OUTH OF THE SACS AND FOXES, ON THE BANKS OF THE LITTLE OSAGE NEAR
its confluence with the main Osage River in present Missouri, lived the
tribe which gave its name to these streams. They called themselves
Wah-Sha-She, meaning Water People. The French explorers corrupted
the tribal name to Osage, by which American frontiersmen knew them.
They were one of the five tribes in the Dhegila group of the Siouan
linguistic family which had migrated from the west to the Atlantic Coast
several centuries before the coming of the white men. After occupying
the Piedmont region between the James River in Virginia and the Savannah River in the Carolinas they migrated or were driven westward to
the mouth of the Ohio, where they lived for many years in a single
village. Then, according to their own legend, the Mississippi overflowed
its banks and forced them to flee in panic to the safety of a steep hill,
where they established a temporary camp. Soon they separated in three
groups. One called itself the Quapaws and went downstream to the
Arkansas River. Another, the Osages, remained on the river named for
their tribe. The third, including the Omahas, Poncas, and Kansas, ascended the Missouri. Later, in frontier times, the Osages resided in two
villages in present Vernon County, Missouri. One was located on the east
side of the Little Osage, near its confluence with the Marmaton. The
other was six miles farther up on the west side of the Little Osage. But
the region of their activities was much wider. John Joseph Mathews,
who has written beautifully of this tribe, says that they "claimed all the
territory east of the Mississippi, south of the Missouri, north of the
Arkansas and west to the Rocky Mountains. They not only claimed this

69

great country but were quite able to protect it from the encroachment of other tribes."[1] From their two villages they conducted hunting and warring expeditions which took them as far away as parts of Arkansas, Kansas, and Oklahoma.

George Catlin, who lived among them and knew them well, described them as—

> the tallest race of men in North America, either of red or white skins; there being very few indeed of the men, at their full growth, who are less than six feet in stature, and very many of them are six and a half, and others seven feet. They are at the same time well-proportioned in their limbs, and good-looking; being rather narrow in the shoulders, and, like most all very tall people, a little inclined to stoop; not throwing the chest out, and the head and shoulders back, quite as much as the Crows and Mandans, and other tribes amongst which I have been familiar. Their movement is graceful and quick; and in war and the chase, I think they are equal to any of the tribes about them.[2]

Thomas Nuttall, who visited their villages in 1819, found them practicing a "curious species of polygamy, which prevails among some other Indian nations, . . . by which, the man who first marries into a family, from that period possesses the control of all the sisters of his wife, whom he is at liberty either to espouse himself, or to bestow upon others."[3] Measuring them by his own yardstick of Protestantism, he found them "more than usually superstitious," with an "ominous dream . . . often sufficient to terminate the most important expedition."[4] Though they were no mean warriors, they were essentially religious people whose cultural pattern was bound up in innumerable rituals, ceremonies, and legends, many of which are poignantly beautiful.

Often they referred to themselves as Ni-U-Ko'n-Ska, meaning the Children of the Middle Waters; but in their humility they preferred the nickname of The Little Ones. They believed that originally they dwelled in a heavenly home or Sky Lodge and were all Tzi-Sho, meaning Sky People. Eventually Wah'Kon-Tah or the Great Mysteries sent them down in three divisions to the earth, which they called the Sacred One and which they found divided into land and water. One division retained the name of Sky People; the other two divisions called themselves Wah-Sha-She, meaning Water People, and Hunkah or Honga, meaning Land People. On the earth they found an indigenous division, which they

70

called U-Tah-No'n-Ssi, meaning Isolated Earth People. Now that all of them together symbolized the elements of the universe, they became a complete tribe for the first time.[5]

All of these things were revealed to them by their seers, No'm-Ho'n-Shinkah, Little Old Men, who originally sat under the shade of elms and began to study the stars—

> . . . and talk of the constancy of the sun, the wheeling of the Big Dipper; of the moon and the Morning and Evening Stars, and of the Pleiades, which they called Deer Head and the Galaxy.
>
> They talked of the swiftness of the bank swallows and of the courage and ferocity of the striking falcon; of the old-wise-man look of the tranquil pelican, who traveled slowly and unafraid across the loops and swamps and oxbows and crescent moon-shaped lakes abandoned by the whimsical river.[6]

Intrigued by their powers of observation, the Little Old Men came to believe that the Great Mysteries had gradually given them the genesis of their tribe. It was created in the Sky Lodge, they preached, because the sky was permanent and the sun and moon and stars never changed in their orderly progress. The Great Mysteries had sent it down to the Sacred One to safeguard its destinies.

These things they put down and discussed little by little, always broadening their ideas and embellishing them with details. At times, when they doubted or disagreed, two of them would seclude themselves and seek aid and guidance from the Great Mysteries. And gradually, through patient reflection, they saw the book of nature opening before them. They knew now how it had all happened. While they lived in the Sky Lodge they had neither human bodies nor souls, but they somehow managed to exist. When they slid from the lowest chamber of the Sky Lodge they obtained souls from the bodies of birds. As they continued downward toward the Sacred One, they saw the branches of a huge red oak spreading before them. Down they glided to its uppermost branches, their legs outstretched and their arms spread like the wings of an eagle. Loosing acorns that clattered down among the leaves of the tree, they reached the Sacred One, where they divided into three divisions and found the fourth division that made them a unified tribe.[7]

According to their *wigies*, as they called their chants, the three initial divisions found the Isolated Land People only after long marching. One day the leaders of the Water People and the Land People suddenly halted. Looking over their shoulders they said to their followers and to the leader of the Sky People: "We have come to the village of a strange people." The leader of the Isolated Land People sent a messenger to the strangers to ask the purpose of their visit. He was satisfied with their answer and invited them to enter the village. The Land People and the Sky People declined because they noticed with revulsion that the bones of animals and men lay scattered and bleaching around its walls. The Water People were less squeamish and accepted the invitation, only to learn to their horror that they had come, not to the village of life, which they were seeking, but to the village of death.[8]

The leader of the Water People was conducted to the leader of the Isolated Land People, with whom he exchanged friendly words. The leader of the Water People presented his host with a ceremonial pipe. Then, in an easy manner, they talked of the customs and manners of their peoples. The leader of the Water People told his host that the Land People as well as the Sky People wanted to dwell with him and his people, but disliked his habits of destroying life. He suggested that they all move to a new country, where the land was pure and free from signs of death. The leader of the Isolated Land People accepted the invitation. So they all moved to a country free of decaying carcasses and any signs of destruction. There they united themselves in friendship, each pledging to the other its strength and support in resisting dangers that might beset them in the course of their united tribal life.[9]

By smoking a pipe of red clay they sealed their pledge to support each other as long as their tribe endured. Before he accepted the pipe from the leader of the Water People, the leader of the Land People asked: "Who are you?" And the leader of the Water People replied:

> *I am a person who has verily made of a pipe his body.*
> *When you also make of the pipe your body,*
> *You shall be free from all causes of death, O Honga.*

The leader of the Land People took the pipe and said in response:

> *I am a person who has made of the red boulder his body.*
> *When you also make of it your body,*

The malevolent gods in their destructive course
Shall pass by and leave you unharmed, O Wah-Sha-She.

By its purifying smoke, the red clay pipe symbolized the life of the
Water People. The red boulder, which had the color and durability of
the sacred sun, symbolized the life of the Land People. The Little Old
Men recited the chants of each division in one of their *wigies*.[10]

In time the term, "move to a new country," came to denote a period
that preceded a change in the government of the tribe. Such a move, for
example, occurred when the civil branch of the tribal government was
instituted. They agreed that two chiefs, one from each of two great tribal
divisions, should govern the people. The Little Old Men laid down ten
principal laws for the two chiefs to follow:

When two men quarrel, come to blows, and threaten to kill each other,
the chief shall compel them to cease fighting.

When a murder is committed and a relative of the person slain threat-
ens to take the life of the murderer in revenge, the chief shall compel the
relative to keep the peace.

If the relative persists in his effort to take the life of the slayer, the
chief shall expel him from the tribe.

If the relative takes the life of the slayer when the chief has already
offered him the sacred pipe to smoke, the chief shall give the order for him
to be put to death.

The chief shall require the murderer to bring gifts to the relatives of
the man he has slain as an offering of peace.

If the murderer refuses to do this, the chief may call upon the people to
make the peace offering and then expel the murderer from the tribe.

If a man's life is threatened by another and he flees to the house of
the chief, he shall protect the fleeing man.

If a murderer pursued by the relatives of the slain man flees into the
house of the chief, he shall protect the man.

If a stranger, although he be from an enemy tribe, enters the house of
the chief for safety, the chief shall protect him.

When a war party comes home with captives, the chief shall give
them their lives and have them adopted into the tribe.[11]

The house of each chief was held sacred because it represented two
life-giving powers, earth and sun. It had two doors, one opening toward

the rising sun and the other toward the setting sun. The pathway of the sun was understood to symbolize endless life. The fireplace, which was consecrated and which stood midway between the two doors, represented the sun. Its fire, by which the people started their home fires, was also thought to be holy and to have the power of giving life and health to those who used it. The two doors, which represented the continual flow of life, were forever closed to any man who contemplated murder as he approached them.[12]

The symbol of the tribe was the hawk, which the Little Old Men sanctified because of its courage, swiftness, silence, and cleanliness. From the skin of this sacred bird the Osages made *waxobes* or shrines to symbolize the courage of the warriors of each group or "fireplace" in the tribe. As hereditary caretakers of the *waxobes* the Little Old Men chose the buffalo and the thunder. These were imbued with the authority to redecorate the sacred hawk, an act equivalent to reconsecration for the benefit of the initiate.

According to a well-known Osage legend, the buffalo and the thunder obtained their holy offices when they protested to the Little Old Men that they had been ignored as possible tribal symbols. One day, while the seers sat working on the *waxobes* in their council house, they were startled by the terrifying bellowing of an animal. Looking up at their *shoka*, or messenger, they saw an angry buffalo. Its head was lowered; its tail quivered in the air; it pawed the earth, throwing clouds of dust toward the sky. They asked, "Who are you?" And the bull replied, "I am Tho-xe, the buffalo bull; lift up your heads!" At that moment a crash of thunder, which seemed to come from the end of the ridgepole, shook the earth. The frightened Little Old Men picked up the skin of a hawk on which they had been working and threw it at the bull. The bull, though angry, seemed awed and the seers thought it was Wah'Kon-Tah in disguise. Looking at the hawk skin the buffalo stopped bellowing, lowered its tail, and became friendly. At that moment the heavy clouds which had been creeping over the sky vanished; the sun shone again with its usual brilliance; and the thunder, which only a few moments before had made the earth tremble, growled with seeming contentment in the distance. The Little Old Men reasoned that the buffalo and the thunder were angry at the Tzi-Sho or Sky People for failing to make them symbols. The buffalo had been one of the first animals that the Little Ones had encountered on the Sacred One after their descent from the Sky

74

Lodge. It had given them so many good things: sinew, robes, bedding, lodging, food, and utensils. Should they not therefore regard the buffalo as a part of Wah'Kon-Tah and try to placate it? And had it not evoked the thunder, which was a manifestation of Wah'Kon-Tah's wrath? The Little Old Men placated both the buffalo and the thunder by appointing them hereditary caretakers of the *waxobes*.[13]

Some *waxobes*, such as the portable *waxobe tonga*, were made from the skins of the cormorant and pelican, the feathers of several birds, and other objects. A number of these *waxobes* were circulated among the members of the tribe without regard to the tribal divisions or to the gentes to which the candidates belonged. A leading Osage scholar, Francis La Flesche, describes in detail a *waxobe tonga* which the National Museum acquired from one of the chiefs of the tribe:

> The tattooing waxobe, which is the skin of a cormorant, is split down the entire length of the back. Around the base of the tail is wound a string of scalp locks, 10 or 12 in number, that hang down like a skirt. Within the body of the skin are placed eight tattooing instruments, the points toward the head and the tops toward the tail. The shafts of some of the instruments are flat, others round, and about the length of a lead pencil. To the lower ends of the shafts are fastened steel needles, some in straight rows and others in bunches. To the tops of some of the shafts are fastened small rattles made of pelican or eagle quills. The needle parts of the shafts are covered with buffalo hair to protect them against rust. The skin of the cormorant was folded over the tattooing instruments, the neck of the bird doubled over the back and tied down. The skin of a pelican, split down the back, is wrapped around the cormorant and tied around the middle with a band of woven fiber. The bill, head, and neck of the pelican are missing.
>
> Within the woven rush case, placed without any particular order, are seven weasel skins; one tobacco pouch made of a buffalo heartsack; bits of braided sweet-grass; half of the shell of a fresh-water mussel for holding the coloring matter; four tubes, one of bamboo and three of tin, worn by the operator on his fingers as guides for the instruments when he is at work; two bunches of the wing-feathers of small birds used in applying the coloring matter; an old burden-strap; four wing-bones of a pelican or an eagle, tied together with the twisted horn of wood or nettle fiber; two rabbits' feet, used for brushing the skin of the parts that have been gone over with the instruments when the subject becomes nervous by the irritation of the wounds; and a large brass ring worn by the operator around his neck as a part of his symbolic paraphernalia.[14]

The military arm of the Osages was known as the Grand Hunka or Honga. It was composed of members of the Land People and the Isolated Land People. Legend says that, when the Grand Honga was first established, it became so arrogant with power that it greatly displeased the Little Old Men. Its members strutted with their war clubs "decorated into uselessness, as they themselves were too encumbered with decoration to be of any military use."[15] They hurled taunts at the women and shouted obscenities at the girls. They laughed and clowned. Heedless of the insults to Wah'Kon-Tah, they often painted themselves diabolically, armed themselves, and sought excitement on the plains. Vying with one another on buffalo drives, they sometimes set fire to the brush or waved a robe too soon, thereby scaring the herd away while they laughed uproariously. In pursuit of self-glorification, they further offended Wah'Kon-Tah by singling out a buffalo bull in the herd and making him a target for their arrows and spears.[16]

These delinquencies mortified the Little Old Men. They shook their heads in disapproval, and after much deliberation they agreed that they had given the Grand Honga too much power. They resolved to diminish it by giving equal power to the Tzi-Sho or Sky People. This they achieved by appointing two grand chiefs of equal power for the tribe, one from the Tzi-Sho and one from the Grand Honga. The Little Old Men decreed that these chiefs should rule their people together, though each was to have his own prerogatives and his own province of action.[17]

The legend goes on to say that shortly after they were appointed to their offices these grand chiefs separately sought some sign of approval from Wah'Kon-Tah. They fasted seven days and six nights, spreading earth on their faces as a sign of the vigil. On the last day of the fast, as darkness spread over the land, one of the chiefs washed the earth from his face and sat down to rest for the night. He was still awake and in deep thought when he heard approaching footsteps. Looking up he beheld a man standing before him, as though in the light of day. "I have heard your cry," said the stranger. "I am a person who can heal all the pains and the bodily ailments of your people. When the Little Ones make of me their bodies they shall always live to see old age. In the morning, when the mists have cleared away, go to yonder river, follow its course until you come to a bank, and, there, in the middle of it, you will see me standing in the midst of the winds."

When morning came, the chief followed the course of the river as the stranger had requested, until he came to a sharp bend where the waters had washed away the earth and left a high bank. There stood a Medicine Man in the shape of a root. The chief removed him from his place without breaking any part of him. Since this was the seventh and last day of his fast, the chief started homeward, following the course of the river. Soon he came to another high bank in the bend of the stream. In the middle of it he saw another root. He examined it and he found it to be of the female sex. This, too, he removed from its place without breaking any part. He carried these two roots home, and afterwards they cured the Little Ones of many of their bodily ailments.

Meanwhile, on the evening of the sixth day of his vigil, the other chief wiped the earth from his face and sat down to rest for the night. He was still awake when an old man appeared before him. The old man said, "I have heard your cry and have come to give myself to your people. I am Old Age. When the Little Ones make of me their bodies they shall always live to see old age. When morning comes, go to yonder river, and in a bend where the water, sheltered by a high bank, lies placid, you will find me. Take from my right wing seven feathers. Let your people make of them their bodies and they shall always see old age." Accordingly, at dawn of the seventh day, the chief rose and rubbed his face with earth as a sign of his vigil. He went down to the bend of the river where the water was sheltered from the winds by a high bank. On the water's edge he saw a white pelican so cold it could not move. The chief recognized his visitor of the night before. He plucked seven feathers from the right wing of the pelican and walked homeward. Near a brook he met an eagle, which gave him a downy feather as a symbol of old age. As he neared home he saw lying on the ground a piece of black metal, which he also regarded as a symbol of old age. Henceforth, the Little Old Men of the tribe recited the follow-ing *wigie* in which they celebrated the art of healing by scarring and cupping as it was revealed to the grand chief by the pelican and the eagle:

He said: Behold my wings
They also
Are not without meaning.

I offer them for use as awls.
When the Little Ones make use of them as awls,
They shall always have awls that are sharp, indeed.
When they make use of them as awls,
The Little Ones shall always live to see old age.

When they take to making awls of my wings,
They shall have awls that will be sharp, indeed.
Even if any of the Little Ones pass into the realm of spirits,
They shall, by the use of awls, bring themselves back to
*   consciousness.*
When they use the awls to bring the Little Ones back to life,
They shall always live to see old age.

In another *wigie* the Little Old Men indicated that the wing bones
of the pelican and the eagle had been abandoned in favor of the metal
instruments introduced into the tribe by white men:

The Little Ones have nothing of which to make their bodies.
The metal spoke, in quick response: O Little Ones,
You say the Little Ones have nothing of which to make their
*   bodies.*
They shall make of me their bodies.
I am difficult to overcome by death.
When the Little Ones make of me their bodies,
They shall be as I, difficult to overcome by death.
Verily, at that time and place, it has been said, in this house,
He also said: The Little Ones shall make awls of me.
When the Little Ones take to making awls of me,
They shall have awls that will be sharp, indeed.
When the Little Ones make of me their bodies,
When they take to making awls of me,
And should any of them pass, even to the realm of spirits,
They shall, by the use of awls, bring themselves back to
*   consciousness.*
When, by this means, they bring themselves back to life,
They shall always live to see old age.

When the Little Ones make of me their bodies,
They shall always be free from all causes of death.
When the Little Ones make of me their bodies,
They shall know that there is no god whose skin is as hard
as mine.[18]

Henceforth the two chiefs directed their labors toward understanding bodily ailments and finding suitable remedies for them, and all future chiefs emulated them. They maintained the population of their tribe by combating disease, thereby securing the infinite trust of their people. The pelican was formally consecrated as the sacred symbol of old age.[19]

Before the grand chiefs led their warriors against enemies, they performed a war ceremony. This consisted of innumerable songs, recitations, and symbolism designed to enlist the omnipotence of Wah'Kon-Tah against the possibility of defeat. At the beginning of this ceremony a member of the war party killed a bull buffalo with a consecrated arrow. Then with a special knife, his comrades cut into the buffalo's hump and tasted its fat. From its left hind leg each cut a round piece of hide, painted it red to symbolize the sun, and tied it on his breast as a sacred fetish for protection against his enemies in battle. Each of them also cut a number of narrow strips of hide, dried them, painted them with blood-root juice, and carried them for the purpose of binding any possible captives. Then they laid a sacred pipe before the Little Old Men, who selected a Do-Do'n Honga, meaning the Sacred One of the war party. He acted as leader for the war party and as a kind of liaison officer between the tribe and Wah'Kon-Tah. The Do-Do'n Honga accepted the pipe and went west to pray and fast for seven days in a flat prairie with a full view of Wah'Kon-Tah. There he filled the pipe with sumac leaves and lit it. As he smoked he lifted the pipe to Wah'Kon-Tah, and prayed for protection of the Little Ones against their enemies. He prayed also that Wah'Kon-Tah might give an answer during the seven days of fasting and vigil. During the vigil he received many messages from Wah'Kon-Tah through hawks and owls. Then, at dusk on the seventh day he dragged himself back to the Little Old Men who had gathered to wait his return. As he reached the firelit lodge in which they had built a fire he was conducted to the seat he had left seven days before.

He confirmed for the seers the signs that Wah'Kon-Tah had given him by taking the skin of the sacred hawk carefully from the *waxobe*. The Little Old Men painted his face red, had him stand facing east toward the rising sun, then west toward darkness and war. While the women placed the blue clay of mourning on their heads and foreheads, the Little Old Men chose eight officers to assist the Do-Do'n Honga in the war movement. Just before dawn two of the Little Old Men ordered two fires built of redbud and sang a number of ceremonial songs. Then they gestured to the warriors, who showed their zeal for war by rushing toward the fires, and struggling with one another for charcoal with which to paint their faces. Before they departed to meet the enemy, however, they took time to ride around their village eight times while their officers chanted in an exultant tone:

> *Our brave young men have found in me their leader,*
> *Our brave young men have found in me their leader,*
> *Our brave young men have found in me their leader,*
> *I go forth in obedience to their call.*

> *O! Do-Do'n Honga, they are eager to meet the foe,*
> *To defeat and to triumph over him;*
> *Our brave young men have found in me their leader,*
> *Our brave young men have found in me their leader,*
> *Our brave young men have found in me their leader.*[20]

They moved toward the enemy's country in parallel columns. Their Do-Do'n Honga kept a considerable distance in front so that he might be able to perform his military duties undisturbed.[21]

At night they performed a number of ceremonies before pitching camp. In the morning they sent out scouts, who returned only after finding the enemy. If immediate attack was unnecessary, the Do-Do'n Honga opened his *waxobe* without ceremony and put the pelican skin on one of his officers. Meanwhile his warriors opened a little deerskin pouch containing powdered charcoal symbolic of their zeal for war, and hastily painted themselves and their horses with it.[22]

If the enemy was near, one of the chiefs ordered the warriors to battle. If the enemy was at a distance, one of the officers led the warriors until they came within attacking distance and he ordered them to charge. The Do-Do'n Honga remained in his headquarters to continue his military duties, while his aides took care of the pack horses and the camp utensils.

If the attack was successful, the warriors who had taken scalps stretched them on small hoops made from saplings and attached them to slender poles. They approached the Do-Do'n Honga and presented him with the scalps, captives, horses, and any other booty they had taken. Then at his command they hastened homeward.[23]

As they came within sight of their village, one of the officers sent a messenger to notify the grand chiefs and the Little Old Men of their approach. On hearing this news all the villagers rushed forward to greet the warriors. The Do-Do'n Honga, who had been carrying the mounted scalps, now transferred them to one of his officers and took his place at the head of his warriors. While villagers cheered the warriors the Do-Do'n Honga met with the Master of Ceremonies who asked, "Have you come home?" The Do-Do'n Honga replied, "Yes, my father, I have come home," and turning over his horse to one of his assistants he marched toward the village, attended by the officer who carried the scalps. The Master of Ceremonies, warriors and villagers followed them, dancing and singing a song of victory:

> *We appealed to the god of the earth,*
> *Behold, by the grace of our grandfather,*
> *Our warriors come home in triumph, the, the, the, he the,*
> *By the grace of our god of the sky they come home in triumph,*
> *By the grace of the god of the sky they come home in triumph.*
> *We appeal to the god of the earth.*

Arriving at the outskirts of the village, the Do-Do'n Honga approached the residence of the Little Old Men. There he sang another song known as *Entering the House:*

> *It is I who now return, who now return,*
> *It is I who now return, who now return,*
> *Lo, I come to the border of the village,*
> *It is I who now return.*

81

By this song he expressed his joy at having returned safely to the outskirts of his village. He and his officers marched into the village, passed
a spot of ground which the villagers had worn bare with their feet, and
entered the residence of the Little Old Men, where he thanked Wah'-
Kon-Tah for his victory. Then he walked to the left of the room and
paused for a moment, walked to the opposite side of the room and
paused again, before walking to the fireplace in the middle of the room
where on a pole hung a kettle from which the villagers were fed. Walking again to the door, he looked at the sky, while one of his officers
thrusted with the slender poles on which the scalps were mounted. The
Do-Do'n Honga ended the ceremony with a victory song in which he
told figuratively of his return from the darkness of war and death to the
light of day and the joys of life.[24]

6

The Quapaws, a Stone-Age People

THE QUAPAWS WERE ONE OF THE DHEGIHA TRIBES WHO HAD MIGRATED eastward in prehistoric times and had located on the James and Savannah rivers. Attacked there by the Iroquois, they fled westward to the mouth of the Ohio, where they crossed the Mississippi. There they divided, one band going downstream into present Arkansas, and the other going northward and finally settling on the Missouri River in present Nebraska. The northern Algonkins, and especially the Illinois, called them Arkansas, a name Father Marquette bestowed on them. The tribe called itself Ouaguapas, which the French rendered Quapaws. The name Arkansas itself is of uncertain origin.[1]

What little we know of their customs and traditions have come down to us from a few white men who came in contact with them. In May, 1541, Hernando de Soto and his men crossed the Father of Waters at present Sunflower Landing, in northwestern Mississippi, and marched northward to the principal village of the Quapaws, near the mouth of the St. Francis River, in what is now Arkansas. The Gentleman of Elvas, who wrote one of the chronicles of the expedition, called the tribe Pacaha, a name the chronicler Garcilaso de la Vega more accurately rendered Capaha, a variation of Quapaw. He described their village as consisting of five hundred large and good houses standing on elevated ground and almost surrounded by a moat. A canal connected the moat with the Mississippi, which flowed about nine miles from the village. The canal was wide enough to accommodate two large canoes. The moat and canal provided the Spaniards and their Indian carriers with a steady supply of several kinds of fish, one of which, says Elvas, was "a third part head, with gills from end to end, and along the sides were great spines, like very sharp awls." Apparently a catfish, it weighed one hundred fifty pounds. Garcilaso added the charming detail that the Spaniards found fish so numerous that they feasted on them until they were surfeited.

De Soto conquered the Quapaws, reconciled their chief with his hostile neighbor, Gasqui, and was rewarded by both chiefs with comely girls. He pushed westward toward Tanico, on the present site of Hot Springs, Arkansas, in his ceaseless quest for gold. After months of searching, he decided to retrace his steps toward the gulf to build two brigantines, one of which he planned to send to Mexico for assistance, and the other to Cuba with an order to sell a part of his property to refit the expedition. But in the following spring, while he was at Guachoya, near present Ferriday, Louisiana, he died of a fever.[2]

No other white man visited the Quapaws until 1673, when Father Marquette and his companions found them living at the junction of the Mississippi and the Arkansas. In his account of his visit to them he called them Arkansea and Akensea, but on his original map of the region, which John Gilmary Shea found in St. Mary's College, Montreal, he spelled it Akansea. He placed their village on the east bank of the Mississippi; but on another map it appeared on the west bank, higher up and near the mouth of the St. Francis River.[3]

Seeing the Frenchmen approach their village, some Quapaws in a canoe motioned to them to land. Through an old man who understood a few words of the Illinois tongue, they offered the strangers shelter for the night and promised to escort them in the morning to their principal village, which Father Marquette indicated stood about twenty miles down the river on its eastern bank and just above the Arkansas. True to their word, in the morning ten paddled ahead of the white men to the village and interceded with the chief, who sent out a welcoming committee in two canoes. When the Frenchmen arrived, the chief held forth the customary calumet, presented them with tobacco and a loaf of corn bread, and sang "quite agreeably." Then he escorted them to his lodge, where he had clean mats spread out for them to sit on. Soon the whole village gathered around them, while Father Marquette gave them gifts and spoke to them of God and the mysteries of the Holy Catholic faith. Through a brave who understood Illinois, the Quapaws expressed

84

a great desire to keep Father Marquette with them and to learn more of his religion.[4]

Fear of their enemies prevented the Quapaws from hunting wild animals to augment their meager food supply. But they were generous with what they had. Father Marquette learned that they grew abundant corn, which they sowed at all seasons. He saw some that was ripe, some that was sprouting, and some that was already in ear. They cooked it in large, tastefully fashioned earthen jars and plates. From baked earth they fashioned plates which they used for various purposes. They feasted the Frenchmen with sagamite, corn on the cob, and roasted dog meat, which they regarded as a great delicacy and served only on special occasions. The men cropped their hair, wore no clothes, and adorned their noses and ears with pendant beads. The women dressed in shabby skins and braided their hair in two plaits which fell behind their ears. They banqueted without ceremony and served their meats in large dishes, eating as much as they pleased and sharing the remains with one another. Father Marquette found their language difficult to master; try as he might, he never succeeded in pronouncing some of their words. They lived in wide, long cabins or lodges made of cypress and thatched with bark and they slept in corners, on platforms raised about two feet from the ground. They kept their corn in large baskets made of cane or in gourds as large as half barrels. They had never seen or heard of a beaver and counted their riches in terms of buffalo hides. They had never seen snow and knew winter only by the rain, which fell more often than in summer.[5] The Frenchmen remained only a few days with them before the friendly Quapaw chief, learning that a few of his men schemed to plunder and kill them, came with his interpreter to warn them of the danger by dancing with the calumet and presenting it to them.[6]

Hitherto the voyagers had believed that they were traveling westward and that, therefore, the Mississippi flowed into the Gulf of California. Now, however, they were convinced of their error. They realized that they were really traveling southward in the direction of the Spaniards, who were the enemies of France and who boasted many savage allies. So they held a council as to what they should do. They resolved to turn homeward, thereby precluding the possibility of capture and of losing their well-kept records which they knew would be of inestimable value to future French explorers. On July 17, 1673, they departed for Canada.[7]

No white man visited the Quapaws again until 1682, when Sieur de la Salle voyaged from the Illinois country toward the mouth of the Mississippi. He and his men heard the shrill cries of a war dance as they descended on the western side of the river. They crossed to the opposite bank where, under cover of a heavy fog, they erected a rude palisaded fort of felled trees in less than an hour. After giving the Quapaws time to gain confidence, La Salle sent some of his men to the river bank to beckon to them to come to see him. They sent out a few of their braves in a *periagua* or dugout canoe, which came within gunshot of the fort. La Salle displayed the calumet and sent a Frenchman with two Indians to meet them. They received the white men with many tokens of friendship and advanced to meet La Salle and to receive from him presents of tobacco and some goods. They reciprocated with slaves, while their chief invited the visitors to go to the village to refresh themselves. Father Zenobius Membré, a member of the party, wrote a vivid account of what then took place:

> All those of the village, except the women, who had at first taken flight, came to the bank of the river to receive us. Here they built us cabins, brought us wood to burn, and provisions in abundance. For three days they feasted us constantly; the women now returned, brought us Indian corn, beans, flour, and various kinds of fruits; and we, in return, made them other little presents, which they admired greatly.
>
> These Indians do not resemble those at the north, who are all sad and severe in their temper; these are far better made, honest, liberal, and gay. Even the young are so modest, that though they had a great desire to see La Salle, they kept quietly at the doors not daring to come in.
>
> We saw great numbers of domestic fowls, flocks of turkeys, tame bustards, many kinds of fruits, peaches already formed on the trees, although it was only the beginning of March.
>
> On the 14th of the same month, the Sieur de la Salle took possession of this country with great ceremony. He planted a cross, and set up the king's arms, at which the Indians showed a great joy. You can talk much to Indians by signs, and those with us managed to make themselves a little understood in their language. I took occasion to explain something of the truth of God, and the mysteries of our redemption, of which they saw the

arms. During this time they showed that they relished what I said, by raising their eyes to heaven, and kneeling as if to adore. We also saw them rub their hands over their bodies after rubbing them over the cross. In fact, on our return from the sea, we found that they had surrounded the cross with a palisade. They finally gave us provisions and men, to conduct us, and serve as interpreters with the Taënsa, their allies, who are eighty leagues distant from their village.[8]

According to George E. Hyde, a leading scholar of Indian cultures, the Quapaws in the seventeenth century had a ruder culture than that of the tribes living below them on the Mississippi. They had no religious temple; their gods were the moon, the sun, the stars, and the animals with which they were acquainted. Every family chose its *penates* or guardian spirits from among those animals which they regarded as wise, useful, or strong. Some worshiped the snake, the buffalo, the owl, or the raven. Many of them venerated the eagle whose feathers were regarded as being empowered to protect their wearers. All of the members of a hunting expedition returned home in deep dejection if one of them accidentally killed an eagle.[9]

Their lack of a satisfactory religion may account for their eagerness to accept Christianity and to protect its symbol, the cross. They practiced, too, a kind of faith in the ceremony of the peace calumet which symbolized their friendship. The Quapaw calumet was a wooden tube pierced through its entire length. It was about four feet long, ordinarily painted in different colors, and ornamented with porcupine quills usually dyed red and yellow. From the middle of the tube hung a tuft of white and red feathers to which were fastened vermilion-dyed hairs from a horse killed in war. At one end of the calumet was a pipe fashioned in different styles and made either of red stone resembling coral or of black stone resembling marble.[10]

When a chief wanted to establish friendship with a tribe or nation, he sent a commission of from fifteen to twenty of his men to its leader to request permission to come to the village in the morning with the peace calumet. If the chief granted the strangers their request, he ordered the women of the village to make preparations to receive them. The women then crushed corn, made bread, festooned their lodges, and cleaned and swept the paths. The strangers, too, prepared themselves suitably for the occasion. They daubed their faces with red paint, or painted one side red and the other side black. Each man usually put on either a shirt open at the neck or a breechcloth. They adorned their heads with eagle feathers of different colors, and even wore them in their ears, which were pierced. Sometimes they wore belts with rattlers or adorned themselves with bells and horse tails. In their opinion, they dressed magnificently; in the opinion of Frenchmen, they dressed like masqueraders.[11]

Early next morning the strangers would approach the village. The bearer of the calumet led the way. Some were in charge of the gifts to be presented to the chief. These included dressed buffalo skins, deerskins, bear's oil, and a few slaves. Some shook rattlers or empty calabashes with some semblance of cadence. One beat time with a drumstick on an earthen pot over which a dressed deerskin was stretched, while his comrades answered him with cadenced cries. The bearer of the calumet threw it in the air, caught it and swung it cleverly around his legs as he contorted and gyrated madly. Arriving at the chief's cabin, he handed him the calumet. The chief lit it, drew two or three mouthfuls of smoke from it, and passed it to his neighbor. In this manner the calumet reached every spectator of the ceremony and slowly made its way back to its original bearer. He then smoked it and, after observing a few moments of silence, addressed the chief, explaining the reason of his arrival. The chief granted or refused what was asked of him as he saw fit, but he always received the presents with apparent or real pleasure. The calumet remained with him as a pledge. The calumet bearer removed only the pipe, for future ceremonies. The ceremony closed with a feast for the strangers, who were served from different dishes expressly prepared for them by the women of the village.[12]

Father Jacques Gravier, who visited the Quapaws in 1700, said that they accorded to the calumet the honor and reverence white men accorded to crowns and sceptres. "It seems to be the god of peace and war," he wrote, "the arbiter of life and death. To carry and show it enables you to march with assurance amid enemies who in the heat of the combat lay down their arms when it is shown."[13] The Quapaws distinguished between a calumet of peace and a calumet of war simply by the colors of the feathers with which it was trimmed. Red was the color of warfare, diplomacy, and alliance. The calumet was, indeed, the supreme symbol of religion to them, just as much as the cross is to Christians. They offered a calumet for the sun to smoke when they desired calm, rain, or fair weather. "They would scruple," wrote Gravier, "to bathe in the beginning of hot weather, or to eat new fruits till after they had danced the calumet, that is to say, the chief holds it in his hands singing airs, to which the others respond, dancing and making gestures in time with the sound of certain instruments of the fashion of small drums."[14]

They had innumerable dances, one or more for every occasion, including religion, medicine, joy, ritual, war, peace, marriage, death, play, hunting, and copulation. The dance of copulation was held secretly at night by the light of a large fire. Every man who participated in the ceremony struck a post with his tomahawk to signify that he would keep his promise never to reveal what he had done or seen. The French traveler Jean-Bernard Bossu learned that both men and women danced completely nude at this ceremony, "accompanying their obscene poses and gestures with lewd songs, although they are merely light and witty in the original Indian language."[15] He does not say whether they actually performed the sexual act or merely simulated it.

He greatly admired their feats of magic which he said "would probably astound our magicians." He saw one of them swallow a stag's rib which was seventeen inches long, hold on to one end of it, and then pull it out of his stomach. He sent the juggler to New Orleans to perform before the governor and all the officers of his garrison. [16]

The young or unmarried woman was distinguished from the matron by the manner in which she braided her hair. She wound it around each ear and decorated it with beads, wampum, or silver. After she was married she let her hair hang in a single knot behind, and laid aside her decorations for her daughters.[17]

At marriage the husband gave his wife an uncleaned leg of deer to show that he would furnish the meat and that she would clean it. The wife, in turn, gave her husband a basket of corn to symbolize her willingness to raise corn and vegetables. Thomas Nuttall, who visited the tribe in 1819, wrote that the women, before the spring corn planting, devoured a live dog as "an offering to the Indian Ceres."[18]

Dog meat constituted the chief dish in the Quapaw's pre-war feast. Dogs were known to lay down their lives for their masters, so the warriors believed that dog meat would make them strong. A man proved he had killed the dog by bringing in its scalp, as though he were dealing with a man. The chief then rewarded him by making him a warrior. After the feast, which was always held in his cabin, the chief called a council of war in the middle of the village. There he and his leading men sat on mats or wildcat skins in a circle, in accordance with their ranks. Rising in the middle of the circle, the chief made a loud speech telling them that they had been insulted by another tribe, and that if they remained passive they would be disgraced and would be considered "women." This epithet in Indian parlance was tantamount to calling them cowards. A chorus of guttural "Ugh! Ugh!" indicated their approval of war. The chief then held out a bundle of twigs and each man took one as an expression of his desire to go to war. The next morning women ran through the village, shouting: "Young men and warriors, you have received the twigs. Leave! Go to war! Avenge the death of our relatives, our allies, and our friends. Do not come back until you are covered with our enemies' blood and have their scalps!"[19] Every man who had taken a twig went to a designated meeting place, where he carefully daubed his war club or "head breaker" before he was taken to the edge of the enemy country. There he cut a notch in a tree. In the notch he drew two crossed arrows in red, the color of revenge and war.[20]

Before setting out to seek his enemies the chief held a war feast for his allies which included singing, dancing, and much beating of drums and rattling of gourds. In one of these war dances a small group of warriors would whip themselves into fury by chanting: "I am going to war to avenge the death of my brothers. I'll kill, exterminate, rob, and burn the enemy. I'll bring back slaves, I'll eat their hearts, I'll roast their flesh, I'll drink their blood, I'll take their scalps, I'll make cups of their skulls." Then followed a surprise dance which was performed by two braves. Club in hand, one of them crouched and pretended to spy on his "enemy." Suddenly he jumped up, screamed, and attacked his victim. The victim fell immediately, stiffening his arms and legs like an epileptic. In a third dance, the victor pretended to make an incision in the forehead and around the neck of his victim. Kneeling on his shoulders, he went through the motion of digging his long fingernails into the "incision." He then shoved in and yanked, removing the "dead man's" scalp, hair and all.[21]

Like other Indian tribes, the Quapaws never went to war without consulting their *manitou,* which was usually a dried crow, snake, amphibian, or a quadruped. If the *manitou* led them to defeat, they abandoned it and chose another. Before leaving for war they fasted severely and painted their bodies black. At the end of their fast they washed off the black and re-painted themselves red. Then the chief harangued them in the presense of their *manitou* and ordered the food and supplies he needed for his campaign. Each man carried a bear skin, a buffalo hide, a little ax, a rifle, a powder horn strung over his shoulder, a bow, and a quiver full of hunting arrows. He refrained from using his rifle for fear of alerting the enemy. The chief aim was to surprise the enemy, a type of warfare in which the Quapaws were very skillful.[22]

The Quapaw warrior gave little or no thought to food. He could travel three or four days without eating. "They just tighten their belts," wrote Bossu, "and go on their way." Only when they approached the enemy did they make a meal by mixing a little water with corn flour or maize roasted in just about the same manner in which white men roast coffee.[23]

If he defeated the enemy, the chief sent several messengers to carry the victory news to his village. Even before he returned, he announced through a system of criers how many prisoners he had taken, how many he had killed, and how many scalps he had brought back. The women greeted the prisoners by beating them with sticks. They bound the prisoners and painted them black, then met to determine whether they should live or die. Any Quapaw family which had lost a husband or son had the right to choose a prisoner to replace him. The adopted men were immediately set free.[24]

The other prisoners, however, were subjected to the horrible fate of being burned alive over a slow fire. Venting their anger on the prisoners, the braves scalped them and tied them to a wooden frame, where they subjected them to horrible torture. The captives, far from complaining, sang until they died, declaring their fear neither of death nor of fire. Sometimes they even taunted their executioners, saying that they were not suffering enough, and pointing out where the fire should be built up more and which parts of their bodies were most sensitive.[25]

One of the best authorities on the Quapaws was Bossu, who was so much admired that he was made a member of the tribe. On his thigh they tattooed the picture of a deer as a sign that they had made him a warrior and a chief. He sat on a wildcat skin—

. . . while an Indian burned some straw. He put the ashes in water and used this simple mixture to draw the deer. He then traced the drawing with big needles, pricking me until I bled. The blood mixed with the ashes of the straw formed a tattoo which can never be removed. After that, I smoked a pipe and walked on white skins which were spread under my feet. They danced for me and shouted with joy. They told me that if I traveled among the tribes allied to them, all that I had to do to receive a warm welcome was to smoke a peace pipe and show my tattoo. They also said that I was their brother and that if I were killed they would avenge my death. I am now a noble of the Arkansas nation. By adopting me, these people have showed me the greatest honor they can pay to a defender of their land. I consider it similar to the honor received by Marshal de Richelieu when his name was inscribed in the golden book among the names of the nobles of the Republic of Genoa.

It is true that there is some difference between having your name inscribed in a book and having to undergo the operation which the Indians performed on me. I cannot tell you how much I suffered and how great an effort I made to remain impassive. I even joked with the Arkansas women who were present. The spectators, surprised by my stoicism, cried out with joy, danced, and told me that I was a real man. I was truly in great pain and ran a fever for almost a week. You would never believe how attached to me these people have become since then. This is all that I can tell you about them.[26]

7

The Caddo Confederacy

W EST AND SOUTH OF THE QUAPAWS, IN THE RED RIVER BASIN OF PRESENT Arkansas, Louisiana, and Texas, lived the Caddoes. This name applied collectively to a people now regarded as a single tribe. When they were first known to Europeans, they consisted of about twenty-five tribes forming three or more confederacies. Some units of the Caddo family were entirely independent. Caddo is a popular name contracted from Cadohadacho, a word which the whites used to include all the tribes in the confederacies. The French explorers and even American frontiersmen after them used different names for the Cadohadachoes. Tonti called them Cadodaquis, Joutel called them Cadaquis, and John Sibley, Indian agent of Natchitoches, called them Caddoes. How many tribes were formerly included in the Caddo confederacies is unknown. Only a small number of the Caddoes survive, and these have little or no knowledge of the organization of their tribe. In present Louisiana resided many dependent and independent tribes, most of whom followed more or less a common culture.[1] Here we treat two of the most important: the Caddoes and the Taënsas.

One of the Caddo units, the Natchitoches, once lived near the town on the Red River that bears their name today. Originally they formed a powerful group; but war and disease, particularly smallpox and measles, almost wiped them out. By the beginning of the nineteenth century they numbered twelve men and nineteen women living in a village near a lake twenty-five miles north of present Natchitoches. Another unit, the Yatasi, made its first home on the Red River, northwest of Natchitoches, and then at Bayou River or Stony Creek which flows into the Red River

about fifty miles above Natchitoches. Still another unit, the Adai, resided in the neighborhood of what is now Robeline, Louisiana, and
sometimes camped along the Red River above Natchitoches. The Cadohadachoes, meaning real or proper Caddoes, may have resided on the
Red River from time immemorial. According to tradition their original
home was the lower Red River, from which they migrated westward and
northwestward. Pénicaut reported in 1701 that the Caddoes lived on the
Red River about one hundred and seventy leagues above Natchitoches.
This places them a little above the big bend of the Red River near
present Texarkana and Fulton, Arkansas. A century later they moved
down the Red River near Caddo Lake, about a hundred twenty miles
from present Natchitoches. Sibley says that—

> They formerly lived on the south bank of the river, by the course of the
> river 375 miles higher up, at a beautiful prairie, which has a clear lake of
> good water in the middle of it, surrounded by a pleasant and fertile coun-
> try, which had been the residence of their ancestors for time immemorial.
> They have a traditionary tale, which not only the Caddoes, but half a
> dozen other smaller nations believed in, who claimed the honor of being
> descendents of the same family; they say, when all the world was drown-
> ing by a flood, that inundated the whole country, the Great Spirit placed
> on an eminence, near this lake, one family of Caddoques, who alone were
> saved; from that family all the Indians originated.[2]

The Cadohadachoes, the leading tribe of the confederacy, wielded a
great influence over many of the tribes belonging to the southern Caddoan family. By the beginning of the nineteenth century their influence
extended over the Yatasi, the Nacogdoches, the Adai, the Natchitoches,
and many other units. These tribes looked on the Cadohadachoes as
their father, visited and intermarried with them, and joined them in all
their wars.[3]

The Caddoes have given their name to a large lake in northwestern
Louisiana, to one of the parishes in that state, and to a number of places
which they formerly occupied. The name of the great state of Texas,
too, is derived from the western Caddoes or Tejas who made a lasting
impression on the missionaries there. Father Juan Antonio Padilla described them as a strongly built, well developed, brave, vigorous people.
Though a number of travelers or explorers have written contradictory
opinions of their morals, nearly all of them praise their diligence. Never-

94

theless, they did seek gifts as rewards for labor. Father Francisco Casañas de Jesus Maria found this characteristic so strong that, in their opinion, only "the person who gives them something is good while all others are bad."[4] Two other missionaries, Father Francisco Hidalgo and Father Isidro Felis de Espinosa, called them good humored and joyous. Generally, added Espinosa, they were "quick, intelligent, friendly, [and] high minded."[5] Espinosa also found them "ready for war expeditions and of good courage. They preserve an inviolable peace, but they never form a truce or make friends with an enemy."[6] He learned that they were peacefully disposed toward all white men, but that they liked Spaniards better than Frenchmen. "It is not necessary," he wrote, "to prove the friendship of these Indians by any proof save that of the experience of those who have lived among them for some time. For, up to this time, I have never seen anyone who has left the country of these poor Indians who does not speak of their kindness."[7] Father Padilla, too, found them morally sound. He wrote that they enjoyed social intercourse, disliked theft, and treated Spaniards well, "entertaining them in their houses and aiding them in every possible manner." The merchants of Natchitoches, finding that the Caddoes kept their promises and paid their debts punctually, exchanged munitions, trinkets, and liquor for furs at a good price. Padilla called them the most civilized and most sociable Indians he had ever known.[8]

They lived in cabins shaped like bee-hives which stood from forty to fifty feet high. Like other tribes, they slept in beds which were built around the cabins three or four feet from the ground. Father Anastasius Douay, who accompanied La Salle in one of his expeditions, surmised that only two families lived in each cabin. Joutel's estimate was more liberal. Joutel wrote: "There are usually eight or ten families in these cabins, which are very large, for they are some sixty feet in diameter; they are made in a different way from those we had seen before. They are round . . . like big haystacks, being of the same material except that they are taller; they are covered with grass from bottom to top. They made the fire in the middle, the smoke escaping above through the grass."[9]

The Caddo women, like those of many other tribes, undertook much of the heavy labor in home and field. Most of them were so strong that even pregnancy in no way interfered with their daily chores. When a woman saw that her time was drawing near, she built a little hut near

95

the river. She thatched it and covered three sides with the bark and branches of trees. In the center of the hut she fixed a forked stick firmly in the ground which she grasped to help her endure the pangs of child-birth. After her baby was born she rose, bathed him and herself in the river, returned to the village as if nothing had happened and resumed her chores.[10] Sometimes, however, mothers killed their newborn children because their husbands did not want them.[11]

The naming of the child entailed a ceremony which resembled that of Christian baptism. When he was from six to eight days old, his mother summoned one of the medicine men who sat in a designated seat and took the child in his arms. He caressed him and whispered in his ears for a long time. Then he bathed him in a big vessel and asked his parents what name he was to give him. Usually the name his parents or relatives bestowed on him was a diminutive form of one of their own. Sometimes, later in life, this name was replaced by another such as that of his guardian spirit. A decrepit old woman performed the same ceremony for a female child. After the ceremony was concluded, the child's parents offered the medicine man or woman various presents as gratuities and prepared a feast with all the food they had in the cabin.

The Caddoes hardened and toughened their boys by forcing them to bathe in streams, even icy ones, and by requiring them to participate in arduous war parties and foot races. Their most important relatives were not their parents but their maternal uncles, especially those who were warriors and medicine men. They entertained the utmost respect for them and obeyed all their wishes. Thanks to the rigorous training to which their maternal uncles subjected them they had become successful warriors, skillful hunters, or respected medicine men by the time they reached marriageable age.[12]

The marriage practices of the Caddoes departed drastically from Christian custom. Like other Indians, the Caddoes exchanged or bartered their wives. Sometimes they swapped them with their friends or sold them for a horse, gunpowder, balls or beads of glass, or other trinkets they esteemed. Father Casañas frowned on their marriage customs, though he admitted that their arrangements sometimes seemed good ones:

If a man wants a certain woman for his wife who he knows is a maiden, he takes her some of the very best things he has; and if her father and mother give their permission for her to receive the gift, the answer is that they consent to the marriage. But they do not allow him to take her away with him until they have first given notice to the [governor or] *caddi*. If the woman is not a maiden, there is no other agreement necessary than that the man say to the woman that she is willing to be his friend and that he will give her something. Sometimes this agreement is made for only a few days. At other times they declare the arrangement binding forever. There are but few of them who keep their word, because they soon separate from each other—especially if the woman finds a man who gives her things she likes better than those the first man gave her.[13]

Under these circumstances, marriage endured only as long as it was satisfactory to the contracting parties. Though it entailed no particular ceremony, each man obtained beforehand the good will of his intended wife's father or brothers by leaving deer meat at their door. Their taking the meat inside and eating it was tantamount to agreeing to the marriage. Because the woman was almost always amenable to the wishes of her parents, her consent was never required. Most Caddoes were monogamous, but this did not mean that they had a horror of polygamy.

They practiced the levirate in which a man inherited his dead brother's wife and children, if he had any. Father Juan Agustín de Morfi wrote that affinity among them was no obstacle to matrimony, though they carefully avoided consanguinity. Joutel learned that the women of one of the Caddo tribes were loose and that those of another changed their husbands often. Morfi reported the existence of *beraches* or hermaphrodites in at least one of the Caddo tribes.[14]

The death ceremonies depended on the social position of the deceased. As soon as a man died his relatives prepared his body for burial by bathing it carefully and dressing it in fine clothing. An ordinary man was usually buried within a few hours after death; an important one was allowed several days to give his entire confederacy time to witness his last rites. Before the burial members of the household displayed their grief by copious weeping. Two men served as priests and directors of the last rites of one chief. When his coffin had been completed they placed tobacco, herbs, bows, and arrows in it, while they prayed in voices so strenuous that they sweated profusely despite the cold weather. Then they went to the burial place, and prayed again in a low voice. After determining how the dead chief's coffin was to be placed, they dug his grave. Returning to the chief's house, they gave directions as to how his body should be placed in the coffin, then moved aside to pray to the Great Spirit.

At this point the supreme priest of the confederacy, known as the *xinesí* or *chenesí*, delivered a mighty eulogy on the dead chief and ordered the crowd to mourn for him. The eulogy emphasized the industry, military glory, and hunting prowess of the chief. When he was finished talking he sat near the dead man and repeated the eulogy to him, assuring him everybody loved him and was weeping for him. The priest also requested him to go to "that other house" to join his dead brethren. As he completed his homily he had the body taken to its grave, informing the dead brethren of its approach by having volleys of arrows shot into the air. After the mourners had wept over the closed grave they surrounded it with large quantities of food, tobacco, fire, and a pot of water. Dead women received flowers and a number of household utensils.[15]

The *xinesí* was the supreme authority of Caddoan society in political as well as religious matters. His office was hereditary in the male line and normally passed to his oldest son. He commanded infinite respect and complete obedience. His disapproval was dreaded more than a thousand lashes. Indeed, everybody tried to keep him satisfied by giving him most of everything they had, and by hunting so that he could feast whenever he wanted on the choicest meats. He derived much of his power and authority from his role as religious leader and chief liaison officer between his people and their gods. He told his people that he spoke to Ayo Aymay, the "great captain" or sureme god of the tribe. He claimed to do this through two small boys who were kept in small houses a short distance from the Fire Temple and who were invisible to every person save himself. In the Fire Temple he met with his officers and advisers around a perpetual fire. Over the fire he mixed a concoction of buffalo fat and tobacco which he burned as a kind of offering to the two boys. As soon as he offered the incense he spoke to the boys, asking them to assure Ayo Aymay that his people had improved in their conduct. He also begged them to bless the tribe in the future with an abundance of corn, good health, swiftness in hunting deer and buffalo, invincibility in battle, and many women to serve them. On one occasion Father Casañas noticed that the *xinesí,* as soon as he finished his prayer, seized a small calabash and threw it to the ground. Because it made no sound it indicated that Ayo Aymay was angry and that he disdained any intercourse with them. Frightened, the people promised that they would bring the *xinesí* and the two boys anything they desired. Casañas observed that, as soon as the *xinesí* heard their promise, he picked up the calabash he had thrown down, rattled it with his finger, and told them in the voice of a boy that he would give them anything they requested if they fulfilled their promise. Then in his normal voice he repeated the same message. And he told them to bring meat and everything else they could find so that neither Ayo Aymay nor the boys should be angry again.[16]

Subordinate to the *xinesí* were the *caddices* or tribal chiefs who, like their superiors, inherited their offices. Each *caddi* ruled over a specific tribe. He was assisted by subordinates known as *canahas,* who numbered from three to eight depending on the size of the tribe. They assisted him in his duties, published his orders, and summoned the elders' councils. Whenever the *caddi* went on the warpath or on a hunting expedition, his *canaha* looked after his camp site, his food, and his sleeping quarters. Whenever the *caddi* wanted to smoke, his *canaha* brought him a pouch full of tobacco and put the peace pipe into his mouth. The *canahas* had subordinates, called *chayas,* who speedily carried out all of their orders. Another group of petty officials, the *tammas,* had duties roughly equivalent to those of sergeant-at-arms or sheriffs. They whipped the legs and stomachs of all laggards. Like the *caddi,* braves who had won renown on the battlefield enjoyed a special place in Caddoan society. At all times they wore the skins and scalps of the men they had killed as the insignia of their rank. Another privileged class consisted of the wives of the *xinesí* and of the *caddi.* Each was called *aquidau,* meaning great lady or queen, a title which set them apart from the rest of their sex. Each lived in a house of many rooms, attended by servants and priests called *tammas conas,* who continually brought gifts.[17]

Much like the American frontiersmen, the Caddoan masses moved in a society of mutual needs and benefactions. This won Father Casañas' admiration. They helped one another, he wrote,

> . . . in such a manner that if one's house and all his possessions are burned up, they all gather together, build him a new house, and furnish him

whatever he needs for his subsistence and comfort. All these things they do together. At planting time, they come together and plant whatever each one has to plant, according to the size of the family—beginning first at the home of the grand *xinesi* . . . . Next, they plant the corn and other crops for the *caddi*. Then they work for the other officials and the old men. In this way they continue working from the highest to the humblest until each has planted what he needs for the year. . . . Those who hunt work steadily, for they are obliged to supply food until the planting is finished. During sickness, these Indians visit and aid each other with great kindness, trying to give to the sick all possible consolation by taking them something nice to eat. Some of them present the trinkets they own, others lend them. Among them there is no exchange, save by bartering. It seems that everything they own they do not hold as personal property but as common property. Therefore, there is no ambition, no envy to prevent peace and harmony among them.[18]

A good example of their communal living is the manner in which they built their houses. To the place in which a house was to be built the *caddi* sent two of his mounted *tammas* with long flexible poles and bark. The bark, though thin, was so strong that a man could not break it with his hands. The *tammas* left a pole with each father of a family, with instructions to cut, clean, and place it in a designated hole. Another group tied the poles together with thongs made of the bark. One or two women from each house had the duty of bringing in a load of grass, coarser and tougher than wheat stalks and which was admirably suited for roofing. When they had completed these arrangements the *tammas* went to bed on the spot on which the house was to be built. At daybreak they rose and summoned the workmen together. As soon as he arrived to supervise the construction, the *caddi* sent each workman to place his pole. Soon a circle of poles arose in the middle of which was set a very tall pole with a crosspiece at its top and with climbing knots. Two men went up, seized the tops of the poles with a noose, brought them together, and tied them firmly with the strong thongs of bark.[19]

Then the workmen on the ground began covering the poles with heavy timbers. Working from bottom to top, they finished their tasks within an hour. Then other workmen covered the house with grass to the thickness of three hand spans. They cut off the long middle pole at the bottom, and the house stood complete by noon. During all this time the *tammas* walked around them, hurrying them on by threats of beatings with rods made of two or three fresh and flexible branches. All morning long the *tammas* came and went, reprimanding all those who had arrived after the work on the house had begun. They gave the delinquent men four or five strikes across their chests and lashed the delinquent women on their bared shoulders. "This is done," wrote Father Espinosa, "without exception of persons, for even though it be his own wife or sisters who is at fault, she receives her punishment. No one is offended at this, but rather laughs at it. During all the time the people are working the householders are busy preparing food for everybody, having previously provided quantities of deer meat and many pots of ground corn, which in this section of the Indies is called *atole*." They served everybody from the *tammas* down to the humblest workman from earthen jars which they fashioned with great care. Thus refreshed, the crowd scattered, each returning to his or her home much pleased.[20]

At the end of the seventeenth century when the French explorers first visited them, the Caddoes depended for their livelihood more on the products of their fields than on what they could find in the wilderness. The men advised the village women to provide food for planting day. When the day arrived all women met with their leader, who ordered them to weave reed mats. These they offered to the *caddi*, who presented them to the Fire Temple so that the people would be assured of an abundant crop. At the end of this ceremony they feasted on what the women had brought.[21]

The men and women then met at the Fire Temple, usually in the house of the *caddi*, and celebrated the ceremony of constructing their hoes. These were fashioned by cutting down black walnut trees and burning them down to the desired sizes. Then they cleared the field in a circle measuring one stone's throw in diameter, filled the circle with wood, and set fire to it in preparation for the great feast in which they served each other equal portions of venison, corn meal, and a variety of vegetables. Next morning the entire community participated in the sowing in soil which was no deeper than the span of a hand. Most of them sowed only a few seeds and then departed, leaving the chore to the old women.[22]

One of the crops they cultivated with care was tobacco, though they never let it get perfectly ripe. When the time came to pick it, one of their *tammas* went from hut to hut collecting it and delivering it to the *caddi*. With a few incantations the *caddi* drove away future storms, assured rain at the proper seasons, and blessed the anticipated crop.

The Caddoes sowed two crops a year, one at the end of March, when the rains ceased, and the other at the end of May. The first crop was what they called "little corn," perhaps a popcorn, the stalks of which grew no taller than three feet, though they were covered with ears. As soon as the "little corn" was harvested, they cleared the ground and replanted with "the big seed" or flour corn, which took until the end of July to ripen perfectly. Thus in four months the Caddoes usually gathered two abundant crops of corn. In addition, they planted climbing beans, which were stored, as the shelled corn was, in strong reed baskets, called *otatillos*. Sometimes they mixed some well sifted ashes in the baskets as a preventative against worms, and carefully covered them to keep out rats or mice.[23]

The Caddoes were farsighted in acknowledging the unpredictability of the future. They selected the largest and fullest ears, leaving on them the leaves which were immediately next to the grain. Placing the ears on a long string, they hung them up in places where they would get smoked. This corn they kept for future planting. Anticipating possible ruin of their crops, they saved enough corn for two years of sowing and placed it in a sacred deposit, which they opened only in times of great distress.[24]

In wartime much of the food they raised was offered to their god Ayo Aymay. For seven or eight days they prayed and sang to him, asking for strength and valor. They also prayed for swiftness to run away from the enemy, for they regarded flight as no disgrace. They prayed, too, to a god who resembled a demon and who in turn offered to Ayo Aymay the incense they concocted by throwing tobacco and buffalo fat into a fire. Their warriors assembled around the fire. Each rubbed his body with a handful of smoke in the belief that Ayo Aymay would grant them either the valor to conquer their enemies or the swiftness to run away from them. Before they took the warpath they performed many dances. Casañas observed that at the time a dance began, a brave would step forward to advise the warriors what they were to request of Ayo Aymay. The missionary wrote that they prayed—

> to the fire, to the air, to the water, to the corn, to the buffalo, to the deer, and to many other similar things, asking some of them to permit themselves to be killed for eating. To others they pray for vengeance. They ask

the water to drown their enemies, the fire to burn them, the arrows to kill them, and the winds to blow them away. On the last day of such a meeting the *caddi* comes forward and encourages the men by saying, "Well, now, if you really are men, think of your wives, your parents, or your children, but I charge you not to let them be a hindrance to our victory."[25]

They obeyed him implicitly. They traveled for whole days without food, and ignored any water holes they passed until the *caddi* made his camp. And the *caddi* did not do this until he had explored the country to determine the position of the enemy. Around the *caddi's* camp they built cabins in which they held alternate fasts and feasts. These sometimes lasted from sunset to dawn. The women followed the warriors on the warpath, brought food and tobacco, and, with the consent of the *caddi*, trained the young men in racing.[26]

The Caddoes fought their enemies ferociously, giving them no quarter and bringing in many scalps as trophies. These were later tanned very neatly and displayed in their cabins. When it was necessary to share a single scalp, they divided the long hair on it into little tresses which they attached to sticks. When they conquered they usually took a large number of prisoners. They put to the knife all of the old men and women. The smallest children were carried off to be eaten on the way home. The larger children were sold to other tribes. They tied the vagabonds, women, and young girls to stakes, dancing fiercely and uttering funereal cries to the accompaniment of a harsh reed instrument. Sometimes they tortured their victims with poles of burning resinous pine before roasting them whole. Or they might cut from the still-live bodies chunks of flesh which they half roasted and ate with great relish. Sometimes hungry warriors simply bit off pieces of flesh and ate them raw. The orgy continued until the gory bodies were reduced to skeletons. Then, hair and all, the scalps were cut off and placed around sacrificial poles. Each warrior took a bone and sucked on it, until all the bones of each skeleton were distributed.[27]

This cannibalism was inspired by the medicine men or shamans, who exercised a profound influence over many of the social and martial activities of the Caddoes. The medicine men, who were organized in societies or guilds, were numerous, and their numbers increased with each passing year. One of their duties was to initiate young men into manhood. Dressed in official regalia, which included bunches of feathers and necklaces made of the bright-colored skins of coral snakes, they met their assembled candidates, each of whom was about twenty years old. They drank many strong drinks and smoked endless quantities of tobacco as part of the ceremony of initiation. The candidates soon lost consciousness or pretended to do so. When they regained their senses, usually at the end of twenty-four hours, they related in a languid voice all they had dreamed or pretended to have dreamed. Then for eight days they cast their experiences into song, while women onlookers responded with weird cries. At the end of this part of the ceremony, wrote Father Espinosa, "the Indians attack the pots which they do not cease stirring on the fire and fill their stomachs while the candidates entertain the crowd with their songs and dances."[28]

The primary duty of the medicine men, however, was to cure diseases. Their therapy was based on the assumption that disease was caused by insects or arrows which certain enemies had planted magically in the bodies of their patients. So they resorted to sucking the affected areas, performing sleight-of-hand tricks, and sweating their patients in an endeavor to rid them of infections. Before they began treatment they invoked the medicine men of their friends the Bidais, who allegedly came to their assistance in the shape of *tecolotes* or owls sent by benevolent demons. They recognized these owls by their hoots; hearing them they were impelled to utter shouts of joy, as though they had won a martial victory. To this superstition they added one of a false god, Ynici, who helped them in therapy with songs and prayers.[29]

The medicine man began treatment of his patient by drinking certain brewed herbs topped with foam. Then he played on a reed instrument and danced furiously. This lasted from mid-afternoon to near dawn. At intervals he would stop to sweat his patient on a grate covered with live charcoal. To his patient's protestations he replied that the treatment was very mild. With a knife or flint he made an incision in his patient's stomach and quickly sucked out the blood. In the case of a snake bite he sucked out the venom. In the case of a tumor or swelling he sucked out the pus. "One must concede," wrote Morfi, "that, in spite of so much error and extravagance, they do sometimes succeed in very singular cures because the land has an abundance of medical herbs, and, knowing many of them, they probably apply them with skill, especially in the healing of wounds, in which they have the greatest practise."[30] Sometimes the medicine man could foretell accurately the death or the recovery of his patient. Before he treated a prominent man he held a consultation with his colleagues, each of whom suggested his own remedy.

The medicine man did not confine his functions to healing; he also presided over the construction of houses, the distribution of crops, and the programs of festivities, so that he combined the character of social administrator with that of physician. He was also the priest of the tribe, for he blessed the houses when they were completed and the corn when it was harvested. To eat new corn before the medicine man mumbled his prayers over it was a sacrilege punishable by inevitable snake bite. And this punishment extended to the animals, especially dogs, whose forefeet were tied to their muzzles to prevent them from eating fresh corn, of which they were very fond. In his capacity as priest, the medicine man never failed to attribute a snake bite to an infraction of his teaching, even though the region was snake-infested and the victim had never thought of the crime. The medicine man taught that the presence of many ticks on the mountainside foretold an abundant crop of beans. The frequency of rains in March and April forewarned of a drought in June, July, and August. The sight of many small *banit*, birds, after a buffalo hunt or a campaign against an enemy, assured the Caddoes that they neared their homes.

When they decided to go out on a campaign, they usually held a general meeting at the house of the *caddi* or of the medicine man. The host chose the most valiant among them and regaled him with brewed drinks until he lost consciousness or pretended to do so. He remained in this state for twenty-four hours. When he regained his memory, he was able to describe the whereabouts of the enemy, his intentions, and the extent of his preparedness.[31]

The medicine man predicted events with the help of an astrolabe made of fox tails. He told his followers that, if in summer they fanned a fire with a blower or with a feather fan, enough snow would fall in the ensuing winter to cover and crush them. Once when a medicine man saw a missionary use these objects to make a fire, he took them from his hands and reprimanded him for the danger he might precipitate. The missionary assured him that no danger would result from that manner of fanning a fire. The medicine man replied that this was doubtless due to the fact that the missionary's fire was different from his own and that it had been produced with steel and flint. Father Espinosa once asked a medicine man why all the tribes of the Ainais and Nechas did not go out together on buffalo hunts, as did the Nasonis and Nacogdoches. The medicine man replied that this was a precaution to prevent the sacred fire in the temple from going out during the absence of those who guarded it. The Nasonis and Nacogdoches, he said, had a different kind of fire which they lit by rubbing two little sticks together. By leaving these in the temple they were confident of finding the fire still burning when they returned to their homes. The Ainais and Nechas, on the contrary, had kept their sacred fire burning without interruption from the time their forefathers gave it to them, a tradition which they recounted often with great pride.[32]

The medicine men of the Ainais nation, which comprised more than fourteen or fifteen tribes of one of the Caddo confederacies, believed in the omnipotence of Ayo Aymay, whom they worshiped as the creator of the universe. The several legends which describe his birth disagree about the details surrounding it, though they concur in stating that in the beginning only three persons existed, a woman and her two daughters. One daughter was a virgin; the other was pregnant. Since these legends deal with the miraculous, they need not explain how the mother and her daughter became pregnant without the assistance of a man or men. One day when the girls were alone, a *caddaja* or ogre appeared suddenly and snatched the pregnant girl as she rested her head on her sister's lap. He was huge and misshapen, having a ferocious countenance, claws as sharp as an awl, and horns so long that their tips extended beyond sight. In no time at all he tore the hapless girl to pieces and devoured her. The virgin, fearing that the same thing was about to happen to her, climbed to the safety of a very tall tree. The ogre, still hungry, looked for her and seeing her up there among the branches tried in vain to climb after her. Forgetting in his greed that he could have reached her easily with his horns, he tried with his claws and teeth to cut down the tree at its roots. The virgin, her wits sharpened by her plight, flung herself into a deep creek that conveniently ran past the foot of the tree. The ogre began to suck the water to drain the creek dry. But the virgin was too clever for him; by swimming under water she deceived his cunning and foiled his evil intentions. Running to her mother, she told her of the tragic end of her sister.

The two went to the place where the pregnant girl had met her doom. There they found a drop of her blood in an acorn shell. The mother covered the shell with another shell, put it in her bosom, and carried it home. She put the first shell in a large jar which she covered carefully and placed in a protected corner of her room. That night she heard faint scratching sounds which came from the jar. At dawn she found that the drop of blood had changed into a shapely and beautiful male child who, however, was no bigger than one of her fingers. Excited at her discovery, she covered the jar carefully. That night she again heard the noise in the jar. Again investigating it, she found that the child, who was Ayo Aymay, had grown to splendid manhood. Elated, she hurriedly made a bow and a quiver full of arrows and before she took him out of the jar gave them to him. In the language of his tribe, which he spoke perfectly, he asked for his mother. His grandmother informed him of her tragic death. Enraged, he went out to seek the ogre. He quickly found him, wounded him badly with his bow and arrows, and drove him from the face of the earth. Having thus avenged his mother's death, Ayo Aymay returned to his grandmother and aunt. He told them that to live in a land where they would be constantly reminded of the death of his mother would spoil their joys; and he persuaded them to accompany him to *cachao ayo* or great sky, where they dwelled from then on in great happiness and splendor. So Ayo Aymay became an adored divinity, to whom the Caddoes attributed the distribution of rewards and punishments.[33]

As we have mentioned, the Caddoes worshiped Ayo Aymay in their Fire Temples, which were usually large and round buildings thatched with rush mats painted red. Assisted by his *caddi,* the *xinesí* kept the eternal fire burning with four very long, thick, and heavy logs which were thoroughly inspected and then arranged "in the direction of the four principal winds." The Caddoes believed that if they allowed the fire to go out they would all perish. They built a small fire with little sticks which they piled up in the form of a pyramid just outside the temple. Near the fire on small benches and tables they kept tobacco, a pipe, some feathers, and little clay pots in which they offered incense to Ayo Aymay. Here, too, the *xinesí* deliberated with the medicine men on peace, war, the scarcity of rain, or any menace to their crops. They were very careful in removing the ashes of the sacred fire and made

107

little mounds of them to contain the bones of their enemies. A short distance away from the temple stood the little houses in which the *xinesí* said dwelled the two boys who served as messengers between himself and Ayo Aymay.[34]

The most famous feast of the Caddoes was called the *sacabbi,* which they celebrated in February. At this feast their medicine men foretold the events of the coming year. Some days before the feast occurred, the Caddoes hunted rabbits, wildcats, wild birds, and badgers which they dressed and took to the Fire Temple. Two or three of the women spent the morning brewing a laurel leaf tea which the medicine men drank in incredible quantities. Then, in a drunken state of ecstasy, they turned to the wall and wailed a chain of prayers to Ayo Aymay. One of them reverently picked up an elaborately decorated, specially prepared eagle wing, called *ygui,* and paraded it before his colleagues while they continued their wailing. Symbolically, the eagle wing ascended to heaven, where it consulted with Ayo Aymay about the events of the year. The medicine men sat in a secret chamber, muttered between their teeth, and formed an almanac in accordance with the replies they received from Ayo Aymay. Meanwhile, the congregation smoked a pipe and saluted the sacred fire by throwing ground tobacco on it. As soon as the medicine men completed their labors they left their chamber to disclose the contents of the almanac to the people. Then they all returned to their homes, resigned to the fate their god had decreed for that year.[35]

At the end of the seventeenth century, when French explorers first visited the Lower Mississippi, the most dominant and influential tribe north of the Red River in what is now Newellton, Louisiana, was the Taënsas. Their neighbors on the west bank of the Mississippi were the Quapaws, and their neighbors along the east bank of the river were the Yazoos, Ofafoulas, Tunicas, Natchez, Koroas, and other small tribes, all of whom were akin in blood and culture. The Taënsas are little known, though they are perpetuated in the names of the Tensas River and Tensas Parish. In the chronicles of the French explorers and missionaries, the name of the tribe is variously spelled; but Taënsas is the generally accepted form. As in the case of the Quapaws, what we know of the Taënsas is derived from French writers, for not a word of Taënsa is known to exist.

The first unquestioned knowledge concerning the Taënsas is found in the chronicles of La Salle's voyage down the Mississippi in 1682. The explorer sent his friend, Henri de Tonti, with a party of Frenchmen and Quapaws to take gifts to the chief of the tribe. After carrying a birch canoe for several miles and then launching it on the small lake where the chief's village stood, Tonti and his companions arrived at a number of mud cabins thatched with cane mats. "The cabin of the chief," wrote Tonti later, "was 40 feet square, the wall 10 feet high, a foot thick, and the roof, which was of a dome shape, about 15 feet high."[36] Entering the cabin, Tonti saw the chief seated with three of his wives on a camp bed and surrounded by more than sixty old men dressed in large white cloaks which the women made from the bark of the mulberry tree. The women, clothed in the same manner, showed their respect for the chief by prefacing their answers to his questions with howls of "O-o-o-o-o-o!" Nobody drank from the chief's cup or ate from his plate or passed in front of him. When he walked his attendants cleared the path before him.[37]

The chief bade Tonti and his companions sit down on a delicately worked cane mat which was spread on the ground. He told Tonti of the pleasure he felt at the arrival of the French. Tonti's Quapaw interpreter rose to his feet, made a speech, and presented his buffalo robe to the chief, who reciprocated by offering his own robe. Through his interpreter Tonti informed his host that they had come to make an alliance with him and that their leader needed provisions. The chief immediately commanded the women of the village to make corn meal and fruit pastry, from *paquimina* fruit. Tonti acknowledged this hospitality by presenting the chief with a knife, which was gladly accepted as a very considerable gift. Tonti noticed that the chief wore sixteen pearls in each ear and asked where he had found them. The chief replied that he had obtained them from shells in the sea and that he had many of them.[38]

One of the chief's wives wore a pearl necklace. Tonti offered her ten yards of blue glass beads for it. She was reluctant to part with it and would not until her husband ordered her to do so. Tonti carried the pearls to La Salle, gave him an account of all he had seen, and advised him that the chief had promised to make a visit on the following day. The chief arrived next day in a wooden canoe accompanied by the beat of a drum and the chanting of women. La Salle received him with great courtesy and gave him some presents. The chief reciprocated with buffalo robes and the provisions which the women had prepared. On the next day the Frenchmen continued their journey toward the Gulf of Mexico.[39]

In both custom and language the Taënsas belonged to one of the three known tribes of the Natchez division of the Muskhogean stock, from which they later separated.[40] Father Membré described their country as "covered with palm trees, laurels of two kinds, plums, peaches, mulberry, apple and pear trees of every kind. There are also five or six kinds of nut trees, some of which bear nuts of extraordinary size. They also gave us several kinds of dried fruit to taste; we found them large and good. They have also many other kinds of fruit trees which I never saw in Europe; but the season was too early to allow us to see the fruit." He found the people "docile and manageable, and even capable of reason. I made them understand all I wished about our mysteries. They conceived pretty well the necessity for a God, the creator and director of all."[41] Father François Joliet de Montigny, who descended the river from Canada to their country early in 1699, saw nothing "debauched" about their pattern of living. "On account of the great heat," he wrote, "the men go naked, and the women and girls are not well covered, and the girls up to the age of twelve years go entirely naked. They are so mild and have so much deference for what we told them, that I persuade myself that it will not be very difficult when I know their language a little to reform their abuse, which among them makes no impression, they being accustomed to it from childhood."[42]

They believed in a sun god and worshiped in sun temples. Some of these were imposing structures shaped like earthen ovens. They had well made columns and images of snakes and other reptiles on their roofs. The roof of one was adorned with crude forms of eagles made of wood and painted red, yellow, and white. Another, perhaps the principal temple of the tribe, had strong clay walls on which were placed the heads of enemies as sacrifices to the sun. This temple had no windows and its only door was about four feet high and about three feet wide. At the door was a great shell, standing on a block of wood and covered with a plait of hair as thick as a man's arm and about twenty fathoms long. This hair had been taken from scalped enemies. Two old priests

110

who were the directors of the temples once told Tonti of a small shed of cane mats built within one of the clay walls. When Tonti asked to look inside the shed, however, the priests refused, implying that their god resided there. Later Tonti learned "that it is the place where they keep their treasure, such as fine pearls, which they fish up in the neighborhood, and European merchandize."[43]

Inside the temple were a number of shelves. On one shelf were oval cane baskets containing the bones of ancient chiefs and of men "who had caused themselves to be strangled to follow their masters into the other world." On another shelf were many gorgeously painted flat baskets in which their idols were preserved. These included figures of men and women made of stone or baked clay, heads and tails of unusually large snakes, stuffed owls, pieces of crystal, and the jawbones of large fish. In these temples the Taënsas (like the Caddoes) kept a perpetually burning fire. They used nothing for it but dry hickory or oak. Each priest or temple guardian was obliged to carry a large log into the shed. Each served three moons during the year. The priest on duty was placed like a sentinel near the shed in order to prevent the fire's going out. He fed it with two or three large logs which he burned only at the ends, never placing one on top of the other for fear they would burn too quickly.[44]

No women were allowed in the temple save the sisters of the great chief. Moreover, no common man was permitted to enter it, not even to carry in food to celebrate the memory of relatives whose bones lay there. He could give the food to the priest, who placed it near the basket containing the beloved one's bones. Later the food was either placed on the wall or abandoned to fallow deer.[45]

In March, 1700, the principal temple was struck by lightning and burned to the ground during a heavy rainfall. An old man, who was perhaps the principal priest, stood near the fire crying aloud, "Women, bring your children to sacrifice them to the spirit in order to appease him." Some pious women obliged him by throwing five of their small children into the fire. They would have thrown in many more had not some Frenchmen prevented them. The priest regarded the action of these women "as one of the finest one could make." The priest led them with ceremony to the cabin of the new leader, successor to the great chief who had recently died.

111

At this chief's death they had, in accordance with custom, strangled fifteen or twenty persons who volunteered to serve him in the next world. The priest tried to encourage more persons to follow their example. He explained that because no man or woman had been willing to follow the late chief's predecessor into the next world, the "spirit" had become angry and burned down the temple. For this misfortune he blamed Father Montigny, who had prevented the tribe from fulfilling its ancient custom.

The priest consecrated and sanctified the women who had sacrificed their children to appease the angry god. At the new chief's house the priest embraced them, clothed them in white garments made of mulberry bark to denote purity, placed a great white feather on the head of each, and set them on huge white mats in the doorway. Then he converted the chief's cabin into a temple by ordering a perpetual fire to be lit in it. The priest and the holy women stayed in the chief's doorway, in view of the rest of the tribe, and chanted intermittently for three days.[46]

Within a few years the tribe suffered a calamity even more serious than the destruction of their principal temple. The English traders from Carolina, anxious to supply their countrymen in the West Indies with as many Indian slaves as possible, incited their allies, the Yazoos and the Chickasaws, to make war on the Taënsas. In the ensuing struggle the Taënsas, being very much inferior in numbers and in weapons, were practically exterminated. The survivors persuaded Sieur de Bienville, French governor of Louisiana, to permit them to leave their old villages and to settle among the Bayagoulas, thirteen leagues above the site of New Orleans. No sooner were the Taënsas newly situated than their benefactors attacked and nearly destroyed them. Fearing the vengeance of the Colapissas, the Houmas, and other small tribes who were allies of the Bayagoulas, they sought Bienville's protection, begging him to let them settle at Fort Mobile. The governor granted their request and they remained near Fort Mobile until 1715. Then, tired of warring against their implacable enemies, the Houmas, they moved again. This time they went to Manchac, where they helped Antoine de la Loire des Ursins to defeat an English trader who presumably had been sent with a strong force to make alliances with the tribes of the Lower Mississippi.

Before 1744 the Taënsas migrated once more, from Manchac to the

Tensas River. There they would have been happy to settle had not the region been ceded to the English by the Treaty of Paris of 1763. Loyal to the French, the last few survivors of the tribe crossed to the west bank of the Mississippi into Louisiana. They never entirely accepted Christian teachings, but remained closely wedded to their native cult.[47]

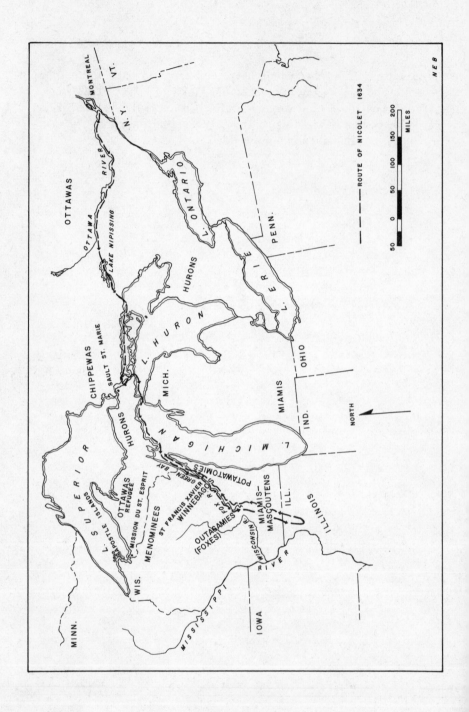

OTTAWAS

MONTREAL

VT.

N.Y.

OTTAWA RIVER

LAKE NIPISSING

L. ONTARIO

CHIPPEWAS

SAULT ST. MARIE

HURONS

HURONS

L. HURON

L. ERIE

PENN.

OHIO

L.   S U P E R I O R

APOSTLE ISLANDS

OTTAWAS REFUGEE

MISSION DU ST. ESPRIT

MENOMINEES

MICH.

L. M I C H I G A N

MIAMIS

IND.

NORTH

MINN.

WIS.

ST FRANCIS XAVIER

GREEN BAY

WINNEBAGOES

FOX R.

POTAWATOMIES

ILL.

OUTAGAMIES (FOXES)

MIAMIS-MASCOUTENS

WISCONSIN R.

MISSISSIPPI

IOWA

ILLINOIS

RIVER

N E B

ROUTE OF NICOLET 1634

50   0   50   100   150   200
MILES

8

Jean Nicolet in Search of the
China Sea

THE FIRST WHITE MEN IN THE MISSISSIPPI VALLEY WERE SPANIARDS. THEY sought gold, found none, and withdrew. The great valley held the story of their romantic episodes, their frenzied searches, their incredible hardships, their crushing disappointments. But all they left were some abandoned cooking and eating utensils, occasional wooden crosses, heaps of bones, and innumerable graves. They had not sought the Mississippi; they merely stumbled on it, and had overlooked its significance. Exploration, the glory of uncovering for the world one of its greatest river valleys, was left to another people of another era. The fur traders and missionaries of New France sought the Mississippi because it would enable them to extend their fur routes, and because it promised them greater ease in carrying Christianity to the more remote Indian tribes. They persevered, and realized generous dividends when they eventually attained their goals.

The history of civilization is largely the history of the civilization of great river valleys. Each of the ancient peoples who founded civilizations on the Euphrates, the Ganges, and the Nile knew the necessity of possessing a fertile and well-watered region with its large potential for prosperity. The early English settlers, being excellent colonizers and shrewd farmers, availed themselves of the rich ground along the river valleys. The founding fathers of Virginia built homes and established plantations along the banks of the James and its tributaries, which

115

became "almost their only highway of trade and social intercourse." The history of New York began at the mouth of the Hudson; that of Maryland, on the banks of the Potomac; and that of Pennsylvania, on the banks of the Delaware and of the Susquehanna. When the Massachusetts colonists became crowded, they spread to the broad and beautiful valley of the Connecticut. And the first settlements in the south rose along such important rivers as the Cape Fear and the Roanoke in North Carolina, the Ashley and the Cooper in South Carolina, the Savannah in Georgia, and the St. Johns in Florida.

In the first part of the eighteenth century, when the Scotch-Irish and the German immigrants braved the cataracts of the Fall Line or streamed through Cumberland Gap to establish themselves in the present Appalachian states, they too saw the wisdom of settling along swift streams. This pattern was repeated by those of their descendents who, in the next century, moved westward to the Mississippi Valley. To it they brought an intensification of the social and political principles which they had acquired in their former homes and which their fellow pioneers had accepted. Before them stretched an area of about a million and a quarter square miles which in its fertility, its variable climate, its transportation facilities, its abundance of wild game—in its great promise of wealth and prosperity in general—was surpassed by no region of similar size in the whole world. Its frontiersmen were destined to play an important role in the history of the United States. For here occurred some of the most dramatic and significant events of our nation.

Like many great adventures, the search for the Mississippi Valley began with a dream. The dreamer was Samuel de Champlain, founder of Quebec and, later, governor of New France. He dreamed of reaching the "Sea of China" by way of the upper Ottawa. In his younger days he had voyaged up that river and on to Lake Huron by way of the Mattawa River, Lake Nipissing, the French River, and Georgian Bay. This route became the main highway between New France and the Indian tribes with whom the Hundred Associates or, as they were sometimes called, the Company of New France, conducted a lucrative fur trade. Champlain had journeyed toward the west for nearly four hundred and fifty miles, half his estimate of the distance from Montreal to the Pacific Ocean. Then, during his sojourns with the Indians, he heard

116

that the distance between Montreal and the Pacific Ocean must be much greater; the inland seas, of which Georgian Bay was a part, stretched for a thousand miles, and on the western extremity dwelled a people who were enjoying the benefits of an advanced civilization. He yearned to reach the "Men of the Sea," as the Indians called the people of that country, which he guessed to be China, or at least some part of the Orient. He heard, too, that the "Men of the Sea" traded with another race, a beardless people whose costumes and manners somewhat resembled those of the Tartars, and who journeyed from the west on a great river in large canoes. He guessed the river to be a channel leading to Asia. A romantic adventurer, he had no difficulty imagining these beardless people to be Chinese or Japanese, though they were really the ancestors of the Sioux Indians. The "Men of the Sea" were none other than the tribe which white men later called the Winnebagoes.[1]

But Champlain's desire to visit the west was a dream. He was an old man now, and such a task needed the vigor and recklessness of youth. As commissary of the Hundred Associates he had trained a number of young men in the life of the wilderness and in the languages, manners, and customs of the Indians. Among them was Etienne Brulé, who explored the northern shore of Lake Huron and who may even have ventured into Lake Superior. Another was Jean Nicolet, son of Thomas Nicolet, a mail carrier between his native Cherbourg and Paris. Soon after young Nicolet had come to the New World in 1618, Champlain added him to the list of men trained in Indian life. Endowed with profound religious feeling and a remarkable memory, Nicolet inspired the admiration and confidence of his superior, who sent him to the village of the Ottawas on the Isle des Allumettes in the Ottawa River. He remained with them for two years, following them in their wanderings and sharing their dangers and privations with a fortitude equal to that of the boldest and bravest man of the tribe. He learned their language and accompanied them on a peace mission to the Iroquois. He returned to Quebec only to go back to the Nipissings, with whom he made his home for the next eight or nine years. He built his own cabin, fished and traded, learned the language and customs of his hosts, and often served in their councils. Yet he yearned for the Christian sacraments, which he knew would be denied him as long as he remained in the wilderness. Feeling at last that he could no longer do without them, he bade farewell to his Indian friends and returned to Quebec.[2]

Such was the man whom Champlain now chose to lead an expedition to the unknown west. Its purpose was to hold "talks" with the "Men of the Sea" and their neighbors, to smoke the peace pipe with them, and to see if profitable trade routes might be opened between them and the Hundred Associates. Perhaps he was instructed, too, to keep a sharp lookout for mineral deposits, for as early as 1610 two friendly Indians had presented Champlain with a foot-long piece of copper which they said they had obtained on the banks of a river near a great lake.[3]

At last, sometime in July, 1634, the expedition got underway. In its party were six Jesuits whom Nicolet was to conduct as far as the Huron villages, where Champlain had established the first western mission in New France some years before. Nicolet left Three Rivers, on the upper St. Lawrence, ascended the Ottawa, and proceeded to Lake Nipissing, where he stayed a short time with his old friends. Then he continued toward the Huron villages on the border of Georgian Bay. He was so inured to the difficulties of wilderness travel that he bore with equanimity what would have required the fortitude of the most courageous Indian. But his unseasoned Indian paddlers and the tenderfoot monks suffered severely. The monks were so afraid that they made the trip crouched in the bottom of the canoes. The Indians grew weaker and weaker as they alternately paddled their canoes and carried them, along with the baggage, over a number of portages, sustained only by a meager diet of Indian corn. But eventually the expedition arrived at the country of the Hurons, where Nicolet informed the Indians that Champlain wanted them to establish friendly relations with the Winnebagoes. They showed their willingness to support his mission of peace by giving him seven men to guide him to the next tribe. Bidding farewell to the monks, he continued along the northern shore of Lake Huron to St. Mary's River, now through narrow rapids, now across little lakes, now around beautiful islands, and soon arrived at Sault Ste. Marie, between Ontario and the upper peninsula of Michigan. Before him, only fifteen miles away, Lake Superior stretched westward for fully four hundred miles. He was the first white man to set foot on what became, a century and a half later, the Northwest Territory, including the present states of Ohio,

Indiana, Illinois, Michigan, Wisconsin, and that part of Minnesota lying east of the Mississippi River. He journeyed in a desolate country of dark forests, wild animals, and a few dirty wigwams.[4]

From Sault Ste. Marie the expedition turned southward, passed through the Straits of Mackinac, and entered Lake Michigan. No white man had ever seen it before. As he glided along its northern shore, which is the upper peninsula of Michigan, he stopped frequently until he arrived at those northern arms of Green Bay, Big Bay de Noc and Little Bay de Noc. Here he visited an Indian tribe which later was classed with the Chippewas. The language of this tribe, being Algonkian, he understood. Entering Green Bay, he journeyed to the Menominee River, where he encountered another tribe of the same name. He found that they were of a lighter complexion than any other Indians he had ever seen and that their language, though a derivative of Algonkian, was difficult to understand. Their food was largely wild rice, which grew in abundance in their country. They were skillful in hunting and fishing.[5]

By this time he had sent one of his Huron guides to the Winnebagoes with a formal announcement of his approach and of his mission of peace. They received the message and the messenger with great courtesy and dispatched several of their young men to meet Nicolet and to escort him and carry his baggage to their village. Having seen nothing but Indians all along his route, he had no illusion that he was landing in China. Yet he pretended that he had arrived in that country. From Quebec he had brought a gorgeous Chinese costume of heavy damask or silk, embroidered with birds and flowers of many colors, such as mandarins wore. He put it on, armed himself with pistols, and stepped majestically ashore, as though he were a fully accredited envoy of France to the Grand Khan. No mandarins greeted him, of course, only primitive and curious men, women, and children. Suddenly he fired his pistols in the air. The Indians scampered like frightened rabbits in all directions, screaming or shouting that he was a *manito* who carried thunder in his hands. A resourceful man, Nicolet quickly indicated his good intentions: he placed sticks in the ground and put gifts on them to indicate to the Indians that he was really their friend. Cautiously they approached him, a few at a time. And when they saw no more thunder in his hands they quickly spread the word of his presence to the neighboring tribes. Gradually he found himself surrounded by four or five thousand admirers and a great feast was laid out in his honor by the tribal chiefs. One of them regaled him and his companions with a hundred and twenty roasted beavers! The chiefs made a number of speeches that he could not understand, for they spoke Siouan, not Algonkian. Then he spoke, finally succeeding in conveying to them the advantages of forming an alliance with the tribes to the east of them.[6]

But he was not yet ready to return to Quebec. Instead he ascended the Fox River to the country of the Mascoutens, perhaps in what is now Green Lake County, Wisconsin, where he was glad to hear Algonkian spoken once more. From them he learned of a "great water" only three days' journey to the south. He could reach it by continuing up the Fox and then crossing a short portage to the Wisconsin, which was a tributary of the "great water." But the confusing way in which they described the "great water" made him believe that they were talking of a sea rather than of a river. He decided against making the passage, for he was confident that he had just about realized the purpose of his expedition. Yet he still did not turn homeward. Instead he visited the Illinois, who lived on the beautiful prairies of the state that now bears their name, and who answered a question that had long perplexed him. He discovered that the people who came in large canoes to trade with the Winnebagoes were none other than the Sioux. He learned much about the customs and manners of that tribe, that he was to take back to Quebec and that proved invaluable to the French explorers of another day.[7]

And now, at last, he turned toward Quebec. At the islands on the mouth of Green Bay he visited the Potawatomies, who assured him of their loyalty to the king of France. Then he passed on to Lake Huron, where he joined the expedition which came down from Quebec every summer to trade with the Ottawas. In July, 1635, after an absence of precisely a year, he reached Quebec. Champlain rewarded him by appointing him commissary and interpreter at Three Rivers. These appointments, though significant, were not commensurate to the recognition he deserved. In 1632 Champlain had drawn a map of the known west. To it Nicolet added the Straits of Mackinac, Lake Michigan, and Green Bay. But on Christmas Day, 1635, Champlain died, and his immediate successors showed little of Champlain's love of exploration. Had he lived he would have continued the work begun by Nicolet and he would have been able, perhaps, to add to his map the name of the Father of Waters. Nicolet survived Champlain by only seven years. In October, 1642, he was drowned on the St. Lawrence during a storm while he was on his way to rescue an Indian ally from imprisonment and torture by the Hurons.[8]

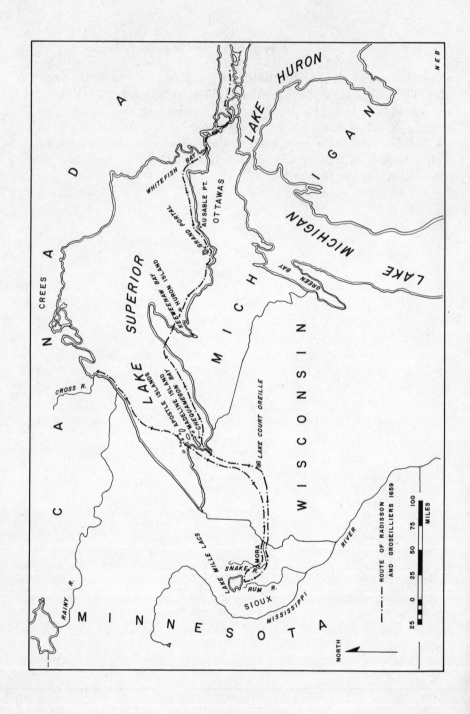

LAKE HURON

NEB

WHITEFISH BAY

AU SABLE PT.

OTTAWAS

GRAND PORTAL

KEEWEENAW BAY

HURON ISLAND

LAKE SUPERIOR

LAKE MICHIGAN

GREEN BAY

M I C H

CANADA

CREES

CROSS R.

APOSTLE ISLANDS

MADELINE ISLAND

CHEQUAMEGON BAY

LAKE COURT OREILLE

W I S C O N S I N

RAINY R.

LAKE MILLE LACS

SNAKE R.

MORA

RUM R.

SIOUX

MISSISSIPPI

RIVER

M I N N E S O T A

ROUTE OF RADISSON
AND GROSEILLIERS 1659

— · · —

25 0 25 50 75 100

MILES

NORTH

9

Radisson and Groseilliers, Explorers of the Upper Valley

THE CHIEF OCCUPATION IN NEW FRANCE DURING THE FIRST HALF OF THE seventeenth century was fur trading. At first it was confined to the small tribes living along the rivers that flow into the St. Lawrence from the north. Gradually it extended to the more populous region of the Hurons and to the Ottawas on Manitoulin Island. Every spring representatives of these tribes would arrive in Montreal and Three Rivers with their canoes full of peltries, which they exchanged at small fairs for utensils, tools, ornaments, and other objects offered by French merchants. This trade became so profitable that in 1645 the Hundred Associates obtained from the government a monopoly on it. They did not, however, enjoy their new privileges for long. In 1649 some bands of the Iroquois confederacy, chiefly Mohawks and Senecas, made a surprise attack on the defenseless Hurons. They fought bravely and won a few encounters, but were finally forced to disperse. Some wandered westward to the region of Green Bay and some went as far as the Mississippi Valley. For a time the Iroquois war made exploring enterprises and fur trading impossible and missionary work very dangerous. One by one the Huron missions, including St. Joseph, St. Ignace, and Ste. Marie, fell to the Iroquois. But slowly they rose again, thanks to the zeal of the missionaries, who were willing to risk ambush and even death to minister to their Indian converts and to bring Christianity to remoter tribes. From fleeing Hurons the missionaries heard stories of the "great water" in the west and recorded the stories when they returned home. They estimated that the sea between America and China was only nine days' journey from Green Bay and that it was narrow and easy to cross. They wrote that one Father Grelon, a Jesuit missionary, had encountered in Chinese Tartary a woman who had been a member of his congregation on Lake Huron. It was explained that she had been sold from tribe to tribe until she had passed from America to Asia. This story strengthened the prevailing notion that the two continents were quite near each other.[1]

The tales of the missionaries encouraged the *coureurs de bois*, a group of carefree, tough young men who had conducted independent trading expeditions since Champlain's death in order to extend their activities to hitherto unexplored regions. The missionaries availed themselves of their protection and went along, hoping to introduce Christianity in these regions. In 1654 Hurons and Ottawas brought a caravan of canoes laden with furs from the islands in the mouth of Green Bay to Three Rivers. They also brought news of their victory over the fierce Iroquois and of the natural richness of the country beyond the Great Lakes. Soon two fur traders penetrated the region beyond Lake Michigan. Two years later they returned with a valuable cargo of furs and an abundance of stories regarding the geography of the west. Pierre Esprit Radisson, the chronicler of this and three other expeditions, claimed to have participated in the expedition, though historians now claim that he did not. The other fur trader was his brother-in-law, Médard Chouart, better known by his assumed title Sieur des Groseilliers or, as the English later called him in derision, "Lord Gooseberry Patch." A few years later the two men did make a voyage together to the west and by so doing contributed greatly to our geographical knowledge of that part of the continent. They opened up a route to Lake Superior, to Wisconsin, and to the Mississippi Valley for the fur traders of a later day. Later they deserted France for England, whose claim to the continent of North America they strengthened by their explorations. They were aware, too, that France, as well as other nations, had been seeking a Northwest Passage since the days of Cartier. At times Radisson was unrealiable in reporting what he saw. Nevertheless, he may be considered a kind of prophet in that he heralded the greatness of the Mississippi Valley several centuries before it became known to countless American frontiersmen and European immigrants. He quaintly called the valley "a laborinth of pleasure." His chronicle is regarded as worthless by some unimaginative scholars, but it is by far the most original and vivid account of Indians living in stone age fashion and of life in interior America long before frontiersmen made their homes there and fashioned the stable society that led them to statehood.[2]

Radisson is one of the most controversial figures in the history of exploration in North America. For many decades historians have waged verbal warfare among themselves over his hopeless chronology, his lengthy and confusing digressions, his habit of plagiarizing other travelers' experiences for the purpose of dramatizing his own, and his usage of hearsay reports of distant places as though he had seen them himself. Some scholars have defended him; others have derided him as a kind of Baron Münchausen of the Mississippi Valley. To complicate matters, they have disagreed as to whether the manuscript that has come down to us is the original or only a copy of it, and as to whether Radisson wrote his chronicle in English or in French. A. T. Adams declares that it was written in English; Grace Lee Nute and Theodore C. Blegen say French. Bernard DeVoto accepts French, but with characteristic tongue in cheek. Writing in French, he says, makes "more mysterious the odd and charming language of the book. The translator, whoever he was, could not cope with English idiom and syntax and was repeatedly baffled by English vocabulary."[3]

This is undeniably true. What we have is written in the execrable English of one possessing scarcely a rudimentary knowledge of the language. But its rampant Gallicisms and its grotesque and crude syntax constitute, as we shall see, one of its great charms. Radisson proved that a man may fabricate and still be valuable, even to historians. Adams is charitable toward Radisson and defends him on the ground that his defects are the result of deficient knowledge of the English language and of an imperfect memory of events which he recounted from nine to seventeen years after they occurred. Perhaps, adds Adams, "some of the mistakes were due to the human shortcomings of a copyist or to possible disarrangement of sheets upon which original notes were made."[4] Adams states that if Radisson had written his account of the first four voyages in French and if it had to be translated into English, surely in London somebody who understood the language well could have been found to make a translation less encumbered with errors and crude expressions than is the manuscript as we have it. Radisson's accounts of his fifth and sixth voyages, written independently in French and translated into English, "are free of nearly all the errors occurring in the earlier voyages."[5]

The manuscript has had almost as adventurous a life as had the man who wrote it. Completed in 1669, perhaps for the purpose of providing Charles II of England with information regarding the importance of the fur trade in the Hudson Bay country, it became the property of Sir George Carteret, Vice-Chamberlain of the King and Treasurer of the Navy. He passed it on to Samuel Pepys, the famous diarist and Secretary of the Admiralty to Charles II and James II. Sometime after his death in 1703, Pepys' collection of manuscripts was dispersed into the hands of various London businessmen, who bought parcels of it to use as wastepaper or wrapping paper. The most valuable portions were carefully reclaimed by the celebrated collector, Richard Rawlinson, and after his death found their way to the Bodleian Library at Oxford. There Radisson's chronicle reposed with the rest until 1885, when it was published by the Prince Society of Boston in an edition of only two hundred and fifty copies. "These," says Adams, "were distributed chiefly among the public libraries throughout the country, and some copies are in the possession of individual owners, who value them highly. This small edition of the narratives was received with much interest by historians, and before many years a spirited controversy arose in regard to the times, duration, and order of the first four voyages narrated in the manuscript."[6] Only two of these voyages are pertinent to this history. Like the others, they contain controversial topics which we shall discuss one by one as we come to them.

Radisson was born in 1636, probably in Avignon, France. He came to the New World with his parents when he was only fourteen or fifteen years old. In the spring of 1652, while he and a few of his friends were hunting ducks and geese near Three Rivers, where his father had settled, they were captured by the Mohawks and taken to the Mohawk village. The Indians killed his companions but spared him, probably because he submitted to torture stoically and was willing to do a little more than his share of work. These qualities won him the indulgence of an old chief, who adopted him. The chief's wife, who was a Huron, called him

Orimha, which like the French Pierre meant a "stone." She bestowed on him the affections of a mother. Though he almost became an Indian in his pattern of living, he still longed for his real parents. One day he and another prisoner, an Algonkin, managed to escape by killing the three sleeping Mohawks with whom they shared a cabin. They crossed both the St. Lawrence and Lake St. Peter, only to bump into a band of Iroquois. These Indians, though unaware of their prisoners' crime, promptly returned them to the Mohawks along with their own prisoners: three white men, a white woman, and a dozen or so Hurons. On the first day of Radisson's capture they tore off four of his fingernails. On the second day, an unusually brutal Mohawk forced him to put the end of his thumb into a calumet full of burning tobacco and to keep it there while he puffed furiously until the tobacco was reduced to a cinder. On the third day, they burned his feet, through which they then thrust a skiver of hot iron. Finally, they tied him to a stake and set fire to the wood they had piled around him; but within a few minutes the flames ate the thongs, momentarily freeing him and giving his Indian father a chance to rescue him. In gratitude Pierre vowed that he would never again try to escape. Once the Dutch governor of Fort Orange, at the present site of Albany, visited the Mohawk village at Auriesville, near the present town of Fonda, and, speaking excellent French, urged Pierre to take off his paint feathers and return to civilization. Pierre refused and even turned down the offer of a ransom. Proclaiming his love for the Mohawks, he said he wanted to travel with them and see the world. So he went off with a war party, which made an extensive tour of what is now the state of New York. Starting from their village, they visited all the principal villages of the Iroquois confederacy. Probably they saw Niagara Falls, traveled eastward by way of Lake Ontario, arrived at Lake Champlain, and then, marching westward, returned home.

By now Radisson had forgotten the vow he had made to his foster father. In October, 1653, he escaped the Mohawks again and reached Fort Orange, where the governor welcomed him, dressed him as an Indian, and hid him in the fort for three days. Then the governor sent him to New Amsterdam, a town Radisson described condescendingly as "a towne faire enough for a new country."[7] From there he embarked on a Dutch ship for Amsterdam, Holland, which he reached six weeks

127

later. In January, 1654, he sailed for La Rochelle, and from there to New France. There Radisson met his new brother-in-law and future associate, Groseilliers. The two men became fast friends.

In August, 1654, the pro-French tribes, having recently made peace with the Iroquois, were able to resume their trade relations with the French settlements. During the summer representatives of these tribes had arrived in Quebec with word of "a great river which empties into a great sea, which is believed to be the China Sea." Groseilliers, who was present when they arrived, was greatly impressed by their cargo of furs as well as by their report; he planned to accompany them when they were ready to return to their homes. Radisson's chronicle, completed in 1669, includes a description of this expedition. In it he claims that he accompanied his brother-in-law's expedition. Grace Lee Nute shows, however, that he was in Quebec in 1655 and that he either falsified his description of the expedition or confused it with another he had made. He undoubtedly obtained information of the expedition from his brother-in-law, who also gave an account of it to the Jesuits. John Bartlet Brebner, one of the best authorities on exploration in North America, surmised that Groseilliers' companion was Jean Péré,[8] a half-breed who later was chosen intendant of New France, perhaps because of his knowledge of the Lake Superior region.[9] Radisson could have learned the details of the expedition from Péré. Years later, when he wrote his chronicle, he perhaps reported Péré's experiences, or what he could remember of them, as his own, in order to impress Charles II into granting him and his brother-in-law support for an expedition to the Hudson Bay region.[10]

At the head of the chronicle on this expedition Radisson wrote a word which puzzled historians for several generations: "*Auxoticiat.*" In 1926 Edward C. Gale of Minneapolis at last put scholarly minds at rest by explaining that *aux* is the French word meaning "to the," and that the remainder of the word, *oticiate,* is an imperfect form of the French word *ottouats,* meaning Ottawas. The complete word, therefore, means "to the Ottawas." Commenting on Gale's explanation, Grace Lee Nute states that the English translator misread the two French words and, concluding that they belonged together, produced "*Auxoticiat.*" Two slightly different variants of the word occur in the narrative of this expedition, which came to be known as the *Auxoticiat* or Mississippi Voyage.[11]

128

The travelers took the route that French, English, and American traders used for centuries in journeying from Montreal to the west. They followed the Ottawa to the Mattawa, up that stream and by portage to Lake Nipissing, down the French River, and into Georgian Bay. Radisson's description to this point is perfectly clear; but when he tries to recall what he learned from his brother-in-law or Péré or the Jesuits, he begins to generalize; and he becomes increasingly obscure as he shifts imaginatively from place to place. He recalls Indian tribes, lakes, rivers, and islands, and the general direction of the expedition. But the only sure guide in his narrative is its title. Groseilliers and his companion voyaged to the Ottawa country, to the region of Green Bay, and to the shores of Lake Huron. From careful reading of the narrative some scholars have deduced that the voyagers visited southern Michigan and Illinois as well as the region of Green Bay. But only one place can be identified with certainty. "We came to the strait of the 2 lakes of the stinkings and ye upper lake, where there are litle isles toward Norwest, ffew towards the southest, very small. The lake towards the North att the side of it is full of rocks & sand, yett great ships can ride on it w^thout danger."[12] Here Radisson is describing the Straits of Mackinac. For many years the French knew Green Bay as *Baie des Puants,* meaning Bay of the Stinkards. And in some of their early maps they failed to distinguish Lake Michigan from Green Bay. The "upper lake" is simply the English for *mer supérieure* or Lake Superior.[13]

The most interesting passage in the narrative is that which describes what is probably the Mississippi River. "By the persuasion of some of them we went into ye great river that divides itselfe in 2, where the hurrons wth some Ottanake [Ottawas] & the [Indians] that had warrs wth them had retired. . . . This nation have warrs against those of [the] forked river. It is so called because it has 2 branches, the one towards the west, the other towards the South, wch we believe runns towards Mexico, by the tokens they gave us."[14] Some scholars are convinced that this describes the junction of the Mississippi and the Missouri, while others contend that it is inconclusive. Perhaps Jean Péré learned of the Father of Waters from Indian tribes who crossed it as they fled the Iroquois. Or perhaps Péré reached it himself and later told Radisson about it. In any case, Radisson was the first Frenchman who understood the greatness of the Mississippi Valley and who heralded its natural wealth and beauty. In describing the country around Lake Michigan, which he called "the delightfullest lake in the world," he anticipated the sentiments that countless frontiersmen felt when, a century and a half later, they set eyes on the great valley:

> the country was so pleasant, so beautiful & fruitfull that it grieved me to see y^t ye world could not discover such inticing countrys to live in. This I say because that the Europeans fight for a rock in the sea against one another, or for a sterill land and horrid country, that the people sent heere or there by the changement of the aire ingenders sickness and dies thereof. Contrarywise those kingdoms are so delicious & under so temperat a climat, plentifull of all things, the earth bringing foorth its fruit twice a yeare, the people live long & lusty & wise in their way. What conquest would that bee att litle or no cost; what laborinth of pleasure should millions of people have, instead that millions complaine of misery & poverty! What should not men reape out of the love of God in converting the souls heere, is more to be gained to heaven then what is by differences of nothing there, should be so many dangers committed under the pretence of religion! Why so many thoesoever are hid from us by our owne faults, by our negligence, covetousnesse, & unbeliefe. It's true, I confesse, that the accesse is difficult, but must say that we are like the Cockscombs of Paris, when first they begin to have wings, imagining that the larks will fall in their mouths roasted: but we ought [to remember] that vertue is not acquired w^thout labour & taking great paines.[15]

In midsummer, 1656, Groseilliers and his companion returned with their expedition to Quebec. Hjalmar R. Holand says that Groseilliers, on returning from the voyage, bought a piece of wild land near Three Rivers known locally as *des groseilliers*, meaning "the gooseberry patch." Hitherto he had been known simply as Médard Chouart; but now, having acquired land and wealth and dignity, he felt he should have at least a baronetcy. He began to call himself Sieur des Groseilliers, a title immediately adopted by the people who knew him, "probably as good-natured derision of his vain pretensions."[16] Blegen, however, says that the title was probably taken from the name of a farm near his birth place in the Marne Valley of France.[17]

On their arrival in Quebec they were hailed as heroes by the town, for each had returned with from fourteen to fifteen thousand *livres* in furs for themselves and with a flotilla of thirty canoes, laden with skins. This was the largest consignment ever to reach the lower St. Lawrence, and it revived the sagging economy of the colony. They found themselves not only possessors of a respectable fortune; they had the satisfaction of learning that they had opened up for their countrymen a new world of enterprise. They inaugurated the greatest period of activity and prosperity that the colony had ever enjoyed. They brought back, too, detailed accounts of the tribes they had met. These were so alluring that when the Indians who had come with the expedition were ready to return to their homes, thirty-one French fur traders departed with them. They soon learned, however, that the Iroquois were waiting for them. Dismayed by the dangers that threatened them, they turned back, glad to crawl ashore before they reached Montreal.[18]

By summer, 1659, Groseilliers was ready to start on another expedition to the west. This time it is certain that Radisson accompanied him. Their purpose, says Radisson, was to explore the possibility of obtaining furs in the Hudson Bay region. They called this voyage the "Superior" because they used a route across Lake Superior to the Mississippi Valley. For the dates of this voyage scholars have ignored Radisson's muddled history and have turned to Father Jerôme Lalemant, who in the *Jesuit Relations* of 1660 describes the return of the expedition, which had lasted a year. Adams, however, dissents from these findings, declaring that an examination of Canadian records shows that the only governor who could have authorized the expedition was Avaugour, whose term extended from August 31, 1661 to July 23, 1663. In Adams' opinion the Superior Voyage could not have ended in 1660, for that date would place it in the administration of Avaugour's predecessor.[20] Other scholars reject this argument as inconclusive. They prefer Lalemant, who wrote his account of the expedition soon after its return and who had no reason to want to give a false picture of it.[21]

A contest of dates may intrigue a few scholars. Much more important is narrative which, because it uncovers and illuminates human experience and therefore commands men's hearts and minds, enjoys a perennial vitality denied to other forms of historical writing.

The brothers-in-law approached the governor, Pierre de Voyer, Viscount d'Argenson, for leave of absence. The governor, doubtless loving money and mindful of the governmental policy which always appointed two men to carry on any enterprise, insisted that two of his servants go with them. The Jesuits, too, wanted to send a representative or two, not only to preach the gospel to the Indians but to negotiate with them on matters of the beaver trade. Groseilliers turned down both the governor and the Jesuits. He told the governor that he and his brother-in-law "knewed what we weare, Discoverers before governors." The governor, annoyed, flatly ordered them not to leave without his permission. Whereupon the two men sought the intercession of the Jesuits who, of course, were little disposed to speak up for them. In his narrative Radisson does not blame them, indeed, he praises them for their charity and kindness, even though he at that time was addressing English heretics for the sake of obtaining their support.[22]

Ignoring the governor's orders, Groseilliers and Radisson resolved to slip away unnoticed. Groseilliers as captain of Three Rivers held the keys to its fort. That night, says Radisson, they went with an unnamed Frenchman to the fort and "embarked ourselves. . . . Being come opposit to the fort, they aske who is there. My brother tells his name. Every one knows what good services we had done to the countrey, and loves us, ye inhabitants as well as the souldiers. The Sentrey answers him, 'God give you a good voyage.' "[23] With this blessing the expedition departed. It included about sixty Frenchmen and some Indians who had recently brought a load of peltries to Quebec and were returning to Sault Ste. Marie. At Montreal two more Frenchmen and eight Ottawas joined them. On their way up the St. Lawrence an Indian appeared on its bank and warned them against using their rifles. They ignored the warning, and the next day a handful of Iroquois attacked them, killing thirteen and scattering the rest. All the white men returned home save Radisson and Groseilliers who continued their journey with the Indians. Later Governor Argenson, perhaps on the basis of this incident, accused them of betraying their countrymen to the Iroquois. The governor suspected that they led their white companions into a trap because they were unwilling to share the profits of the expedition with them.[24]

Radisson's chronicle of this voyage is as explicit as his earlier chronicle is vague. For scholars, this confirms his participation. Lake Nipissing, Georgian Bay, St. Mary's River, and Sault Ste. Marie are all accurately described. They entered Lake Superior, fishing and camping along its southern shore as they journeyed westward. The region of Whitefish Bay yielded bear, beaver, and moose, as well as beautiful

132

weather. Radisson described it as an earthly paradise. Soon they came to a small river which the Indian guides called *Pauabickkomesibi,* meaning Little Copper River. Radisson asked why it was so called, and the Indians led him two hundred paces into the woods, where he found many large pieces of copper. The mountain, he wrote, was made of nothing else. "Seeing it so faire & pure, I had a minde to take a peece of it, but they hindered me, telling my brother there was more where we weare to goe. In this great Lake of myne owne eyes have [I] seen [great nuggets of copper] wch are admirable, and can maintain of a hundred pounds [and] will not be decayed."[25]

At Au Sable Point they paddled along high sandbanks. One of their Indians climbed to the top of one of these banks. To his companions below he appeared no bigger than a crow. A few days later they saw canoes ahead of them. Knowing that they had no enemies in this region, they paddled to overtake the strangers. When they overtook them they learned that the strangers were Indians who belonged to a small tribe consisting of no more than a hundred persons. Some of them knew Groseilliers, and were astonished to see him again so soon. They admired the merchandise he and his brother-in-law had brought with them, including "hattchetts and knives and other utensils very commodious, rare, precious, and necessary in those countreys."[26] All of them camped together, feasting and exchanging news. Some of the Indians mourned for their dead friends and danced the scalp dance over their fallen enemies. Later the "strangers" and the expedition party separated. Radisson and Groseilliers presented gifts to those who were leaving and received in return "great store of meate, wch was putt up in barrills, and grease of bears and [moose]."[27]

They paddled now along banks which boasted high rocks of variegated forms. At one of the rocks, *Nanitoucksinagiot,* meaning Evil Spirit or Ghost, the Indians left tobacco and other offerings. This rock resembled a human figure clothed in a long, flowing garment, showing its eyes and nose but concealing the lower part of its face as though with a bandage. Its color was yellow, and it assumed from a distance a strange phosphorescence, especially when it was drenched with summer sunlight.

They skirted Pictured Rocks, a formation of elevated grey sandstone with sides resembling variously fluted pillars and with a perforated base which suggested upside-down bowls that had others piled on top of them. The voyagers marveled at this natural architecture but the waves that crashed at its base invited no close inspection save on windless days. Close by stood Doric Rock, a vast entablature resting on two immense, rude pillars chiseled through many ages by the waves. From a distance the rocks in this forest suggested towns, castles, forts, and cottages. On closer view they assumed the shapes of men and animals. The voyagers passed by pinnacles, towers, caverns, and rocks resembling a sloop in full sail.

One of the most awesome points was the Grand Portal, a vast wall of rock more than a hundred feet wide and almost twice as broad. It formed a kind of gateway to a cavern which had been cut out by waves and which Radisson believed was large enough to permit the passage of a five hundred ton ship. In rough weather the waves crashed into the cavern, tearing into foam and spray, sending countless jets into the air, and making a deep, sullen roar "like the shooting of great guns" that could be heard ten miles away. Radisson named it the Portal of St. Peter after his patron saint.[28]

Some days later they reached the Huron Islands, which Radisson named the Islands of the Trinity because of their number and because they formed a kind of triangle. Soon they entered Keweenaw Bay and then portaged Keweenaw peninsula, where Radisson found enormous deposits of copper. He learned, too, that beavers had turned into swamp more than sixty miles of country and had cut down all the trees, leaving none to make a fire. The voyagers had to drag their canoes over this swampy ground. Sometimes they sank to their waists, sometimes to their heads, and they pulled themselves out of one hole only to find themselves in another. "I must with my hands," wrote Radisson, "hold the mosse, and goe [forward] like a frogg, then to draw my boat after me."[29] Five days of such misery brought them to a Cree encampment where they were warmly received. The Crees were to guide Groseilliers and his brother-in-law to Hudson Bay, and were presented with large gifts. This aroused the jealousy of Groseilliers' own Indian guides, who often acted as middlemen in the fur trade. Radisson and Groseilliers allayed this resentment by making their stay as short as possible. They paddled to the small Montreal River, where some of the Indians found a short cut and returned to their own people. Still twenty-three canoes remained, for various Indians had joined them all along the route in the hope of getting steel knives which, wrote Radisson, "they love better than we serve God, wch should make us blush for shame."[30] Seven of these canoes belonged to the Chippewas, who had joined them to observe their trading operations. A half-day's paddling brought them to land. They portaged it to Chequamegon Bay, passed to one of the Apostle Islands, perhaps Madeline, then reached a pyramidal point which they regarded as an ideal place to build a fort in the spring. There they caught many fish, including enormous sturgeons and pikes seven feet long. The Indians gave thanks to their gods and the explorers to their God for protecting them and preserving their health during the journey.

The Indians, tired of carrying the heavy supplies and anxious for their families' safety, now decided to return to their tribe. Radisson and Groseilliers remained but gave the Indians freedom to go home. Radisson records what he and his brother-in-law told them before they departed:

> We will build us a fort here. And feeling that you are not able to carry all your merchandizes att once, we will keepe them for you, and will stay for you 14 dayes. Before the time expires you will send to us if your wives be alive, and if you find them they will fetch what you have here & what we have; ffor their paines they shall receive guifts of us. Soe you will see us in your countrey. If they be dead, we will spend all to be revenged, and will gather up the whole countrey for the next spring, for that purpose to destroy those that weare the causers of their death, and you shall see our strenght and vallour. Although there are seven thousand fighting men in one village, you'll see we will make them runne away, & you shall kill them to your best liking by the very noise of our armes and our presence, who are the Gods of the earth among those people.[31]

This resolution pleased the Indians. They went off, leaving the two white men alone in the wilderness. On the waterfront Radisson and Groseilliers built a triangular fort walled with logs and thatched with branches. It had a fireplace, a bed, and a gate that faced the bay. Around the fort they piled boughs crosswise and ran a strong cord along them on which they tied at intervals little bells to warn them if anybody approached. They celebrated the completion of the fort by feasting on some fish they had saved. Then Radisson, being the younger and fitter of the two, went hunting, leaving his brother-in-law to guard the fort. Walking three or four miles into the forest, he saw, on a meadow surrounding a brook, a number of bustards or Canadian geese. He crept toward them:

> the poore creatures, seeing me flatt uppon the ground, thought that I was a beast as well as they, so they came neare me, whistling like gosslings, thinking to frighten me. The whistling that I made them heare was another musick then theirs. There I killed 3 and the rest scared, wch nevertheless came to that place againe to see what sudaine sicknesse befeled their comrads. I shott againe; two payed for their curiosity.[32]

At the end of the day he carried back to the fort enough fowl to feed him and his brother-in-law for five days.

Neighboring Indians came to admire the fort, though they were not allowed to enter it. Radisson wrote proudly that they were ready for any intruder, for they had five guns, three fowling-pieces, two musquetons, three pair of great pistolets, and two pair of pocket pistols, in addition to their swords and daggers. "Mistrust is the mother of safety," became their motto, and they abided by it. They had several night alarms caused by squirrels, foxes, and other small animals. One night one of these animals carried away Radisson's bracer, which he had left outside. Eventually their patience with the animals was exhausted. They had done so much damage to the fort and had so often endangered their lives that they resolved to make open war on them. With their large game catch, and with the meat and fish the Indians supplied they always had more than enough to eat.[33]

On the twelfth night they saw fifty young men approaching them from a distance. They soon recognized their former companions among them. They invited them into the fort and amazed them with its contraptions, which to the newcomers were works of the devil. The Indians offered to carry the explorers' baggage and furs. By this time the voyagers had accumulated so much that, fearing an Indian attack, they had buried half on the other side of the bay. They told the Indians, however, that they had sunk that portion in the bay, thereby placing it in the charge of the devil, who would see that no part of it would spoil or be stolen until they should return to recover it from his hands. Radisson wrote that they believed this cock-and-bull story as readily

as Christians believe the Gospel. Knowing that they could not bring
their canoes with them and fearing that they might be stolen in their
absence, the Frenchmen tied them in a row and set them on fire. The
birch bark blazed so quickly that it gave the appearance of fireworks,
which greatly astonished the Indians. "We weare Cesars," wrote Radisson, triumphantly, "being nobody to contradict us."[34]

They all departed southward for the Indian village. The Indians
were happy to carry the equipage in the hope of being remunerated for
their services with a brass ring, an awl, or a needle. Journeying for four
days through a beautiful country of clear forests and a few hills, they
came to within a league of the village, where they encamped so that in
the morning they could enter it in style. At dawn they repaired to a
small lake, which has been identified as Lake Court Oreille in present
Sawyer County, Wisconsin. From there they paddled in dugouts and
canoes to the village. It was an unpalisaded place of about a hundred
lodges. Its inhabitants welcomed them with cheers and shouts. The
women threw themselves backwards on the ground as a gesture of
friendship and welcome. To win their good will the Frenchmen chose
three categories of gifts, one for the men, one for the women, and the
other for the children. The first category consisted of a kettle, two
hatchets, six knives, and a blade for a sword. The kettle, they explained,
was to unite all tribes to the Feast of the Dead, which they celebrated
every seven years to renew friendships. The hatchets were to encourage young men to fight bravely at all times, to guard their wives, and to
show themselves men by knocking their enemies on the head. The knives
were to show that the French were their great and mighty friends. The
sword signified that the Frenchmen would be masters of both peace and
war, ready and able to destroy their enemies with superior arms.

The category for the women consisted of twenty-two awls, fifty
needles, two "gratters of castor" for cleaning beaver skins, two ivory
combs and two wooden ones, some red paint, and six tin looking glasses.
The awls, they explained, were to remind them that they must always
be courageous, protect themselves, and follow their husbands to the
French settlements when weather permitted. They were to use the
needles to help them make beaver robes, which the French loved. The
"gratters" were to enable them to dress skins, the combs and paint to
help them beautify themselves, and the looking glasses to allow them to
admire themselves.

137

The third category, given to the children, consisted of brass rings, small bells, and drinking cups of different colors. They assembled the children and made them scramble for the gifts, while they bade them make merry and to remember their benefactors, who would protect them throughout childhood.

The Indians then held a council, laid out a grand banquet for their guests, and entertained them by dancing over the scalps of their enemies. Radisson and Groseilliers, of course, availed themselves of their prestige to direct the affairs of their Indian friends.

At first they made their home with the principal chief, who came with them on the voyage; but, not caring for his company, they soon transferred their packs to the cottage of a witty old man with a large family and a handsome old wife. The chief wondered why they left, but says Radisson, "durst not speake, because we weare demi-gods." He took the old man for his father, the wife for his mother, and their children for his brothers and sisters. They adopted him into the family and exchanged gifts with him.[35]

By now winter had arrived. Snow began to fall, giving the villagers and their guests warning that they must all leave their homes and seek their living in the forest. Because game was temporarily scarce, they scattered in all directions, agreeing on the place for a point of rendezvous at the end of two and a half months to make plans for the coming summer. At the same time they sent messengers in all directions to inform persons and tribes that within five moons they should meet at a designated place to celebrate the Feast of the Dead and to distribute presents of peace and union.

All together they numbered about sixty hunters. In the space of two and a half moons, wrote Radisson, with Gallic ebullience, they killed enough bears to last them a thousand moons. In winter, they ate the grease of these animals to keep themselves warm, supple, and swift; in summer, to protect themselves against the bites of mosquitoes. Sometimes they varied their otherwise monotonous diet with the meat of deer, caribou, moose, stags, fallow does, bucks, and panthers. Radisson must have had some trouble with these animals, for he called them children of the devil.[36]

For a time they led a good life. But soon new snow fell on the old, forcing them to make snowshoes, "not to play att ball, but to exercise ourselves in a game harder and more necessary. They are broad, made like racketts, that they may goe in the snow and not sinke when they runne after the [moose] and other beast."

At the end of the hunt Radisson and his party went to the point of rendezvous, where they found some of their friends awaiting them. They built cabins and awaited the arrival of the rest, who came straggling in day after day. The snow kept piling up, sticking to the pines, cedars, and thorns, and darkening the forest until it seemed like a prolonged eclipse of the sun. The snow was so light that it looked like sifted flour. It could not bear men even on snowshoes which were six feet long and eighteen inches broad. They staggered and swayed, only to slip and fall in the drifts on their backsides or on their heads. There they remained until their friends rescued them.

And the snow whirled relentlessly down, turning the landscape more and more into a Sahara of fleecy whiteness and blinding the travelers with its fierce glare. They became snowbound for two weeks. Then their misery increased. They had to take in a band of about a hundred and fifty Ottawas who came from an island on which they had been living with the Hurons. The Ottawas had quarreled with the Hurons and were planning to make war on them in the coming summer. Being fishermen and traders rather than hunters, they had brought no food with them. Well armed with knives and hatchets, they terrified their hosts. They were so hungry that they insisted on taking much of the remaining food. Sometimes they even snatched it from the mouths of children. Their behavior disgusted Radisson, who described them as "the coursedest, unablest, the unfamous & cowardliest people that I have seene amongst fower [four] score nations that I have frequented."[37]

He recalled with bitterness the ample provisions they had once enjoyed. "Where is the time past? Where is the plentynesse that yee had in all places and countreys? Here comes a new family of these poore people dayly to us, halfe dead, for they have but the skin & boans. How shall we make strength to make a hole in the snow to lay use downe, seeing we [cannot carry] our racketts after us, nor to cutt a little woad to make a fire to keep us from the rigour of the cold, wch is extreme in those Countreyes in its season."[38] The misery became more pervasive, more intense, more unbearable as day followed day. Every morning people awakened to find some member of the family or some relative stiff and dead. The crying and wailing that rang through the cabins was

139

hideous enough to make one's hair stand on end. "Good God," prayed Radisson, "have mercy on so many poore innocent people, and of us that acknowledge thee, that having offended thee punishes us." But, he continued bitterly, they could not free themselves of "that cruell Executioner." Those who could still move searched for roots, which they could find only with great difficulty, for the earth was frozen three feet deep and snow lay six feet high. They were reduced to eating the bark of vines which twined around trees. They cut the vines into two-foot lengths, tied them in faggots, and boiled them in a kettle until the bark came off with ease. Then they dried it in smoke, reduced it to powder between stones, and boiled it into a kind of broth. It nourished them but made them very thirsty.[39]

In desperation they seized their dogs and then killed, stewed, and ate them. When that food was gone they moved back and forth, over and over again, looking for anything that they could put into their mouths to assuage the gnawing pain in their stomachs. They were elated when they found a bone or two of the animals they had killed many days before. "And happy," wrote Radisson, "was he that could gett what the other did throw away after it had been boyled 3 or foure times to get the [marrow] out of it." Starvation made them keenly resourceful. They reduced the bones of crows and dogs to powder which they buried six inches in the ground. On this they burned a fire until the heat brought more subsistence to the powdered bones. Then they dug them up and made broth with them.[40]

Soon they began to eat their clothes—their moccasins, their stockings, most of the skins of the cabins, and even the beaver skins which the children had "beshit above a hundred times." They singed the hair off furs and chewed the hides so heartily that their gums bled. Now nothing remained for them to eat except dry wood. By this time they were reduced to mere skeletons. They mistook the living for the dead, the dead for the living. Those who could still walk were not strong enough to draw their dead comrades out of the cabins to bury them, or, if some succeeded in doing so, could not carry them more than four steps in the snow. More than five hundred men, women, and children perished.[41]

Suddenly the weather changed. A strong wind and heavy rain brought new hope to the survivors of the famine. The snow melted gradually from the evergreens; mottled patches of brown sage began to

140

form on the thinning blanket of snow; animals emerged from their dens; and the men who had not eaten the strings from their bows mustered what little strength remained to them to stagger out to the forest to search for game. In three days what little snow remained had hardened so much that they could walk on it with their snowshoes. They killed a number of deer which had broken through the crust of snow and floundered. But some of the men had gone without food for so many days that they could eat only small quantities of meat at widely spaced intervals. The Indians, thinking that Groseilliers' physical condition seemed unchanged throughout the famine, said that some devil had provided him with food. "But," comments Radisson, "if they had seene his body they should be of another opinion. The beard that covered his face made as if he had not altered his face. For me that had no beard, they said I loved them, because I lived as well as they."[42] Grace Lee Nute finds in this last statement strong evidence that Radisson was still a beardless youth in 1659. "No Frenchman of Radisson's day," she wrote, "would have been without his beard, especially in the woods, if he had been capable of raising one. Besides being difficult to shave off in the wilderness, a beard was a distinct protection against severe cold in winter and the hordes of mosquitoes that made life almost unendurable in spring and early summer."[43]

As spring advanced the travelers slowly regained their strength. One day they were pleased to receive eight representatives of the Sioux from the region of present Minnesota. They had come to form an alliance. Each representative brought two wives carrying packs of wild rice, Indian corn, and other foods, which, writes Radisson, "had been welcome if they had brought it a month or two before." They made a ceremony in which they anointed the legs and feet of the Frenchmen with buffalo grease. The Frenchmen in turn painted their guests with vermilion. The Sioux showed their delight in this procedure by stripping the Frenchmen of their clothes and dressing them in buffalo robes and small white skins, perhaps ermine. Then, in accordance with a tribal custom, the Indians wept and wailed to gain pity. They brought out red stone calumets and smoked them to show their peaceful intentions. When they had finished smoking they burned every garment belonging to the white men and threw tobacco into the fire to please the gods.[44]

The Frenchmen had never received such a welcome from any tribe before. They responded with equal hospitality. Summoning the Indians through an interpreter, they impressed them by speaking from elevated seats. They borrowed one of the calumets, held it up, and told them that they were forbidden to carry away any such articles from their own country. They removed the eagle's tail which hung from the stem of the calumet and supplanted it with twelve iron arrowheads. They said that these arrowheads would pass over the whole world to destroy their mutual enemies. Then the Frenchmen pointed to a sword and said that by means of it they would vanquish their enemies. They stuck a hatchet in the ground and pointing to it assured the Indians that they would kill those who made war on them and that they would make forts to protect them in celebrating the Feast of the Dead. Then the Frenchmen tossed some gunpowder into the fire, pretending that it was merely French tobacco. It filled the lodge with flying embers, smoke, and firebrands. The Indians were so frightened that they fled in all directions, for, says Radisson, they "never saw a sacrifice of tobacco so violent." The Frenchmen followed immediately to reassure them and found them trembling with fright.[45]

The place appointed for the Feast of the Dead lay between a meadow and a small lake. This may have been Spring Brook Hill near the confluence of the Snake and Ann rivers, two miles south of Mora, in Kanabec County, Minnesota. There assembled about five hundred Indians belonging to eighteen different tribes. The fort, probably made of brush, was a large square building six hundred paces long and six hundred paces wide. A brook which emanated from the lake ran past the fort, and attracted many deer. Soon a group of thirty Sioux warriors arrived. They were armed with bows and arrows and dressed in short garments so that they could readily hunt deer. In a short while they were able to kill a great many deer. They scraped off the snow, covered the earth with boughs, and brought kettles full of meat. For five hours they feasted without saying a word. Then the Sioux called for attention by shooting arrows and uttering weird cries. They announced that their elders and warriors would soon arrive to make a treaty with the Frenchmen and to inform them of their desire to take the warpath against the Crees. The Frenchmen shoveled snow from a large piece of ground near the fort and laid the framework of the tipis in which the expected Sioux would be housed.[46]

They arrived on the next day with great pomp and circumstance.

142

Their appearance reminded Radisson of the entrance of the "Polanders at Paris," though they wore feathers instead of jewels. The warriors arrived first and were equipped with bows, arrows, and round shields on which were painted all sorts of figures, including moons, suns, and animals. Their faces were daubed with paints of many colors and their ears were adorned with copper rings. Each had his hair singed short save for a tuft that turned up like a crown. The tuft was decorated with small pearls, turquoise, buffalo horns, bears' paws, or snakes' skins. The grease that covered their bodies was heavy and mixed with red clay. Their clothing was of buckskin. Probably because they belonged to the *Kangi-yuha* or Crow-Owners Society, which continued to exist throughout frontier days, they wore skins of crows hanging from their belts. Their moccasins and leggings were adorned with pearls and porcupine quills. Their swords and knives, which were a foot and a half long, were made of wood and had rounded, decorative handles which aroused Radisson's admiration. Some of them wore the scalps of men they had killed in recent battles.[47]

The elders, who followed the warriors, were dressed in handsome buffalo robes that hung to the ground. Each wore a grave countenance as he approached. He carried a calumet adorned with "precious jewells" in his hand and a sack containing all his earthly possessions on his shoulders. Next came their women, carrying packs heavier than themselves. They seemed to Radisson as "laden [as] so many mules." Conducted to the appointed place, they unfolded their bundles and pitched their tipis so quickly that "they had howses [in] lesse than half an houre."

Near a large fire their spokesman made a long speech in which he avowed their friendship for the Frenchmen, whom he declared masters of peace and war. He said his people had come purposely to ask their protection. Then the Sioux presented them with beaver skins while they invited them to visit their villages:

> ye mountains weare elevated, ye valleys rise, the ways very smooth, the bows of trees cutt downe to goe wth more ease, and bridges erected over rivers, for not to wett our feete; that the dores of their villages, cottages of their wives and daughters, weare open at any time to receive us, being wee kept them alive by our merchandises.[48]

With these words they made preparations to lay out a great feast. The white men, mindful that Sioux custom required each man to furnish his own dish, went back to their baggage to get their wooden bowls. They took the precaution, too, of bringing back a pair of pistols and a sword and dagger, which they laid down beside them. Soon they were approached by four elderly men with a lighted calumet, and by four beautiful young girls with bearskins for them to sit on. A spokesman set the calumet before them, drew the kettles from the fire, and gave thanks to the sun for friends so powerful that they could make the earth tremble. He sang as he stripped off his robes and put them on the Frenchmen. Standing naked save for his legs and feet, he said, "Yee are masters over us; dead or alive you have power over us, and may dispose of us at your pleasur." He handed them the calumet, which they smoked. Thinking that the occasion called for a song, Radisson responded with one, perhaps a French *chanson*. He promised, through his interpreter, that he and his brother-in-law would protect them as though they were all brothers. The white men attested to the sincerity of their words by giving a twelve-gun salute and unsheathing their swords. The Indians, interpreting these flourishes of military might as manifestations of sudden hostility, became so terrified that they hardly knew whether to run away or stay. Observing this, Radisson intensified their superstitious dread by repeating his trick of throwing gunpowder into the fire.[49]

They feasted on wild rice which grew in water three or four feet deep. "There is a God," philosophized Radisson, "that shews himself in every countrey, almighty, full of goodnesse, and ye preservation of those poore people who knoweth him not." He described their method of gathering rice. "They have a particular way to gather up that graine. Two takes a boat and two sticks by wch they gett y^e [stalk] down and the [grain] out of it. Their boat being full, they bring [the rice] to a fitt place to dry it, and that is their food for the most part of the winter, and doe dresse it thus: ffor each man a handfull of [it] in the pott, . . . swells so much that it can suffice a man."[50]

When they had finished eating, Radisson made a long speech in which he urged them to keep peace with the Crees. He said that the French had also adopted the Crees as their children. Mindful that the fur trade flourished best in times of peace, he threatened to reduce to "powder with our heavenly fire" all those who took to the warpath.

144

Then he distributed gifts which included "gratters," awls, ivory combs, small bells, and vermilion. He gave sword blades to the elders and necklaces and bracelets to the girls who had served him. The Sioux were overwhelmed with gratitude, which they attempted to express with a chorus of "Ho! Ho! Ho!"

Leaving his brother-in-law and the Indians to celebrate the Feast of the Dead, Radisson led a party of fifty men to inform the Crees of the treaty he had just concluded. Their camp lay three days' journey to the north in the region of Lake Mille Lacs. There he found such quantities of meat that he was reminded of the markets of Paris and London. However, as he was suffering from snow blindness, he could not attend the Crees' councils. As soon as he regained his sight he hurried back to his brother-in-law and to the sham battles, dancing, and singing of the Feast of the Dead. When the feast ended, each band which had attended went home. The Frenchmen set out to visit the Sioux village, perhaps Issati, southwest of Lake Mille Lacs, where Father Hennepin later was held prisoner. At the end of six weeks they returned with a band of friendly Chippewas to Chequamegon Bay, where they found the furs and supplies they had hidden in good condition. On the site of the old fort they built a new one. They soon discovered that the Ottawas had built a fort near their cache on the opposite side of the bay. Fearing for the safety of their furs and supplies, they decided to remove them on sleds to the fort. When they were returning with overladened sleds and were only four leagues offshore, Radisson fell through the ice up to his knees. In so doing, he injured his legs and perhaps other parts of his body. He stripped off his wet clothes and, covering himself with skins, lay down on his sled. Groseilliers, weak from a recurring disease, went slowly on with his load to the Ottawas. He asked them to help him rescue his brother-in-law. The Ottawas seized on the white men's misfortune to make exorbitant demands which Groseilliers was forced to grant. The rescued man lay for eight days in such dreadful pain that he thought he would die. In his chronicle he recalls that he rested neither day nor night. His brother-in-law tended him faithfully, rubbing his legs with hot bear's oil and binding his thigh to keep him as comfortable as possible. Slowly he regained his strength.[51]

As spring advanced they set out to visit the country of the Crees on the northern shore of Lake Superior, in keeping with a promise they had made to them. The tribe sent a delegation to accompany them to its

145

camping ground. But the Frenchmen, seeing the Ottawas hanging around their valuable cache, sent the delegation ahead across Lake Superior. Next day, taking care to tell the Ottawas that they were going hunting, they slipped away in a single canoe. They crossed the lake, perhaps at La Pointe, on Madeline Island, Wisconsin, to the vicinity of the Cross River. According to Radisson the distance was about fifteen leagues, or forty-five miles. They were constantly in danger because the ice was breaking up. They feared it might either smash their canoe to pieces or cause it to founder. Almost miraculously they escaped, though they wandered, confused or lost, for several hours before they came out of a deep bay. There they saw smoke and the tents of the Crees. As soon as the Indians saw them they came out in their canoes and conveyed them ashore, where they gave them a rousing welcome.[52]

Radisson says that later in the spring he and his brother-in-law made a journey from the northern shore of Lake Superior, presumably to James Bay and Hudson Bay. They went by way of Lake Nipigon and the Albany River, the Michipocoton and Moose rivers, or one of the other routes known to the Crees. Most scholars doubt that the Frenchmen ever made such a journey. By the time Radisson wrote his chronicle he and his brother-in-law had deserted France for England. His motive in fabricating a journey to the salt waters of the north was to impress his new employer, Charles II. He wanted Charles II to grant him and his brother-in-law the support they needed to promote a lucrative fur trade in that region. Again, as in other parts of his chronicle, Radisson betrays himself by his vagueness of language, his lack of detail, and his confused chronology and itinerary in trying to invent or recount experiences which were derived largely from hearsay. A journey to James Bay and Hudson Bay would, moreover, have required more time than was available to them, for they claimed to have returned to Montreal by the latter part of August. The probability is that Radisson derived his general knowledge of the region from an Algonkin named Awatanik. In 1658 Awatanik had traveled from Green Bay to Lake Superior, from Lake Superior to Hudson Bay. From Hudson Bay he had gone along the coast to other rivers and by portage to the Saguenay River, where he met Father Gabriel Druillettes. Later he returned with Druillettes to Quebec. There they met Radisson and Groseilliers who obtained from the Indian an account of his experiences in the region of Hudson Bay.

146

Blegen surmises that the two men did not spend their time journeying to James Bay and Hudson Bay. Rather, he says, they canoed along Lake Superior, whence they returned to Montreal. There they were welcomed by the booming of cannon. They had brought home a tremendous flotilla of sixty canoes laden with furs which Mère Marie de l'Incarnation, leader of the Ursulines in Quebec, hailed as "true manna from heaven." Moreover, their diplomacy had won over the Ottawas, Hurons, and Chippewas. Consequently, they were able to push as far as the country of the Sioux along the Father of Waters and to establish markets for French goods. This cargo met the needs of most of the people. It particularly helped the merchants who, because of a recent dearth of furs, had seriously entertained thoughts of leaving the country.[53]

Ironically, triumph led to misfortune. Governor Argenson had not forgotten how Groseilliers had slipped away without permission. He promptly threw him into prison and fined him and his brother-in-law 4000 livres, which he spent in building a fort at Three Rivers. Ironically he permitted them to place their coat of arms on it "as the only compensation for their expense." In addition, Argenson made them pay a customs duty amounting to a fourth of the value of their entire cargo. After these merciless fleecings they found they had left about 22,000 livres. Needless to say, they were extremely bitter. "Was not he a Tyrant," exclaims Radisson in his chronicle, "to deal so with us, after wee had so hazarded our lives." Seeing themselves so wronged, he and his brother-in-law sailed to France to demand justice, but they had no success there. Eventually they resolved to sell their services to England, where they landed in 1666. They succeeded in interesting Charles II, his cousin Prince Rupert, and other noblemen in the potential riches from Hudson Bay furs. They obtained two ships, one under Radisson and the other under Groseilliers, in which they reached Hudson Bay in 1668. Radisson soon encountered a fierce storm which forced him to return to England. But Groseilliers reached the mouth of the Rupert, wintered there, and brought back to England a rich cargo of furs. His success led to the establishment of the Hudson's Bay Company, which played a leading role in the economic development of Canada as well as in that of the Mississippi Valley. The company survives to this day.

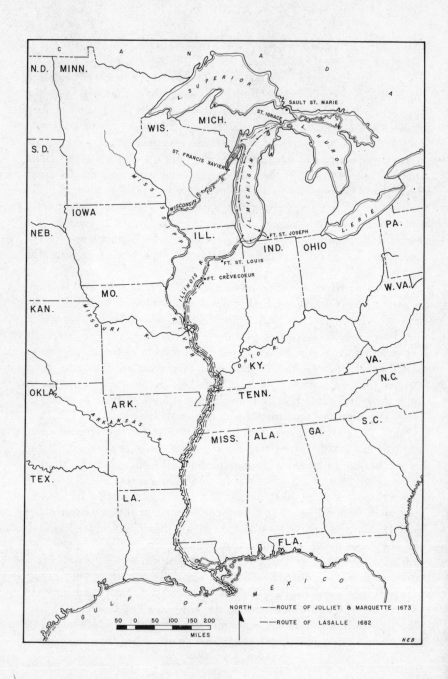

N.D. MINN.

S.D.

IOWA

NEB.

KAN.

OKLA.

TEX.

L. SUPERIOR

WIS.   MICH.

SAULT ST. MARIE

ST. IGNACE

L. HURON

ST. FRANCIS XAVIER

WISCONSIN R.   FOX R.

ILL.

FT. ST. JOSEPH

L. MICHIGAN

MISSISSIPPI R.

ILLINOIS R.

FT. ST. LOUIS

FT. CRÈVECOEUR

MISSOURI R.

MO.

ARK.

LA.

ARKANSAS R.

OHIO R.

KY.

TENN.

MISS.   ALA.

IND.   OHIO

L. ERIE

PA.

W. VA.

VA.

N.C.

S.C.

GA.

FLA.

GULF   OF   MEXICO

CANADA

NORTH

—— ROUTE OF JOLLIET & MARQUETTE 1673

—— ROUTE OF LASALLE 1682

50 0   50 100 150 200

MILES

NEB

10

Jolliet and Marquette

In 1665 NEW FRANCE ACCELERATED HER INTEREST IN THE DISCOVERY and in the fur trade of the Mississippi Valley. At that time Louis XIV's great minister, Jean-Baptiste Colbert, appointed Jean-Baptiste Talon intendant of New France. This office gave him charge of the financial, police, and judicial affairs of the colony. It was, therefore, the most powerful office next to that of the governorship itself. Young, vigorous, fearless, imaginative, and stern, Talon became the guiding genius of French exploration. For the first time since the days of Champlain a leading authority of the colony regarded the Mississippi Valley as worthy of exploration and occupation at any cost. Talon resolved to follow up the explorations begun in 1634 by Jean Nicolet and to extend French authority gradually over the entire interior of North America. So pronounced was this determination that the Spaniards, learning of it, expressed a fear that he would succeed in driving them from the entire valley—a fear which eventually became reality, though not in Talon's administration. The intendant urged Louis XIV to lay claim to all territory traversed by French explorers, missionaries, and traders, and to assert supremacy over all its Indian tribes.

Already the Mississippi Valley was becoming better known to New France, thanks to the zeal of missionaries interested as much in exploration as in teaching Indians the Word of God. One of such missionaries was Father Claude Jean Allouez who often welcomed Chippewas from the region of the Mississippi at his Mission of the Holy Spirit at La Pointe in Chequamegon Bay. Allouez, indeed, bears the distinction of mentioning the name of the river for the first time in French annals.

149

"These are people," he wrote of the Chippewas, "dwelling to the West of this place, toward the great river named Messipi. They are forty or fifty leagues from this place, in a country of prairies, rich in all kinds of game. They cultivate fields, sowing therein not Indian corn, but only tobacco; while Providence has furnished them with a kind of marsh rye [wild rice] which they go and harvest toward the close of Summer in certain small lakes that are covered with it."[1] He prayed that God would some day give him an opportunity to bring the Gospel to them.

But God had other plans for Father Allouez. In 1669 his superior sent him to establish the Mission of St. François Xavier among the Potawatomies on Green Bay. He went, he said, not merely for the sake of ministering to the Indians, but also to exercise some repressive influence on the lawless independent traders known as *coureurs de bois* who often gathered there in considerable numbers. Some months later he and Father Claude Dablon, a trained and talented geographer and Superior of the northwest missions which he directed from Sault Ste. Marie, ascended the Fox and portaged to the Wisconsin. They failed to complete this route to the Mississippi. During their travels, however, they gathered from Indians detailed information of the great river which, though not always accurate, proved of some use to future explorers. Dablon wrote of the Indians he met that they lived—

in the midst of that beautiful region mentioned by us, near the great river Missisipi, of which it is well to note here what information we have gathered. It seems to form an inclosure, as it were, for all our lakes, rising in the regions of the North and flowing toward the south, until it empties into the sea—supposed by us to be either the vermilion or the Florida sea, as there is no knowledge of any large rivers in that direction except those which empty into these two Seas. Some Savages have assured us that this is so noble a river that, at more than three hundred leagues' distance from its mouth, it is larger than the one flowing before Quebec; for they declare that it is more than a league wide. They also state that all this vast stretch of country consists of nothing but treeless prairies,—so that its inhabitants are all obliged to burn peat and animal excrement dried in the Sun,—until we come within twenty leagues of the sea, when Forests began to appear again. Some warriors of this country who tell us they have made their way thither, declare that they saw men resembling the French, who were splitting trees with long knives; and that some of them had their houses on the water,—for thus they expressed themselves in speaking of sawed boards and of Ships. They state further that all along that great river are various Tribes of different Nations, of dissimilar languages and customs, and all at war with one another.[2]

Allouez' successor at the Mission of the Holy Spirit in Chequamegon Bay was Father Jacques Marquette. During his first winter there he met some Sioux who said they lived on the banks of a great river. Marquette, whose interest in geography almost equaled his priestly zeal, planned to make a journey to the river to ascertain its size, direction, and commercial value. Allouez thought it flowed into the Atlantic; Marquette thought it flowed into the Pacific through the Gulf of California. "If the Savages who promise to make me a Canoe do not break their word to me," wrote Marquette to his superior, "we shall explore this River as far as we can, with a Frenchman and [a young Indian they have] given me, who knows some [Indian] languages and has a facility for learning the others. We shall visit the Nations dwelling there, in order to open the passage to such of our Fathers as have been awaiting this good fortune for so long a time. This discovery will give us full knowledge either of the South Sea or of the Western Sea."[3]

His plans, however, were spoiled when the Hurons took the warpath against the Sioux. Then, in 1670, Talon ordered Simon François Daumont, Sieur de Saint-Lusson, a soldier of fortune who had crossed to Canada with him, to take formal possession of the whole interior in the name of the king. With Saint-Lusson was Nicolas Perrot, whom he sent to summon the regional tribes to Sault Ste. Marie. There, in the following spring, Saint-Lusson planned to hold a pageant of possession. The tribes around Green Bay received Perrot, who had lived with them and who knew Algonkian well, with clamors of welcome. The Miamis staged a sham battle in his honor and entertained him with a game of lacrosse. Seventeen tribes and subtribes in all agreed to send delegates to the scheduled ceremony.[4]

On the appointed day, June 14, 1671, the Indian delegates and their white friends gathered on a small hill that overlooked the falls, the mission, and the forest beyond. The Indians contrasted sharply with Dablon, Allouez, and several other Jesuits who wore black robes. The Indians were painted with their clan marks or symbols. Their hair was

151

greased and perfumed, their ears were adorned with copper rings, and they were dressed in their best decorated deerskins or in the colored woolens they had bartered for pelts. Near the Jesuits stood Perrot, Louis Jolliet, and twelve or thirteen bearded traders in green, violet, and yellow costumes. Saint-Lusson doubtless wore the holiday costume of his day: plumed velvet hat, long curled wig, bright, velvet, skirted breeches to the knee, short jacket, long shirt, lace and ruffles at knee and elbow, and a short ceremonial sword. The Indians stood or crouched or reclined as Dablon, superior of the regional missions, pronounced a solemn blessing over a large wooden cross, which was then reared and planted in the ground. Meanwhile the white men chanted, *"Vexilla Regis prodeunt"*—the Standard of our King comes forth. Then they planted by the cross a post of cedar with a metal plate including an engraving of the royal arms, while they chanted, *"Exaudiat te Domine in die tribulationis . . ."* When they had finished this hymn and the Jesuits had uttered a prayer for the king, Saint-Lusson, holding his ceremonial sword in one hand and a sod of earth in the other, proclaimed the sovereignty of France of "all the countries, rivers, lakes and streams . . . both those which have been discovered and those which may be discovered hereafter, in all their strength and breadth, bounded on one side by the seas of the North and the West, and the other by the South Sea." At the end of the speech the Frenchmen fired their guns and shouted, *"Vive le Roi!"* The Indians yelped with joy.

When the clamor subsided Allouez addressed the Indians in a long speech which has few equals in frontier oratory for its vividness and force. In his endeavor to impress them with the greatness of France he painted a hyperbolic portrait of her king, whose sway had just been proclaimed over a limitless but yet unconquered and even unknown expanse of territory:

> He lives beyond the sea; he is the Captain of the greatest Captains, and has not his equal in the world. All the Captains you have ever seen, or of whom you have ever heard, are mere children compared with him. He is like a great tree, and they, only like little plants that we tread under foot in walking. You know about Onnontio, that famous Captain of Quebec. You know and feel that he is the terror of the Iroquois, and that his very name makes them tremble, now that he has laid waste their country and set fire to their Villages. Beyond the sea there are ten

152

thousand Onnontios like him, who are only the Soldiers of that Great Captain, our Great King, of whom I am speaking. When he says, "I am going to war," all obey him; and those ten thousand Captains raise Companies of a hundred soldiers each, both on land and on sea. Some embark in ships, one or two hundred in number, like those that you have seen at Quebec. Your Canoes hold only four or five men—or, at the very most, ten or twelve. Our ships in France hold four or five hundred, and even as many as a thousand. Other men make war by land, but in such vast numbers that, if drawn up in a double file, they would extend farther than from here to Mississaquenk, although the distance exceeds twenty leagues. When he attacks, he is more terrible than the thunder: the earth trembles, the air and the sea are set on fire by the discharge of his Cannon; while he has been seen amid his squadrons, all covered with the blood of his foes, of whom he has slain so many with his sword that he does not count their scalps, but the rivers of blood which he sets flowing. So many prisoners of war does he lead away that he makes no account of them, letting them go about whither they will, to show that he does not fear them. No one now dares make war upon him, all nations beyond the sea having most submissively sued for peace. From all parts of the world people go to listen to his words and to admire him, and he alone decides all the affairs of the world. What shall I say of his wealth? You count yourselves rich when you have ten or twelve sacks of corn, some hatchets, glass beads, kettles, or other things of that sort. He has towns of his own, more in number than you have people in all these countries five hundred leagues around; while in each town there are warehouses containing enough hatchets to cut down all your forests, kettles to cook all your moose, and glass beads to fill all your cabins. His house is longer than from here to the head of the Sault and higher than the tallest of your trees; and it contains more families than the largest of your Villages can hold.[5]

At the end of this speech Saint-Lusson began a speech of his own in which he told them in martial and eloquent language the reasons for which he had summoned them. He emphasized that the king, whose panegyric they had just heard, had sent him to put them under his protection. The ceremony closed with a great bonfire, which was lighted toward evening and around which the *Te Deum* was sung to thank God on behalf of the Indians who were now the subjects of so great and powerful a king.

Talon next took steps to send an expedition to discover the Missis-

sippi Valley. He was desirous of ascertaing the mineral wealth, especially the rumored copper and iron, of the Great Lakes region. This, of
course, would lead to increased government control of the region, which
hitherto had been under the jurisdiction of the Jesuits. Talon had been
directed to pursue a policy that would win the region for the crown,
even though it might precipitate a contest with the Jesuits. He had been
directed, too, to send out an expedition that would ascertain whether
the Mississippi flowed through North America into the Gulf of California or into the Pacific Ocean. If it did it would enable the French to
outflank the Spaniards on the west. If, on the other hand, it flowed into
the Gulf of Mexico, as some missionaries believed, it would enable
France to weaken Spain in the east, where, over a hundred years before,
she had built St. Augustine, the oldest town in the present United States.
Finally, Talon hoped to hem in the English, who had already reached
Hudson Bay, by building a chain of forts and trading posts connecting
the fur centers on the Mississippi with those of the St. Lawrence.[6]

The man entrusted with the leadership of the expedition was Louis
Jolliet, a talented surveyor and cartographer and a fearless fur trader
and explorer. As we have seen, he had accompanied Saint-Lusson to
the pageant of possession at Sault Ste. Marie. By this time New France
had a new governor, Louis de Baude, Count of Frontenac. Shortly after
his arrival in the colony he had quarreled with Talon, who had soon
been recalled. Already, however, Frontenac had accepted Talon's
advice to appoint Jolliet as leader of the expedition. Frontenac, indeed,
was happy to appoint a layman, for he had secret orders to curb the
Jesuits. Judiciously, he did decide to send one of them, Father Marquette, with the expedition. In the previous year, when the Sioux overran La Pointe, Marquette had fled with the Hurons and Ottawas to
St. Ignace, on the narrow Straits of Mackinac, where he performed his
priestly duties in "a rude and unshapely chapel, its sides of logs and its
roof of bark." Frontenac informed Colbert that Jolliet had promised to
lead his expedition as far west as the Mississippi by way of Green Bay
and that he would in all probability discover that the great river flowed
into the Gulf of Mexico.[7]

In October, 1672, Jolliet left Quebec, probably alone in a birch bark
canoe. Toiling through the turbulent Ottawa and Mattawa rivers, across
the dangerous portage path to Lake Nipissing, down the French River,
and across Georgian Bay and the upper reaches of Lake Huron, he

reached the northern shore of the Straits of Mackinac. There on December 8 he found his destined companion. Marquette, who for two years had constantly invoked the Blessed Virgin to obtain from God the grace that would enable him to visit the tribes of the Mississippi Valley, received word of his new mission with joyous gratitude. On May 17, 1673, he and Jolliet, supplied with smoked meat and Indian corn, embarked with five men in two canoes. Paddling westward, they passed the Straits of Mackinac, crossed the northern section of Lake Michigan, and reached a village of the Menominies. The Menominies, having acted as middlemen in the fur trade and jealous of their profits, tried to frighten them into turning back. Undaunted, the explorers pushed on to the south end of Green Bay, entered the Fox River, portaged along the long and noisy rapids, skirted Lake Winnebago, and drifted up the Fox to a Mascoutin village which Dablon and Allouez had visited several years before. Calling a meeting of its chiefs and elders, they announced that Frontenac had sent them to explore the great valley and to bring the light of Christianity to its people. The chiefs and elders listened to their message with attention and gave them guides who would facilitate their route to the Wisconsin River. Paddling down this stream, on June 17 they reached the Father of Waters. The journal of this expedition was ostensibly written by Marquette in the first person, but it really was written by Dablon from Marquette's notes and a copy of Jolliet's journal. In it, the pious missionary is made to say that he first looked on the magnificent river "with a joy which I cannot express."

This was a momentous day in the history of France and in that of the colony. Here was the real discovery of the Mississippi, despite the controversial views of a number of scholars. Here at last its mystery was solved. It flowed southward, just as the Indians had said, and French policy in its relations with foreign nations could be fashioned accordingly.[8] Here the river was walled in "by picturesque cliffs, with lofty limestone escarpment, whose irregular outline looks like a succession of ruined castles and towers of the Rhine." Jolliet called the river Baude, in honor of the new governor of Canada, while Marquette, in keeping with his religious nature, preferred to designate it Conception. Both men, however, realized that the authorities were primarily interested in its direction, and they resolved to follow it southward, leisurely paddling along by day and resting in mid-stream by night.

In this manner on June 25 they discovered along its western bank a path which they followed to an Indian village. The inhabitants swarmed from their huts to see the white strangers. Four chiefs told them that they were Illinois and gave them calumets decorated with feathers. The Illinois had heard of the French and had desired an alliance with them against their enemies, the Iroquois, who had made merciless raids on their country. They laid out a great feast for their guests, took them to see the whole village of three hundred huts, marched them through the streets, and presented them with belts, garters, and "other articles made of the hair of the bear and wild cattle, dyed red, yellow, and gray." The next day six hundred persons escorted them to their canoes and, as they bade them goodbye, evinced in every possible way their pleasure at knowing them.

They were now at the mouth of the Des Moines River and they were probably the first white men to see the present state of Iowa. They continued to descend the Mississippi to the mouth of the Missouri, to that of the Ohio, and to that of the Arkansas. There, as we have seen in an earlier chapter, they visited the Quapaws, who received them with great hospitality and who advised them that the river continued southward to the sea. Thus they assured themselves of its direction and its outlet—considerations of primary importance to Frontenac. Realizing that it flowed toward the domain of the Spaniards, who were enemies of the French and who boasted of innumerable savage allies, they wisely decided to turn homeward. At the mouth of the Illinois friendly Indians persuaded them that this river would provide them with a quicker and easier route to Lake Michigan. Father Marquette wanted to remain to Christianize them, but he had to bow to Jolliet's wishes to return with him to Quebec. They followed the Illinois and the Des Plaines rivers, portaged to the Chicago River, reached Lake Michigan, and skirted its western shore to the mission of St. François Xavier on Green Bay. There Jolliet wrote a report and made a map of his explorations.

In the spring of 1674 Jolliet resumed his journey homeward, leaving Marquette, who was dangerously ill with dysentery, at the mission on Green Bay. He attempted to shorten his route by shooting the rapids between Montreal Island and the southern bank. His canoe was upset, his two paddlers and an Illinois Indian boy were drowned. His report and map were lost, and he himself barely escaped. Rescued by fishermen, he completed his journey to Quebec, where Frontenac and Dablon welcomed him warmly. Though his written report was gone, his oral report was exciting enough to win for him the admiration of the Canadians. The governor had a *Te Deum* chanted in the cathedral and rewarded him with the seigniory of the island of Anticosti.[9]

Meanwhile Marquette, who thought he had regained his health, decided, with Dablon's blessings, to carry the message of salvation to the waiting Illinois. In good spirits he traveled southward from Green Bay. But in early December, 1674, when he reached the Chicago River, he suffered a severe hemorrhage which forced him to remain that winter in a cold and damp hut built for him by two servants. Always in the hands of the Blessed Virgin, he overlooked every discomfort. "The blessed Virgin Immaculate," he wrote, "has taken such care of us during our wintering that we have not lacked provisions, and have still remaining a large sack of corn, with some meat and fat. We also lived very pleasantly, for my illness did not prevent me from saying holy mass every day."[10]

In the early spring of 1675 he felt well enough to travel to the principal village of the Kaskaskians. They received him, says Dablon, "like an angel from Heaven." Joyously he established a new mission, which he called the Immaculate Conception of the Blessed Virgin, the same name he had bestowed on the Mississippi River. But his illness soon returned. Believing that he was dying he decided to return to Canada. He celebrated Easter with his Indian friends, many of whom accompanied him on the river as far as Lake Michigan. With his servants he journeyed along the eastern shore of the lake, bound for the mission of St. Ignace on the Straits of Mackinac. He never reached his destination. On May 19 he died near the present town of Ludington, Michigan, at the mouth of the little river that now proudly bears his name. Marquette had always entreated God that he might end his life in the trying labors of his missions and that, like his beloved St. Xavier, he might die in the wilderness, bereft of every comfort. His prayers had been heard.[11]

11

Robert de la Salle

During the next few years France gave little encouragement to further exploration of the Mississippi Valley. In 1672 Louis XIV became involved in a series of wars which brought him small additions of territory, but which seriously damaged his colonial empire and ultimately wrecked most of his plans. To finance his military aspirations he called on his colonial governors and other officials to alter their policies. He urged Frontenac to forego temporarily his interest in exploration in favor of more lucrative enterprises. Even Colbert, that prophet of mercantilism who proclaimed the exploitation of the colonies for the enrichment and glory of the crown, found reasons to justify the king's war policies. So the funds which might have been used to develop French power in America and in India went to equip armies in Europe. Under these circumstances Frontenac had to do what he could with the meager budget at his disposal. Colbert forbade him to spread his resources thin by setting up a new colonial empire on the Mississippi. Frontenac himself had been disappointed to learn that the great river led to the country of the hostile Spaniards and that it afforded no passageway to flank them on the Pacific. So Jolliet received no encouragement when he proposed the establishment of a trading post on the Mississippi. The French people were now concentrating their energies on the king's military campaigns and on the possibility of war with England. Under such circumstances all plans for western exploration and settlement were held in abeyance.

Even so, René-Robert Cavelier, Sieur de la Salle, was laying careful plans to make the Mississippi a French river from its source to its mouth.

He may have been born in 1643 in Rouen, Normandy, of wealthy parents. From his Norse ancestors he inherited an unusually tall and muscular frame which proved of inestimable advantage to him in combatting the countless dangers of frontier life. Primarily interested in the fur trade, he hoped to expand and even revolutionize it by using cargo vessels instead of canoes on the Great Lakes, the Ohio, and the Mississippi. Yet he himself was no businessman. He was a dreamer, a patriot, a Ulysses of the wilderness. He wrote to a friend that he had "neither the habit nor the inclination to keep books, nor have I anybody with me who knows how." He was not destined to garner with his own hands the great wealth that lay all around him.

The wilderness was his true home. It possessed his imagination from the time he landed in Canada in 1667 at the age of twenty-three. Exceedingly diffident, he had a great fear of meeting people. He preferred the solitude of the wilderness to the associations of civilized society. He disdained to win over the merchants of Canada to his plans, which included lucrative privileges in the fur trade. So he never inspired confidence in them. La Salle never applied the strategic force of conciliation. Among his very few but steadfast friends was Count Frontenac, who understood him and greatly appreciated his abilities. The governor realized that La Salle had lived with the Iroquois for several years and had learned their language and traditions thoroughly. Frontenac knew that this was the man he needed to succeed in his plans to control the Iroquois and their allies. These Indians had forced the western tribes to carry their furs to the Dutch and English merchants in New York. To intercept this trade and turn it to the advantage of Canada, Frontenac planned to build, on his own initiative and without royal permission, a fort at the present site of Kingston, on the northern bank of Lake Ontario. He planned to secure its command for La Salle. In these plans the governor often consulted La Salle who, "ever alive to strategic advantages, perceived the importance of the place both as a trading post and as a base of operations in the work of western discovery."[1]

In 1673 Frontenac journeyed to the place on which he proposed to build the fort. He met the Iroquois chiefs, won their respect, and turned their traditional hostility toward the French into friendship. Here he raised a palisade fort which was first known as Cataraqui but which

160

was subsequently rechristened Frontenac. Then he sent La Salle to France to explain the situation to the king and his ministers and to petition for the position of commander of the new fort. To Colbert he addressed a letter introducing La Salle: "I cannot but recommend to you, Monseigneur, the Sieur de la Salle, who is about to go to France, and who is a man of intelligence and ability, the most competent of anyone I know here to accomplish every enterprise and discovery which may be intrusted to him, as he has the most perfect knowledge of the state of the country, as you will see, if you are disposed to give him a few moments' audience."[2]

La Salle made such a profound impression on both Colbert and the king that they quickly granted his requests. He received a patent of nobility for the seigniory of Fort Frontenac on condition that he rebuild it with stone, maintain its garrison at his own expense, and clear its environs of wilderness. In 1675 he returned to New France accompanied by his faithful friend, François Daupin, Sieur de la Forest, and "the egregious and garrulous" Recollect friar, Father Louis Hennepin. Both men were to figure prominently in his explorations. He spent the next two years at Fort Frontenac, which he reconstructed as he had promised. He cleared away the wilderness around it, planted grain fields, established a school of Recollect missionaries, and built ships with which to navigate Lake Ontario in pursuit of the trade. In 1677 he returned to France, this time to petition the king for permission to lead an expedition to the Mississippi Valley. Jolliet and Marquette had discovered that the Father of Waters flowed southward. La Salle desired to ascertain the practicability of maintaining commerce with the interior by means of the lakes rather than by means of the river. Again his petition was favorably considered. On May 12, 1678, Louis XIV and Colbert signed letters patent granting him permission "to discover the western part of our country of New France, and for the execution of this enterprise, to construct forts wherever you shall deem it necessary," provided that he complete his task within five years. He was granted, too, a monopoly in buffalo hides, though he was forbidden to trade with the Ottawas, who customarily brought their beaver skins and other peltries to the merchants in Montreal.[3]

Since he received no financial assistance he had to depend on his monopoly of the future trade in buffalo hides to support his expensive enterprise. Meanwhile he induced a number of merchants, officials, and relatives to advance him large sums of money either by making them shareholders of his venture or by offering them large rates of interest. From a notary, Simonet, he borrowed four thousand livres; from an advocate, Raoul, twenty-four thousand; from Dumont, six thousand; from his cousin, François Plet, a merchant of rue St. Martin, about eleven thousand at forty percent interest; from members of his family, even larger sums. When he returned to Canada he mortgaged Fort Frontenac for another fourteen thousand livres. He also found a useful ally in La Motte de Lussière, who became a partner in his venture and who joined him just before he embarked for Canada.[4]

On July 14, 1678, he sailed from La Rochelle with thirty-two men, an ample supply of stores, and implements for building ships. Reaching Quebec two months later, he increased his resources and strengthened his position by forming a kind of league with several Canadian merchants. These merchants had once been his enemies and, jealous of his success, they were to become his enemies again. Father Hennepin came down from Fort Frontenac to greet him.[5]

Of the men whose services La Salle had secured in Paris, none was more passionately devoted to him than Henri de Tonti. He was an Italian by blood, a Frenchman by service, and an American in spirit. To few explorers of North America is the saying that "truth is stranger than fiction" more applicable than to Tonti. His exploits in the Mississippi Valley contained, in the words of his able biographer Edmund Robert Murphy, "all elements of adventure and romance." His indomitable energy mastered his weak constitution, endowing it with a physical endurance superior to that of most men. His fidelity to La Salle transcended every adversity, every intrigue of their secret and open enemies. He was at home in every environment, as much in the polished and brilliant court of Louis XIV as among the coarse, picturesque *coureurs de bois, voyageurs,* squaw men, and renegades of the frontier.[6]

Tonti was the son of Lorenzo de Tonti, a banker who joined the revolt of the Neapolitan *lazzaroni* under Tomaso Aniello, better known as Masaniello, against Spanish tyranny. Though Masaniello entered Naples in triumph, his despotic rule lasted only seven days. Lorenzo de

162

Tonti fled to France, where he became a financier and inventer of the Tontine system of insurance. His son, who was probably born in Naples, entered a French military academy, served four years as a midshipman at Marseilles and Toulon, and made seven campaigns, four in ships and three in galleys. While he was serving as a cavalry officer at Libisso, in Sicily, his right hand was blown off by a grenade. He was taken prisoner and detained for six months. He replaced his lost hand with one of iron or copper. Later, on the American frontier, this awed his Indian friends, who dubbed him Iron Hand. On gaining his release in an exchange of prisoners, he returned to France. Louis XIV rewarded him for his heroism by granting him a pension of three hundred livres. Returning to Sicily, he participated in a new campaign until 1678 when the Treaty of Nymwegen ended the war. When his regiment was disbanded he went to Versailles. There the Prince de Conti presented him to La Salle, who enlisted his services for the projected expedition of discovery.[7]

With the aid of Tonti's expert knowledge of naval construction, La Salle built a small ship on the northern shore of Lake Erie. The ship was named *Le Griffon* because she bore at her prow a grotesque griffin representing the escutcheon of Count Frontenac's family. On August 7, 1679, while the crew chanted the *Te Deum* and fired salvos of light artillery, La Salle and his men embarked. In the next few weeks *Le Griffon* entered Lake Huron, weathered a terrible storm, and anchored at the Mission of St. Ignace, in the Straits of Mackinac. There La Salle, dressed in a scarlet coat trimmed in gold lace, landed his men and gave thanks to God for delivering them from the elements. In a few days La Salle sailed to Green Bay, where some of his men who had been sent ahead had collected a large store of furs. The furs were loaded onto the ship. On September 18 La Salle sent her back to Niagara with orders to return to the head of Lake Michigan as soon as she had discharged her cargo. La Salle hoped that the revenues from these furs would appease his creditors, who were threatening to seize his property on the St. Lawrence. This transaction violated his contract, which prohibited him from trading with the Ottawas or other tribes who brought their furs to Montreal; but his financial circumstances were so pressing that perhaps he felt justified in giving it as liberal an interpretation as he could.[8]

Next day he embarked in four canoes for the mouth of the St. Joseph

River. He had fourteen remaining men including Father Hennepin. Paddling bravely against a series of gales along the western and southern shores of Lake Michigan, they reached their destination. There La Salle expected to find Tonti, who had started from Mackinac with a party of twenty men and had made his way slowly along the eastern shore of the lake. He had not yet arrived. La Salle was also waiting for *Le Griffon* with twenty recruits from France. To divert his men from mutinous thoughts during their idleness, he put them to work on a fort which would protect *Le Griffon* on her arrival and serve as a storehouse for her cargo. Three weeks passed and still neither Tonti nor the ship appeared. Greatly troubled, La Salle sent two men down the lake to look for her and, if she appeared, to pilot her to the mouth of the river. The men expressed various opinions regarding her fate. Hennepin believed that she had foundered in a storm that was then raging in the northern part of Lake Michigan. Others thought that the Indians might have boarded and burned her. La Salle himself suspected that her Danish pilot and her crew, who had never been friendly toward him, had disposed of her cargo and had sunk her. In any case, the loss of *Le Griffon* was irreparable; it proved a serious blow to the success of the expedition.[9]

Tonti arrived before November ended. He brought no reassuring news of *Le Griffon*. He said that the ship had never reached Mackinac and that even the Indians, who came from all parts of the lake, knew nothing about her. Tonti, moreover, came with only half of the expected number of men. His provisions had failed, forcing him to leave half of his men thirty leagues behind to sustain themselves by hunting. La Salle sent him with a companion to hasten them forward. They soon encountered a storm, lost their canoe, and returned to the fort. All but two of the lagging hunters soon rejoined the party.

Fearing that the gathering ice on the river would eventually impede or even halt his progress, La Salle resumed his journey southward on December 3. The thirty-four men ascended the St. Joseph in eight canoes which they often had to drag through the shallow, icy current. They neared the present site of South Bend, Indiana, where they took a short portage to the Kankakee River. They formed a rather picturesque company of soldiers, friars, artisans, laborers, *coureurs de bois,* and a

164

few Indians. They toiled through snow-mantled country down the narrow, tortuous stream which flowed through reedy and frozen marshes. Discontented and half starved, they began to complain and to threaten to desert. But soon their straitened circumstances were relieved; they found a buffalo that had floundered in the slough, threw a rope around it, pulled it out, and slaughtered it. Eventually they came to more cheerful country. Without accident they reached the junction of the Kankakee and the Des Plaines, which unite to form the Illinois River.[10]

Gliding down the Illinois, they entered a region of bolder and more striking scenery. On their right they saw the high plateau of Buffalo Rock which stood out like an island in the valley and which Indians worshiped in many ceremonies. Farther down, on their left, they passed many wooded islands and came in sight of Starved Rock, so called because of a tradition that here a band of Illinois had defended themselves against their enemies until they all died of starvation. Starved Rock was a tall cliff crowned with stately trees whose branches extended to the bank of the river. On its right bank stood a large Indian village of four hundred sixty lodges. They were made in the shape of long arbors with a framework of posts and poles. The roofs were constructed of double rush mats so well sewn together that they insured protection against snow and rain. Here, about Christmas Day, the hungry voyagers landed to procure some maize, but they discovered that its inhabitants were absent on their winter hunt. Taking thirty *minots* of maize from a supply hidden in the ground, they continued downstream.

On New Year's Day, 1680, they heard Father Hennepin celebrate mass. The friar made what he later called a "very touching" sermon in which he assured them that patience, faith, and constancy would eventually crown their labors with success. Four days later they reached Peoria Lake, an expansion of the Illinois River. A little later they arrived at the site of present Peoria, where they camped. The following morning they resumed their journey and arrived at the point where the river resumes its regular size. There they discovered a village of about eighty lodges. La Salle, having heard that the Illinois were hostile toward Frenchmen because of the suspicion that they were allies of the Iroquois, ordered his men to prepare for possible trouble by forming their canoes into a line across the river, as though in battle array. Seeing the

Frenchmen approaching in this manner, some of the Indians fled. Others took up their bows and arrows. Amid this confusion, La Salle, flanked on his right by Tonti and on his left by the others, sprang ashore. Their bold action awed the Indians, who sent two chiefs to present La Salle with a calumet. La Salle recognized it by presenting them with a calumet of his own and began a friendly discourse with them. They were so pleased with what he said that they regaled the Frenchmen with a feast. Some of them rubbed Hennepin's uncovered feet with bear's oil while others fed their guests buffalo meat, ceremoniously putting the first three morsels of it into their mouths as a mark of the esteem in which they held them. La Salle told Nikanopy, brother of the head chief, that in descending the river he had stopped at their village and had taken some maize from their pits to supply his men with bare necessities. He promised that he would make full restitution or ample payment as soon as he could. He had come, he said, to build a fort for the protection of his men and a large canoe in which to descend the river and to bring back goods to trade for their peltries. He warned them, however, that, if they refused to support his plans and to sell corn and meat to his men, he would pass them up and trade instead with the Osages. Under such circumstances they would be left destitute and at the mercy of the Iroquois, while the Osages would enjoy all the privileges of protection and trade. Jealous of the Osages, the Illinois agreed, with profuse expressions of friendship and good will, to support his plans.[11]

Yet La Salle soon learned that secret enemies were always ready to destroy him by any means at their disposal. One evening Monso, a Mascoutin chief, secretly arrived in the village with four or five Miami braves. Bearing gifts of hatchets, knives, and kettles, he held secret meetings with the leading men of the village. He told them that certain Frenchmen, whom he named, had sent him to warn them that La Salle was an intriguer, a spy of the Iroquois, whose mission was to incite the tribes of the Mississippi Valley against the Illinois. Having filled them with distrust, suspicion and alarm, Monso and his companions departed as secretly as they had arrived. The next morning one of the chiefs whom La Salle had befriended informed him in secret of what had occurred. La Salle was not surprised, therefore, at what followed. Before food was served to La Salle and his men, Nikanopy suddenly addressed him a long speech. He told with terrifying eloquence of the dangers of

166

continuing the voyage to the mouth of the Mississippi. That country, he said, was full of serpents, alligators, and monsters of all kinds which would allow only the largest boats to escape them. The river itself raged around rocks and whirlpools before it "plunged headlong . . . into a fathomless gulf, which would swallow them and their vessel forever." La Salle waited until Nikanopy had ended his speech. Then, with a calm demeanor, he thanked him for the friendly warning, though he chided him for allowing himself to be duped by Monso's lies:

> We were not asleep, my brother, when Monso came to tell you, under cover of night, that we were spies of the Iroquois. The presents he gave you, that you might believe his falsehoods, are at this moment buried in the earth under this lodge. If he told the truth, why did he skulk away in the dark? Why did he not show himself by day? Do you not see that when he first came among you, and your camp was all in confusion, we could have killed you without needing help from the Iroquois? And now, while I am speaking, could we not put your old men to death, while your young warriors are all gone away to hunt? If we meant to make war on you, we should need no help from the Iroquois, who have so often felt the force of our arms. Look at what we have brought you. It is not weapons to destroy you, but merchandise and tools for your good. If you still harbor evil thoughts of us, be frank as we are, and speak them boldly. Go after this imposter Monso, and bring him back, that we may answer him face to face; for he never saw either us or the Iroquois, and what can he know of the plots that he pretends to reveal?[12]

With these words, which have the ring of truth, La Salle regained the friendship of the Illinois. In his letters he attributed Monso's aspersions to Father Allouez who resented him for supplanting his order in influencing the tribes of the Mississippi Valley. La Salle learned that the priest had visited the Illinois only a few months before.

No sooner had La Salle settled one trouble than he was confronted by others. One night six of his own men, among whom were two of his best carpenters, deserted to the woods with the intention of joining *coureurs de bois* and perhaps of eventually returning with them to their homes in New France. A few days later La Salle's breakfast was poisoned. He suffered severe abdominal pains, but an antidote which his friends in Paris had given him saved his life.[13]

167

By now he and his men were facing bitter winter weather which made the continuation of their journey impossible. He provided them with shelter and security for the rest of the winter by building another fort on a low hill or knoll perhaps in the northern suburbs of present Peoria. On one side it was defended by the river and on two other sides by two ravines which a succession of rains had made very deep. The hill on its accessible side was deepened and strengthened with large pieces of timber. Around the fort ran an earthen embankment and a stockade of pointed logs twenty-five feet high and a foot thick. Inside the fort were two barracks and a little cabin which served as the sleeping quarters and chapel of the friars. Father Hennepin lamented the lack of wine that prevented him from celebrating mass. But each morning and evening he summoned La Salle and his men to the chapel for prayers and a sermon, and on Sundays and holidays for the chanting of vespers. La Salle christened the fort Crèvecoeur, meaning heartbreak. This did not signify his dejection at the desertion of his men, as Father Membré believed. Rather, the name was given in honor of the Dutch stronghold which fell to Marshal Turenne in July, 1672. Tonti had served as one of Turenne's minor officers.[14]

In March, 1680, La Salle departed Fort Crèvecoeur for Canada to try to ascertain the fate of *Le Griffon* and to secure needed supplies for his intended expedition down the Mississippi. Before he departed he sent out a side expedition to explore the upper valley. It was under Michel Ako or Accault, a prudent, courageous, and unexcitable man who, though illiterate or almost illiterate, understood the customs and manners of some of the regional tribes. With Accault went Picard du Gay, a native of Picardy whose real name was Antoine Auguelle, and Father Louis Hennepin, whom most historians erroneously regard as the leader of the expedition. Both Accault and Auguelle were robust and hardy, though they were somewhat smaller than Hennepin. They were supplied with a good canoe, a large calumet, and about one thousand livres in goods. Some of the goods were to be traded for furs and some were to conciliate the tribes they might meet on the river. On February 29 La Salle and his men quietly escorted them to the river bank to see them off and wish them a *bon voyage*. With a parting benediction from

168

Father Gabriel Ribourde, who stood on the water's edge to bestow it, "the voyagers plied their light paddles, and were soon lost to sight in the shadows and bend of the stream."[15]

Two days later La Salle himself left the fort under Tonti with sixteen men. He set out with five men in two canoes on a journey fraught with a thousand hardships and uncertainties. They dragged their canoes over ice, braved swift currents, paddled through cold rain that froze the clothes on their bodies, and they endured hunger and innumerable other discomforts. At last they reached the fort on the St. Joseph. Two Frenchmen whom La Salle had sent to Mackinac to search for the missing ship told him that they had looked for her in vain in every section of the lake. His experiences in the next two months attest to his incredible physical vigor and moral courage. He ordered the two men to Fort Crèvecoeur and resumed his journey with his companions. Caching their canoes, they crossed the St. Joseph on a raft, walked across southern Michigan through woods and brambles that tore their clothes and covered their faces with blood. They eluded an Indian hunting party and found a small river, perhaps the Huron, that took them to Lake Erie. They crossed the Detroit River on a raft, walked along to the northern shore of Lake Erie through torrents of rain and flooded woods, and on Easter Monday reached the French fort at Niagara Falls. Here La Salle received the depressing news that *Le Griffon* had never returned to the fort on the St. Joseph and that her fate was unknown. He also learned that another ship, the *St. Pierre*, had sunk at the mouth of the St. Lawrence with a cargo valued at twenty-two thousand livres sent to him from France.[16]

On May 6, having covered a thousand miles in sixty-five days, he reached Fort Frontenac, where he received a most depressing letter from Tonti. This steadfast friend wrote that "most of his men had mutinied, wrecked Fort Crèvecoeur, torn down its palisade, pillaged its storehouse, thrown into the river all arms and ammunition—save those they could carry away—and fled," leaving him "with five men, two of whom were friars."[17] A few days later La Salle learned that some of the deserters with a few recruits from Mackinac and Niagara had departed for Fort Frontenac to kill him. They thought that this was the surest way of escaping punishment. He boarded the brigantine

169

which was to carry him back to the Illinois country, sailed to Cape Gull, concealed his ship in a wooded area, and began to patrol the shore with five men. When seven of the deserters appeared in two canoes, he and his men darted from the cape, surprised them, and took them as prisoners to Fort Frontenac. The next day he captured and imprisoned the rest of the deserters in the same way.[18]

No sooner had he removed this danger to his person than he prepared to return to the Illinois country. He enlisted the services of François Daupin, Sieur de la Forest, with twenty-five men, including a surgeon, ship's carpenters, joiners, masons, soldiers, and laborers, and journeyed with them to Mackinac, where he left his friend La Forest with instructions to gather a store of supplies and to follow him as soon as possible. With ten Frenchmen, two Indian hunters, and a small number of dogs, he pushed southward. On reaching the fort at the mouth of the St. Joseph, he left five men with supplies for La Forest. Then he ascended the river with his remaining men, crossed the portage to the Kankakee, and followed that river to the northern branch of the Illinois.[19]

An expression of horror seized their faces when they approached the familiar site of the Illinois village. Death and destruction pervaded the countryside. The numerous arbor-like lodges with their coverings of rush mats had been reduced to charred poles and stakes on which hung human skulls. Here and there crows and buzzards picked at skulls and wolves tore at pieces of flesh. As the astonished voyagers approached, the wolves fled and the crows and buzzards circled in the sky or perched on the branches of trees. Cornfields had been reduced to rows of parched stalks or charred heaps on the ground. The bodies of illustrious warriors had been rifled and flung down from the scaffolds which served as their final resting places. The ground was strewn with kettles and pots dug up from the trenches in which the Illinois kept their belongings while they were away from home. All this was the fiendish work of the Iroquois, who had invaded the Illinois country and had wiped out its peaceful tribes.[20]

One thought engrossed the stunned and horrified La Salle: what had happened to his friend Tonti and his few loyal men? One by one he turned over the ghastly corpses, only to find that they were those of Indians. When darkness fell he crouched with his men around a campfire, keeping vigil throughout that dreadful and seemingly endless night. The next morning he continued to search for his lost friend. Near the river bank he discovered six posts on which the Iroquois had drawn with black paint the forms of men with bandaged eyes. Surmising that these represented six French prisoners alive in their hands, La Salle decided to continue his search downstream. He concealed three of his men on an island near the ruined village, instructing them to refrain from firing their guns and to put out their fires at night. With the remaining men he swept down the silent banks in a single canoe, witnessing everywhere fresh evidences of savage cruelty.

They passed a number of the deserted camps of the Illinois and the more recent camping grounds of their pursuers, finally reaching demolished Fort Crèvecoeur below Peoria Lake. An unfinished boat, begun before La Salle's departure for Canada, was still intact, though its iron nails and spikes had somehow been pulled out. On one of its boards somebody, perhaps one of the deserters, had scribbled: *Nous sommes tous sauvages: ce 15, 1680.* The surrounding countryside resembled a vast graveyard. Tied to stakes here and there were the half-charred bodies of Indian women and children. Perhaps the young braves and the older men had fled before the invading Iroquois, leaving their families to the mercy of their dreadful foes. Still finding no trace of Tonti and his men, La Salle continued to the mouth of the Illinois River. There, perhaps for the first time, he beheld the great and mysterious river of his passionate striving; but "now, ironically, it meant little to him: all his thoughts he reserved for his lost friend. The latitude and the flora and fauna of the surrounding country; the river's course; the bluff at the mouth of the Illinois which afforded an ideal location for a fort; the fertility of the surrounding plain, so inviting to settlers: what were all these compared with such a friend as a man can have once in a lifetime?"[21]

His mind uneasy about Tonti's fate, his men scattered, and his resources depleted, he had no heart to continue his journey. Instead he returned to the devastated village, where he found the three men he had concealed on the island. Unable to proceed because of the ice on the river, he put the men to work harvesting the corn from the charred stalks. One night they saw a huge comet blazing on the rim of the desolate prairie. At that moment it was terrifying a large part of the world; but to La Salle, surrounded as he was by death and destruction, it was an entirely impersonal matter. Calmly he made notes of the phenomenon for the scientists of his country.[22]

Before the end of the year he resumed his journey. Beyond the junction of the Des Plaines and Kankakee rivers they entered a rude cabin in which La Salle found a piece of wood which renewed his hope that Tonti was still alive. Observing that the wood had recently been sawed, he persuaded himself that it had belonged to Tonti or to one of his five men and that they had escaped the carnage behind them. He left two of his men to guard his supplies, concealed his canoes, and made his way with the others on foot slowly through a prolonged snowfall toward the site of the fort at the mouth of the St. Joseph. The snow, he wrote,

> fell in extraordinary quantities all day, and it kept on falling for nineteen days in succession, with cold so severe that I never knew so hard a winter, even in Canada. We were obliged to cross forty leagues of open country, where we could hardly find wood to warm ourselves at evening, and could get no bark whatever to make a hut, so that we had to spend the night exposed to the furious winds which blow over these plains. I never suffered so much from the cold, or had more trouble in getting forward; for the snow was so light, resting suspended as it were among the tall grass, that we could not use snowshoes. Sometimes it was waist deep; and as I walked before my men, as usual, to encourage them by breaking the path, I often had much ado, though I am rather tall, to lift my legs above the drifts, through which I pushed by the weight of my body.[23]

At last, after gnawing hunger and unbearable fatigue, they came, through bitter cold and waist-deep snow, to their destination. They found shelter in the fort, which La Forest and his men had strengthened; but La Salle despaired to learn that his friends had received no word of Tonti. La Forest and his men accorded him some measure of consolation by clearing the ground for the spring planting and by hewing out planks for a vessel to ply the lakes in place of the lost *Griffon*.[24]

That winter he fought off despondency with large and bright plans for the future. He was resolved to relieve his men, explore the Mississippi, and colonize the Illinois country. To realize these aims he planned an alliance of the Algonkin tribes with himself as their leader. He hoped to settle them in and around a fort in the valley of the Illinois. There, protected by French arms and Indian allies, they could keep the Iroquois in check while they would be converted to Christianity and taught the arts of civilization. He planned to supply them with goods in exchange for furs, which he was confident would find a ready market in France and in other parts of Europe.

The allies he needed to realize his aims were close by. Along the St. Joseph dwelled a band of Abenakis and Mohicans. These had been defeated by the Puritans in King Philip's War and, in consequence, had migrated from New England to the territory of the more sympathetic French. La Salle found them ready to participate in any undertaking he might propose. Indeed, they begged for the privilege of calling him their chief. Next he obtained the allegiance of a band of one hundred and fifty Shawnees. Seeking protection against possible Iroquois depredations, the Shawnees accepted La Salle's advice to migrate to the Illinois country and agreed to join him in the fall at the mouth of the St. Joseph. Even more important was his success with the Miamis. They had fought with the Iroquois in conquering the Tamaroas, but they had been so brutally handled by their allies that, on returning home, they determined to support the Illinois and their French friends. They sent La Salle a delegation of friendship which, of course, he received with an expression of gratitude. Lastly, he set out with fifteen men on snowshoes to obtain confirmation of support from the Illinois, many of whom had returned to their homes on the heels of their departing Iroquois enemies. The snowshoes glided swiftly over the prairie, but its glare in the bright sunlight gave La Salle and some of his men snowblindness. This forced the entire party to halt before it reached its destination. The men camped at the edge of a forest while one of them sought pine needles with which to make a decoction useful in relieving the afflicted men. The man followed fresh tracks to a camp of Foxes, who informed him that they had seen six white men traveling from a Potawatomie village toward Green Bay. The six men had kept themselves alive on a diet of elderberries and, later in the year, on that of wild onions they grubbed up out of the snow. The man carried this information back to La Salle, who received it with joy. He was certain now that the six white men were none other than Tonti and his companions and that, while he had come down the east shore of Lake Michigan in the previous autumn, his lost friends had been ascending the opposite shore.[25]

As soon as he and his companions regained their sight, La Salle led his entire party to the St. Joseph. He put his men to work planting corn and vegetables while he himself completed negotiations with the Abenakis, Mohicans, and Miamis. Then, late in May, 1681, he journeyed up Lake Michigan to Mackinac, where on Corpus Christi Day he met Tonti, who had arrived from Green Bay on the previous day. He was overjoyed to see his friend, though he suppressed any expression of his emotion. Tonti regaled him with a detailed account of his nightmarish experiences with the Iroquois and of his subsequent hardships. He and his companions had been captured and condemned to death, but their lives had been saved by the intercession of an Onandaga chief who knew and admired La Salle. The chief allowed them to ascend the Illinois in a leaky canoe. When they had journeyed fifteen miles they stopped to repair the canoe and to dry their supplies. One of the friars, old Gabriel Ribourde, strolled to an adjacent grove to say his breviary. He never returned. Later Tonti and one of his men learned that a band of young Kickapoos, who had been hovering around an Iroquois camp for scalps, had knocked the friar on the head, scalped him, thrown his body into a pit, and had carried off his breviary and diurnal. At their village they danced around the friar's scalp as though it belonged to one of their Iroquois enemies.[26]

After Father Ribourde's death Tonti and his four companions resumed their journey up the Illinois River. They turned up the Des Plaines, and continued to Lake Michigan with the intention of finding asylum with the friendly Potawatomies. But, says Tonti, on "All Saints' Day we were wrecked" twenty leagues from the nearest Potawatomie village, and, "our provisions failing us, I left a man to take care of our things and went off by land." They traveled slowly, for Tonti was burning with fever and wracked with pain from swollen legs. But they managed to walk sixty miles to the village, living on nothing save wild onions "which we were obliged to grub up from the snow." Much to their chagrin, they found that the Indians had deserted their village for their winter quarters. So Tonti and his friends "were obliged to go into their wilds, where we obtained hardly as much as two handfuls of Indian corn a day and some frozen gourds, which we piled up in a cabin at the water's side."[27]

Soon they returned to the lake, journeyed to Green Bay in a canoe they had found, and entered Green Bay's estuary, called Sturgeon Cove, which they ascended until a strong wind stopped them for a week. Consuming all their food, they despaired of ever reaching the next Potawatomie village. So they decided to return to the deserted village, but they could not travel to it because the stream had frozen during the night. Having by now worn out their shoes, they covered their feet with pieces of Father Ribourde's cloak. They were on the point of setting out overland when two Ottawas arrived in their camp and conducted them to the next Potawatomie village, which "received them kindly." Soon one of the friars, Father Zenobius Membré, went to spend the winter at the Jesuit mission on Green Bay. Tonti and his remaining men stayed on in the village until spring, when they journeyed to Mackinac where, as we have seen, they saw La Salle.[28]

Despite his experiences Tonti was as determined as ever to follow his friend in the projected expedition to the mouth of the Mississippi. Since this great enterprise necessitated fresh supplies, they set out to obtain them at Fort Frontenac. In this endeavor La Salle was again successful, though he was obliged to forego some of his monopolies and to offer larger rates of interest to merchants and relatives. In Montreal he made his will in favor of François Plet, his cousin. He mustered men and supplies, and in November, 1681, set out for the west. Resolving to place no more trust in agents, he led his followers in a united body under his own personal command.[29]

The following month saw him again at the mouth of the St. Joseph, where he chose eighteen Abenakis and Mohicans to accompany his party of twenty-three Frenchmen and Canadians. The Indians insisted on taking along ten of their squaws to cook for them and three of their children, swelling the entire company to fifty-four persons. On December 21 the advance party, led by Tonti and Father Membré, departed in six canoes, leaving La Salle with a few men to cache the supplies that could not be taken along. A few days later La Salle rejoined the expedi-

175

tion as it crossed Lake Michigan to the Chicago River which was found to be covered with ice. Undaunted, the travelers "made sleds, strapped their canoes and supplies to them and, in straggling procession, dragged them wearily mile after mile over the glistening surface until open water below Peoria Lake permitted them to take to their canoes."[30]

On February 6, 1682, they entered the Mississippi, where floating ice stopped their progress and where they waited for their Indian friends, who had fallen behind. Within a week the river had cleared and the laggards had arrived. Then La Salle led his small flotilla past the mouth of the tawny Missouri and that of the placid Ohio. There he stopped for a short time to replenish his food supply. The new supply lasted until they arrived at Chickasaw Bluff, near the present city of Memphis, Tennessee. Then they again scoured the wilderness for game. All of them returned save Pierre Prudhomme. La Salle feared that he had been seized by the Chickasaws who often prowled in the region. So he sent a few men to search for him, while he employed the remaining men in building a stockaded fort at the high bluffs near the river. Nine days later the search party found Prudhomme, who had lost his way, and brought him half-famished to camp. To console him La Salle named the stockade Prudhomme and left him with a few others in charge of it.[31]

Spring was now in the air. More and more delicate greenery was appearing on the trees and the fragrance of peach blossoms and azaleas pervaded both banks of the river on which the voyagers were descending toward their goal. They found the tribes friendly and gay—"pleasantly different from the morose and taciturn northern tribes." They "generally plied the travelers with dried plums and persimmons and a drink made of sweet raisins crushed in water."[32] As we have seen in an earlier chapter, they visited first the Quapaws in present Arkansas and then the Taënsas in present Louisiana, both of whom received them with boundless hospitality.

At last, on April 6, they neared their journey's end. They found that the river divided itself into three broad channels or passes. They camped on the most westerly. The next day La Salle divided his men into three groups: one under Tonti, another under Dautray, and the third under himself. He proceeded with them to explore the channels of the river. As they paddled down the turbid current past friendly villages through a country of tall canebrakes and cypress trees, the water gradually changed from brackish to brine. Dining almost entirely on the musky flesh of alligators, they arrived three days later at their journey's end. Before them spread the great Gulf of Mexico "tossing its restless billows, limitless, voiceless, lonely as when born of chaos, without a sail, without a sign of life."[33] On a spot of dry ground near the mouth of the river La Salle gathered his company and readied a column which bore the arms of France and on which were inscribed the words: *LOUIS LE GRAND, ROY DE FRANCE ET DE NAVARRE, RÈGNE; LE NEUVIÈME AVRIL, 1682.* Then, while the Abenakis and Mohicans looked on in silent wonder, the Frenchmen mustered under arms and chanted *Te Deum,* the *Exaudiat,* and the *Domine salvum fac Regem.* While his men fired volleys of musketry and shouted, "*Vive le Roi,*" La Salle took formal possession of the vast country which he called Louisiana in honor of his king:

In the name of the most high, mighty, invincible and victorious Prince, Louis the Great, by the grace of God King of France and of Navarre, Fourteenth of that name, I, this ninth day of April, one thousand six hundred and eighty-two, in virtue of the commission of his Majesty, which I hold in my hand, and which may be seen by all whom it may concern, have taken, and do now take, in the name of his Majesty and of his successors to the crown, possession of this country of Louisiana, the seas, harbors, ports, bays, adjacent straits, and all the nations, people, provinces, cities, towns, villages, mines, minerals, fisheries, streams, and rivers, within the extent of the said Louisiana, from the mouth of the great river St. Louis, otherwise called the Ohio, . . . as also along the . . . Mississippi, and the rivers which discharge themselves thereinto, from its source beyond the country of the [Sioux] . . . as far as its mouth at the sea, or Gulf of Mexico, and also to the mouth of the River of Palms, upon the assurance we have had from the natives of these countries that we are the first Europeans who have descended or ascended the said river [Mississippi]; hereby protesting against all who may hereafter undertake to invade any or all of these aforesaid countries, peoples, or lands, to the prejudice of the rights of his Majesty, acquired by the consent of the nations dwelling herein. Of which, and of all else that is needful, I hereby take to witness those who hear me, and demand an act of the notary here present.[34]

To these words his followers responded with volleys of musketry and shouts of "*Vive le Roi!*" Then they planted a cross beside the column and buried at its foot a leaden plate bearing the arms of France with a Latin inscription: *LUDOVICUS MAGNUS REGNAT, NONO APRILIS, M.D.C. LXXXII.* And the ceremony ended with all of them singing the grand hymn of the *Vexilla Regis:*

> *The banners of Heaven's King advance,*
> *The mystery of the Cross shines forth.*

What were the specific boundaries of Louisiana? It had none. Neither La Salle nor his immediate contemporaries could, of course, have any definite conception of the magnitude of the territory. The source of the Mississippi was unknown as were the entire lengths and directions of many of its most important tributaries, including the Missouri, the Ohio, the Arkansas, and the Red. Jean-Baptiste Louis Franquelin was a Canadian cartographer interested in recording the progress of western exploration. In 1684 he made a large map of a portion of North America on which he marked off the great region included in the French claim. On this map Louisiana extended from the Alleghenies on the east to the Rocky Mountains on the west, and from the Great Lakes and central Minnesota on the north to the northern boundary of Spanish Florida and the western coast of the Gulf of Mexico on the south. Doubtless it was inspired by the geographical terms of La Salle's proclamation which were, perforce, quite vague. Yet La Salle realized that the dimensions of the Mississippi Valley were very great and that, therefore, it needed every protection against possible English or Spanish encroachment. That his country failed to provide it cannot be laid to any lack of effort on his part.[35]

Lack of provisions prevented La Salle and his men from tarrying long at the mouth of the great river. No sooner was the ceremony of possession completed than they turned homeward. They encountered little trouble with the Indians as they journeyed upstream toward Fort Prudhomme. But before they reached the fort La Salle came down with a protracted and dangerous illness characterized by high fever. Unable to continue his journey, he sought rest at the fort, where Father Membré nursed him with tender care. Sometime during his illness, which lasted forty days, La Salle sent Tonti to Mackinac to relay word of their new discovery to eagerly waiting creditors and friends in Canada and France. By the end of July La Salle was well enough to travel by slow stages with Father Membré to the mouth of the St. Joseph. From there they continued to Mackinac. At Mackinac La Salle and Tonti discussed plans to build a fort in the Illinois country. It was to serve as the nucleus of what they hoped would be the first permanent settlement in Louisiana. Tonti soon departed for the Illinois country, while La Salle prepared to return to Quebec for the purpose of taking ship for France; but hearing that the Iroquois were about to renew their raids on the western tribes, La Salle decided to rejoin Tonti instead. He sent Father Membré to Quebec with letters to officials and friends. In them he described the great country he had recently discovered and the abundance of its products. He told of great furs, pearls, odoriferous gums, sugar, tobacco, cochineal, and timber with which to build ships on the Mississippi and on the Gulf of Mexico for the protection of Louisiana.[36]

In December, 1682, he and Tonti met at a great Indian village near the present town of Utica, on the northern bank of the Illinois, in La Salle County, Illinois. Along the southern bank of the river rose a range of irregular sandstone bluffs. They culminated in the natural abutment of Starved Rock, which rises perpendicularly to an altitude of one hundred twenty-six feet and is accessible on only one of its sides. Here La Salle put his men to work. They built a rude storehouse of stunted pines. Around it they put up a stout palisade of timbers which had to be dragged up the rugged ascent of the bluff. It was completed sometime during the winter. La Salle called the stronghold Fort St. Louis in honor of his king's patron saint. By right of his patent, the explorer ruled the fort and its environs as a seigniory which he parceled out to his followers. However, these men "were too indolent and profligate to improve or derive any benefit from such grants" and they preferred dallying with Indian women to cultivating their wild lands.[37]

Their attitude only complicated matters for their leader whose enemies had increased with his success and fame. To add to his woes, he could no longer count on Frontenac, who had always given him strong support. The governor had recently lost to his political enemies and had been recalled. His successor, Antoine le Febvre, Sieur de la Barre, was a headstrong and avaricious old naval officer who hated La Salle and regarded his monopoly of trade as particularly objectionable. In vain did the explorer try to win La Barre's support. In several letters he recounted all the sacrifices he had made and all the hardships he had surmounted before success had crowned his enterprise. But La Barre preferred to disparage La Salle and to doubt the reality of his discovery in letters to the minister of marine and colonies, Jean-Baptiste Colbert, Marquis of Seignelay and son and successor of Louis XIV's great minister. "With a score of vagabonds," he wrote in one letter, "he has pillaged his countrymen and put them to ransom, and was about to set himself up as king." Seignelay repeated this piece of calumny to the king, who, mistaking the true state of affairs, supported La Barre. "I am convinced like you," wrote the king, "that the discovery of the Sieur de la Salle is very useless, and that such enterprises ought to be prevented in the future, as they tend only to debauch the inhabitants by the hope of gain, and to diminish the revenue from beaver skins."[38]

Emboldened by his success, La Barre seized Fort Frontenac on the ground that La Salle had forfeited his patent by failing to maintain an adequate garrison there. Then he proceeded to eject La Forest, its commander, and to replace him with two of his own men, Aubert de la Chesnaye and Jacques Leber. Unsatisfied with this demonstration of his power, the governor sent Chevalier de Baugy to assume command of Fort St. Louis and to deliver to La Salle a letter requesting his presence in Quebec. La Salle, convinced that he could gain nothing from further correspondence with the governor, had decided to appeal his case to the king in person. Relinquishing his command at Fort St. Louis to Tonti and bidding farewell to the hundreds of Indians who had collected around the fort, he departed in October, 1683, for Canada. Enroute he met Baugy, who informed him of the nature of his errand. The circumstances permitted La Salle no choice but submission to the indignity imposed on him. He sent a letter to Tonti to receive Baugy with courtesy. The two men passed the winter at the fort, one commanding for La Barre and the other for La Salle. They were assaulted by a band of Iroquois whom, however, Tonti defeated and drove away. During the crisis Baugy had sent a messenger to Mackinac begging for aid.

The sixty men who came proved unnecessary, but they brought Tonti an order to report to Canada.[39]

Early in November La Salle reached Quebec and almost immediately embarked for France. He was destined never to return to a region in which he had played such a great role as an explorer, an entrepreneur of the fur trade, and a diplomat among the western tribes.

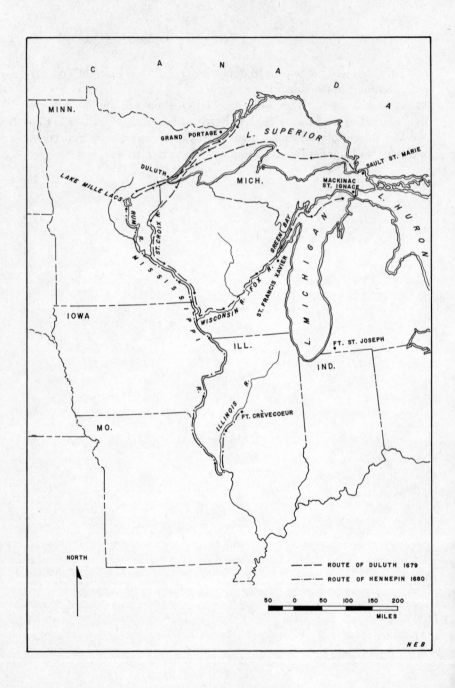

C A N A D A

MINN.

GRAND PORTAGE

L. SUPERIOR

DULUTH

SAULT ST. MARIE

LAKE MILLE LACS

MICH.

MACKINAC
ST. IGNACE

L. HURON

RUM R.

ST. CROIX R.

MISSISSIPPI

WISCONSIN R.

FOX R.

ST. FRANCIS XAVIER

GREEN BAY

L. MICHIGAN

IOWA

ILL.

FT. ST. JOSEPH

IND.

R.

ILLINOIS R.

FT. CREVECOEUR

MO.

NORTH

— — — ROUTE OF DULUTH 1679
— · — · — ROUTE OF HENNEPIN 1680

50   0   50   100   150   200

MILES

N E B

12

Father Louis Hennepin

THE BROAD AND DEEP ILLINOIS RIVER FLOWED WITH A GENTLE CURRENT, reminding Father Louis Hennepin of the Seine at Paris. He overlooked little in the raw March landscape as he voyaged with his two companions Accault and Auguelle toward the Mississippi. Later, when he wrote the chronicle of this journey, he recalled vividly the patches of snow, the leafless forest, and the prairie studded with trees as regularly spaced as those in orchards. No less keen was his sense of drama in reporting his first adventure. Soon they approached the mouth of the Illinois, where they met a group of Tamaroas who invited them to their village on the west bank of the nearby Mississippi; but they preferred to continue downstream. This incensed the Indians who suspected them of carrying iron and arms to enemy tribes. The Indians pursued the travelers in dugout canoes and fired arrows at them. Escaping unharmed, the voyagers reached the Mississippi on the following day. Floating ice from the north kept them idle there for three days. After that they were able to make rapid progress up the river. They passed by many of its tributaries, including the Des Moines, the Iowa, and St. Peter's, the Wisconsin, and the Chippewa. They admired the beautiful islands covered with trees and interlaced with so many vines that they seemed impassable.[1]

Inscrutable history shows that the chronicle of an expedition is sometimes infinitely more important than the expedition itself. Such is the case with Father Hennepin's chronicle of his journey to the Upper Valley of the Mississippi. This singular man was born in Ath, a village in the province of Hainault, which was then in the Spanish Netherlands but which is now in Belgium. Feeling at an early age "a strong inclina-

183

tion to leave the world and live in the rule of strict virtue," he became a Franciscan friar and made his novitiate in the Recollect convent of Bethune, in the province of Artois, France. His master of novices was Father Ribourde who, as we have seen, later earned a martyr's crown in the American wilderness. But Hennepin soon found monastic life very irksome; he longed to travel to foreign lands. While studying Dutch in Ghent he felt strongly tempted to visit the East Indies, though he had to find appeasement by a tour through the Franciscan convents of Italy and Germany. Returning to Hainault, he served as a preacher in the convent of Halles. Then he roamed to Artois, whence he traveled through several Dutch towns, including Maestricht, where for eight months he was in charge of a hospital. Here he developed such an ardor for military life that he was delighted to serve as assistant chaplain in the obstinate and bloody battle of Séneffe. Returning to convent life, he found it intolerable. He relieved his frustration by skulking behind the doors of restaurants to listen to sailors talk of their adventures —an occupation he found so agreeable that he was happy to tolerate their smoking, which nauseated him, and to go without food for several days. In 1674 he was one of the five Recollect monks whom Louis XIV, yielding to an appeal of Governor Frontenac, sent to Canada to reinforce those of that Order who were already there. Receiving the required authority from his superior, he went to the seaport of La Rochelle, where in July, 1675, he embarked in the same ship with Bishop François de Laval of Quebec. Among other fellow passengers was La Salle, who was returning from France to Canada and who enlisted Hennepin's services as a missionary in future expeditions.

Had Hennepin been content to report truthfully what he had seen and experienced he would have carved for himself an enviable niche in the Valhalla of honored explorers. But his fame is besmeared by his vanity, his excessive boastfulness, his garrulity, and his desire to cover himself with glory without earning it. After he returned to France he published books containing plagiarisms and untruths. In his first book, *Description de la Louisiane nouvellement découverte au Sud-Ouest de la Nouvelle France,* published in January, 1683, he speaks of himself as though he were leader of the expedition, "not only during the voyage up the Mississippi but from the very beginning."[2] In the first two hundred pages of the book he relegates La Salle to the background. Once,

184

in describing a party of Fox Indians which threatened to attack the French, Hennepin depicted La Salle, not as the leader but as the follower of his men.[3] The book included a map which traced the Mississippi with remarkable accuracy as far south as the present site of St. Louis. It was irregular in its longitudes and latitudes and it marked the probable course of the rest of the river with a dotted line. So zealous was he to record Recollect successes that he placed an imaginary mission of his Order on the map far to the north of the source of the Mississippi.

The book contains a plagiarism which has led scholars in Europe and in America to formulate theories regarding its real authorship. Pierre Margry, eminent editor and collector of documents dealing with French explorations in the New World, theorized that the *Description* was a plagiarism of an undated work, *Relation des découvertes*, written by Abbé Claude Bernou and based on three autographed letters of La Salle. On the contrary, Father John Gilmary Shea who, says the noted Jesuit scholar Jean Delanglez, "was determined to avoid by every possible means, the necessity of being on the same side of the fence with Margry," declared that Bernou plagiarized Hennepin's *Description*. Another scholar, Father Hugolin Lemay, followed Shea, though he added that Bernou plagiarized only the first section and a part of the third section of Hennepin's *Description*. Still another historian, Marc de Villiers, presented the hypothesis that Hennepin had some two hundred pages of the *Relation* "recast for his use by a man who was both an able writer and a devoted friend of the explorer."[4] More recently Delanglez made a line by line comparison of the two narratives. He compared the statements contained in each with the letters of La Salle, and he compared the style and the use of words in the first two parts of both the *Description* and the *Relation*. His research convinced him that Hennepin in compiling his *Description* "lifted bodily" two-thirds of the *Relation*. He noted the literary superiority of the *Relation* over the *Description*:

> Anyone who reads the *Relation* will clearly realize its homogeneity, and the same homogeneity is apparent in the first two-thirds of the *Description*. If, as Buffon said, "le style est l'homme même," then two men composed the *Description*: one of them is the author of the whole *Relation*, and the other's name appears on the title page of the *Description*. Not

only is there a striking difference in the contents of the two sections of the *Description,* but also in the manner in which the events are expressed in each. This stylistic difference is marked, in spite of the evident changes introduced by the author of the *Description of Louisiana* in that part of of the *Relation des decouvertes* which he made use of. The first part of the *Description* is obviously in the style of Bernou; there is no trace of this style in the second part.[5]

In 1697, ten years after La Salle's death, Hennepin published his second book, *Nouvelle Découverte d'un tres grand Pays, situé dans l'Amérique, entre le Nouveau Mexique et la Mer glaciale,* which was an enlargement of his first book. By this time he had incurred the displeasure of his Provincial by refusing to return to America. In consequence, he had pledged his allegiance and fulsomely dedicated his new book to William III, King of England, whom he had met at the Hague. In this book he advanced what Francis Parkman calls the "new and surprising pretention" of stating that he descended to the mouth of the Mississippi. Hitherto, wrote Hennepin, concern for his personal safety had compelled him to remain silent. But now he was ready to reveal the truth:

> I am resolved to make known here to the whole world the mystery of this discovery, which I have hitherto concealed, that I might not offend the Sieur de la Salle, who wished to keep all the glory and all the knowledge of it to himself. It is for this that he sacrificed many persons whose lives he exposed, to prevent them from making known what they had seen, and thereby crossing his secret plans. . . . I was certain that if I went down the Mississippi, he would not fail to traduce me to my superiors for not taking the northern route, which I was to have followed in accordance with his desire and the plans we had made together. But I saw myself on the point of dying of hunger, and knew not what to do; because the two men who were with me threatened openly to leave me in the night, and carry off the canoe and everything in it, if I prevented them from going down the river to the nations below. Finding myself in this dilemma, I thought that I ought not to hesitate, and that I ought to prefer my own safety to the violent passions which possessed the Sieur de la Salle of enjoying alone the glory of this discovery. The two men, seeing that I had made up my mind to follow them, promised me entire fidelity; so, after we had shaken hands together as a mutual pledge, we set out on our voyage.[6]

To support his revelation Hennepin included in the book a revised map which showed the Mississippi throughout its entire course to the Gulf.

His story fooled few people. He lacked the long memory required of successful mendacity. In his earlier narrative he had stated that "We had some design of going to the mouth of the river Colbert [Mississippi], which more probably empties into the Gulf of Mexico than into the Red sea; but the tribes that seized us, gave us no time to sail up and down the river."[7] This contradiction, together with others regarding the length of his journey and the time needed to arrive at certain points of his itinerary, later involved him in serious embarrassment. In 1698 he attempted to relieve it by publishing his third book, *Nouveau Voyage d'un Pais plus grande que l'Europe*, which only involved him in additional contradictions.

In view of these findings, what value can we attach to Hennepin's writings? We censure him for maligning La Salle, for attempting to deprive La Salle of his just fame, for belittling his friends, and for seeking glory at the expense of truth. But we must praise him for his graphic descriptions of his experiences and of the places and persons he saw. Europeans read him with lively curiosity because he described vividly a world that was unknown to them. His books became best sellers and were translated into a number of foreign languages. The world will easily forgive inaccuracies and even untruths in a historical narrative that is ably written and that contains the stuff of humanity, and the world regards Hennepin's books as classics of American frontier history, as infinitely more important than his travels themselves. In the part of *Description* which deals with his ascent of the Upper Mississippi, and with which we are chiefly concerned here, Hennepin, though not as polished a stylist as Bernou, from whom he borrowed much without acknowledgment, is largely himself—robust, human, and entertaining. We are indebted to him for his fine word-pictures of the Upper Valley and of the manners and customs of the Sioux. They have the ring of sincerity. When we read them we get the impression that he could not have written them if he had not seen them.

The voyagers prayed morning, noon, and night that they might meet the Indians by day, "for when they discover people at night, they kill them as enemies, to rob those whom they murder secretly of some

187

axes or knives which they value more than we do gold and silver; they even kill their own allies, when they can conceal their death, so as afterward to boast of having killed men, and so pass for soldiers."[8] On April 11, perhaps when they were near the mouth of the Chippewa, their prayers were answered. While cooking a freshly killed turkey they suddenly saw thirty-three bark canoes manned by a hundred and twenty Indians coming swiftly down the great river. They were on their way to war on the Miamis, Illinois, and Tamaroas. The Indians shot arrows at the voyagers while they surrounded them. But some of their old men, seeing one of the white men (perhaps Hennepin) holding up a calumet, prevented their young men from killing them. Nevertheless, the Indians leaped from their canoes, some on to the land, some into the water. Approaching with frightful cries and yells, they wrenched the calumet from the voyager's hands. Hennepin hastened to quiet them by offering them a piece of Martinique tobacco which they accepted, knowing that it smoked better than their own. Some of the warriors kept repeating the name *Miamiha* to make the voyagers understand that they were a war party on the way to attack the Miamis. Hennepin told them by signs and by drawing pictures on the sand that their enemies had gone across the Mississippi to join the Illinois. This information was bitterly disappointing to some of the minor chiefs. They put their hands on Hennepin's head and began to wail dismally. Hennepin tried to show sympathy for their cause by wiping away their tears with a handkerchief which he describes as dirty. Yet they refused to smoke the calumet with him, and they forced him and his companions to cross the river. The Indians followed them yelling and crying so loudly that they filled the voyagers with dread. Hennepin appeased them by offering them a tomahawk, which they accepted. In turn they offered the white men beaver's flesh and, in accordance with tribal custom, put the first three morsels of it into their mouths and blew on it before offering more of it on bark dishes.[9]

Yet they returned the calumet, an act which the white men regarded as a forecast of their doom. "Our two boatmen," wrote Hennepin, "were resolved to sell their lives dearly, and to resist if attacked; their arms and swords were ready. As for my part, I determined to allow myself to be killed without any resistance, as I was going to announce to them a God who had been falsely accused, unjustly condemned, and cruelly crucified, without showing the least aversion to those who put him to death."[10] Their fears were unjustified. The Sioux were divided as to what should be done with them. Some advocated killing them and taking their supplies. Others, mindful of the trade they had carried on with the French, advised that they refrain from deeds of violence that would rob them of the hatchets, knives, guns, and other articles. This advice must have prevailed, for early next morning a young chief named Narrhetoba, naked and painted from head to foot, appeared before them and asked them for their calumet. He filled it with tobacco and made them and every member of his band smoke it. By signs he told the white men that, since he could not make war on the Miamis, he would lead his warriors homeward and that they must accompany them. Hennepin agreed. His chief purpose, he said, was to explore the region, even if he had to do so in their company.[11]

The friar, however, soon encountered difficulties by saying his prayers in the presence of his captors. Seeing him move his lips, some of them exclaimed with terror that his book was an evil spirit which made him mutter words of doom. Therefore, they said that he must stop communicating with it. Accault, whose sense of safety greatly exceeded his piety and who lost no love on the talkative and boastful friar, remonstrated to his companions that all three of them would be killed unless they could stop him from saying his breviary. Picard, who disliked him a little less than did Accault, advised him to say his prayers alone in the wilderness. Hennepin begged forgiveness for endangering their lives and heeded Picard's advice. But the more he concealed himself the more he found the Indians at his heels, for now they believed that he had gone into the forest to hide something in the ground. At last Hennepin hit on a device by which he welded devotion to prudence. Instead of saying his breviary he opened his book in the canoe and began to chant the litany of the Blessed Virgin. This appeased his listeners. Naturally fond of singing, they supposed that the book was teaching its owner to sing for their amusement. They smiled and nodded in approval.[12]

They journeyed for nineteen days, covering a distance which Hennepin estimated at two hundred and fifty leagues. Afraid that the prisoners, who were traveling in a heavy and slow canoe, would lag far behind and perhaps escape, several warriors were placed in it to help paddle. Hennepin stated that the Indians could cover thirty or forty leagues a day, "when at war and pressed for time, or anxious to surprise some enemy." The white men, observing that some of the Indians often showed hostility toward them, did not yet feel entirely safe. They journeyed from morning until night. On rainy days they sheltered themselves by building crude cabins. On fair days they slept in the open air, where Hennepin says he and his companions had a good opportunity to contemplate the moon and the stars. They took the precaution of sleeping by Narrhetoba, the young chief who had asked for their calumet, and of putting themselves under his protection. Even so, they were still in danger. One of the party, a minor chief named Aquipaguetin, had lost a son in the war against the Miamis and singled out the white men as the target of his revenge. Moreover, he was enraged with Narrhetoba for abandoning the expedition. He alternated between fits of great fury and dismal laments which he kept up half of the night. At or near Lake Pipin his grief became so conspicuous that the Frenchmen dubbed it the Lake of Tears. Sometimes Aquipaguetin shed tears and wailed all night long. When he grew weary of his lugubrious exertions, he persuaded his surviving son to take up his demonstrations of sorrow "in order to excite his warriors to compassion, and oblige them to kill us and pursue their enemies to avenge his son's death." But cooler tempers prevailed. Those who were fond of the articles they had obtained from French traders "were much disposed to preserve us, so as to attract other Frenchmen there and get iron, which is extremely precious in their eyes; but of which they knew the great utility only when they saw one of our French boatmen kill three or four bustards or turkeys at a single shot, while they can scarcely kill only one with an arrow."[13] They learned that the words *manza ouachangé* which the Indians often uttered meant "iron that has understanding." This was their name for a gun, because it could break a man's bones, while their arrows only glanced through the flesh, "rarely breaking the bones of those whom they strike, and consequently producing wounds more easily cured than those made by French guns, which often crippled those whom they wounded."[14]

Aquipaguetin often resumed his tearful exhibitions. One day he halted in a large prairie and resolved to regale the chiefs of the party with a very fat deer he had killed. When the feast ended, the warriors, their faces marked with pictures of various animals in different colors,

190

began to dance. Arms akimbo, they stamped with such force that they left the imprint of their moccasins on the hard prairie earth. While Aquipaguetin's son, acting as master of ceremonies, passed around the calumet, his father wept so bitterly that his whole body shook. Then, in a doleful voice broken by signs and sobs, he addressed sometimes the warriors, sometimes Hennepin, while he kept placing his hands on the Frenchmen's heads or raising his eyes toward heaven as he uttered the Sioux word for the sun and complained to it of the death of his son. Though the Frenchmen could not understand what Aquipaguetin was saying, they feared that the ceremony portended their destruction. Later they learned that the chief's men had several times refused to obey his orders to kill them.[15]

But one day Aquipaguetin's tears, wails, yells, laments, and pitiful complaints to the sun gained the compassion of all of his men. They agreed to kill the Frenchmen and they seized them. In an attempt to save themselves the Frenchmen flung them twenty knives and some tobacco. Aquipaguetin asked his men one by one to advise him as to whether he should accept or refuse the gifts. Meanwhile the Frenchmen gave him an ax with which to kill them and accommodatingly bowed their heads. At this crucial moment Narrhetoba appeared, took them by the hand, and led them away to his cabin. There he had one of his brothers break some arrows in their presence to indicate to them that he had prevented Aquipaguetin from killing them.[16]

Aquipaguetin carried with him a relative's bones which he preserved with great care in dressed skins adorned with several rows of black and red porcupine quills. One day he contrived by means of the revered bones to deprive the Frenchmen of their goods without robbing them outright. He assembled his men in a circle, placed the bones in the center of it, and ordered the Frenchmen to cover them with gifts for several days in succession. He also demanded from them a special gift to help him dry up the tears he might still shed over the death of his son. Hennepin obliged him with several fathoms of Martinique tobacco, axes, knives, beads, and some black and white wampum bracelets. In this manner Aquipaguetin stripped them of much of their goods. They could not reproach him, for he declared that what he had asked for was only for the deceased and for his men. Indeed, he distributed among them all that the Frenchmen gave him. [17]

On the nineteenth day of their journey they arrived at a place fifteen miles below the falls which they named in honor of St. Anthony of Padua. They smashed to pieces the canoe in which the white men had been traveling to prevent their possible escape to any enemy tribe. Their own canoes they hid in the brushwood to use them later in hunting. Though they could have reached their village by water, the Indians forced the white men to march every day from daybreak to two hours after nightfall until they reached their destination one hundred and eighty miles away. These exertions proved the physical superiority of Indians over Europeans. Hennepin wrote that on leaving the water,

> I could scarcely stand; our legs were all bloody from the ice which we broke as we advanced in lakes which we forded, and as we ate only once in twenty-four hours, some pieces of meat which these barbarians grudgingly gave us, I was so weak that I often lay down on the way, resolved to die there, rather than allow these Indians who marched on and continued their route with a celerity which surpasses the power of Europeans. To oblige us to hasten on, they often set fire to the grass of the prairies where we were passing, so that we had to advance or burn. I had then a hat which I reserved to shield me from the burning rays of the sun in summer, but I often dropped it in the flames which we were obliged to cross.[18]

On approaching their village they seized and divided equally among themselves all the goods belonging to the Frenchmen's two paddlers. Esteeming Martinique tobacco more than Europeans esteemed gold, they almost killed themselves in their mad scramble to obtain as much of it as possible. The more humane assured the paddlers by signs that they were willing to give them beaver skins for what they took. Acquipaguetin took Hennepin's vestments, including a brocade chasuble. He also took all the articles on the portable altar save the silver chalice, which he observed glittered in the sun and which, therefore, he regarded as a kind of evil spirit. With sharp stones they broke the lock and key of a box which they expected to contain valuable goods. To their disappointment they found only books and papers in it.

A journey of five days, during which they suffered hunger, thirst, and many humiliations, brought them to the village. Its inhabitants, mostly old men, women, and children, swarmed from their cabins to welcome home the war party and to gaze curiously at the white strangers. Hennepin saw in front of the cabins a number of stakes to which were attached bundles of straw. Did they intend to burn him and his companions? His concern increased when he saw Picard, his hair and face painted in different colors and his head decorated with a tuft of white feathers. He entered the village with a group of Indians who compelled him to sing and keep time to his own music by rattling a dried gourd containing a number of pebbles. Usually this was the treatment they meted out to a person whom they were about to burn at the stake. Hennepin trembled and invoked his favorite saints. They speedily came to his rescue. Instead of leading him and Picard to the stake, the Indians took them to a cabin, bade them sit on the ground, and placed before them birchbark dishes containing wild rice boiled with dried whortleberries. This was the best food, says Hennepin, that he had tasted in seven or eight days. Then three minor chiefs adopted the three Frenchmen on the spot. Aquipaguetin adopted Hennepin to replace the son over whom he had spent so much energy and shed so many tears. Now all his evil intentions toward him were gone, and he showered him with paternal affection.[19]

But the other Frenchmen still felt uncertain of their own safety. Picard confessed himself to Hennepin, but Accault, who had little faith in the efficacy of prayer, especially from one who allowed his tongue to wag so indiscriminately, refused to do so. Hennepin nevertheless embraced them both with what he called "great tenderness." Then Aquipaguetin took his foster son through several miles of woods and marshes toward his cabin, which lay on an island in a lake. On approaching the edge of the lake they were met by five of Aquipaguetin's wives in three canoes and taken to the island. The chief told them to call Hennepin by his first name and to regard him as a son. One of the chief's younger sons greeted him as a brother. The friar was scandalized to find the boy wearing the vestments which his father had taken some days before. The girdle, which was made of red and white wool with two tassels hanging from its hem, served as the boy's suspenders. And on his bare back he was carrying the brocade chasuble in which were wrapped a deceased relative's bones. A little later he gave the chasuble to allies who lived five hundred miles away and who had sent his father a delegation of peace.[20]

Next day Aquipaguetin covered Hennepin with a robe made of ten large dressed beaver skins adorned with porcupine quills. The strain of constant and forced travel had weakened him so much that he could scarcely stand under the weight of his new robe. Aquipaguetin had four of his men take the friar to a tightly covered hut where, by a pile of heated stones, they sweated him three times a week until he felt better. Despite his meager diet of wild rice and smoked fish roes five or six times a week, he gradually regained his strength. By this time the chief had spread the word far and wide that his foster son was *wakan* or a spirit. He was often requested to show an assemblage of elders the compass which he always carried in his sleeve. Of course he did all he could to encourage their belief in his occult powers. He made the needle of the compass turn with a key and told his audience that it enabled him and all other white men to travel magically all over the world. Proud of his son's wondrous gifts, Aquipaguetin waxed eloquent in telling his people that the friar was a spirit capable of doing anything beyond their reach. The friar had an iron pot which the Indian women would not allow inside their cabins. They thought it was *wakan* because it had three feet and resembled a lion's paws. He was obliged to hang the receptacle on the branch of a tree.[21]

Hennepin tried to be as useful as he could. In a nearby village he found a sick little girl who seemed to be on the point of death. Curiously, for a priest, he conferred with Accault and Picard, who lived in separate villages but whom he saw occasionally, on the expediency of baptizing the child. Accault refused to accompany him to the village in which the sick child lived. Picard alone consented to go with him and serve as the girl's godfather. Hennepin christened her Antoinette in honor of St. Anthony of Padua and her godfather's patron saint. After receiving the sacrament Antoinette revived; but she soon relapsed and died.[22]

Early in July the Sioux of the neighboring villages, numbering two hundred fifty warriors with their wives and children, set out on a buffalo hunt to gather hides for French traders whom they expected in the early fall and to lay away a quantity of meat for the winter months. The chiefs granted Accault and Picard permission to participate in the hunt. But somehow they overlooked Hennepin who, fearing that he would be left behind, stood on the river bank and begged each passing canoeman to give him a ride. To his entreaty Accault, who went by with Picard, called back that he had taken him too many times already. But God, who never abandoned him in that painful voyage,

> inspired two Indians to take me in their little canoe, where I had no other employment than to bale out with a little bark tray the water which entered by little holes. This I did not do without getting all wet. This boat might, indeed, be called a death-box, from its lightness and fragility. These canoes do not generally weigh over fifty pounds; the least motion of the body upsets them, unless you are long habituated to that kind of navigation. On disembarking in the evening, . . . Picard, as an excuse, told me that their canoe was half rotten, and that, had we been three in it, we should have run a great risk of remaining on the way. In spite of this excuse I told him, that being Christians, they should not act so, especially among Indians, more than eight hundred leagues from the French settlements; that if they were well received in this country, it was only in consequence of my bleeding some asthmatic Indians, and my giving them some orvietan and other remedies which I kept in my sleeve, and by which I had saved the lives of some Indians bit by rattlesnakes, and because I had neatly made their tonsure, which Indian children wear to the age of eighteen or twenty, but have no way of making except by burning the hair with red-hot flat stones. I reminded them that by my ingenuity I had gained the friendship of these people, who would have killed us or made us suffer more, had they not discovered about me those remedies which they prize, when they restore the sick to health. However, . . . Picard only, as he retired to his host's, apologized to me.[23]

On reaching the Mississippi River the entire hunting party camped opposite the mouth of the Rum River. The young men separated in bands to hunt stags, deer, and beavers. Unfortunately they killed so few of them that they seldom had meat to eat and had to limit themselves to broth every twenty-four hours. Bored by his idleness, Hennepin decided to set out for the mouth of the Wisconsin, more than three hundred miles away. He went to ascertain, as he says for the first time in his narrative, whether La Salle had kept his promise to send to that point a reinforcement of men with powder, lead, and other munitions. Thanks to the friendship of a great chief, Ouasicoudé, Hennepin was permitted to do as he wished. Picard consented to accompany him, but Accault, who had a better opinion of the Indians than of the friar, stoutly refused.

Supplied with a gun, a knife, and a robe of buffalo skin, they took off in a small canoe the Indians had given them. At the Falls of St. Anthony, whose length Hennepin miscalculates, they saw five or six Indians who had preceded them. One of them climbed an oak tree whence in a loud and lamenting voice he apostrophized the cataract as a spirit. He beseeched it to grant his people many buffaloes, victory over their enemies, and slaves that he might sacrifice them to it whenever he saw fit. Three miles below the Falls Hennepin saw a snake, which he describes as six feet long, writhing up a hill toward young swallows in their holes. He and Picard pelted it with stones until it fell into the river.

The two men paddled down the Mississippi for one hundred and eighty more miles, still seeking the mouth of the Wisconsin. They killed a small deer, and trapped many huge turtles. On July 11 they were greatly surprised to see Aquipaguetin, whom they thought at least four hundred miles away, approaching with ten men. They believed that he was coming to kill them because they had left the hunting party without his permission; but they were delighted to find him well disposed toward them. He gave them some wild rice and a slice of buffalo meat and asked them whether they had found the Frenchmen they sought. When he learned that the Frenchmen had not yet arrived he continued downstream toward the mouth of the Wisconsin to find them and to trade with them on as good terms as he could get. Failing to find them, however, he rejoined Hennepin and Picard. The three men soon joined a large band of Sioux who were hunting on the Chippewa, which enters the Mississippi from the east at Lake Pepin.[24]

One day two old Indians who had been standing guard on top of a mountain ran into the hunting camp with the word that they had seen two warriors in the distance. The bowmen hastened there, but they brought back only two of their own women. The women said that one of the bands, while hunting at or near the Falls of St. Anthony, had seen five "spirits," as they called Frenchmen, paddling upstream in a single canoe. The Frenchmen had somehow learned that three white men were among the hunting party and had sent an Indian requesting permission to come and ascertain whether they were English, Dutch, Spaniards, or Frenchmen. They also wanted to know by what roundabout way they had reached the region. On July 25 the five "spirits" overtook the Sioux as they were ascending the river toward their villages after the hunt. They proved to be Daniel Greysolon, Sieur du Lhut (or du Luth or Duluth, as his name is spelled in American history books) with two white men, his Indian interpreter, and another Indian who for a present had consented to guide him to the place where the Sioux were hunting.[25]

Brave and enterprising, Duluth belongs to that class of lesser nobility which contributed so many illustrious names to the history of French exploration in the New World. Though born at St. Germain-en-Laye, near Paris, in 1636, he grew up in Lyons, where his father became a wealthy merchant. Like his cousin Henri de Tonti, young Duluth adopted a military career. He served in the king's guard until he was thirty-six years old. Then, in 1672, he migrated to Canada and settled in Montreal, where his uncle was a successful merchant. There he busied himself with plans to find copper mines and a route to the mysterious Western Sea, which later explorers found to be Lake Winnepeg. Knowing that peace among the tribes was essential to the success of his plans, in the fall of 1678 he added a new chapter to western exploration by traveling with seven companions from Montreal to Sault Ste. Marie, where he won the friendship of the Chippewa. Then, "fearing not death, only cowardice and dishonor," he led his companions to the western end of Lake Superior. Near the present site of the city which bears his name, he held a council with the Sioux who promised to keep peace with the Chippewa. Accompanying the Sioux delegation to its village on Lake Mille Lacs, he followed Saint-Lusson's example of eight years before by claiming the region for the king of France. The Sioux, awed by his description of the power of Louis XIV, made him solemn promises of peace. Into the interior he sent three men who traveled perhaps as far as the western limits of Minnesota. Meanwhile Duluth, having retraced his steps to Lake Superior, held another council in September, 1679. This one was between the Sioux and the Assiniboins, who promised to abandon the warpath they had so long pursued. That winter Duluth sojourned at Kaministikwia, at the site of present Fort William, Ontario.[26]

In the spring he resolved to resume his search for the Western Sea, sometimes called the Vermilion Sea. He was encouraged in his plans, he wrote later, by the return of the three Frenchmen whom he had sent the previous year into the interior of present Minnesota. These three had "brought me some . . . salt, having reported to me that the savages had told them that it was only twenty days' journey from where they were to the discovery of the great lake whose water is not good to drink. This is what makes me believe that it would not be at all difficult to find it, if one were willing to give permission to go there."[27] He started out in two canoes with four of his companions and his interpreter, and followed Lake Superior to its southern shore, where he entered the mouth of the Brulé River in present Douglas County, Wisconsin. Cutting down some trees and about a hundred beaver dams, he ascended the turbulent river, portaged to the placid Upper Lake St. Croix, and descended the picturesque river of the same name "through all its foaming rapids," and eventually reached its junction with the Mississippi. There he learned that the Sioux were holding three white men prisoners. Without hesitation he went with two of his companions and his interpreter in a single canoe to rescue the unknown strangers.[28]

They met with mutual cordiality. Duluth was delighted when Hennepin recalled that they had served some years before in the bloody but indecisive battle at Séneffe. All the more was he enraged at the Sioux for mistreating the Frenchmen and especially for grossly insulting "Father Louis" by stealing his priestly vestments. He reproved the Sioux for breaking the peace treaty they had signed with him in the previous year. He demanded and obtained custody of the three Frenchmen, whom he boldly conducted to the great Sioux village at Lake Mille Lacs. There he denounced the Indians for their perfidy, scornfully rejected the peace calumets they offered him, and announced that he would conduct his newly freed friends to Canada. Even the great chief Ouasicoudé feared his wrath. He consented to all his wishes and traced on paper which Hennepin gave him the route the white men should take for the first twelve hundred miles. The chief also advised Hennepin to soften the blow his foster father, Aquipaguetin, would feel at his departure by offering him a fathom of Martinique tobacco. The gift had a surprising effect on the usually tearful man—he and his men leaped with joy, shouting the Indian word for the sun several times.[29]

Abandoning for the present his plans for further exploration, Duluth led his friends homeward. He descended the Mississippi, entered the Wisconsin, ascended that river, portaged to the Fox, and arrived at Green Bay. There they found a company of *coureurs de bois* engaged in illicit trade with the regional tribes. "We remained two days to rest,"

198

wrote Hennepin, "sing the *Te Deum,* high mass, and preach. All our Frenchmen went to confession and communion, to thank God for having preserved us amid so many wanderings and perils."[30] A large canoe which they traded with an Indian for a gun enabled them to continue their journey across Lake Michigan to Mackinac, where they decided to spend the winter. In the spring Duluth set out alone for Montreal to answer the governor's charge of his having led a party of unlicensed traders. He was cleared of this charge only after he had spent some time in prison. The other white men also returned to Montreal. Count Frontenac, chancing to be in town and looking out of a window, saw a Recollect father approaching alone in a canoe. The monk's face was worn and sunburned and his Franciscan habit was tattered, dirty, and patched crazily with scraps of buffalo hide. Recognizing him at last, the governor embraced him "with all the tenderness which a missionary could expect from a person of his rank and quality." He kept him for twelve days in his own house, listening "with interest to such of his adventures as the friar saw fit to divulge."[31]

Soon Hennepin returned to Europe, where, probably in the monastery of Saint-Germain-en-Laye, he compiled the first narrative of his adventures and achievements in America. It brought him ephemeral fame. Then he traveled from France to Rome, where he lived for a time in the celebrated convent of Ara Coeli on Capitoline Hill, and where he became a favorite of Cardinal Spada. Suddenly we lose sight of him. Nobody knows where and when he died.

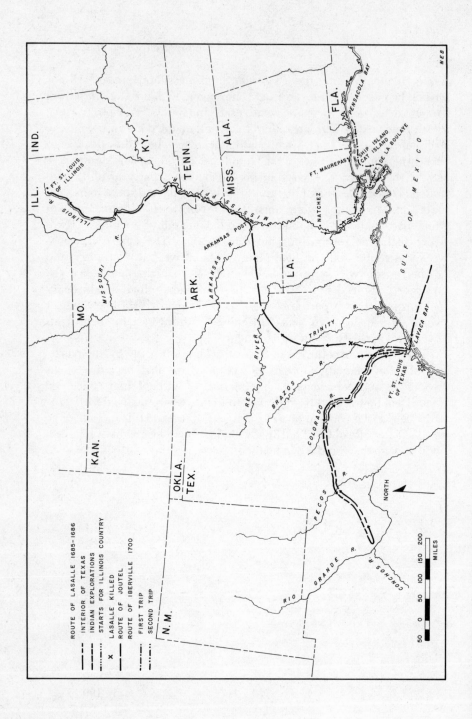

13

La Salle's Last Expedition

L ATE IN DECEMBER, 1683, LA SALLE LANDED AT LA ROCHELLE AND ALMOST immediately took a stagecoach to Paris. He was soon joined by La Forest and Father Membré, both of whom had preceded him from Canada. He also conferred with his old friend and supporter Frontenac, who was instrumental in obtaining for him audiences with Louis XIV and interviews with Seignelay, the minister of marine and colonies.

La Salle laid before the minister a petition for redress of grievances and two memorials setting forth his plans for the colonization of Louisiana. In the memorials he proposed to establish a fortified colony on the Mississippi, some one hundred and eighty miles from its mouth, and to make it the principal depository for the fur trade of the great valley. He stated that he could accomplish this with one war vessel of thirty guns, a few cannon for the forts, and two hundred men who were to be armed and maintained for a year at the king's expense. He further stated that the Mississippi was close to the rich silver mines of New Spain. He said that the conquest of that colony would be easy because its defense had been entrusted to a small number of men weakened by pleasure and idleness and incapable of waging war.[1]

Privately La Salle realized that the Mississippi River was actually too far from New Spain to be useful in any project of conquest. But he realized, too, that Louis XIV and his minister might not be disposed to support his plans to colonize the Mississippi Valley unless he coupled them with plans to acquire the silver mines of New Spain. To make certain that his plans of colonization would not be rejected, he drew a map of Louisiana which showed the mouth of the Mississippi some six hundred miles west of its actual course. On the map the course of the river turned sharply westward between the mouth of the Missouri and that of the Arkansas. This brought it close to New Mexico and, therefore, to the coveted silver mines in the present state of Durango, Mexico. Only then did the river flow reluctantly into the Gulf of Mexico. La Salle was clever, too, in drawing a mountain range between the river's delta and its sudden turn toward New Mexico as explanation of its strange course. When Pierre Lemoyne, Sieur d'Iberville, rediscovered the river for France in 1699, he recalled its misplaced course on La Salle's map and readily understood.[2]

The times and circumstances were propitious for La Salle's project. Since 1679 Louis XIV's hostility toward Spain had increased with his interests in colonial expansion. In that year some Spaniards had captured a French frigate in the Gulf of Mexico, which the French regarded as exclusively their sea. Highly offended, Louis ordered his fleet in the West Indies to pursue and punish the Spaniards and to demand restitution of the captured frigate. This order was duly carried out. But the king's real reason for ordering the pursuit of the offending Spaniards was to obtain information of their Gulf towns, which he planned to capture. In this endeavor he was encouraged by Diego Dionisio, Count of Peñalosa, a Peruvian who, while serving as governor of New Mexico, had aroused the enmity of the Inquisition, which had sequestered his property and sent him to prison. On gaining his release he had migrated to Spain, but had failed to obtain there a redress of grievances. Burning with revenge, he had tried in vain to interest Charles II of England in an expedition against the Spanish colonies. Then he had offered his services to Louis XIV. Through his friend, Abbé Bernou, whom we have met elsewhere, Peñalosa presented to Seignelay a proposal to conquer "Thegayo" and "Quivira," imaginary kingdoms lying east of the upper Rio Grande towns. He said these kingdoms contained the richest gold and silver mines in the world. To add weight to his proposal he submitted to Seignelay a journal of an imaginary expedition he had made to Quivira in 1662.[3]

Early in 1684, while France and Spain were at war and after La Salle's arrival in France, Peñalosa proposed to attack the Spanish town of Panuco with twelve hundred buccaneers from Santo Domingo. He planned to march into the interior of the viceroyalty of New Spain, seize its silver mines, conquer Durango, and occupy New Mexico. Seignelay seemed to favor his plan and proposed to combine it with that of La Salle who, however, refused to accept him as a partner in the enterprise. He had discussed it with him and had expressed distrust of him. The truth was that he wanted to pursue his own plan of colonization and would not, therefore, have consented to play second fiddle to anybody. So he submitted a new memorial in which he reverted to his original plan of building a fort on the Mississippi River. In it he criticized Peñalosa's plan to attack Panuco, stating that Indians hated Spaniards and that they would not follow him. He hastened to exaggerate the number of his Indian allies, who, he said, would follow him "wherever he would like to lead them." And he proposed that New Spain be invaded by "three armies" simultaneously from three directions—a plan which he declared was superior to Peñalosa's. Furthermore, he said, Peñalosa's buccaneers would fail because their lack of respect for Spanish women would infuriate the inhabitants of the colony.[4]

To put matters at rest, Seignelay decided to combine the two plans; but both became unworkable when, in 1684, Louis planned to make peace with Spain. The new plan, of course, made no mention of an attack on Spanish territory; it merely spoke of bringing the light of the Gospel to the heathen tribes of the Mississippi Valley. In such a project Peñalosa, of course, could have no part. The king then made La Salle commander of the territory between the Illinois River and New Mexico. At about the same time, he directed Governor La Barre by letter to restore to the explorer possession of Fort Frontenac and Fort St. Louis. A little later he sent La Forest back to Canada with authority to reoccupy the two forts in La Salle's name.[5]

Seignelay easily won a generous policy for La Salle. Instead of the single vessel which he had requested, he received four, including two frigates, *Le Joly* and *La Belle,* and two ketches or merchantmen, *L'Aimable* and the *Saint François*. The passengers, numbering about three hundred, consisted of men, women, and children, of whom only one hundred and eighty were destined to remain with La Salle to his tragic death.[6]

From the very beginning the expedition incurred a series of mistakes and misunderstandings which forecast a ruinous conclusion to La Salle's great career. The passengers were mostly vagabonds and beggars entirely lacking in the diligence and hardiness required of successful colonists. La Salle's agents, like those of other such enterprises, entertained the delusion that any kind of people could establish and maintain a colony. But Father Christian Le Clercq, who was one of the missionaries as well as one of the chroniclers of the expedition, knew better. He found only two or three passengers of whom he fully approved:

> Would to God the troops and the rest of the crew had been as well chosen! Those who were appointed, while M. de la Salle was at Paris, picked up a hundred and fifty soldiers, mere wretched beggars soliciting alms, many too deformed and unable to fire a musket. The sieur de la Salle had also given orders at Rochelle to engage three or four mechanics in each trade; the selection was, however, so bad, that when they came to the destination, and they were set to work, it was seen that they knew nothing at all. Eight or ten families of very good people presented themselves, and offered to go and begin new colonies. Their offer was accepted, and great advances made to them as well as to the artisans and soldiers.[7]

As if this were not enough, Seignelay had chosen Sieur de Beaujeu as captain of the fleet. Beaujeu secretly despised La Salle because of his ignorance of naval affairs. Each man mistrusted the other and they quarreled from the very beginning of the voyage. To add to their troubles, Spanish pirates one night captured the *Saint François*, which had lagged behind the other ships and which was laden with provisions, ammunition, and tools. Still worse, La Salle, when he arrived at Petit-Goâve, in present Haiti, came down with a high fever. Perhaps it was a recurrence of his old disease, which may have been either malaria or yellow fever. All these luckless experiences depressed him as well as his colonists. To relieve their troubled minds, some of them plunged into every kind of debauchery. Others contracted tropical diseases of which they either died or which they carried along with them.[8]

By this time La Salle's illness had perhaps aggravated his mistrust of Beaujeu. His letters and actions show increasingly paranoid characteristics, either real or designed. He resented Beaujeu as a partner who had been thrust upon him and whom he suspected of planning an incursion against New Spain, regardless of peace between Spain and France. He wanted no part of it. He merely wished to be let alone to pursue his original intention of establishing a colony on the lower Mississippi. Therefore, after many unpleasant encounters with the captain, he requested him to return to France with the king's soldiers. The captain realized that, if he obeyed, La Salle could later accuse him of deserting the expedition, so he asked La Salle for a written order. La Salle refused to give it to him.[9]

Yet he still hoped to get rid of Beaujeu. Probably for this reason, he had embarked with his colonists, his own men, and his own supplies on *L'Aimable* and *La Belle,* leaving Beaujeu and the king's soldiers on *Le Joly.* Now he hoped to lose the captain in the Gulf of Mexico, leaving him to return to France.[10]

On November 25, the three remaining ships of the fleet left Petit-Goâve, passed the Caymen Islands, took on water at the Isle of Pines, and sailed to Cape San Antonio, on the western end of Cuba. There they anchored and appropriated some casks of wine left by Spanish pirates. Resuming their voyage, on December 27 they noticed that the water had become "whitish," indicating that they were nearing the Mississippi. Though La Salle must have realized that he could not be too far from the mouth of the river he had discovered less than three years before, he gave orders for the two ships to continue westward. He hoped thereby to elude Beaujeu and leave him to return to Santo Domingo and on to France. On January 18, 1685, after sailing for three weeks westward from the mouth of the Mississippi, he ordered the two ships to turn northward. He was confident that by this time he had freed himself of Beaujeu forever. Needless to say, he was profoundly vexed when, on the following morning, he saw *Le Joly* approaching on the rim of the sea. He had no choice but to pretend to Beaujeu that he had been following Seignelay's original plans and that, at last, he believed himself near Spanish territory. He entered Matagorda Bay, which he had passed a few days before and which he now pretended was the mouth of the Mississippi.[11]

Here he decided to disembark his colonists. On February 18 *La Belle* entered the harbor and discharged her cargo and crew without incident. Two days later *L'Aimable* weighed anchor and, while La Salle watched from shore, started through the narrow channel that led to the bay. Her captain, Sieur d'Aigron, had quarreled with La Salle and nursed a sullen dislike for him. Now he disregarded his orders. He neglected to guide the ship through the markers and ordered the pilot to pull through the shoals, even though a sailor watching from the fore lookout had shouted to keep in the offing. The ship became stranded in the shoals, furled her sails, careened, and shot off a cannon to signal her peril. Aigron might have cleared her had he taken his pilot's advice to drop anchor. Instead, says Henri Joutel—La Salle's nephew and the most reliable chronicler of the expedition—Aigron let fall her mainsail and set her foresail to catch the wind and make sure that she would be wrecked. Joutel added that all her passengers believed that the accident had been premeditated. As further proof of their belief they pointed out that the captain had ordered all his personal belongings, including his jars of jam, to be removed to *Le Joly,* as though he had planned the accident in collusion with Beaujeu.[12]

The misfortune was all the greater because the ship contained most of the ammunition, utensils, tools, and other supplies which La Salle needed to start his colony. Yet, says Joutel, "his Intrepidity did not forsake him, and he apply'd himself, without grieving, to Remedy what might be."[13] Some sacks of flour and about thirty hogsheads of wine and brandy were saved. The passengers, sick with nausea and dysentery, camped on the inlet of the bay, made a fire of bramble bushes, and tried to sustain themselves with the messes of porridge which they made by boiling the flour. From uprooted trees and rotted logs they found on the shore they made a kind of rampart in which to protect themselves against the elements and Indian attacks. Here, says Parkman, "among tents and hovels, bales, boxes, casks, spars, dismounted cannon, and pens for fowls and swine, were gathered the dejected men and homesick women who were to . . . hold for France a region large as half Europe."[14]

A few weeks later Beaujeu, declaring that he had fulfilled his mission to transport the colonists to what La Salle said was the mouth of the Mississippi, prepared to return to France. With him went Aigron, an engineer named Minet, and some discontented colonists. In his parting words Beaujeu—always the cold, correct, and dignified man of order—assured La Salle of his unfailing devotion and admiration. In France, Seignelay, realizing that the captain had been prejudiced against La Salle from the very beginning, received him coldly and warned him "to say nothing in disparagement of the enterprise, under pain of the King's displeasure."[15] As for Aigron, he fared much worse. Beaujeu refused to defend Aigron's conduct from fear of exposing himself. Seignelay ordered his arrest and had him imprisoned in the tower of La Rochelle.[16]

Left in the wilderness of Texas with one hundred and eighty sick and starving colonists, La Salle built a temporary shelter for them as well as for his supplies. The shelter was on Lavaca Bay which adjoins Matagorda Bay in present Calhoun County, Texas. As soon as it was completed, he set out with fifty men in five canoes to find a suitable location for a permanent settlement. Joutel was left in charge of the rampart. At the same time La Salle began exploring in a northwesterly direction, though he led Joutel to believe that he was going to seek the mouth of the Mississippi. His real purpose was to try to ascertain from Indians the reaction of the Spaniards to his presence. He knew that they were west and not east of the great river.[17]

In June, after a month's absence, he returned to the rampart. Though the Indians he met had given him no satisfactory information, he had found the location he sought. It was fertile and elevated ground affording a magnificent view of surrounding plains that extended beyond sight and that, in certain seasons, swarmed with buffalo and wild goats. Francis Parkman and most of the historians who came after him erroneously stated that the fort stood "on the river which [La Salle] named La Vache, now the Lacava, which enters the head of Matagorda Bay."[18] But in 1914 Herbert Eugene Bolton, availing himself of newly discovered records in the Spanish archives and corroborating them by archeological and topographical investigation, discovered that the permanent fort was located, not on the Lavaca, but on the west bank of Garcitas Creek, about five miles above its mouth, on the site of some ruins traditionally known only as "the Old Mission."[19]

To this place La Salle transported by *La Belle* and by canoes all of his colonists, ammunition, and supplies. Countless obstacles beset their efforts to build the fort. Weakened by disease and fever, unskilled and clumsy in felling and squaring trees, they labored painfully and endured many frustrations and privations as they made slow progress against approaching winter weather. Thirty men died, some from fatigue, some from the tropical diseases contracted in Santo Domingo, some from eating an unknown fruit that resembled an apple and that grew abundantly in the surrounding forest. But at last, thanks to La Salle's unsleeping direction, the fort was completed. He called it by his favorite name, St. Louis, and gave its command to Joutel. A fleur-de-lis waved from its roof as missionary priests and monks in their crude chapel gave thanks to God in masses and vespers.[20]

No sooner were the colonists ensconced in the fort than La Salle resumed his exploratory journeys. On October 31, 1685, he set out with fifty men, including his brother Jean Cavelier, an abbé of St. Sulpice. Some of them, though lightly equipped, wore corselets made of staves as protection against arrows. They walked along Garcitas Creek for a time, then northwestward into the interior of present Texas. They encountered many hostile bands of Indians, whom they scattered like chaff by the terror of their firearms. They crossed a number of rivers, including the Colorado and the Pecos. Eventually they arrived at a village of a more peaceful tribe perhaps less than seventy Spanish leagues from the Mission of La Junta de los Ríos, which stood at the juncture of the Rio Grande and the Conchos rivers, some two hundred miles southeast of present El Paso, Texas.[21] La Salle inquired if Spaniards resided in the region of El Parral, where silver was mined. He asked if the trails that led to it were in good condition. When they answered both questions in the affirmative, he told them

the Spaniards were not good people, but that they themselves were, and that they would be brothers to the Indians and would come with provisions and wagons and would enter as far as El Parral, since the road was good; that they [the Indians] should not come here [to trade] for they would bring to them from their country very excellent goods with which to clothe themselves. They gave the [chiefs] some shirts, and within three days set out on their return down the river, after having embraced all with much pleasure.[22]

During their journey homeward they repeated many of their old adventures. At the end of March, 1686, they approached Fort St. Louis. Joutel from a housetop had seen seven or eight men far off across the prairie and had hastened with a few of his soldiers to meet them. Among

208

them were La Salle, his brother, and their nephew Moranget. La Salle had, a few days before, sent the rest of his men to look for *La Belle*, for whose safety he had become very anxious. Joutel noticed that La Salle and his companions were in rags. The abbé's cassock was so badly tattered that no piece of it was large enough to wrap a farthing-worth of salt. An old cap replaced the hat he had lost on the way. Some of them were carrying parts of a buffalo they had recently killed to assure themselves of food during the last days of their journey.[23]

Rejoicing filled the fort; but it was of short duration. The next day the men La Salle had sent to look for the ship returned to the fort with information that she had disappeared from her anchorage. They plunged into the deepest gloom. Without the frigate they were lost. How could they now send to Santo Domingo for sorely needed supplies? How could they now inform their country of their whereabouts and circumstances? La Salle, thinking that the ship was a safer place of deposit than the fort, had transferred to her thirty-six barrels of flour, ammunition and tools, some of his personal belongings, and all of his valuable papers. Always surrounded by persons of questionable loyalty, he suspected that the ship's crew had either deserted her or had sailed away to the West Indies or to France. Later, in La Salle's absence, Joutel learned that, through carelessness on the part of her crew, she had wrecked on a sand-bar with all her stores. Her pilot, four of her crew, and a priest managed to save some of La Salle's luggage and papers and returned with them in a canoe to the fort.[24]

Distressed by his loss and weakened by the rigors of his journeys, La Salle came down with a recurrence of malaria. But his responsibility to his colonists and his determination to succeed in his enterprise soon brought him to his feet. He resolved to try to reach the Illinois country, and eventually Canada, by land. Choosing twenty of his best men, including his brother, their nephew Moranget, Father Anastasius Douay, and Nika, a Shawnee guide, he equipped each of them with powder and lead, as well as hatchets, knives, awls, beads, and kettles for presents to the Indians. On April 22, heartened by a celebration of the divine mysteries, they set out in a northeasterly direction. Crossing the Colorado River, they journeyed through a pleasant region of alternating prairie and woodland. To La Salle, marching ahead in silence and solitude, this

209

journey was an accursed necessity. But to Father Douay, who wrote its only detailed and usually reliable chronicle, it was a glorious adventure. In his black robe of St. Francis and in his sandals, he trudged along with the others, exulting in the beauty of the region through which they were passing and recording their daily adventures as they crossed river after river. He tells us—

> One of our men, with an axe on his back, swam over to the other side, a second followed at once; they then cut down the largest trees, while others on our side did the same. These trees were cut so as to fall on each side into the river, where meeting, they formed a kind of bridge on which we easily passed. This invention we had recourse to more than thirty times in our journeys, finding it surer than the Cajeu, which is a kind of raft formed of many pieces, and branches tied together, on which we passed over, guiding it by a pole.[25]

Eventually they crossed the Brazos, the Trinity and several other smaller rivers to the villages of the Cenis, a tribe of the Caddo confederacy, who received them, says Father Douay, "with all possible friendship." The good priest observed that all of the Indians, when they gained sight of the white men, began to "weep bitterly for a good quarter of an hour. It is their custom when they see any who come from afar, because it reminds them of their deceased relatives whom they suppose on a long journey, from which they await their return."[26]

Accepting some of the pirogues of their hosts as parting gifts, they paddled down a small river to larger and friendlier villages, where, says Douay, they were surprised to find "many things which undoubtedly came from the Spaniards, such as dollars, and other pieces of money, silver spoons, lace of every kind, clothes, and horses. We saw, among other things, a bull from Rome, exempting the Spaniards in Mexico from fasting during the summer." They had so many horses that they traded them for an axe apiece. One Indian took a fancy to Father Douay's cowl. He would have given a good horse for it had the priest consented to the trade.[27] Cavelier, who also wrote an account of this journey, reported that he saw silver lamps, old muskets, and a rusty sword, all of which had been made in Spain. He asked by signs whence these things came. In reply "they drew on the bark of a tree with a piece of charcoal the figure of a Spaniard, houses, steeples, and showed us the part of the heaven under which New Mexico is situated."[28]

La Salle requested them to draw a bark map of their country, one of their neighbors', and one of the Mississippi, with which they were acquainted. "They reckoned themselves," wrote Douay, "six days' journey from the Spaniards, of whom they gave us so natural a description that we no longer had any doubts on the point, although the Spaniards had not yet undertaken to come to their villages." A master of Indian psychology, La Salle filled them with admiration by telling them, says Douay, "that the chief of the French was the greatest chief in the world, as high as the sun, and as far above the Spaniard as the sun is above the earth. On his recounting the victories of our monarch, they burst into exclamation, putting their hand on their mouth as a mark of astonishment. I found them very docile and tractable, and they seized well enough what we told them of the truth of God." The priest was delighted to see some visiting ambassadors from the Comanche country make the sign of the cross, kneel as if in prayer, and clasp their hands and, from time to time, raise them to heaven. They also kissed his habit,

> and gave me to understand that men dressed like us instructed tribes in their vicinity, who were only two days' march from the Spaniards, where our religious had large churches, in which all assembled to pray. They expressed very naturally the ceremonies of mass, one of them sketched me a painting that he had seen of a great lady, who was weeping because her son was upon a cross. He told us that the Spaniards butchered the Indians cruelly, and finally that if we would go with them, or give them guns, they could easily conquer them, because they were a cowardly race, who had no courage, and made people walk before them with a fan to refresh them in hot weather.[29]

Equipped with horses loaded down with melons and grain, La Salle and his men resumed their journey eastward with renewed confidence and courage. Unfortunately, malarial fever attacked him and his nephew when they reached either the Neches or the Sabine. This delayed them for more than two months and dealt a crushing blow to the entire expedition. When La Salle recovered, he found that his ammunition was nearly exhausted, that four of his men had deserted, and that the rest were too weak and too scantily clad to continue their journey. He had no choice but to return to Fort St. Louis. The horses greatly facilitated their progress homeward without any serious accident save that of the loss of La Salle's servant, Dumesnil, who was seized by an alligator as he attempted to cross one of the rivers, perhaps the Colorado.[30]

The colonists rejoiced at the return of their leader, only to give way gradually to restless despair. Week followed week without bringing any sign of a ship to rescue them from their weariness and from the wretchedness of their barren colony. "We had imagined," wrote Abbé Jean, "that the king would send us two or three ships. But after having waited for years, we did not know what to think. Sometimes we thought that a ship might well have entered the Mississippi without our knowing it, and at other times we imagined that the king believing us lost had forgotten all about us."[31]

In all this uncertainty La Salle saw the necessity of making another attempt to reach Canada and then France by way of the Illinois country. Of the one hundred and eighty persons who formed the original colony only about forty remained. "The weary precincts of Fort St. Louis," says Parkman, "with its fence of rigid palisades, its area of trampled earth, its buildings of weather-stained timber, and its well-peopled graveyard without, were hateful to their sight."[32] None of them wanted to be left behind to guard the fort. All clamored to become a part of the expedition and to follow their fearless leader. But with that equanimity and eloquence which always came to his support in crucial times and which constituted his most engaging traits, La Salle showed them the impossibility of providing, by hunting, enough food for so many persons traveling together. He chose seventeen of his best men to go with him. The rest, including three friars, a surgeon, soldiers, laborers, seven women or girls, and several children, were to stay behind, "doomed," says Parkman, "in this deadly exile, to wait the issues of the journey, and the possible arrival of a tardy succor."[33] They cobbled their shoes, made shirts from sheets, and suits from the sails of the ship they had recently lost. They celebrated a wineless Christmas and at midnight heard mass in the chapel. They were ready to depart on their journey when their leader became ill with a flux which delayed them for several more weeks. Then, on Twelfth Night, in accordance with old French custom,

212

they gathered in the hall, lifted their cups of cold water as though they were filled with the best Spanish wine, and cried, one and all, the jovial old toast: "The king drinks! The king drinks!"[34]

Next morning, January 7, 1687, La Salle mustered his little band in the enclosed area of the fort. They loaded the five horses they had purchased from the Cenis. Around them gathered those who were to stay behind. La Salle needed Joutel on the expedition and had replaced him as commander of the fort with Sieur Barbier, whose wife, having just miscarried, required his presence. "We took our Leaves," wrote Joutel, "with so much Tenderness and Sorrow, as if we had all presaged, that we should never see each other more. Father [Membré] was the Person who express'd it to me most significantly, saying, He had never been so sensibly touch'd at parting with any Body."[35] Sadly they filed from the gate, crossed the Garcitas Creek that flowed along the fort, and slowly marched northeastward over the prairie. Soon an intervening forest shut the fort from their view.

Following the same route as before, they advanced over a level country of grassy prairies and wooded river bottoms, killing buffalo whose flesh they ate and whose skins furnished them with shelter against the rain. When their shoes wore out they substituted raw buffalo hide, which they had to keep wet to prevent its hardening like iron around their feet. At a village of friendly Indians they obtained a number of dressed skins from which they made tolerable moccasins and a boat in which two or three men could cross a stream at one time. Nearly every day they met Indians, some of whom were hunters and fishermen living in a winter camp on the slope of a hill or under the sheltering rim of a forest. Abbé Jean reports that one day he and his companions saw a hundred and fifty mounted Indians, each of whom was vigorously attacking a bull buffalo with a lance pointed with sharpened bone:

> We approached them little by little, and when they saw us, a few among them left the party and came to meet us. After they had dismounted to embrace us, they looked at us and examined us, uttering extraordinary exclamations. They then made us mount to see the end of the bull fight. It was truly an admirable sight, and I am very much persuaded that more interesting or more diverting chases can hardly be seen in Europe. Such was the reflection my brother made, when he said that marvellous things were found in every corner of the universe. When the combat ended, after

213

each of the attackers had floored his bull, they came to us at full speed, and having given us every mark of surprise and joy, they forced us to go to their village. As their affectionate manner showed only much good faith, we felt no great hesitation in following them.[36]

There the Indians washed the heads, the hands, and the feet of the travelers in warm water. They brought boiled and roasted meat, and then a fish six feet long cooked whole and served in a sort of dish of the same length.[37]

At the end of January they arrived at a village which Abbé Jean calls Sassori. There they saw a group of Indians capture an alligator twelve feet long with a hook made of a buffalo bone on which was stuck a large piece of meat:

> The cord which held the hook was also studded with bones of animals to prevent the alligator from cutting it with his teeth. All these Indians amused themselves for three or four hours tormenting this poor alligator. They dragged it from the river into a prairie with three thick ropes made of bark of trees, that passed in slip knots around its head, its tail and the middle of its body. They then let it loose, but without untying the ropes. Each Indian approached it to strike it in the mouth, and as they had put out its eyes, there was no risk in doing this. After having thus tormented it, they turned it belly up and fastened it to eight stakes which pressed its body right and left from the head to the tail. They then skinned it. There were thick knots on its scales. After they had very skillfully removed the said skin from the body with wooden tools made for that purpose, except the skin of the head to which they did not touch, they made it run about stark naked. As the blows given hurt it to the quick, it yelled fearfully. At the end they killed it and gave it to their dogs.[38]

Resuming their course in a northerly direction, they traveled in the next several weeks through the regions of the Brazos and the Trinity rivers, which they crossed in the boat they had made from buffalo hide. Spring rains intermittently impeded their progress. February gave way to March before they arrived in the country of the Cenis, who welcomed them as before and helped them on their way. But two of them, Liotot and Duhaut, had slept with Indian women against La Salle's strict orders. This had aroused the anger of their immediate officer, Moranget, who had reprimanded them. A few days later Moranget added to the

214

resentment the two men felt toward him. He berated and threatened them for cutting up without his permission two buffaloes which Nika, the Shawnee hunter, had killed, and for laying the meat on scaffolds for smoking before it was properly dried. Burning with revenge, the two men reviewed and magnified their grudges until they resolved to kill Moranget, together with Nika and La Salle's faithful servant Saget, that very night. Into this conspiracy they enlisted Hiens or Jam or James, a German or English buccaneer whom La Salle had hired in Santo Domingo; Tessier, who had served as a master on *La Belle;* and a lad of seventeen named Jean l'Archevêque. After supper, when the three men lay down to sleep, Liotot struck each of them a blow on the skull with a hatchet. Nika and Saget died instantly; but Moranget sat up, gasping and trying to talk, until the conspirators wakened another of their companions, De Marle, who knew nothing about the plot, and forced him to deal the stunned man a fatal blow.[39]

Now that they had committed murder, how could they face La Salle? Motivated partly by revenge and partly by desire to escape punishment or to save their own lives, they resolved to kill La Salle also. At that time La Salle was in his camp six miles away. When, two days before, he had been told that Nika had killed several buffaloes, he had sent Moranget to the hunting place to obtain some fresh meat and he had expected him to return within a few hours. But the whole day passed without a sign of him. When nearly another day went by and his nephew still did not return, La Salle, mindful of his quarrelsome nature, began to fear that some evil might have befallen him. He resolved to go to the hunting place and look for him. Since he did not know his way, however, he induced an Indian to guide him. Next morning when he prepared to set out, La Salle asked Joutel to accompany him and the Indian. But fearing on second thoughts that Duhaut and some of the other men might form some plot against him, he changed his mind. Instead he decided to take Douay and two Indians with him and to place Joutel in charge of the camp. Nevertheless, he borrowed Joutel's gun as well as his pistol, which were the best in the camp, for the occasion. All the way to the hunting place, wrote Douay, La Salle

conversed with me on matters of piety, grace, and predestination; expatiating on all his obligations to God for having saved him from so many dangers during the last twenty years that he had traversed America. He seemed to me peculiarly penetrated with a sense of God's benefits to him. Suddenly I saw him plunged into a deep melancholy, for which he himself could not account; he was so troubled that I did not know him any longer; as his state was far from being usual, I roused him from his lethargy.[40]

Seeing two eagles flying over his head, La Salle guessed that he was approaching the hunting ground. He saw L'Archevêque standing at the river bank. He approached him, asking what had happened to his nephew. The solemn youth kept on his hat. "Back yonder," he said in an insolent tone. La Salle rebuked and menaced him as he advanced to chastise him. The youth drew back toward the river bank, where Duhaut and Liotot lay concealed behind a clump of tall weeds. Duhaut fired two shots. One of them pierced La Salle's brain; he fell, face downward, to the ground and died without saying a word. The shot that killed him was also the signal for the murderers to gather at the spot where his tall and large body lay. They stripped it naked and kicked it into deep grass. "There you are, you big Pasha!" muttered Liotot, triumphantly. "There you are!"[41]

So died René-Robert Cavelier, Sieur de la Salle, the most famous French explorer in the annals of the American frontier. Many men, admirers as well as detractors, have analysed his achievements and character. Henri de Tonti, who perhaps understood him better than any other man, praised him as "one of the greatest men of this age, a man of an admirable spirit, and capable of undertaking all sorts of explorations."[42] His nephew, Henri Joutel, who was always reserved in his language and in his estimates of even his closest friends, wrote that La Salle had

> a Capacity and Talent to make his Enterprize successful; his Constancy and Courage and his extraordinary Knowledge in Arts and Sciences, which render'd him fit for any Thing, together with an indefatigable Body, which made him surmount all Difficulties, would have procur'd a glorious Issue to his Undertaking, had not all those excellent Qualities been counterbalanced by too haughty a Behaviour, which sometimes made him insupportable, and by a Rigidness towards those that were under his Command, which at last drew on him an implacable Hatred, and was the Occasion of his Death.[43]

216

Though this estimate seems just and impartial, Joutel really never understood his uncle and knew him only when his constitution was broken down by disease and his temper soured by many reversals. The haughtiness which Joutel and many others attributed to La Salle was really a defense against his great fear of meeting people. He deprecated his own diffidence and believed that it stemmed from self-love and from a need to defend himself against the possibility of making mistakes. Rigorously schooled by Jesuits, whom he resented for the rest of his life, he became puritanical and overly correct in his personal conduct. He required these qualities in others. He never married. He never expressed affection, not even to La Forest and Tonti, whom he genuinely liked. In an age remarkable for its licentiousness, he maintained a moral rectitude that must have seemed odd to his friends and business associates. Some five years before his death he defended himself from the charge of harshness and cruelty toward his men in a letter to a business correspondent: "The facility I am said to want is out of place with this people, who are libertines for the most part; and to indulge them means to tolerate blasphemy, drunkedness, lewdness, and license, incompatible with any kind of order. It will not be found that I have, in any case whatever, treated any man harshly, except for blasphemies and other such crimes openly committed. . . . I am a Christian, and do not want to bear the burden of their crimes."[44]

Yet his general austerity proved no deterrent in inspiring unquestioned loyalty among those to whom he gave his confidence and who understood the lofty quality of his genius. Though he required every sacrifice from men in his employ, he never shrank from leading them through every difficulty, through every danger, at the risk of his life. Because he was an idealist, some of his schemes and enterprises seemed visionary and impractical to his contemporaries, until he proved, by his persevering energy, that he could succeed where others had faltered and failed. His failure to establish a colony at the mouth of the Mississippi was due to circumstances beyond his control.

In his relations with the Indians he showed that his knowledge of them was superior to that of contemporary explorers. The great respect in which they held him was attributable to his conciliatory policy in dealing with them and to his grave and taciturn manner which comported well with their ideas of dignity and decorum. He was nearly always accompanied by missionaries, especially his favorite Recollects, who served him as his most efficient and faithful coadjutors. But because he was no business man his transactions as a fur trader nearly always ended in financial losses. His only real ambition was to acquire fame as a discoverer of unknown lands—an ambition for which he was always ready to sacrifice his means, his comfort, his health, and even his life. He failed because the resources at his disposal were too meager for his extensive and complex schemes. Even his uncommon energy and fortitude fell short of saving him from the enmities and jealousies that were constantly arrayed against him. The misunderstanding he aroused in his contemporaries was the price he paid for genius. His career was a notable contribution to that sense of tragedy which since ancient times has inspired great historians to write the most moving pages of their art. Francis Parkman, whose imaginative appeal, solid scholarship, and —what is always the final preservative—literary style won him a special place among American historians, characterized La Salle as "a tower of adamant, against whose impregnable front hardship and danger, the rage of man and of the elements, the southern sun, the northern blast, fatigue, famine, disease, delay, disappointment, and deferred hope emptied their quivers in vain."[45] Such was the initiator of Louisiana, a region which eventually became American and which quickly attracted a pioneer society characterized by an "exuberant animal vitality and pride in its own worth."[46]

La Salle's murderers imposed a terrorizing rule over his little party. Ranging aimlessly for several days, the group found itself at a village of the Cenis, who received it with much ceremony and regaled it with nuts, sagamite, corn cakes, beans, and sunflower seeds. The travelers found a young Frenchman who had deserted La Salle on his last journey and who invited them to a neighboring village, where he traded with them. Next morning Duhaut ordered Joutel to continue to trade with the Indians while he and his companions returned to their camp. During his sojourn in the village Joutel met two French sailors, Ruter and Grollet, who had also deserted La Salle but who, on learning of his death, expressed surprise and regret. They joined Joutel and returned with him to the French camp, where all of them soon witnessed a violent quarrel between Duhaut and Hiens. Hiens was so afraid of being punished for his part in the conspiracy against La Salle that he refused Duhaut's request to proceed to Canada by way of the Illinois country. Instead he requested his part of the plunder. When Duhaut failed to comply, Hiens killed him almost instantly with a pistol shot. At the same time Ruter, who had been with Hiens, fired his pistol at Liotot three times. He lived long enough to make his confession before Ruter put him out of his misery with another pistol shot. "We dug a Hole in the Earth," wrote Joutel, "and bury'd him in it with *Duhaut*, doing them more Honour than they had done to Monsieur *de la Sale* and his Nephew *Moranget*, whom they left to be devour'd by wild Beasts."[47]

Strutting about in an embroidered scarlet coat which had belonged to La Salle and which he had seized, Hiens now assumed command of the surviving men, but he had no intention of leading them in the direction of Canada. Instead he gave Joutel a good share of the plunder, which included hatchets, knives, beads, and six Spanish horses. Then he bade them all a good trip, and wandered off with a band of Indians. Joutel's party, which consisted of six men, including Abbé Jean and Father Douay, soon departed from the Cenis village, urged their horses through forests and across prairies studded with villages belonging to various tribes, crossed the Red River, where one of his men, De Marle, was accidentally drowned, and in July penetrated a cypress brake near the southern side of the Arkansas River at a point some distance above its junction with the Mississippi. On the opposite or northern bank they saw an object that overwhelmed them with joy. It was a tall, wooden cross, near which stood a small palisaded house evidently raised by white men. They fell on their knees and raised their hands to heaven, while two men in European dress appeared at the door of the house and saluted their arrival with volleys of musketry. Soon two canoes crossed the river, picked them up, and ferried them to the house. There they were elated to hear two Frenchmen, Jean Couture and Jacques Cardinal, called Launay, greet them in their own tongue.[48]

These men were two of Tonti's followers. That brave and generous man had, in 1685, been reinstated as commander of Fort St. Louis of the Illinois and had soon received word of La Salle's landing on the shore of the Gulf of Mexico. Resolving to seek out his old friend, he descended the Illinois and the Mississippi to the Gulf. There he dispatched canoes to reconnoiter as far east as Florida and as far west as

Mexico, a range of ninety miles. He built on an island a temporary post which he named Fort St. Henry in honor of his patron saint. When the search parties returned to the island without finding any trace of La Salle, Tonti proposed that they make the return journey by following the seacoast around to New York and thence overland to Montreal. But his men were unwilling to risk the possible dangers of such an itinerary. Instead they all ascended the Mississippi to the Arkansas, where, Tonti claimed, La Salle had granted him a seigniory in 1682. There he built above the junction of the two rivers a palisaded house which was to serve as a trading post for beaver skins. This station, which was known to the French as Poste aux Arkansas and, as evident, to American frontiersmen as Arkansas Post, is the oldest settlement in the Lower Mississippi Valley. Tonti left it in charge of five men under Couture with orders to report to him any information they might gather from the natives or otherwise concerning his friend. Tonti also wrote a letter for La Salle which he left in the hands of a Quapaw chief, "who," says Parkman, "preserved it with reverential care, and gave it, fourteen years after, to Iberville, the founder of Louisiana."[49]

Couture and Cardinal were the only Frenchmen present at Arkansas Post to welcome Joutel and his men. They feasted the travelers with corn bread, dried buffalo meat, and watermelons, and listened tearfully to their account of the disasters and of La Salle's death. Joutel left behind the horses, which they no longer needed, and one man who complained of poor health. Then the voyagers descended the Arkansas to the Father of Waters which Joutel called the "fatal river" and which, indeed, rolled "like a destiny, through its realms of solitude and shade." Upstream they toiled, slowly winning their way against sweltering heat, rapid current, knee-deep mud, and unwholesome jungle through which they were often forced to drag their canoe. In the next few weeks they passed the Ohio, the Missouri, and the lofty and irregularly lined limestone escarpment which Frenchmen called the Ruined Castles. Then they entered the more peaceful current of the Illinois. Eleven more days of toilsome paddling brought them to the cliff where the palisades of Fort St. Louis of the Illinois stood towering above forest and river. As they approached, a Frenchman, accompanied by a troop of Indians, saluted them with a volley of musketry. Tonti was away in the east fighting the Iroquois. However, his lieutenant, Sieur de Bellefontaine, and his little garrison received the voyagers. Meanwhile Indians from neighboring villages yelped and yelled as they ran down to the river to meet them. Abbé Jean prevailed on his comrades to conceal his brother's death in the hope that he might realize some remuneration by acting as his brother's agent. They told Bellefontaine that La Salle had been with them nearly as far as the Cenis villages and that, when they last saw him, he enjoyed good health. As autumn was already in the air, they were eager to press forward in order that they might be in time to take passage to France on the autumn ships. Bidding farewell to Bellefontaine and his men without disclosing La Salle's death, they journeyed to the site of present Chicago, where they departed toward Canada in a canoe; but stormy weather soon forced them to return to Fort St. Louis.[50]

They found that Tonti had returned from the Iroquois war. He listened with deep interest as they told him of their troubles and tribulations in Texas. Again they refrained from mentioning La Salle's death, though Tonti knew Abbé Jean quite well and had every claim to his confidence and affection. The priest carried a letter of credit from La Salle—some historians have regarded it as spurious—requesting Tonti to furnish him with supplies and to pay him nearly three thousand livres in beaver skins. On the strength of this letter he drew from Tonti the amount of four thousand livres in furs, besides a canoe and a quantity of other goods, all of which were delivered to him as soon as he left the fort and for which in return he gave only his promissory note. In the spring of 1688, after living on Tonti's hospitality for six months, Abbé Jean and his companions again set out for Canada, reached the present site of Chicago, and proceeded to the Straits of Mackinac. There the priest sold some of Tonti's furs to a merchant who gave him in payment a draft on a Montreal firm. This supplied Abbé Jean with funds for the rest of the journey. Traveling by the familiar route of the French and Ottawa rivers, they reached Montreal, bought much-needed clothes, and descended the St. Lawrence to Quebec. In Quebec they stayed with monks of various orders to avoid the questions of curious people. At the end of August they embarked for La Rochelle, which they reached in the following month. Now, for the first time, they revealed their gloomy secret to Louis XIV, who, however, did nothing save to issue an order for the arrest of the murderers should they appear in Canada. Joutel was greatly disappointed. He had hoped that the king would send a ship to the relief of the little group that La Salle had left at Fort St. Louis. Occupied with weightier matters, the king left them to their fate.[51]

Relief, however, would have arrived too late. That the colony no longer existed was known when Alonso de León, governor of Coahuila, pushed with a small force to the site of the fort in the spring of 1689. In the previous year he had captured a Frenchman, Jean Jerry, who was perhaps a deserter from La Salle's force and who had been living with the Indians. Jerry told León of a French town founded "about fifteen years ago" in the province of Texas. His story reached Mexico City, where it created a great stir. The viceroy was mindful that Alexander VI had decreed that part of America to Spain by a papal bull of 1493. He had also forbidden any other nation to occupy it on pain of excommunication. The viceroy sent León to investigate the French activity in Texas.

Crossing the Rio Grande with his men, León soon learned from an Indian that four Frenchmen were living nearby and that the French colony he sought had been destroyed. He summoned the four Frenchmen, but they, learning that Spaniards were approaching and fearing great punishment if they were caught, fled on horseback. León continued his search for the site of the fort for several months, pushing his way over arid and wild plains, rivers, prairies, and forests, until, on April 22, 1689, he suddenly found it. The begrimed and weary Spaniards dismounted before the palisade and surveyed a scene of destruction and death. Doors were torn from their hinges. Smashed chairs, tables, and beds, broken chests, and staved barrels mingled with pieces of rusty muskets and arquebuses. Splattered with mud and stained by rain were several hundred books, many of which still bore traces of costly bindings. A few pieces of artillery still stood on their broken gun carriages like silent guards over the bodies of dead men, women, and children. Close by was a fenced-in garden in which the colonists had planted a little corn and asparagus. One of the soldiers was moved to write a poem in which he visualized life at the fort before its destruction: he saw in poetic fancy beautiful French women picking fresh roses and playing the lyre with hands as white as snow. León and his men, searching the bare and boundless prairie, found three dead bodies. One of these was judged to be that of a woman by fragments of dress that still clung to the wasted remains. Occasionally an Indian, wrapped to the throat in his buffalo robe, passed imperturbably by the ruins and silently moved on.[52]

Returning to his nearby camp, León found a note from two Frenchmen who had been living with a tribe of the Caddo confederacy. One of them was none other than L'Archevêque, the youth who had witnessed La Salle's death. L'Archevêque, who signed the note, begged León to "have the kindness to wait for them," for they were tired of living among the Indians and wanted "to return among the Christians." León, mistrusting the youth's promise to surrender, sent thirty soldiers after him and his companion, who turned out to be the French sailor Grosset. Interrogated in the Spanish camp, L'Archevêque explained that a large band of Indians had attacked the fort and killed all of its occupants save an Italian, a young Parisian named Eustache de Bremen and four children of one Talon. The Italian and the Parisian had managed to escape. The children had been carried away to safety on the backs of Indian women. L'Archevêque said that on the day of the massacre, he and Grosset had been with the Indians but that they had returned to the fort to bury the dead. There they exploded a hundred barrels of powder to prevent the Indians from carrying it away. This explanation satisfied León that his mission had been successful. He had located the French fort and had ascertained that it no longer constituted a threat to Spanish territory. Soon all of the fort's survivors surrendered to him. He conducted L'Archevêque and Grosset to his headquarters in Coahuila. From there he sent them to Vera Cruz and on to Spain, where, despite his assurances of safe conduct, they were thrown into prison with the intention of sending them back to work in New Spain's silver mines. The Italian was imprisoned in Vera Cruz. The eldest of the Talon children, Pierre and Jean, were declared old enough to bear arms and were enrolled in the Spanish navy. The two younger children were taken to Spain by the viceroy.[53]

That fall Couture visited Tonti at Fort St. Louis of the Illinois and informed him of La Salle's death. Couture also told him that the Caddoes, who lived on the Red River near present Texarkana, were confident that they could defeat the hated Spaniards with the assistance of French firearms. Learning that the War of the Palatinate had recently broken out and that his country had declared against Spain, Tonti planned not only to give the Caddoes the assistance they sought but also to join them in their prospective raid. Early in December he set out in a large canoe with five Frenchmen, two Indian slaves, and a Shawnee hunter. Unaware that the garrison at Fort St. Louis of Texas had been killed almost a year before, he planned to enlist its help against the Spaniards. When he arrived at the Red River he heard that Hiens and six other white men were living in an Indian village two hundred and forty miles away. Tonti was preparing to march there when all of his men save a Frenchman and the Shawnee hunter, weary from their ceaseless travel, refused to go any farther. Undeterred, he continued his journey in April, 1690, with two faithful men and five Indian guides; but a few days later the Frenchman, while crossing a river, lost his bag containing most of their powder. Even this incident failed to daunt Tonti's determination to press toward the village in which Hiens and his friends were said to reside. When he reached it, however, he found no trace of them. Its headmen tried to mislead him by telling him different stories of their whereabouts. "I no longer doubted," wrote Tonti, later, "that they had murdered them. So I told them that they had killed the Frenchmen. Directly all the women began to cry, and thus I saw that what I had said to them was true."[54] He refused their calumet, though he bartered with them seven hatchets and a string of large glass beads for four Spanish horses. With these he was ready to join his Indian allies; but León, anticipating him, sent forty mounted Spaniards to attack him in the village. Fortunately Tonti had left the village a few days before the Spaniards arrived. The military strength they displayed, moreover, seems to have convinced him that his puny and ill-equipped force stood no chance of success against them. So he abandoned all thought of pursuing the campaign and decided to retrace his route back to Fort St. Louis of the Illinois. In September, after suffering many hardships and illness which laid him up at Arkansas Post for several weeks, he and his men reached their destination.[55]

14

Iberville, Founder of Louisiana

THE WAR OF THE PALATINATE, KNOWN IN AMERICA AS KING WILLIAM'S War, which broke out two years after La Salle's death, discouraged any further effort Louis XIV might have made in favor of the colonization of the Mississippi Valley. The expense of the new conflict was, perhaps, only his principal deterrent. No sooner did Charles II of Spain learn that La Salle had occupied Matagorda Bay than he ordered Pedro Ronquillo, his ambassador to England, to enlist James II's support against further French advances in North America. Referring to the Papal Bull of 1493, by which Alexander VI had divided the newly discovered lands in the New World between Spain and Portugal, Ronquillo asserted Spain's prior claims. He requested James to convince Louis of the injustice of sending La Salle to the Gulf Coast. He told James, moreover, that no foreign nation could legally own any territory in America unless this was recognized by a treaty with Spain. Spain in 1670 had signed such a treaty with England, but she had none with France. Louis, in deciding against another expedition to the Mississippi Valley, may have been persuaded by James to forego for the present any further encroachment of Spanish territory in North America.[1]

Yet some leading men in France and Canada continued to urge the settlement of the Lower Mississippi Valley. One of these was Tonti who in 1694 offered the French court his services to establish a colony in Louisiana. He pointed out that French occupation of the region would not only prevent the English from seizing the Gulf coast but that it would also serve as a base for an attack on the Spanish colony of New Spain. Furthermore, he said, it would serve as a depository for the fur trade and the lead ore of the Illinois country.[2] His offer fell on deaf ears.

In 1697 the Treaty of Ryswick once more brought peace to Europe. It ended the shooting war, but it started the old war for colonial supremacy. Again leading Frenchmen revived plans to settle and fortify the Lower Mississippi Valley to prevent England or Spain from seizing it. They observed that aggressive fur traders from Carolina were already expanding westward to the Mississippi and southward to Florida. They recalled that the Treaty of Ryswick recognized each of the three powers as possessor of the territory it controlled when the war began, but they agreed that none was content and that each, coveting its neighbor's property, planned to take it as soon as it could repudiate the treaty.[3]

At the end of the same year a book appeared which had a profound influence on the French court and which hastened its plans to colonize the Lower Mississippi Valley. Written by Sieur de Rémonville, a Canadian nobleman and friend of La Salle, it described in glowing terms the natural beauty and resources of the region. Even more important, it stirred Louis XIV and his new minister of marine and colonies, Louis Phélypeaux, Count of Pontchartrain, to activity. This it did by telling of a rumor that William Penn, founder and governor of Pennsylvania, had already dispatched fifty men to found a settlement on the Wabash as a step preliminary to English occupation of the Lower Mississippi Valley.[4]

Rémonville's revelations and glowing descriptions of Louisiana stimulated French merchants into formulating plans for the establishment of what they called the "Louisiana Company." It proposed to ask the Crown to grant it full sovereignty to a tract of land stretching from Apalachicola Bay westward to New Mexico and from the Gulf of Mexico northward to the Illinois country. It also planned to request a monopoly of navigation to and from Louisiana for a period of fifty years, two warships with full supplies for fourteen months, and four hundred soldiers to protect and to keep order among the immigrants. The company itself proposed to furnish four ships to transport from seven to eight hundred immigrants. It intended to employ them in shipbuilding, developing pearl-fisheries, raising crops, and gathering buffalo wool which was falsely considered very valuable. The Crown, however, refused to co-operate in these plans. It feared that a private company would have no chance of success against possible Spanish and English armed opposition to French occupation of the Lower Mississippi Valley.

Furthermore, Pontchartrain needed no private encouragement to his aggressive plans. He was no less interested than his predecessor Seignelay had been in promoting La Salle's project in the Gulf region.[5]

The minister learned that Spain, too, was preparing to colonize the Lower Mississippi Valley which, as we have stated, she claimed as part of her ancient domain. Snce 1689 Andrés de Pez, a naval officer, had strongly advised his king, Charles II, to occupy Pensacola Bay to forestall its possible seizure by the French or English. After five years of hesitation Charles had issued a royal decree ordering the bay to be occupied and fortified; but the powerful Council of the Indies had opposed the plan, and it was never carried out. Then, in April, 1698, Charles learned that the French were planning to send an expedition to the Lower Mississippi Valley. Believing that their primary object was Pensacola Bay, he ordered the Count of Moctezuma, the Viceroy of New Spain, to occupy it without delay and without regard for cost. To assist this operation he sent two ships under Martín de Zavala, an intrepid naval captain. With him went Juan Jordan de Reina, who had accompanied previous expeditions to the bay and who had instructions to organize another expedition in Havana. Early in the fall Reina left Havana for the bay with two ships, fifty soldiers, and six cannon. Finding no French ships in the bay, he concluded correctly that he had won the race for it.[6]

Meanwhile Moctezuma had gathered a fleet in Vera Cruz and had placed it under Andrés de Arriola, who sailed immediately for Pensacola Bay, which he had visited three years before. On reaching it he joined Reina. He had orders to try to dislodge the French with force of arms if he found them in the bay and to return to Vera Cruz if he failed. Though he found no Frenchmen to fight, he feared that eventually they would arrive and that he could not prevent them from occupying another bay along the same coast. For the present, however, he resolved to safeguard Pensacola Bay against possible capture by a more powerful French fleet. He began to build in the harbor a fort and a presidio, while he prayed for further aid from Mexico or Spain.[7]

But what finally urged Pontchartrain to dispatch a fleet to the Gulf coast was the more formidable challenge of England. In 1698 Louis XIV's secret agents reported that Dr. Daniel Coxe, who had served as a court physician to Charles II, had purchased two grants collectively called Carolana. This was an enormous region extending from sea to sea between the thirty-first and the thirty-sixth parallels. There Coxe planned to establish a colony of Englishmen and of French Huguenots, refugees who were flocking to England and to other Protestant countries of Europe. While he seems to have decided to leave unmolested the Spanish possessions at St. Augustine and in New Mexico, he ignored the conflicting French claims in the region of the Mississippi. In his grandiose schemes he derived much propaganda value from Father Louis Hennepin who, in 1697, we will recall, had published his famous book in which he claimed for himself the honor of discovering the mouth of the Mississippi. In October, 1698, Coxe fitted out two ships which left England but which wintered in Charleston, South Carolina. In the spring one of the ships, the *Carolina Galley*, under Captain Bond, resumed her voyage, coasted along the Gulf of Mexico from Florida Cape to Rio Pánuco, entered the Mississippi, and sailed upstream for about one hundred miles. Here Bond learned that the French had already taken possession of Louisiana as a part of New France. Though he protested that the English had discovered and taken possession of the region more than fifty years before, he withdrew quietly and never returned.[8]

Pontchartrain had sent the French expedition from Brest in the previous October in anxious endeavor to beat its two competitors to the prize. To assure its success he avoided a divided command such as had wrecked La Salle's last expedition. The leader of the new enterprise, Pierre Lemoyne, Sieur d'Iberville, was both a sailor and an explorer. He was born in 1661 at Montreal, the third of the eleven sons of Charles Lemoyne, a gallant soldier of Lower Canada. Trained in the French navy and familiar from youth with war on the Canadian frontier, Iberville was eminently suited to his new undertaking. The English forts he had captured in the region of Hudson Bay and in Newfoundland were trophies of his fortitude, endurance, courage, and quick intelligence, and the exploits by which he settled colonies in Acadia and Cape Breton Island disclosed his unusual powers of imagination and diplomatic skill. Later he added new luster to his fame by engaging and sinking an English warship, capturing two smaller vessels, and rescuing Fort Nelson. Returning full of honors to France, he sought and obtained command of the new colonizing venture on the Mississippi.[9]

His fleet consisted of two ketches and two frigates, *La Badine* and

Le Marin, on which were several hundred men, women, and children, including his younger brother Sieur de Bienville, who was destined to succeed him as governor of Louisiana, Father Douay, and veterans of late wars. On December 4, 1698, Iberville arrived at Cape François, in Santo Domingo, where he enlisted the frigate *François* under Joubert, Marquis de Châteaumorant. Reinforced and provisioned, he resumed his journey toward the Gulf of Mexico by way of Cape San Antonio, at the western end of Cuba. On January 24, 1699, he touched at the mouth of the Apalachicola River in northern Florida and two days later he reached Pensacola Bay. There he found Arriola's two ships and his fort, which was still unfinished and which was now called Santa Maria de Galve. Iberville sent one of his officers to the Spanish commander for wood and water. Arriola received him cordially but advised him that the king forbade strangers, friendly as well as unfriendly, to enter the bay. On receiving this reply, Iberville, mindful that his mission was to occupy the mouth of the Mississippi and confident that the river did not flow into Pensacola Bay, decided to move westward. On January 31 he anchored off Mobile Bay, reconnoitered around it for several days, and continued westward along Dauphin, Petit Bois, Horn, and Ship islands which shelter Mississippi Sound. Then, piloting his ships through the deep passage between Cat Island and Ship Island, he anchored them on the lee of the latter within cannon shot of its shores.[10]

On the next day he paddled with his brother, Father Douay, and a small group of sailors to the mainland where, at present Cedar Point, he built temporary huts. Soon some of his men rounded up a few Indians and won their friendship with gifts. At the same time he fired guns "for their edification and amusement," while he invited them to examine the mechanics of his ships. Warming up to the white men, they showed their pleasure by rubbing their hands on their heads and bellies and on those of their guests and then raising them toward heaven. Bienville invited them to his hut, where he regaled them with numerous gifts, including axes, blankets, shirts, and knives, all of which they greatly prized. That evening he served them wine and whiskey, which delighted them, but which, he observed, they used more moderately than did the northern tribes.[11]

Confident that his goal was near, Iberville directed all of his energies toward finding the actual mouth of the Mississippi and ascending it in search of a place for permanent settlement. This he believed he could do without the help of the Marquis de Châteaumorant. He invited that nobleman to dinner on board *La Badine*, told him of his intention to undertake the rest of the expedition alone, and asked him for supplies of flour and wine. Châteaumorant obligingly transferred from his ship to *La Badine* all that Iberville needed and departed for Santo Domingo, which he reached early in April. In the ensuing month, after spending five weeks in extensive repairs on his leaky ship, he sailed for France. As soon as he reached home in the latter part of June he sent a long letter to Pontchartrain, informing him of the events of his voyage from the time he joined Iberville to his return to France. His letter provided the French authorities with their first information concerning the Spanish occupation of Pensacola Bay.[12]

Meanwhile, on February 11, Iberville sent a small group of sailors under Bienville in one of the ketches and a canoe to a point on the mainland twelve miles north of his anchorage on Ship Island. Bienville and his men entered present Biloxi Bay, where they discovered several canoes filled with half-naked Indians, who fled with alarm as they approached. On the next day, however, Bienville contrived to capture a squaw by whom he was able to talk to a number of persons of her tribe. They called themselves Biloxi, a name which Bienville bestowed on the little bay. That evening a band of eighty braves of the Bayogoula tribe arrived and from them Bienville learned by signs that they lived on the shores of a large and deep river. He ascertained, too, the river's probable distance and course. With this invaluable information he returned to his brother, who made immediate preparations to sail in quest of the great river.

On February 27 Iberville was ready. Leaving the two frigates on Ship Island, he sailed with the smaller boats in heavy rain past Cat Island. He turned southward along the low and marshy coast, and at twilight of the third day discovered a line of rocks projecting from the land. He could see a narrow ribbon of water stretching in the center of the rocks, and he steered toward it. This was North Pass, a branch of the delta of the Mississippi, which Father Douay recognized from its thick, whitish appearance and its turbidity. On the next day, Shrove Tuesday, the Frenchmen ascended the river, passed rushes and reeds that gradually gave way to trees, and fired salutes to attract the attention of the Indians. None appeared, however, until March 7, when the Frenchmen approached two men in a canoe who paddled vigorously toward the bank and, reaching it, fled into the woods. Presently they came on another canoe with five Indians. Four of them fled. The other was a curious fellow who dallied long enough to be overtaken. By giving him some trifling gift, which delighted him, they induced his comrades to join him. Iberville persuaded one of them to lead him to their village. There the chief, clad in bearskins and besmeared with mud to enhance his appearance, offered him an unusually large calumet embellished with multi-colored feathers. The chief waited while the Frenchmen smoked. Then, sitting down in one of Iberville's boats, he led them to the place where his braves and some of their wives had assembled to entertain them. There they accorded Iberville their customary abdominal caress, which he returned. They brought sagamite, beans, and Indian corn cooked in bear grease, all of which the Frenchmen hurriedly swallowed, as much from repugnance as from hunger. Iberville in turn offered them whiskey, which he diluted for the benefit of their unaccustomed palates, and made them gifts of needles, mirrors, and knives. While the braves danced and yelled to the sound of pebbles rattling in gourds, their chief appeared before Iberville in a superb blue coat which he said Tonti had given him several years before. Partly by signs and partly by words which Bienville had picked up, Iberville learned the names and locations of the tribes in the Lower Valley. Curious to see more of the valley and its inhabitants, he hastened his departure upstream. Presently he and his comrades came to a collection of huts in which many persons lay ill with smallpox. Nevertheless, the Frenchmen tarried long enough to enable Father Douay to celebrate mass and to present them with trinkets. The chief was given a pair of red stockings, two shirts, and a scarlet coat with gold lace trimmings. The Indians in turn gave the white men a number of buckskins, with which they patched their shoes, and invited them to a dinner of dried meat, which they found unpalatable.[13]

Continuing upstream, they arrived on March 16 at present Scotts Bluff, Louisiana. On the east bank of the river they saw a pole which had been daubed red and which was adorned with heads of fish and bears as a kind of sacrificial offering. This served as the marker separating the hunting grounds of the Bayogoulas from those of the Houmas.

Each tribe hated the other so much that they shot on sight any man caught hunting on the wrong side of the marker. The Indians called it *Istrouma,* which the French translated Baton Rouge, meaning Red Stick, the name of the present capital of Louisiana.[14]

Two days later Iberville and his men arrived at present day Profit Island, where the river forms a loop or cut-off which brings its banks close together. Here, at the Fauss River Cutoff, as it is called, the Indians advised the explorers that they could save a day's journey by dragging their boats across the intervening neck of land. This task alone took two days, for they had to remove a pile of wood and debris thirty feet high and had to clear a path over three hundred feet long before they could launch their boats on the other side of the portage. Presently they arrived at a Houma village just north of Tunica Island, where a delegation of its leading men met Iberville and presented him with a calumet which, being no smoker, he quickly passed to his friends. The Indians feasted and entertained them with dances.[15]

For several days Iberville had been keeping a sharp lookout for a fork of the Mississippi which, Father Membré had written, flowed eastward toward the Gulf of Mexico and which, if it existed, would have provided a shorter route for his return voyage to Ship Island. He asked the Indians, who, however, assured him that no such fork existed. Eventually he was constrained to brand Father Membré a liar and to regard the river before him as the main stream. For another day he proceeded upstream, perhaps to the junction of the Red and the Mississippi rivers at present Pointe Coupee Parish, Louisiana. Then, finding himself short of provisions, he started on the return journey to his frigates on Ship Island. Now that he was traveling with the current, he made better progress than on his outward journey. On March 24 he found himself at Bayou Manchac, a little stream which leads to Lake Pontchartrain, which in turn leads to the Gulf of Mexico. Since this offered a shorter route to his frigates, he decided to take it; but the stream was too shallow for his boats. So he divided his party, sending Bienville and the Sieur de Sauvole down the river with the large boats under instructions to meet him at Ship Island. With four men and an Indian guide Bienville himself launched on the bayou in two birchbark canoes. They found their journey difficult. On the first day, they had to cross two portages. On the second day, they made perhaps as many as fifty portages over masses of fallen trees and brushwood. On the third, their guide complicated matters by deserting. Fortunately, the stream grew wider and deeper as they traveled. They soon passed from the bayou to the Amite River, which was swollen by recent rains. From the Amite they entered a small salt lake which Iberville named Maurepas in honor of Pontchartrain's eldest son. Crossing it hurriedly, they found its outlet. It was a short stream called Pass Manchac that led them to a much larger salt lake which Iberville called Pontchartrain in honor of the minister of marine. Making his way along its southern shore, he reached the Rigolets, a channel of considerable depth that led to the Gulf of Mexico.[16]

On March 30 he camped at a place on the mainland across Mississippi Sound from Ship Island. That night he lighted a blazing fire to attract the attention of the men on board his frigates. The next day, when he approached Ship Island, he met two boats which were coming to investigate the fire and one of which carried him to his flagship. Just two hours later his brother and Sauvole arrived from North Pass. The time that had been saved on mileage had been spent in crossing the numerous and difficult portages on their route between Bayou Manchac and Lake Pontchartrain.[17]

They told Iberville that their voyage down the Mississippi had been largely uneventful. One incident, however, was worthy of mention. They had heard of the letter which, we will recall, Tonti addressed to La Salle in 1685 and left in the care of a chief. Learning from the Houmas that this chief lived in the Mugulasha village farther south, they spared no effort to locate him, for Tonti's letter would furnish incontestable proof that the river was none other than the Mississippi. Before they reached North Pass they sent out messengers offering the reward of a hatchet to the Indian who would produce the letter. In a short time the chief came to the Frenchmen with the "speaking bark," as he called the letter, and gladly exchanged it for a good axe. Indeed, he threw into the bargain a prayer book in which was written the name of one of La Salle's men.[18]

These articles tied loose historical threads together to confirm Iberville's claims to the Mississippi. He now cast about for a suitable location on which to build a permanent settlement. Early in April he visited a small bay a few miles north of Ship Island and named it St. Louis. He liked its appearance, but its entrance proved too shallow for his frigates.

Pascagoula Bay was likewise unsuitable. Eventually he selected a fair, sandy glade of raised coast on the eastern shore of Biloxi Bay, near present Ocean Springs, Mississippi. In making this choice he reasoned that it was strategically located. A fort here could control the northern shore of the Gulf of Mexico as well as the mouth of the Mississippi River. On April 8 he set his men to work to build Fort Maurepas.[19] It had four bastions that looked out over sand as white as silver, over broad, sunny waters that recalled the Mediterranean, and over majestic live oaks and splendid magnolias in whose branches birds of brilliant plumage sang incessantly. Its armament consisted of twelve cannon. Protected on its sides by deep gorges or gullies, on its front by water, and on its rear by a dense forest, it had all the natural advantages of a formidable stronghold. Iberville strengthened its rear, which he thought was its weakest point, with an entrenchment that ran to the gullies. When the fort was completed he ordered twenty-five men to clear the land around it and to plant peas and beans. He also supplied it for the present with a few cows, some pigs, and a bull. On May 3, four days after its completion, he left the fort under Sauvole with Bienville as second in command. He sailed with his frigates for France to enlist new colonies and obtain fresh supplies. His voyage was uneventful. Sailing through the old Bahama Channel and touching on Santo Domingo, he arrived at La Rochelle early in July. [20]

In compliance with Iberville's instructions, Sauvole and Bienville organized Fort Maurepas for the coming winter. They also built a suitable house, opened a hospital, and made a clearing around the fort. Later in the summer Sauvole sent Bienville to visit the Colapisses at the present sites of Mandeville, Houltonville, and Madisonville along the northern shores of Lake Pontchartrain. Guided by a Bayogoula chief and five of his men who had visited the fort and were now returning home, Bienville approached one of the villages to find its inhabitants ranged in battle array. He sent the chief to request an explanation of their hostile attitude. They replied that, just two days before, two hundred Chickasaws under two English slave hunters from Carolina had attacked one of the villages and had carried its inhabitants into captivity. The guide assured them that their present visitors were Frenchmen who sought nothing save their friendship and support against their common enemies. Whereupon the Colapisses laid down their arms and

234

received Bienville and his men with great cordiality. In return for a few presents Bienville gained their promises of reciprocal friendship, alliance, and support.[21]

He returned to Fort Maurepas only to undertake another expedition, this time to Pascagoula bay and river. He also explored Round Island, Mobile Bay, and, at its mouth, Dauphin Island. Everywhere he was accorded receptions which encouraged him to extend his explorations to Bayou Plaquemines and Bayou Chetimachas which his brother had described. Then he crossed Lakes Pontchartrain and Maurepas, ascended Bayou Manchac, reached the Mississippi, and began to descend it. On September 16, when he arrived at a point where the river makes a considerable bend a few miles below the present site of New Orleans, he met an English frigate, the *Carolina Galley* under Captain Lewis Bond. Bond, as we have seen, was in the employ of Dr. Daniel Coxe, proprietor of the Carolina grant. With characteristic boldness Bienville boarded the frigate and informed her captain, whom he had met and fought on Hudson Bay several years before, of France's prior claims to the Mississippi Valley. Whatever his arguments were, they must have been convincing, for Bond turned his frigate and withdrew peacefully. By so doing he bestowed on the bend of the river associated with this incident the name English Turn, which it retains to this day. The incident may be regarded as a harbinger of that bloody struggle which England and France fought intermittently until 1763, when the latter, with a scratch of the pen, surrendered an empire which had taken her two centuries to secure and develop.

Bienville returned to Fort Maurepas, which he found in desperate straits. Six months had now gone by without any trace of Iberville, and the fort was desperately in need of supplies. Some renegade Spaniards from Pensacola Bay had convinced the colonists that Louisiana was another Golconda. Therefore, instead of planting crops, they preferred to explore the region for gold and other precious metals, leaving their homes to an invasion of alligators and snakes that terrified and jeopardized their families. "Unless a mine is discovered," wrote Sauvole, ironically, "the king will not be compensated for his services." The extreme weather intensified the general misery. The summer had been oppressively hot. Marine worms ruined the hulls of the boats. The reflection from the sand was blinding and intolerable. The water was undrinkable. The meat was stringy and, in the absence of refrigeration, sometimes putrid. Then in November the weather suddenly turned so cold that "water, when poured into tumblers to rinse them, froze immediately, before it could be used." But much of their suffering stemmed from their own pride and laziness. Many of them were *coureurs de bois* who delighted in hunting and trapping and who knew nothing, and cared to know nothing, about farming. By December, fever and starvation had reduced the number of persons in the colony to about one hundred and fifty, many of whom were ready to desert or mutiny.[22]

Such was the condition of the colonists when, on December 7, they heard cannon booming from the direction of Ship Island. All of them rushed down to the shore, where they lingered for days that must have seemed like weeks, praying for Iberville to rescue them from their misery. At last, on January 7, 1700, he arrived with two ships, *La Renommée*, fifty guns, and *La Gironde*, forty-six guns, bringing fresh supplies and sixty new colonists. To Sauvole he brought the king's compliments and the commission of governor or commander of Louisiana. To Bienville he brought the rank of lieutenant. Iberville was directed "to breed the buffalo at Biloxi, to seek for pearls, to examine the wild mulberry with a view to silk, timber for ship-building, and to seek for mines."[23] To explore the mines in the country of the Sioux, far to the north, Iberville brought his brother-in-law Pierre-Charles le Sueur, a geologist who had taken part in Canadian explorations and had brought back with him a cargo of green or blue earth which he claimed contained copper.

Learning that the English had threatened to seize the mouth of the Mississippi, Iberville resolved to forestall them from making any such attempt in the future. On February 1, after making a preliminary expedition to Lake Pontchartrain and Bayou St. John, he set out from Fort Maurepas with sixty men. They went in a ketch and two feluccas to search for a suitable site on which to build a fort. About fifty miles upstream, at present Phoenix in Plaquemines Parish, Louisiana, his Bayogoula guide pointed out a wooded bluff which he asserted was never flooded. Here Iberville decided to build the fort. He spent the next two weeks supervising his men while they cleared the ground and cut logs of red cypress for a two-story structure twenty-eight feet square. Father Paul du Ru, who was soon to become chaplain at Fort Maurepas, wrote in his journal that he had "the honor of doing the first formal act of clearing, but not without getting very wet, thanks to the

236

bad weather." High winds and intermittent heavy rains, indeed, impeded them from making any real progress for several more weeks.
When only a house and a powder magazine had been completed,
Iberville, leaving fifteen men under his brother to complete the fort,
departed upstream to visit the Bayogoulas. When he returned six weeks
later he was chagrined to find that the fort was still unfinished. On
December 17 Father Jacques Gravier visited it on his journey downstream from the Illinois country. He observed that it had no "bastion,
entrenchment or redoubt; all consists of a battery of six guns, six and
eight pounders, planted on the brow of the bluff, and of five or six cabins
separate from each other and covered with palm leaves."[24] Eventually
the fort was completed. It was named the Mississippi Fort or Fort de la
Boulaye or Fort Boulaye either from the old French word *boulaie*,
meaning a plot of beech trees which sheltered one of its sides, or, as
Marcel Giraud suggests, in honor of Pierre La Boulaye, a member of
its garrison.[25]

The fort was the first French settlement in present Louisiana.
Though its population never exceeded twenty-five and though it was
abandoned and forgotten within fifteen years, it may have been one of
the most important forts that France built in all of North America. It
secured for that country the vast territory of Louisiana, from which
many American states were eventually carved. Its presence prevented
England from seizing the infant colony at a time when it was in no
position to defend itself. By giving France official control of the Mississippi Valley, it linked Canada with the Gulf of Mexico, thereby realizing
the great dream of Father Marquette, Jean Talon, and Robert de la
Salle. France now definitely owned Louisiana, whose innumerable
Indian tribes she could Christianize and civilize. "The historian of our
own day," wrote Maurice Ries, "could not know how vital was to be
the simple act of building a rude little fort on the river-bank against
the swamp and bayous nearby. And since it endured only a few brief
years, vanishing utterly from the face of the earth, historians of a later
time have neglected it. They have failed to consider what the ultimate
importance of the first French fort in present-day Louisiana might be.
Nothing *happened* there, they say, and dismiss the subject from mind.
It is not what occurred there that matters; it is what that outpost made
possible to happen."[26]

On February 17, 1700, when Iberville's men had scarcely completed preliminary work on the fort, they saw in the twilight several canoes sweeping down the river toward them. The canoes contained twenty-two men, one of whom was none other than Henri de Tonti. He had come down from the Illinois country, had traded with several tribes, had heard that Iberville had established the colony of Louisiana, and had decided to ascertain if he could be of any service to him. The two men were old friends; they were delighted to see each other. When Iberville declared his intention of visiting the Cenis farther up the river, Tonti, who was well acquainted with that tribe, offered to accompany him. Iberville, who greatly needed reinforcements, accepted his services. He decided to try to cultivate friendly relations with the tribes living to the north and west of the fort. He sent Bienville ahead with a felucca and two boats, and left the fort to a garrison of fifteen men under Sieur de Maltot. On February 19, he departed with Tonti and his men for the Bayogoula village. There he stayed for several days, giving its inhabitants a variety of gifts and cotton seed which was perhaps the first to be planted in present Louisiana. Then he continued upstream to the Houmas, whom he reprimanded for breaking their friendship with the Bayogoulas and for making war on them. Though the Houmas blamed the Bayogoulas for beginning the war, they agreed to end it if Iberville would serve as peacemaker. Since he was unwilling to leave these tribes warring behind him, Iberville complied with their request. Constituting himself a diplomat of the Bayogoulas, he persuaded his hosts to release their prisoners in return for a suitable gift, as custom required in such circumstances.[27]

At or near the Houma village Iberville changed his mind in regard to Tonti. He requested him to go to the Chickasaw country and arrest an Englishman who had offered presents to some Chickasaws to murder Father Antoine Davion, one of the missionaries. For ten or twelve years the Englishman had employed a number of Chickasaws in seizing peaceful Indians of other tribes. He was particularly interested in young men and women, whom he sold as slaves to rice planters in Carolina. Tonti disliked this assignment. He suspected that his old enemies, the Jesuits, had disparaged him in a letter to Iberville. He thought that Iberville had consequently cooled toward him because of his devotion to the Jesuits and his unwillingness to offend them. His suspicions were groundless. Iberville's change of mind was determined, not by the Jesuits, but by Tonti's own friend, the Superior of the Foreign Missions.

238

This man was convinced that Tonti was the only man who could intimidate the Chickasaws into giving up the captive missionary without harming him. In the end the Chickasaws allowed Davion to depart in peace, and Tonti, instead of going to his rescue, was free to continue his journey to the Illinois country.[28]

For the present, however, Tonti remained with the Houmas, while Iberville resumed his voyage upstream. On March 11 Iberville reached the Natchez village, which stood on elevated ground near the site of the present city of the same name. Its chief received him with every cordiality and gave him a letter which Father François Joliet de Montigny had addressed to him before setting out for his mission among the Taënsas. The letter contained invaluable information about the Natchez. Next morning Iberville, leaving his brother with a few men to gather a supply of flour which he needed for the journey he had planned to the Cenis, departed with six men in a canoe to the village of the Taënsas, where he found Father Montigny, who had built a house and was planning to build a church. The Taënsas welcomed Iberville warmly and obtained for him a guide who, in return for a handsome gift, consented to lead him overland to the Cenis. But as Iberville was preparing to set out for their principal village, he contracted an illness, perhaps rheumatism or arthritis, which prevented him from walking. This compelled him to curtail his voyage. On March 22 he bade his brother farewell, sending him up the Red River to ascertain if Indian reports were true that Spain had established settlements on its banks. Iberville descended the river to the Houmas, where he found Tonti. Next morning, while Tonti departed for the Illinois country, Iberville proceeded to the Bayogoulas, where Father du Ru had established a mission. From there he hurried to Fort Boulaye. There he came down with a more serious ailment, yellow fever, which was eventually to cause his death. Three weeks passed by before he felt well enough to resume his journey to the Gulf and thence to Fort Maurepas on Biloxi Bay.[29]

Meanwhile Bienville was being guided by a Wichita Indian whose tribe lived west of the Mississippi and who claimed to have visited one of the Spanish missions in eastern Texas. Bienville continued by land and water along the Red River through swampy northern Louisiana, until on April 20 he reached the Yatassi. They told him that the Spanish mission on the Neches was nearby, though in reality it had been abandoned seven years before. This misinformation, however, led him to believe that he was approaching Spanish territory. He therefore returned to the Mississippi, to Fort Boulaye, and, finally, on May 18, to Fort Maurepas.[30]

He found his brother preparing to leave the colony. Iberville needed medical attention and the fort needed fresh supplies. On May 28, placing Sauvole in charge of the fort, he sailed away. But he had no intention of heading for La Rochelle. Always scheming to break English power in North America, he steered *La Renommé* up the Atlantic to New York Harbor, boldly entered it, and enlisted the services of a pilot from New Jersey. Availing himself of official peace between France and England, he headed up the Narrows, apparently to take on wood and water. He stayed there for a month, succeeding in taking complete soundings between Sandy Hook and the Battery despite the sleepless vigilance of the British authorities. Then, satisfied that he could accomplish no more for the present, he sailed for La Rochelle and home.[31]

Tonti's mission to the Chickasaws was the last recorded event of his life. In 1704 he descended the Mississippi and continued to Mobile, where in September he died, perhaps of yellow fever. We know nothing of his last hours. Either record of them has perished or no friend or priest was with him when he died. He was only in his early fifties. But though not old in point of years, he was old in experience and knowledge of the world. His contributions to exploration and to the fur trade played an important part in the eventual settlement of the Mississippi Valley. By emphasizing the economic importance of the valley and by repeated warnings that it might fall to the English, he revived the flagging interest of the French court in the Louisiana country. Though he established no colony himself, his zeal and persistent efforts in behalf of colonization helped to make possible Iberville's expedition and the founding of permanent settlements in Louisiana. We have seen that a letter which Tonti addressed to La Salle enabled Iberville fourteen years later to identify the Mississippi River. In the last seventeen years of his life Tonti made the Mississippi Valley the chief scene of his activities, covering more territory than he had in his ceaseless wanderings with La Salle. He retained his admirable qualities of endurance and leadership to the end. But his crowning virtue was patience, which his great friend La Salle manifestly lacked.[32]

240

15

Le Sueur: Early Mining
in Minnesota

LATE IN FEBRUARY OR EARLY MARCH, 1700, PIERRE-CHARLES LE SUEUR with nineteen men in a shallop, a small sailing vessel, reached the mouth of the Mississippi on their way to explore the Upper Valley for copper mines. He was thoroughly schooled in frontier life. In early youth he had migrated with his parents from Artois to Canada, where he became interested in the fur trade. In 1683 and again in 1689 he accompanied Nicolas Perrot to the region of Lake Pepin. In 1692 Count Frontenac, who was again governor of Canada, commissioned Le Sueur to build a post at La Pointe, in Chequamegon Bay, for the purpose of maintaining a recently concluded peace between the Chippewas and the Sioux and of protecting both the latter and the French against attacks by their Fox and Mascoutin enemies during their lucrative fur trade on the water route between Lake Superior and the St. Croix River. In the following year Le Sueur journeyed to the Sioux country. There he established another post on present Prairie Island in the Mississippi, about nine miles below Hastings, Minnesota. That summer he returned to Montreal with a cargo of beaver skins and a band of Chippewas and Sioux. Among the latter was Tioscate, a chief who, with much ceremonial weeping and yelling, promised Frontenac the loyalty of his tribe in return for protection against his enemies. But Tioscate sickened and died in Montreal. Le Sueur, instead of returning with him to Prairie Island, as he had intended, sailed for France. There he obtained a license to open certain copper mines which supposedly existed in present Minnesota. During his return voyage, however, he fell into the hands of the English, who took him to their country and imprisoned him. When he gained his release a year or more later he went to France, where he obtained a new license to work the copper mines in the Upper Mississippi Valley. For this purpose he came to the New World with his brother-in-law Iberville.[1]

The main chronicler of Le Sueur's expedition was André-Joseph Pénigaut or, as American historians spell his name, Pénicaut, a young carpenter whom explorers sought out as much for his expert shipbuilding as for his aptitude in Indian languages. Though he often erred in his dates and in estimating distances between points of his itinerary, he was nearly always reliable in reporting details and he was often entertaining in his style. Pénicaut tells us that he and his men stopped at Fort Boulaye, where they found Bienville and another young Frenchman, Louis Juchereau de St. Denis. These men gave him a canoe to lighten the burden of his shallop and to enable him to make better progress upstream. Even so, they were unable to cover more than from fifteen to eighteen miles a day, for the river had flooded its banks with the melting snows of spring. At last they reached the country of the Quapaws. The Indians received them with much courtesy and sang the calumet but, being either indolent or indifferent in their agricultural pursuits, were able to give them little food. So they hurriedly resumed their voyage, passing the Wolf River at present Memphis, the Chickasaw Bluffs and Iron Banks below Fort Jefferson in Carlisle County, Kentucky, and the Ohio River. In June the troupe reached Grand Tower, in Jackson County, Illinois, where the French often obtained millstones for their mills. Here their provisions gave out, forcing them to delay their journey for twenty-three days. Every morning each of them went out into the woods to seek his living off the end of his gun. Some of them kept alive by drinking wood sap, others by eating young leaves or shoots from trees. Three of them crossed in their canoe to the western bank where they separated to hunt, probably near the river hills above Cape Girardeau in present Missouri. One of them, Polonis, saw two bears in a little ravine. They were walking toward him, one behind the other. Quickly hiding behind a tree, he wounded one of the bears with a load of shot between its eyes as it approached, almost blinding it. Stunned and unable to see, it turned this way and that, giving Polonis time to kill it with a bullet. His companions, hearing the two shots, hurried to his side and rejoiced at the sight of the dead animal. They

242

cut it up in large pieces, carried it to the shallop, and feasted on it for seven or eight days, for, wrote Pénicaut, "the bears from the banks of the Missicipy are as fat as beeves and very good to eat."[2]

When they were again without food, they fortunately met Father de Bontville. He was going downstream from the Illinois country to visit Iberville. Learning that Iberville had sailed for France, however, he turned homeward. Before his departure he gave Le Sueur and his men what of his own provisions he could spare and promised to send them relief as soon as he reached home. He was as good as his word. Paddling night and day, he reached the Illinois country in record time and immediately started Father Joseph Limoges downstream with a boat full of all kinds of provisions. These reached Le Sueur and his men in twenty-two days, at the time of their greatest need. "We were delighted," wrote Pénicaut, "to find such an abundance of things to eat. . . . Each man threw himself upon them. The Reverend Father thought that we were going to eat so much that we would get sick; and he was very much astonished that each of us did not eat one fourth pound of meat and just as much of a kind of flat cake or pie. But we evened things up by drinking quite a deal of the wine of Spain."[3]

Three days later, when they had regained their strength, they resumed their journey. They passed Cinque Hommes Creek in Perry County, Missouri, the Kaskaskia River in southwest Illinois, two springs where the French and the Illinois usually obtained their salt, and the Meramec River by which Indians journeyed to a lead mine far inland. About fifty miles upstream the voyagers found a village of the Illinois tribe. They headed their boats in under sail,

> firing ten or twelve canister shots, at which the savages were greatly surprised, and they were even more surprised at seeing our [shallop], since they have only small canoes made from the bark of trees, which come to them from Canada, and a few pirogues like those in the Lower Missicipy. When we got off the boat, they approached us, along with more than thirty Canadian traders who had come to barter for pelts. The French that were living among the Illinois armed themselves and gave an agreeable reception to [Le Sueur], whom they had already seen in Canada.[4]

In the village lived three French missionaries. One was Jean Bergier, a priest of the seminary of Foreign Missions in Paris. Another was Jean François Buisson de Cosme, who had supervised the building of the

243

Tamaroa mission in 1699. The Indians sang the calumet to Le Sueur, who gave them substantial presents. They remained for seventeen days with this hospitable company. Four of them left the expedition and went to Canada. Le Sueur, however, took on five others, among whom was Jean Baptiste Chaponga, who spoke a number of Indian languages and whom he hired as an interpreter.[5]

From this village they proceeded to the mouth of the Missouri. They reached it on July 12 and found it overflowing its banks and uprooting and carrying trees away in the raging and rushing current. Nobody, wrote Pénicaut, knew the source of the Missouri or of the Mississippi. He also admitted that he knew nothing about the tribes who lived on the banks of these rivers. Another day's hard paddling brought them to the mouth of the Illinois. On its banks, wrote our chronicler, were the most beautiful and most expansive plains in the world. Heading for one of the banks, they made camp, perhaps in what is now Lincoln County, Missouri. They sent out four men to bring in some meat. Presently the hunters returned with a buffalo and a buffalo cow, cut themselves some steaks, broiled them, and washed them down with several bottles of brandy, which, wrote Pénicaut, greatly restored them. In a jovial mood they continued their journey to a small river and there they met four Canadians who were descending the Mississippi on their way to the Illinois country. A little later they met seventeen Sioux in seven canoes. Their chief told Le Sueur that he and his men were going to war on the Tamaroas, who had killed two of their friends and burned another. Le Sueur, remembering that he promised the Illinois to appease the Sioux, gave the chief a present to dissuade him from his intention. He told him that the king of France did not wish them to make the Father of Waters more bloody and that he had been sent to tell them that, if they did his bidding, they would receive in the future all that they asked of him. The chief accepted Le Sueur's present, thereby signifying that he would do as the white man advised.[6]

During the month of August they traveled over two hundred miles almost without incident to the vicinity of the Wisconsin River. There they met five Canadians, one of whom had a serious wound in his head. They were naked and had no weapons save a rusty gun with five or six loads of powder and balls. They said that, as they were descending from the country of the Sioux to that of the Tamaroas, they had been surprised, beaten, and robbed by ninety Indians of various tribes in nine canoes. They joined the expedition, which now counted twenty-eight men. As it proceeded a little distance upstream the Canadians saw on the river the Indians who had attacked them. One of the white men shouted to them that if they approached any closer they would fire on them. So saying, they drew up on an island at half the distance of a gun shot. Soon they saw four of the principal men of the band approaching in a canoe. Their spokesman asked in a stentorian voice if they had forgotten that all men were brothers and why they had taken arms when they had seen them. Le Sueur replied that he had reason to distrust them, for they had robbed five men in his party. Mindful, however, that he must keep peace with all the tribes for the good of the trade, he demanded no redress for the robbery. He told them, however, that the king, their master and his, wished all of his subjects to navigate the great river without insult or injury and that they had better beware of how they conducted themselves. The Indian who had spoken was silent, but another begged Le Sueur to have pity on them and to lend them a little powder so that they might shoot enough game to keep them from starving until they reached their villages. Le Sueur, remembering that a missionary was about to depart for the country of the Sioux, won their friendship by giving them what they requested.[7]

Early in September they arrived at Lake Pepin, a widening of the Mississippi which they called *Bon Secours,* meaning Harbor of Refuge, because of the numerous buffaloes, elks, and deer they found there. West of it rose a chain of mountains abounding in caverns ranging from forty to seventy feet in depth and from three to four feet in height. Bears hibernated in them during the winter months. In his journal of the expedition Le Sueur wrote that the caverns were also dangerous in the summer time, "for they are filled with rattlesnakes, the bite of which is very dangerous." Le Sueur "saw some of these snakes which were six feet in length, but generally they are about four feet. They have teeth resembling those of the pike, and their gums are full of small vessels, in which their poison is placed."[8]

A few days later they came to the Falls of St. Anthony, which, wrote Pénicaut, they had heard six miles away. He describes the falls as the entire Mississippi falling suddenly from a height of sixty feet and "making a noise similar to thunder rumbling through the air." Unable to pass with their boats over the falls they descended the Mississippi a short distance to the Minnesota River, made their way through its mouth, and ascended it for over a hundred miles to another river, which Pénicaut calls Mankato but which is now called the Blue Earth. Here, near the present city of Mankato, in Blue Earth County, Minnesota, they ended their voyage, for they were "unable to go higher on account of the ice and it was already the last day of September, when winter has already set in, which is quite severe in that region." Here, on a large natural mound overlooking its eastern bank, just below where it joins the Le Sueur, he built Fort L'Huillier, named in honor of a minister of agriculture who had once done him a favor. It consisted of three or four log cabins enclosed by a palisade of bur oaks obtained on or near the mound. A few feet from the fort flowed a fine large stream.[9]

The Sioux told Le Sueur that they greatly objected to Fort L'Huillier because it stood in a region which such hostile tribes as the Sioux of the West, the Iowas, and the Otos claimed as part of their ancient domain. The explorer was unwilling to move, and planned to use the Sioux as workmen in the mines he hoped to open in the spring. He appeased them with numerous presents, including fifty pounds of powder, six guns, ten axes, and twelve armsful of tobacco and a hatchet pipe. At the same time he urged them to abandon their nomadic life and form a village near the fort. There he promised to shield them from their enemies, to provide them with the necessities of life, and even to grant them enough ground to plant corn and wheat. He explained to them that his king and chief had

> forbidden him to purchase beaver skins, knowing that this kind of hunting separates them and exposed them to their enemies; and that in consequence of this he had come to establish himself on Blue River and vicinity, where they had many times assured him were many kinds of beasts, for the skins of which he would give them all things necessary; that they ought to reflect that they could not do without French goods, and that the only way not to want them was, not to go to war with our allied nations.[10]

The Sioux agreed to do his bidding.

The voyagers spent the entire winter in their huts, which they had built inside the fort. They lived on the flesh of four buffaloes they had killed that fall. They skinned, gutted, and quartered them, and hung the pieces on scaffolds to dry. That winter they had nothing to eat save the buffalo meat, which they shared with seven Canadians who, robbed and entirely stripped by a band of Sioux, had taken refuge with them. At first they hated the very smell of the meat, for they had no salt with which to flavor it. For the first two weeks, wrote Pénicaut, "we had trouble enough getting accustomed to it: we had diarrhea and fever and became so squeamish that we could not taste it; but little by little our bodies became so accustomed to it that after six weeks there was not one of us who did not eat more than ten pounds of it daily and drink four bowls of the broth. When we got used to that kind of food, it made us quite fat, and there were no more sick among us."[11]

Le Sueur sprinkled his usually matter-of-fact journal with some interesting pictures of Sioux life. They told him that they had three souls, one bad, one good, and one which guarded their bodies after death. He tells us that they were very jealous and that they often fought duels for their wives. "They manage to bow admirably, and have been seen several times to kill ducks on the wing. . . . They are all great smokers, but their manner of smoking differs from that of other Indians. There are some . . . who swallow all the smoke of the tobacco, and others who, after having kept it some time in their mouth, cause it to issue from the nose."[12]

When spring came Le Sueur went with twelve men and four hunters to a very long mountain that rose from the bank of the Blue Earth River and put them to work at what he thought was a copper mine. "The stratum where the ore is found is a green clay, that is a foot and a half thick. Above, there is dirt as solid and as hard as a rock, which is black and charred, like a coal, from the fumes coming from the mine. We scratched the copper with a knife." What Le Sueur thought was copper ore was nothing but clay, which the Indians had used from time immemorial as pigment. Le Sueur had two tons of it carried to the fort in three canoes for the purpose of transporting it in his shallop to Fort Maurepas and on to France.[13]

A month later, when he was about to begin his return journey, he traded with the Sioux. He gave them Brazilian tobacco, two little horn-handled knives, and four leaden bullets in exchange for four hundred beaver robes, each of which was made of nine skins sewn together. Just before his departure he gave command of the fort to one of his best officers, Daraque, with twelve men. Meanwhile he exhorted three of the leading chiefs to live in complete peace with the garrison. He promised Daraque that he would send him some ammunition as soon as he reached the Illinois country. He kept his word, sending three of his men back to Fort L'Huillier with two thousand pounds of lead and powder. Unfortunately, the canoe that carried this precious cargo was overturned, perhaps during a storm or a flood, in some treacherous point in the river.[14]

On February 10, 1702, Le Sueur reached Fort Maurepas on Biloxi Bay. In the following April he sailed for France with his cousin Iberville, who had completed his third sojourn in Louisiana. We know nothing of what became of the "ore" that Le Sueur took with him. In this case no news was perhaps bad news, for, had the assayers of Paris found any value in Le Sueur's cargo, they surely would have left some record of it to satisfy the curiosity of future writers as well as readers of American frontier history.

Fort L'Huillier, too, came to a sad end. In the winter after Le Sueur departed for Fort Maurepas, a band of Foxes and their Mascouten or Miami allies suspected a band of Sioux of obtaining arms from the Frenchmen. They attacked the Sioux as they were going into or coming out of the fort, killed seventeen of them as well as three members of the garrison and carried away their heads as trophies for the scalp dance. The surviving Frenchmen managed to repel the Sioux and, emerging from the fort with picks and shovels, buried the dead men. But, finding themselves without powder and lead to repel any possible attacks in the future, they hurriedly buried what goods they had, abandoned the fort, and journeyed downstream to Fort Maurepas, where they informed the authorities of what had occurred.[15]

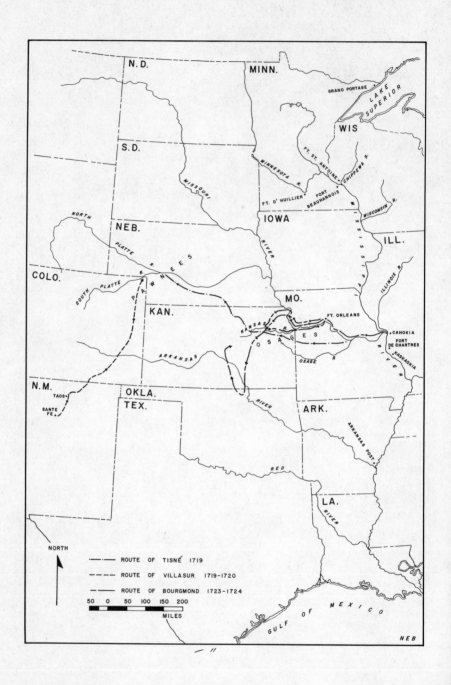

N.D.

MINN.

GRAND PORTAGE

LAKE SUPERIOR

WIS

S.D.

MISSOURI

MINNESOTA R.

FT. ST. ANTOINE • CHIPPEWA R.

FT. D' HUILLIER • FORT BEAUHARNOIS

WISCONSIN R.

MISSISSIPPI

NORTH

NEB.

IOWA

RIVER

ILL.

PLATTE R.

COLO.

SOUTH PLATTE R.

PAWNEES

ILLINOIS R.

KAN.

MO.

FT. ORLEANS

KANSAS R.

CAHOKIA FORT DE CHARTRES

OSAGES

KASKASKIA

OSAGE R.

RIVER

ARKANSAS

N.M.

TAOS •

OKLA.

RIVER

ARK.

ARKANSAS POST

SANTE FE •

TEX.

RED

LA.

RIVER

NORTH

——·— ROUTE OF TISNÉ 1719

——— ROUTE OF VILLASUR 1719-1720

——— ROUTE OF BOURGMOND 1723-1724

50 0 50 100 150 200
MILES

GULF OF MEXICO

GULF OF

NEB

— 11

16

Early Explorers of the Missouri

BY THE ELEMENT OF CHANCE WHICH, LIKE THAT OF ACCIDENT OR IRONY, confounds the application of theory to any general phase of history, the Middle Valley was first settled in the same year, and almost in the same month, as the Lower Valley. While Iberville was building Fort Maurepas at Biloxi Bay, Seminary Fathers of Quebec, or, as they are perhaps better known, the Fathers of the Society of Foreign Missions, were founding the Mission of the Holy Family of the Tamaroas, now Cahokia, Illinois. This mission was located on the east bank of the Mississippi almost directly opposite the site on which St. Louis was to rise more than a generation later. It was the first settlement in the Illinois country, a term which the French gave to the Middle and Upper valleys on both sides of the Mississippi and which included, therefore, present Illinois and Missouri. The founding of Cahokia in 1699 encouraged further settlement of the Middle Valley. In the autumn of the following year the Kaskaskians, perhaps in keeping with Iberville's plan of developing the Mississippi Valley by relocating its tribes, migrated from their village on the Illinois River to the west bank of the Mississippi. There, five or six miles below Cahokia and either on the mouth or close to the mouth of the stream subsequently known as Rivière des Pères, meaning The River of the Fathers, they founded a settlement within the corporate limits of present St. Louis.[1] The river derived its name from their Jesuit pastors, François Pinet and Gabriel Marest, who followed them and built, with the assistance of French traders, a wooden chapel, cabins, and a small fortification. To this village, whose name is unknown, migrated Rouensa, chief of the Kaskaskians, offering his people every inducement to follow him. So many of them agreed to go that Father Jean Bergier, parish priest of Cahokia, was constrained to keep them by laying before them such counterattractions as "a kettle, four pounds of powder, a pound of colored glass beads, four boxes of vermilion, and a dozen knives."[2] These gifts seem to have had the desired effect. Only a third of the Cahokians, including their chief, Long Neck, moved to the village across the Mississippi. Rouensa had expected a much larger number, for in one day in April, 1701, he sent as many as twenty-three pirogues to carry Indians over from Cahokia.[3]

The new settlement was short-lived either because its French traders were "afraid of being killed or plundered by the Sioux" or because, as Moses Austin stated, its climate proved insalubrious. In any case, in the spring of 1703 its inhabitants abandoned it for the new mission which Father Marest had established farther down the Mississippi on the banks of the Kaskaskia. There they helped to found Notre Dame de Cascasquios, known later simply as Kaskaskia. Eventually every vestige of the village on the Des Pères disappeared. It retained only a dim memory of its history, a vague tradition, which "research has only recently verified and placed on a basis of actual fact."[4] Kaskaskia was a focal point in the Mississippi Valley for many decades, and it retained its importance in the political and social life of the Illinois Country even after Illinois reached statehood.[5]

But no region of the Mississippi Valley was more favorably suited for settlement and steady growth than was present Missouri. Its geographic centrality, temperate climate, bountiful river system, fertile plains, luxuriant forests, hordes of wild game, and its rich mineral deposits—all these were irresistible attractions to countless French and American frontiersmen. Its central location encouraged migration from Canada, from the Gulf of Mexico, and from the region of the Appalachians, each of which was the same distance apart. The Missouri climate varied with the seasons, ranging from an average of twenty-six degrees in January to an average of seventy-seven degrees in July. Its growing seasons were very favorable to agricultural pursuits. And its hot winds were less frequent and less destructive than those of some neighboring states. Along its eastern border, a stretch of about four hundred seventy-five miles, flowed the Mississippi. The river was invaluable to early travel and trade, and it made possible a number of important towns along its course and near its junction with the Missouri. The Missouri, too, assisted mightily in settling the future state. The rich and seemingly endless plains along its banks were like a magnet drawing immigrants to, from, and across the state. It could therefore contribute to the development, not only of the Mississippi Valley but also of the Great Plains and of the Far West.[6]

In their journals or letters early travelers described the region of Missouri as a terrestrial paradise. In 1681 Father Membré, descending the Mississippi with La Salle, praised the cedars of the future state as "the most beautiful . . . in the world" and he said that its groves were so clear and unobstructed that a man could ride through them on horseback.[7] Father Marest, writing to a fellow Jesuit thirty-one years later, depicted Missouri as a "very fine" country with a charming variety of great rivers, vast and dense forests, and delightful prairies.[8] Early in the nineteenth century Victor Collot, a former French officer of the American Revolution, pictured the Mississippi Valley as "full of small lakes and villages, and interspersed with woods and natural meadows, strewed with medicinal and odoriferous plants. Across these meadows flow numerous rivulets, sometimes murmuring beneath the flowers, and sometimes displaying their silver beds and their transparent waters, pure as the air which is breathed amidst these romantic spots."[9] In the next century Louis Houck, one of Missouri's best known historians, meditated poetically on her virgin forests and on how mysterious time had spoiled them in the name of progress:

It is difficult for us now to imagine the natural beauty of this virgin landscape. The outline remains—the swelling hills, the valleys, the rocks and streams; but the picturesque clumps of trees, the narrow line of woodlands here and there among the creeks, or on the isolated hilltops, far away, are gone; then, too, bordering these prairies, the immense thickets of wild plum and the varieties of crab-apples, and copses matted with grape-vines have disappeared. From the open oak woods, crowning here and there a hill-top, the emerald prairie then gleamed to the far-away horizon. There was nothing to disturb the serene repose of the scene or divert the mind. In the summer, a green carpet covered the whole landscape. The high wild grass undulated in the breeze like the billows of a southern sea. Here [grew] various prairie flowers, some in purple, some with creamy spikes, some in golden yellow; lilies, some in white, and

253

others tossing and swaying their red cups in the breeze; and some scarlet, made fragrant, when in full blossom in the summer sun.[10]

The early settlers of Missouri found lumber of these primeval forests suitable for any purpose to which it was usefully applied. They made their carriages, wagons, and agricultural implements from oak, hickory, maple, ash, mulberry, locust, linden, poplar, elm, walnut, and pine; their houses and other buildings from pine, linden, poplar, cotton-wood, walnut, cypress, cedar, oak, and gum; their furniture from walnut, poplar, maple, cherry, coffee-tree, locust, gum, mulberry, tupelo, pine, cypress, cedar, birch, hickory, and oak; and their fences from cedar, locust, oak, hickory, mulberry, and pine.[11]

The prairies teemed with wild game of every description. They were undisturbed save for a few Indians who hunted on them for food. Buffaloes, elk, deer, and bears were seen everywhere. In autumn large flocks of migrating wild geese filled the sky with their atonal honkings; and wild pigeons flew in flocks so numerous that they darkened the sky like a passing rain cloud. Turkeys, quails, and woodcocks grew so fat feeding on wild oats that many of them suffocated and died. Most bears stayed deep in the forest, where they could find proper food. In 1700 Father Gravier killed two bears on an island opposite what is now Grey's Point, in Scott County, Missouri. One day he saw, between that island and the mouth of the Ohio, fifty bears crossing the Mississippi River. He found that buffaloes were even more abundant than bears. He and his companions left nearly all of the buffaloes they killed to the wolves. One buffalo defended its life so well that it cost Gravier ten or twelve gunshots.[12]

This abundant and diversified wild life was, of course, an important inducement to the settlement of Missouri. Early settlers derived both meat and clothes from buffaloes, deer, and black bears. Many of the settlers were traders who realized handsome incomes by selling their skins to agents of fur companies in Philadelphia and New York. In regions settled by the French, fur traders and missionaries often traveled together. They blazed trails in the endeavor to ascertain accessible routes and to establish friendly relations with the regional tribes. The fur trade was responsible for the rise of some of Missouri's oldest cities.

254

We shall see later that St. Louis was established by a fur company, that the site of present New Madrid was a rendezvous for Canadian traders, and that Cape Girardeau was a trading post long before it became a settlement. The fur traders, together with the merchants, the hunters, and the missionaries, were the chief agents in the social, economic, and religious history of early Missouri. The fur trade was often the lure that directed immigrants to some particular locality, that provided them with purchasing power, and that exerted among them a leveling influence favorable to democratic principles.

Another strong inducement to the settlement of Missouri was its reputed mineral wealth. French explorers avidly sought tin, lead, salt, copper, and silver. In about 1700 a few of them discovered salt among the banks of the Saline River near what is now known as the Burnt Hill. During the next several years small groups of Frenchmen, mainly from Canada, visited Missouri in search of mines of precious ores. Early in 1703 twenty Canadians ascended the Missouri River on their way to New Mexico, where they planned to trade with the Indians and to ascertain if the mines really existed. This expedition, of which we unfortunately know very little, led Iberville as governor of Louisiana to plan to build on the Arkansas, Ohio, and Missouri rivers a small number of posts around which colonists could settle. In 1705 one Laurain gave Bienville at Fort Maurepas a confused account of a journey he said he had made up the Missouri, of the Indian tribes he had met on its banks, and of Spanish towns in New Mexico. In the following year Iberville died and his brother Bienville became administrator of Louisiana. At about the same time one Derbanne, who later became commander at Natchitoches, journeyed with a small band of Frenchmen up the Missouri for about a thousand miles. On his return he claimed that he had visited Spanish towns and had discovered among Indians priestly vestments and horses they had either stolen or purchased. Perhaps to deceive him, the Spaniards told him that they knew of no silver which had been mined in New Mexico. Later in the same year two Canadians told Bienville that they had spent two years traveling on the Missouri from one Indian village to another. They said that they had seen Spanish mines and had been imprisoned in an Indian village. In support of their story they presented Bienville with samples of copper and an unknown white metal they claimed to have taken from three mines. The Spaniards, they said, had come to the Indian village to trade for buffalo skins with which to make harness for the mules they used in wars against hostile tribes.[13]

All these excursions into Missouri prompted Father Nicolas de la Salle, nephew of the great explorer and commissary for the colony of Louisiana, to write Pontchartrain urging him to continue expeditions with the aim of finding a suitable location for a settlement. The minister failed to follow La Salle's suggestion, though Bienville later sent to Missouri two men under Daraque, ostensibly to distribute gifts to tribes friendly to the French but actually to trade for buffalo skins and for slaves to sell in the West Indies. La Salle, who hated Bienville and who vetoed everything he proposed, wrote to Pontchartrain urging him not to pay Daraque and his men their salaries.[14]

The dissension between Bienville and La Salle grew so bitter that it divided the colony of Louisiana into two hostile camps. La Salle sent to Pontchartrain a torrent of letters accusing Bienville and one of his brothers of numerous misdeeds and branding them as thieves and rogues who squandered the king's property. Bienville countered with letters accusing La Salle of making many mistakes in his account books and of acting like a common miser in refusing to finance a voyage to Havana for the purpose of obtaining badly needed provisions. This flood of contradictory denunciations finally stirred Pontchartrain to action. He appointed a Norman, Nicolas Daneau, Sieur de Muys, to succeed Bienville as administrator of Louisiana and Diron d'Artaguette to succeed La Salle as commissary. The new officials were ordered to investigate the dissension and to send its initiator to France for trial. Muys, however, died in Havana before he reached his destination, and Artaguette, who undertook the investigation alone, vindicated Bienville entirely. But the colony was in such deplorable condition socially, economically, and politically, that Artaguette felt obliged to return to France to inform Pontchartrain that his colonial venture was losing investments and that the colony needed a new policy. His voyage and his advice proved needless, for Louis XIV had already made a change. Unable to finance the colony, he had leased it to a wealthy merchant, Antoine Crozat, for a period of fifteen years. By his grant Crozat enjoyed a monopoly of working and exploiting all the mines of precious metals that might be discovered in the colony, provided he gave the king a fourth of the profit. Crozat chose as governor of the colony Antoine de la Mothe-Cadillac, founder of Detroit. On June 5, 1713, he arrived at Dauphin Island with a group of officers and men and with Jean-Baptiste du Clos or Duclos, who succeeded Artaguette as commissary. Bienville, whose knowledge of the colony was considered indispensable, was retained as lieutenant-governor. Anxious to impress Crozat by his administrative ability and thereby to enhance his governorship, Cadillac sent out parties to open trade relations with New Spain and to explore the Missouri for mines, but none of his efforts accomplished their aims.

The first definite and detailed exploration of Missouri was made by Étienne Véniard, Sieur de Bourgmond. Like so many French explorers, including the great La Salle, he was of Norman blood. Of towering physique, ferocious strength, and a ceaselessly roving appetite, he was a true representative of his Viking ancestors, appearing anachronously in the eighteenth century to perform a vital service for French exploration. In 1706, when he was a very young cadet, he moved from Quebec to Detroit, where its governor, Cadillac, impressed by his military abilities, made him temporary commander to succeed Alphonse de Tonti, younger brother of La Salle's great friend, who had been transferred to the command of Fort Frontenac. With a garrison of only fifteen men Bourgmond repulsed a fierce attack by a large body of Foxes; but at about the same time he succumbed to the charms of a married lady, Madame Tichenet, whom he nicknamed La Chenette. Deserting his post with some of his soldiers, he took La Chenette to the wilderness around Lake Erie, where all of them lived like a small band of savages. Cadillac sent fifty soldiers to break up their camp and bring them back to face court-martial, but the deserters bested their captors and traveled farther east, giving Cadillac the impression that they had gone over to the English. With the approach of snow and ice Bourgmond's romantic ardor cooled, and after two of his companions were drowned, one murdered, and one captured and eaten by the Indians, he, his mistress, and their remaining friends decided to give themselves up. Still fascinated by his great physical strength and military ability, which he badly needed to help frustrate fresh Indian attacks, Cadillac pardoned

257

Bourgmond and reinstated him to his rank. He imprisoned the other deserters and ordered La Chenette to return to her husband. In 1712, when the Foxes again attacked Detroit in the absence of Cadillac, Bourgmond helped his superior Dubuisson drive them off. But soon he fell in love again, this time with a beautiful Indian girl of the Missouri tribe which had come to aid the French. When her people turned homeward Bourgmond again deserted his post and pursued her up the Missouri for several hundred leagues to her village. She bore him at least one child out of wedlock.[15]

For the next five years Bourgmond remained with her people and perhaps with her. He led the life of a *coureur de bois,* journeying by canoe—perhaps with his Indian mistress and a few Indian guides—up and down several rivers, and ingratiating himself with a number of tribes to the extent of becoming their idol. In 1714 he performed the magnificent deed of leading an expedition up the Missouri as far as the villages of the Arikaras and the Caricaras. Then he continued his journey up the Platte perhaps through present Nebraska and into eastern Wyoming. He met the Osages, the Kansas, the Pawnees, the Otos, probably the Omahas, and perhaps the Poncas. All of these tribes furnished him with information about the Padoucas or Comanches, who traded with the Spaniards and who ranged from New Mexico to the Black Hills. Later he wrote a journal of his travels, describing in glowing terms the rich country along his route. The prairies, which he called "the finest lands in the world," stretched constantly before him like endless green seas alive with game and fur-bearing animals in numbers "defying the imagination."[16]

By this time the government of Louisiana had changed again. Cadillac had failed miserably in his efforts to establish trade relations with New Spain and to explore the Missouri for mines. His master Crozat depended on these enterprises as compensations for the large sums he had invested in the colony. The frustrated governor, fearing that his hungry and wretchedly clothed colonists were about to rise up against him, imposed on them a number of restrictions which only intensified their hatred for him. To Crozat he sent letter after letter, complaining of the wretched conditions in the colony and blaming all of them on Bienville, whom he resented for having refused to marry his daughter. But Crozat was undeceived. He replied by blaming

Cadillac for the evils of which he had complained and by dismissing him from office. He sent one Espinay to replace Cadillac, but the new governor also quarreled with Bienville, and each man created around himself a powerful faction that kept the colony in constant turmoil. At last, in August, 1717, Crozat, seeing that conditions under Espinay were "likely to move as lamely as before," asked the Duke of Orleans, who ruled France as regent during Louis XV's minority, to relieve him of his monopoly. Orleans then handed the colony over to the Company of the Indies or the Mississippi Company, as it was popularly known, whose director, John Law, undertook to deliver France from bankruptcy by using the anticipated wealth of Louisiana as security. The Mississippi Company, with its own flag, its monopolies of the French slave trade and of tobacco, and its control of the royal mint and of the national revenues, enjoyed sovereign power. By propagandizing Louisiana as a terrestrial paradise and by displaying in shopwindows of Paris ingots of gold which purportedly had been mined in the colony, it sold hundreds of thousands of its shares to wealth-seeking Frenchmen and other Europeans at skyrocketing prices. The company replaced Espinay with Bienville, who made every effort to strengthen the colony by encouraging further settlement in the Mississippi Valley. Bienville, believing that the capital should be located on the Mississippi to give it direct communication with the French settlements and trading posts in the Illinois country, laid the foundations of the beautiful city of New Orleans, which he named in honor of the regent.

Such were the circumstances in Louisiana when, in 1718, Bourgmond left his Indian friends and perhaps his Indian mistress. He traveled down the Mississippi, and saw Bienville, who was so impressed by his deeds that he wrote to the regent requesting that Bourgmond be rewarded with the Cross of St. Louis. Though he had deserted the king's service twice he was considered so valuable in the great task of exploring Louisiana for its purported mineral wealth that he was again forgiven. In the following year, when the War of the Quadruple Alliance broke out with France and Spain on opposing sides, Bourgmond joined Bienville in attacking Pensacola. Soon after that city was captured, Bourgmond sailed for France, perhaps for the purpose of enlisting the support of the Mississippi Company in another expedition which he planned to make up the Missouri. At about the same time Bienville wrote to the company asking for permission to establish a post on that river.[17]

The company's activities in trade and exploration engendered an estrangement between France and Spain that was reflected in the changed attitudes among officials of both countries in Louisiana and New Spain. At this time Spain claimed the entire region west of the Mississippi River, though her frontier settlements extended no farther north than New Mexico. These circumstances afforded an inviting field of activity for the French in the valleys of the Missouri, the Arkansas, and the Platte. In 1718 Bienville sent Claude Charles du Tisné to establish trade relations with the tribes along the Osage in Missouri.[18]

Tisné was cast in the same mold as Bourgmond: he was an audacious fellow with a ready smile and wit, polished manners, and a keen eye for pretty girls, regardless of their race, creed, or color. Against the wishes of his parents, who were well-to-do Parisians, he sought and found service as a volunteer in Canada. Later a Quebec merchant was so impressed by him that he fitted him out with a canoe, Indian paddlers, and merchandise and sent him off with some other young Frenchmen to trade with the Indians. They learned the Indian language as they went along. But in front of the Indians they pretended they could speak only by signs to encourage them to speak openly in their presence. They met with no success until they went to a remote village which traders had not visited. The chief received them well and gave them a cabin. Next day Tisné laid out all of his goods and led the chief and other Indians to his display room. During a severe illness in his boyhood Tisné had lost nearly all of his hair. Tired of seeing a few straggly tufts on his head, he had shaved them off and thereafter had worn a wig. The wig now saved his life. The chief suddenly became unfriendly. He told the young traders he did not know that they were coming and that, therefore, he had gathered no beaver skins for them. "There is only one way," said one of the Indians, "to get all that pretty merchandise: scalp them, kill them, throw them into the river, and then we shall have all of it." Instead of grabbing his gun, as each of his companions had done, Tisné grasped his wig and threw it to the ground in front of the chief. "Want my scalp, do you?" he shouted. "Pick it up, if you dare!" Instead of doing his bidding, the Indians shook with awe. "We thought you

260

were men the same as we are," said the chief, "but we see now, you are spirits, because you speak the same language that we do, and you can remove your scalp whenever you wish!"[19] Bossu, who gives a slightly different version of the incident, says that Tisné

> told them that they were wrong in wanting to hurt him, that he had come to be their friend, and that if they insisted on acting in this way, he would burn the water of the lakes and the rivers so that they could not sail on them and would set fire to the forest. He poured some brandy out of a little barrel into a dish and lit it with a match. The Indians, who were not yet familiar with brandy, were amazed. He then took a magnifying glass from his pocket and with the aid of the sun set fire to a rotten tree. These people actually believed that the officer had the power to burn the rivers and the forests. They caressed him, showered him with presents, and sent him off with an escort to protect him from harm.[20]

Le Page du Pratz, who knew Tisné well, says that this daring deed won for him military distinction and a wife from the fashionable society of Quebec.[21]

Tisné bears the distinction of being the first explorer to conduct an overland expedition into the interior of what is now Missouri. Complying with Bienville's orders, he intended to ascend the Missouri to the Paniouasas. But the Missouris would not allow him to continue his journey, perhaps because they feared that he would supply their enemies farther west with muskets. So he returned to Kaskaskia, his starting point. There he obtained permission from Pierre Dugué de Boisbriant, commander of the Illinois country, to make the journey on horseback. Early in 1719 he set out with a few men to visit the Osages, Pawnees, and Comanches. Journeying along the Missouri for forty leagues, he reached the mouth of the Osage which he followed, perhaps along an Indian trail, to the Osages. With them he traded some French goods for some skins and horses. These the Indians said they had stolen from their enemies, the Pawnees, who dwelled in several villages one hundred and twenty miles away. They were friendly until he announced that, as an officer carrying out the orders of his superiors, he must journey to the Pawnees, make peace with them, and exchange goods, including muskets, for beaver skins. Afraid that the Pawnees might use the muskets against them, the Osages angrily refused to let him go until with Gallic aplomb he told them that, if they persisted, Bienville would be angry with them and would send them no more French presents. Then they reconsidered and told him that they would not stand in his way if he left most of his guns with them and if he took with him only his interpreter.[22]

A ride of four days brought him to the Pawnees, who lived in two villages on a rich prairie near a forest along the banks of a stream. Mindful that he had just come from the Osages, they suspected him of being their spy and twice threatened to tomahawk him; but when he dared them to strike him down they began to treat him as a friend. Yet they stopped him from continuing to the Comanches for the same reason that the Osages had stopped him from going to the Pawnees. Reluctant to lose their friendship and perhaps his skins, he made an alliance with them and bartered his three guns, some powder, hammers, and knives for two horses and a branded Spanish mule. Then he planted the fleur-de-lis in their village, bade them farewell and, guided by compass, returned to the Osages. He found them surly—they refused to provide him with men to serve as his guides back to the Illinois country. Seeing that his companions were quite frightened, he calmed them by hastening his departure homeward. Burdened with fourteen horses, a mule, and hundreds of skins, he inched overland along the north fork of the Osage to the Missouri and up the Mississippi to the Illinois. The long and hazardous journey cost him six horses and nine hundred pounds of furs which he deplored more than any other reverse of his entire expedition. When he arrived home he wrote Bienville a detailed account of his odyssey. He had to satisfy himself with what information the Pawnees had given him about the Comanches, who, he said, had allowed the Spaniards to come to their villages but not to travel beyond them. He said that the Pawnees and Comanches were engaged in a cruel war in which they ate their captives. He suggested that the Mississippi Company try to reach Spanish territory by making an alliance with these tribes, though he warned that the Comanches would expect presents and the return of all those of their tribe who had been captured and enslaved.[23]

Word of his expedition spread quickly south and west from tribe to tribe until it reached the Spaniards in New Mexico. They took it seriously, for the Indians had made it appear as an imminent French invasion. They realized that the tribes to the north and east were very warlike and that, under French influence and arms, they might become a great menace to the Spanish empire. By furnishing the Osages and Pawnees with muskets, Tisné had, moreover, forced the Comanches, a powerful nomadic tribe living in present western Kansas, to withdraw southward toward New Mexico. In so doing he had created a new threat to Spanish authority. Informed of these unhappy circumstances, the viceroy of New Spain ordered Antonio de Valverde, governor of New Mexico, to reconnoiter the French for their whereabouts and plans. Accordingly, in the fall of 1719, Valverde led an expedition to the Comanches, who provided him with fresh evidences of the French advance toward New Mexico. He was told that the French had built two towns as large as Taos, that they had formed an alliance with the Pawnees and furnished them with muskets, and that they had built forts bristling with cannon.[24]

Valverde relayed this information to the viceroy. In reply the viceroy ordered him to halt the French advance by building a presidio at El Cuartelejo, an Apache stronghold in present Kiowa County, Colorado, and by undertaking an expedition to the northeast of New Mexico to locate the reported French towns. Valverde with the advice of the leading citizens of his province postponed construction of the presidio on the ground that it would be too remote for communication with Santa Fé. Nevertheless, he wasted little time in sending one of his officers, Pedro de Villasur, to penetrate to the French towns. Villasur's force consisted of about one hundred and ten men, including forty soldiers from the garrison of Santa Fé, sixty town Indians, a few servants, and two or three private citizens, one of whom was Jean l'Archevêque who, we will recall, had been one of La Salle's men thirty-three years before. L'Archevêque had returned from a short imprisonment in Spain to follow the Indian trade in the region north of New Mexico. His acquaintance with the terrain and his knowledge of French made him an invaluable addition to the expedition. He took with him ten horses and six mules loaded with goods to trade with the Indians.[25]

On June 16, 1720, Villasur and his men set out from Santa Fé. Their purpose was to look for Frenchmen and French towns, not to attack them, for at the beginning of the year Spain and France had agreed to

263

a truce in the War of the Quadruple Alliance. They took the familiar
northern route, which brought them to Taos, then to the Culebra or
Taos Range, then along the foot of the eastern slopes of La Jicarilla, an
Indian settlement, then to the headwaters of the Purgatoire River, then
northward to the foothills of the Rockies, across the Arkansas by raft
and on to El Cuartelejo. So far their march had been as peaceful as it
was fruitless; they had seen signs neither of Frenchmen nor of French
towns. In the next several weeks, as they approached the Pawnee
country, they encountered increasing signs of Indian hostility. On
August 6, after having traveled about seven hundred miles from Santa
Fé, they arrived at the south fork of the Platte or, as they called it, the
Rio de Jesus María. They crossed the river and then marched about
three miles across a plain to the north fork of the Platte or Rio San
Lorenzo. They continued along its southern bank for eight or nine
miles, until they met one of their own Indian scouts. He informed
them that the Pawnees lived on the opposite side of the river, that they
had replied to his signs of friendship by swinging their tomahawks and
yelling war cries, and that, becoming frightened, he had mounted his
horse and sped away. "Upon this news," wrote Villasur, "order was at
once given to cross to the other side of the stream. It was carried out
with so much good fortune that everything went over without getting
wet, although the mules were up to their girths in the water."[26] They
marched along its northern bank until they neared the Pawnee village.
Unwilling to attack it, Villasur sent his Indian scout to it with a letter
which L'Archevêque had written in French, announcing their friendship and inquiring about the presence of Frenchmen. Some hours later
the scout brought back a reply which, written on a piece of soiled
paper, was unintelligible to both L'Archevêque and the Spaniards. Villasur, thinking that the French were handicapped by a lack of writing
materials, sent back paper, ink, and a quill, together with another letter, written this time in Spanish.[27]

For two days they awaited a reply in vain. Then, convinced by signs
of activity in the village that its inhabitants planned some mischief,
perhaps with the assistance of the French, they decided to end their
unwise search and to retreat across the river. This they hurriedly did,
doubtless at the same ford they had found two days before. Once on
its southern bank they cleared a space in tall grass and, late in the after-

264

noon, pitched camp. At nightfall Villasur charged his sentinels with caution and sought long-deserved rest. About midnight he and some of his men were awakened by the furious barking of their dogs. The unsuspecting leader little realized that the Pawnees were moving cautiously along the banks of the river and were approaching the camp. He quieted the dogs, cautioned the sentinels to redouble their vigilance, and returned to bed.[28]

At daybreak, August 13, Villasur and his men arose, broke camp, and made preparations to continue their journey homeward. Suddenly, amid commands and shouts, amid mutterings mingled with the braying of mules and the neighing of horses, they were swept by a murderous shower of shots and arrows. The horses stampeded, creating further disorder and confusion. Villasur fell before he could organize a defense and L'Archevêque died with him. Father Juan Minguez, chaplain of the expedition, fell into the hands of a few Otos who were attacking with the Pawnees. Most of the Indians of the expedition had scented danger and fled from the field. When smoke and dust cleared, forty-five Spaniards and Indians lay dead in the tall grass. Only thirteen of the Spaniards survived; begrimed and bedraggled, they made their way to Santa Fé and informed Valverde of the terrible fate that had befallen their comrades. The news flew to Mexico City, where the viceroy ordered an investigation. The dead leader of the expedition became a convenient scapegoat. All agreed that he was inexperienced and perhaps incompetent. Valverde tried to divest himself of all blame by accusing the French. He even persuaded himself that "the aggressors must have been heretical Huguenots, as their insolent daring did not spare even the innocence of the priest who went as chaplain."[29] Despite this claim, the most vigorous research has failed to yield any positive evidence that the French had any part in the massacre. "Indeed," wrote William E. Dunn, "the whole affair has all the earmarks of a typical Indian ambush. . . . A few traders may have instigated or even may have been present at the attack, but in the absence of more definite proof," we must "give the French the benefit of the doubt and absolve them from any direct responsibility for the tragedy."[30] Valverde still hoped to escape punishment, but in 1722 he was removed from office. Four years later he was tried and charged with negligence in entrusting the expedition to an inexperienced officer instead of leading it himself, as the viceroy had ordered him to do. He was required to pay fifty pesos for charity masses for the souls of the men who had died in the attack and one hundred and fifty pesos to purchase ornaments for certain missions.

Some of the Pawnees and their allies hurried with word of their victory to Boisbriant, commander of the Illinois country. As proof of it they brought along numerous spoils of the expedition, including some leaves from Villasur's diary. A chief of the Otos sold some of these spoils to Charlevoix, the Jesuit missionary who later wrote a history of early Louisiana. The Missouris presented themselves before Boisbriant in grotesque procession. Dressed in the priestly vestments stolen from the chaplain they had captured, they danced in the Indian fashion as they carried holy vessels used in the mass and offered them to Boisbriant. They told him that the Spaniards of New Mexico intended to return to avenge the defeat of Villasur's expedition and to establish a fort on the Kansas River. Though their tale was without foundation, Boisbriant believed it and relayed it to Bienville, who was quick to realize that such a fort would threaten all Louisiana and perhaps alienate many of its tribes. To protect the allied Indians from Spanish intrusion, he ordered Boisbriant to build a fort on the Kansas. Bienville also wrote to the Mississippi Company, urging it to protect the Missouri country. Heeding his plea, the company took measures to bring the tribes along the Missouri under French influence.[31]

17

Bourgmond's Expedition to the Comanches

THE MISSISSIPPI COMPANY GAVE THE TASK OF WINNING THE INDIANS TO the French cause to Bourgmond. The explorer of the Missouri was then living in Paris, where he had married a very rich widow soon after his return from Louisiana. He would hardly have consented to exchange his newly won comforts and affluence for the hardships and dangers of the American wilderness had not Spanish encroachment, or Indian tales of Spanish encroachment, provoked deep resentment in the directors of the Mississippi Company. He had been recommended to them as the man best fitted to achieve the mission they planned. A memorial from the Illinois country had lavishly praised his abilities: "There is at the moment in Paris a subject highly fitted to govern the Indians. He is a gentleman of Normandy, M. de Bourgmond, a man of incomparable value, whose achievements all the Indians of this quarter know and admire. If they had him at their head they would be equal to any undertaking."[1] Boisbriant had sent a recommendation no less flattering: "He had a great power over the Indians when he was here; they kept asking for him most eagerly on every occasion. If he were placed in command of them, his services would certainly be very useful."[2] The company sent for him, accorded him every mark of respect, and commissioned him captain of the Louisiana Troop and "commander of the Missouri." Later the king conferred on him the Cross of St. Louis. Bourgmond, of course, laid down certain conditions in return for his services. He requested from the company his salary from the date of his commission, a bequest of 2000 livres in merchandise which he said he needed for the voyage, and a formal promise that, as soon as he had accomplished his mission, he would receive a title of nobility. On his part he agreed to try to establish a general peace with the tribes living in the region from Missouri to New Mexico. Such a peace would not only assure him a safe route, but would also enable him to contact the Spaniards to ascertain what trade relations, if any, they were willing to establish with the French. This was very important to the Mississippi Company which envisioned fabulous profits by exchanging its goods for silver from New Mexico. To strengthen his position as well as that of his successors in any contingency that might arise, Bourgmond planned to build a fort somewhere on the Missouri. It would contain the Spaniards if they attempted to encroach on the mines of Illinois, would help defeat them if they resorted to war, and would serve as a meeting point if they were disposed to trade. In giving him final instructions the company told him that, if he succeeded in establishing a settlement on the Missouri within two years, as he promised, and in making an alliance with the Comanches, he should bring several chiefs of each principal tribe to France "to give them an idea of the power of France." The company would then fulfill the formal promise it had made to him.[3] The encouragement which it gave to Bourgmond's plans indicated that it had settled on the Missouri as an approach to the Comanches and Apaches and as the highway to riches and trade with the Spaniards.

Bourgmond's departure for Louisiana was delayed several times by a financial crisis in France. Early in 1720 Law's glittering Mississippi bubble was about to burst. Tales began to filter through to France that Louisiana had neither gold nor silver mines, that large areas of it were barren, and that its inhabitants were dying of starvation and disease. The shareholders in the company, learning that their shares had little or no backing, began to sell them for specie, which they took out of the country as fast as they could. When Law issued a decree devaluating money and shares he incurred such widespread indignation that he feared for his life, resigned his post, and fled the country. Yet the regency decided that the interest of the kingdom required the continuance of the Mississippi Company. It received government support for thirteen more years, making, during this period, slow but steady progress.

268

Not until June, 1722, was Bourgmond able to sail for Louisiana. When he arrived there he was shocked to find that Bienville had radically changed his attitude toward the expedition and that he had done nothing to facilitate its journey up the river. Since Bienville's own stores were badly depleted he hesitated to give up what he had for what he now regarded as a post "so distant and so little necessary." He therefore doubted the wisdom of the enterprise and Bourgmond's ability to make a lasting peace with the Comanches. But Bourgmond, having full authority to make the venture, resolved with admirable tenacity of purpose to carry it out regardless of very inadequate forces and provisions. In February, 1723, he journeyed up the river from New Orleans. Many of his soldiers, being very badly supplied, deserted along the way. At Cahokia he impressed the local garrison into service, gaining three able but quarrelsome officers, Louis St. Ange de Bellerive, Jean de Pradel, and Simars de Belisle. Continuing to Kaskaskia, he found that even Boisbriant, who had once recommended him with the highest praise to the Mississippi Company, had grown indifferent to the enterprise, perhaps because he was jealous of its leader. He grudgingly gave him twenty soldiers "to establish a little post" and an assortment of presents for the Indians.[4]

Bourgmond sent word to the Missouris, his most reliable friends, asking for men and supplies to help him continue his expedition. Eventually they heeded his call. But while he waited for them, he wrote, "all my sailors deserted at this post, through advice or otherwise; three quarters of my ordinary forces were sick." Though this would have discouraged most men, Bourgmond resolved to carry on "without jettisoning five cents worth of merchandise." After waiting in Kaskaskia for forty-nine days, his Indian friends appeared. He readied his convoy, which consisted of three large boats, perhaps pirogues, and several canoes, and proceeded with it across the Mississippi and up the Missouri. On November 5, having passed the Grand and Wakenda rivers, he arrived at the Missouri village on the southern bank of the Missouri in present Saline County, Missouri, where he had lived for at least five years with his Indian mistress and her family. He had left her at his pleasure, in the customary Indian fashion, but he had taken their son with him everywhere—to France and back to Louisiana and to his mother's people, whom the boy now regaled with stories of his travels with his French father. For four days Bourgmond remained with them. Then, transporting his party across the river to Tetsau Bend about two miles above the mouth of the Wakenda in present Carroll County, Missouri, he began to build his post, which he called Fort Orleans in honor of the regent in France.[5]

The exact location of Fort Orleans was unknown until about forty years ago. Before that time historians in giving it a location seemed to have copied each other's errors. Louis Houck stated that the fort "is supposed to have been on an island, long since washed away, but which then existed, . . . near the mouth of Grand river and not far from present city of Brunswick."[6] Clarence W. Alvord thought that the fort "was situated about fifteen or twenty miles from the mouth of the Missouri."[7] Lucien Carr surmised that it was located "on the south side of the river, fifteen or twenty miles above the mouth of the Grand River."[8] Justin Winsor, copying Houck, simply says that the fort stood on "an island (since disappeared) in the Missouri."[9] Bickford Davis, knowing of no such island in the Missouri, looked for it "above the mouth of the Osage River."[10] So went the guess work of the authorities until 1925, when Baron Marc de Villiers du Terrage carefully collated all available documentary evidence in the French archives to arrive at the conclusion that the fort was located where we have placed it. A few years later Louis C. Karpinski of the University of Michigan discovered in several European archives a number of maps pertaining to the early American frontier. One of these, drawn by Dumont de Montigny, a French officer whose published memoirs constitute an important source in the frontier history of the Mississippi Valley, gives the fort a location almost identical with that assigned to it by Villiers. The map shows the fort on the left bank of the Missouri, not on an island but on the mainland, and only a mile or two farther up the river from the location Villiers described.[11]

The difficulties which had plagued Bourgmond from the beginning of his expedition were by no means eased at Fort Orleans. Jealousy and discord divided soldiers and workmen, while Pradel and Belisle quarreled with Bourgmond over what duties lay within the limits of their jurisdictions. The officers and their soldiers proceeded to build barracks for themselves and ignored Bourgmond's orders to help the workmen finish the fort, the warehouse, the church, and the cottage for Father

Mercier, the chaplain. On January 2, 1724, he wrote to the commissaries of the Mississippi Company in New Orleans, laying all his troubles to their indifference toward his expedition and accusing them of giving improper or unclear instructions to his followers:

> We began construction of a warehouse to store our merchandise, which was spoiling in the boats; we had nothing to cover them from the rain or a six-inch snowfall. If your instructions had been for the good of the service, as were mine, you would have given your Negroes and servants so that I could employ them in building the warehouse. Far from that, you ordered most of the soldiers to work on the barracks without even considering that they should first unload the merchandise.[12]

While everybody else was comfortably lodged, he said, he had to abandon a vile cloth tent, which let in rain and snow, for an Indian hut so cold that it had made him ill. He gave a sarcastic description of the hut:

> The ornamentation is beautiful! A house of stakes driven into the ground, and not of carpentry, no boards either on top or below. No fireplace—fire being made in the middle of the house like the savages. A covering of grass, held up by poles as God made them grow in the woods, unadzed and unsquared. The embellishment is beautiful! You might say a market shack of a barn, rather than a frame house. Undoubtedly I give myself the credit for this in all justice, costing me dear as it did.[13]

The officers, being jealous of him, encouraged their soldiers by word and attitude to ignore his orders and even his requests. One of the sergeants, Dubois, ignored his request to build a little enclosure for five pigs and twenty chickens which would protect them from ferocious dogs owned by Indians. Pradel refused to negotiate with the Indians for badly needed wheat and fresh meat, saying that such subjects were outside the scope of his duties as an officer and suggesting that they be performed by some honest Indian. Bourgmond had asked Belisle several times to have the three boats in which they had come put in a safe place to keep them from being carried away by drifting ice. "Three or four days later I asked him if he had the boats removed, and he told me they were all right. Two days later they told me one boat had been sunk by the ice. The next day another was broken through the negli-

gence of . . . Belisle. He cannot deny that at least two weeks ago I told
him it was desirable to draw up the plans of the fort and of the bastions
in order to have a powder magazine installed in the bastions, and that
there were three soldiers, whose names I gave him, who could work on
this." Instead of following these orders Belisle made to the Indians a
lengthy discourse in which he proceeded to praise himself and his
fellow officers at the expense of their leader. "Belisle has told the Missouris, 'I am a good chief, Monsieur Pradel is a good chief, Monsieur de
Saint-Ange is a good chief, and Monsieur de Bourgmond is not worth
anything; he is a fool, an evil chief,' and other invectives." Happily,
Bourgmond was too well known among them for Belisle to make any
impression. He cut off Belisle's discourse by sending him to jail. The
soldiers, of course, sided with the officer. On Christmas Eve and on the
previous day, Bourgmond had to pay each of them forty livres before
they would consent to build a fence around his yard. He commented
sarcastically that Christmas, their day of rest, was well earned, for on
December 22 they had inaugurated work on the fortifications by cutting
down *one* post![14]

Yet by the end of spring he had managed his affairs so well that he
felt he could safely undertake his peace mission to the Comanches. On
June 25 he sent St. Ange with a convoy of heavily laden pirogues upstream toward the upper village of the tribe known as the Kansas. Eight
days later he followed overland with eight Frenchmen, one hundred
Missouris, and sixty-four Osages. Starting very early each morning to
avoid the heat, which sometimes became oppressive by noon, they
marched for five days across small creeks and beautiful prairies bordered
with little hills. Then they arrived near the present site of Doniphan,
Kansas, where they met Kansas scouts whom their chief had sent out
to inform Bourgmond that a delegation awaited him on an elevation in
the middle of an open prairie—a custom that permitted an Indian delegation to see how many persons were in an approaching party. That
afternoon they met the chief of the Kansas and six war chiefs, who
spread out mats for them, brought them red and white peace pipes,
danced and sang with them in a circle, and later, followed them westward. They marched now along the bluffs of the Missouri, above its
twisted or narrow flood plain, sometimes dipping into limestone canyons,
sometimes climbing out bathed in sweat and tormented by mosquitoes.

Soon they descended to the river, where, exhausted by incessant marching in stifling heat, they pitched camp and cooled themselves under the trees. On the opposite bank stood the Kansas village.[15]

The next morning they crossed the river, Bourgmond and his soldiers in pirogues and the Indians on rafts, while they swam their cattle and horses. The villagers accorded Bourgmond the welcome of a conquering hero, carrying him on a buffalo robe to the lodge of the principal chief who "sat like a large bronze bust in kingly dignity, among piled up gift furs and provisions."[16] The chief addressed him in a grandiloquent manner, gave him two fine horses, and presented him to lesser chiefs. Soon Bourgmond received from St. Ange a message stating that some of his men were ill with fever, perhaps typhoid or malaria, and asking that provisions be sent to him immediately. This Bourgmond did, though St. Ange made no better progress upstream. At last he arrived, bringing a small amount of merchandise for the Kansas; they were so disappointed with it that they would have rejected it had not Bourgmond threatened to march to the Comanches without them. Meanwhile some of his own men had contracted fever. The Osages, fearing that they too would become ill if they remained with the party, cautiously camped apart from the others. When more men in the party, including Bourgmond, became ill, the Osages sullenly left the expedition, taking some of the Missouris with them. A few days later Bourgmond, though still ill, led his followers toward the Comanches. It was an impressive procession—drums were beating and flags were flying in battle array. Sieur La Renaudière, standing by the road as the procession moved on, counted three hundred Kansas warriors under two great chiefs and fourteen war chiefs, about three hundred women, five hundred children, and at least three hundred dogs. All but the chiefs and the warriors were laden with provisions weighing more than their own bodies. Under such conditions they of course made very slow progress. And a week later, when they reached the Vermilion River in present Potawatomie County, Kansas, Bourgmond became so ill that he had to abandon the expedition. Too weak to ride a horse, he was carried on a litter back to the Kansas village, whence he continued to Fort Orleans by canoe. Before leaving his followers, however, he sent Gaillard, one of his Frenchmen, with fifty Kansas warriors to conduct two Comanches to their tribe: a young woman and a boy whom the Kansas had captured and enslaved and

273

whom Bourgmond had ransomed. By returning these captives he increased his chances of a favorable reception among the Comanches once he was well enough to visit them.[17]

On September 6 Bourgmond received word that Gaillard had succeeded in his mission. This information cheered him and hastened his recovery. Renewing his effort to visit the Comanches, he journeyed with a much smaller party up the Missouri to the Kansas village. They reached the village on October 8, and then set out across the plains. But their guide lost his way and took them too far southward, perhaps to the Cimarron River in northern Oklahoma, before he realized his error. Then they traveled north and west through stretches of high, rolling, treeless plains until, on October 17, they arrived at an abandoned Comanche camp, perhaps in present Rice County, Kansas, near the source of the Arkansas between Smoky Hill Fork and Cow Creek. Next day, when they unsaddled their horses and made preparations to cook their evening meal, they saw a column of smoke rise in the west. They replied with the friendly signal of setting fire to some dry grass. Soon they saw about eighty horsemen approaching, including Gaillard and La Renaudière, whom Bourgmond had sent ahead to announce his visit. The great chief of the Comanches, who had led the horsemen, dismounted before Bourgmond's tent, warmly grasped his hands, and sat with him on the ground. Joined by their followers, they smoked pipes of peace. Then they rode ten miles to the Comanche camp, where warriors visited Bourgmond in his tent and placed him, his officers, and his half-breed son on buffalo robes. With yells of joy and gratulation, they carried their guests to the great chief, who regaled them with a magnificent feast which lasted until nightfall.[18]

On the next day Bourgmond summoned all the villagers to his tent and unpacked the gifts he had brought them. Here were all the enviable commodities of which they had dreamed: guns, swords, hatchets, kettles, gunpowder, bullets, red and blue cloth, small mirrors, knives, shirts, awls, scissors, needles, bells, vermilion, beads, and many other trinkets! Spreading the gifts on the ground, he gathered his officers around him and unfurled a large fleur-de-lis. He told his Indian friends that the Great White Father, his and their master, had sent him to exhort them to live in peace with their neighbors, including the Missouris, Osages, Kansas, Otos, Omahas, and Pawnees, with whom they had warred on and off since time immemorial. He offered the flag to the great chief, exhorting him to keep it "always as white as I give it to you and . . . without spots!" Accepting the flag, the great chief agreed in behalf of his people to renounce his enmity toward these new allies of the French, to share with them the blessings of trade and alliance, and to give the French free passage through their country to trade with the Spaniards of New Mexico.[19] "Then, with unspeakable delight," says Parkman, "he and his tribesmen took and divided the gifts."

Bourgmond's original plans called for a visit to the Spaniards, but he had to abandon this part of his project because of the advanced season. Confident that his treaty with the Comanches would render the route to New Mexico safe for traders to exchange idle Spanish pesos for much-needed French goods, he turned toward Fort Orleans. A journey of ten days brought him and his men to the Missouri, which they descended by canoe to their destination. When they arrived there Father Mercier gave a solemn *Te Deum* in thanksgiving for the success of the expedition.

Bourgmond now had only one more duty to perform for the Mississippi Company under his current contract—to engage some chiefs of the principal tribes to accompany him to France. He summoned an intertribal council, which met at Fort Orleans on December 15 and which eventually agreed to send a delegation to France with him. It included one Oto, four Osages, five Missouris, and a "princess" of the Missouris who was probably his daughter. Soon Bourgmond and some of his men journeyed to the Illinois country, where they were joined by four Illinois chiefs and Chicagou, chief of the Metchigamias. The officials of the Mississippi Company, who received them on their arrival at New Orleans in July, 1725, were reluctant to provide for so many mouths during their long voyage across the Atlantic. They permitted Bourgmond to take with him only his daughter, Chicagou, and one Indian from each of the tribes represented in the original party.[20]

Late in September they arrived in Paris. They were the sensation of the day; the city swarmed to see them. They met the directors of the Mississippi Company and many members of the French nobility. Among these were the Duchess of Orleans and the Duke of Bourbon, whom Louis XV, attaining his legal majority at the age of thirteen shortly before the death of the Duke of Orleans, had made his first minister. Later they met the king himself. Chicagou presented him with a treaty necklace sent by Mamantonense, chief of the Metchigamias, Cahokians, and

Tamaroas, while he addressed him in a long oration. The chief had, a few days before, charmed the Duchess of Orleans by expressing to her a wish that she would be fertile with many warriors as had been her husband's ancestors and her own. She gave him a snuff box which he cherished for the rest of his life. He and his fellow chiefs, dressed in cocked hats and beautiful blue suits trimmed with gold, were taken to the Italian theatre, where they danced many of their native dances. In the Bois de Boulogne they were allowed to run down a deer, as was their custom in the American wilderness. In the "princess of the Missouris" the Duchess of Orleans found an outlet from her boredom. She had the girl baptized in Notre Dame de Paris, stood as her godmother, and arranged marriage between her and Sergeant Dubois, who had accompanied Bourgmond from Fort Orleans. Bossu says that the princess "was given, among other things, a repeater watch set with diamonds, which the Indians thought was a spirit because of its apparently supernatural movement."[21] She returned with her husband to America, where he was killed, perhaps in a war between the French and the Foxes. She later married one Marin, captain of the militia, by whom she had a daughter.

All of the chiefs save one, who died en route, returned to their tribes. Twenty-eight years later Bossu questioned one of them about France and asked him what he thought was beautiful in Paris.

> He replied that the *Rue des Boucheries* was beautiful because of the quantity of meat he had seen there and that the *Rue Saint Honoré* pleased him, too. . . . When he told [his friends] that he had seen the great village of the French . . . as many people as there are leaves on the trees of their forest, . . . they answered that, since such a thing was impossible, the Europeans must have bewitched his eyes and must have shown him the same people over and over again. He added that he had seen the cabins of the great French chiefs, Versailles and the Louvre, and that they held more people than there were in all the tribal lands. He said that he had also seen the cabin of the old warriors, l'Hotel Royal des Invalides. Since the old man was beginning to be senile, he agreed with the other Indians that the French must have bewitched him.[22]

Another of these chiefs, an Illinois, told Bossu that he had noticed at the Tuileries and in other public places "men who were half women, with curled hair, earrings, and corsages on their chests. He suspected that they wore rouge, and he said that they smelled like alligators."[23]

Bourgmond, so far as we know, never returned to America. In December, 1725, he received his patent of nobility. His coat of arms, designed by Charles d'Hozier, the royal genealogist, showed an Indian resting against a silver mountain on a blue field. Four years later Fort Orleans was abandoned. In 1727 the Mississippi Company, having realized no profit from the post, instructed Governor Pérrier of Louisiana to reduce its garrison from fifteen to eight men, and two years later these were withdrawn and never replaced. Before 1925 most historians stated that the garrison had been massacred by Indians. Villiers dismissed this story as a myth. But he corrected one error only to commit another. He believed that the fort was re-established in 1736 and again between 1740 and 1750. We have no concrete evidence that Fort Orleans was reoccupied after it was abandoned.[24]

18

The Fox Wars

LIKE THE IROQUOIS IN THE SEVENTEENTH CENTURY, THE FOXES IN THE
eighteenth century were determined to resist French paternalism. Proud
of their bravery in warfare, they defied every attempt on the part of
the French to destroy their ancient customs. Through the Iroquois they
received from the Dutch and English at Albany gifts of belts and cheap
rum to incite them to kill French traders and eventually to destroy the
French fort at Detroit, which Antoine de la Mothe-Cadillac had built
in 1701.

Early in 1712, the Foxes and a small band of their Mascouten allies
suddenly appeared on the meadows behind the fort. They approached
to within fifty paces of it and set up their wigwams in the face of protests
from Joseph Guyon Dubuisson, commander of the fort. They numbered
in all about three hundred warriors and seven hundred old men, women,
and children. Since they had come with so many non-combatants, they
perhaps had no hostile intentions; later a French engineer named Léry
recalled that Cadillac, who since had become governor of Louisiana,
had invited them to the fort in order to trade for their furs. Nevertheless,
Dubuisson was convinced that they planned an attack, especially when
he saw them cutting down young trees, surrounding themselves with a
rough fence or palisade, shooting down chickens and pigeons which
belonged to the garrison, and "speaking always with much insolence,
and calling themselves the owners of all this country."[1] Dubuisson's
allies, the Ottawas and the Hurons, were on a winter hunt so he had no
choice but to submit to their insults. But when some of the Foxes entered the fort for the purpose of killing two of the French, a man and a

279

girl, against whom they had taken some offense, Dubuisson could no longer restrain himself. He took arms, he wrote,

> to prevent their accomplishing their object. I compelled them to retire immediately from the vicinity of the fort, in order not to give them time to strengthen their party, as they expected the Kickapoos and other allies, that they might together execute their nefarious designs; hoping to be strong enough to retire without loss among the Dutch and English and Iroquois. They waited but for a favorite opportunity to set fire to the fort.[2]

Soon their arrogance turned to great anger. They learned that a group of Ottawas and Potawatomies had defeated a band of Mascoutens who were wintering on the St. Joseph River. The Foxes avenged the Mascoutens' defeat by setting fire to an Ottawa cabin just outside the fort. Learning of their intention from Joseph, a Fox who had left his people and had come to live in the fort, Dubuisson immediately dispatched a canoe to recall the Ottawas and Hurons from their winter hunting grounds. Meanwhile, he sent another canoe to the other side of the lake to ask the Chippewas and Mississagues for assistance. At the same time, the Foxes tried to seize the church and several houses which stood beyond the palisade. The French fired on them, drove them back, and brought into the fort most of their wheat which had been stored in one of the houses. Then they demolished the church and several of the houses, which would have given their enemies cover and would have enabled them to set fire to the palisade nearby.[2]

On May 13, while Dubuisson waited for his allies, François Margaue de la Valtries, Sieur de Vincennes, appeared before the fort with seven or eight Frenchmen from the Miami country. The reinforcement was so small Dubuisson nearly despaired, but suddenly a Huron ran breathlessly into the fort with the joyful news that both his people and the Ottawas were close at hand. "God has pity on you," said the messenger. "He has decreed that your enemies and ours should perish. I bring you information that four men have just arrived at our fort, not daring to enter yours, on account of the [Foxes] and Mascoutens, who surround you." And he announced that Maisable, war chief of the Potawatomies, and his brother, Tehamasimon, were marching at the head

280

of six hundred men to the aid of the fort and "to eat those miserable
[tribes] who have troubled all the country."[3]

Climbing a bastion, Dubuisson soon saw them thronging through
the forest—Potawatomies, Sacs, Menomonies, Illinois, Missouri, Osages,
and other tribes "yet more remote." During the winter these tribesmen
had learned that the Foxes and Mascoutens planned to go to Detroit in
the spring. They had gathered at the Huron village, where each tribe
had adopted its own flag, then had marched to the assistance of the fort.[4]

The Hurons especially sought revenge for all the wrongs they had
suffered. Raising the war whoop, they charged their enemies. The Foxes
and Mascoutens also raised the war cry. Forty of them, all naked and
well armed, ran against the fort to show their enemies that they were
not afraid. Having little ammunition, however, Dubuisson wisely refrained from attacking them headlong; instead he began a siege that
lasted nineteen days during which he wore them out by continuous fire.
The Foxes and Mascoutens tried to avoid the continuous cannonading
by digging holes four or five feet deep and sheltering themselves in
them. Dubuisson raised two scaffolds, twenty feet high, which enabled
his men to fire inside the palisades of the enemy. Though they were
exhausted by hunger and thirst, the Foxes and Mascoutens fought on.
They raised twelve red English blankets on twelve separate poles in
their camp to show that they intended to fight until they had covered
the ground with blood. They called out that they had no father but the
English and that the other tribes would do well to quit the French
alliance and join theirs.[5]

At this juncture the war chief of the Potawatomies mounted one of
the scaffolds and began to harangue the Foxes and Mascoutens. He
shouted:

> Wicked nations that you are, you hope to frighten us by all that red color
> which you exhibit in your village. Learn, that if the earth is covered with
> blood, it will be yours. You speak to us of the English, they are the cause
> of your destruction because you have listened to their bad councils. They
> are enemies of prayer, and it is for that reason that the Master of Life
> chastises them, as well as you, wicked men that you are; don't you know
> as well as we do, that the Father of all the nations, who is at Montreal,
> sends continually parties of his young men against the English to make

war, and they take so many prisoners, that they do not know what to do with them? The English, who are cowards, only defend themselves by secretly killing men by that wicked strong drink, which has caused so many men to die immediately after drinking it. Thus we shall see what will happen to you for having listened to them.[6]

A small group of Foxes, availing themselves of the general distraction occasioned by the speech, stole to the adjacent river for water. Dubuisson observed them and ordered some of his men to attack them with a fire so violent that it killed more than thirty of them in a few moments. Undaunted, Pemoussa, the Fox chief, seized a house left standing outside the palisade and there erected a scaffold behind the gable end. Dubuisson could not penetrate it until he brought it down with two swivels which he mounted on logs on one of his own scaffolds. Some of the Fox marksmen were killed; the rest scattered as they uttered cries and frightful groans.[7]

Their bravado succumbed to famine and thirst. Toward evening they called out to Dubuisson from their defenses, requesting a parley. Seeing in it an opportunity to rescue three Ottawa women whom they held prisoners, Dubuisson granted their request. Through his interpreter, he told them that they could come in safely and say their last words before they died.

By morning they had pulled down all the red blankets and had mounted a white flag instead. Soon Pemoussa, carrying a white flag and accompanied by two slaves, approached the fort. Dubuisson sent his interpreter to protect Pemoussa and to conduct him to the parade, where all the chiefs and officers gathered to hear him. Presenting Dubuisson with a belt of wampum and his two slaves, he admitted defeat, begged for mercy, and asked for two days in which to hold a council with his wise men. To this request Dubuisson replied in the name of all his followers that, if their hearts were properly moved and if they wished to return to the allegiance of France, they must begin by giving up the three women whom they held as prisoners. Pemoussa agreed to return to the camp and take up the matter with his wise men in council. Several Frenchmen conducted him back to the village.

A few hours later three chiefs—two Mascoutens and a Fox—appeared before the fort with the three Ottawa women, one of whom was the wife of an Ottawa chief. Again Dubuisson had them conducted to the parade; again his officers and chiefs gathered to hear their message. Their spokesman said:

> My father, here are these three pieces of flesh that you asked of me. We would not eat them, thinking you would call us to account for it. Do what you please with them. You are the master. Now we Mascoutens and [Foxes] request that you would cause all the nations who are with you to retire, in order that we may freely seek provisions for our women and our children. Many die every day of hunger. All our villages regret that we have displeased you. If you are as good a father as all your children, who are around you, say you are, you will not refuse the favor we ask of you.

But now that he had gained the three women Dubuisson no longer cared to negotiate with his enemies. He reprimanded them and asked his Indian allies to pass judgment on them. Makouandeby, head chief of the Illinois, replied with great firmness:

> Now listen to me ye nations who have troubled all the earth. We perceive clearly by your words, that you seek only to surprise our father, and to deceive him again, in demanding that we should retire. We should no sooner do so, but you would again torment our father, and you would infallibly shed his blood. You are dogs who have always bit him. You have never been sensible of all the favors you have received from all the French. You have thought, wretches that you are, that we did not know all the speeches you have received from the English, telling you to cut the throats of our fathers and of his children, and then to lead his children into this country. Go away, then. For us, we will not stir a step from you; we are determined to die with our father; we should disobey him; because we know your bad heart, and we would not leave him alone with you. We shall see from this moment, who will be master, you or us; you have now only to retire, and as soon as you shall re-enter your fort, we shall fire upon you.[8]

The French and their allies carried out this threat. Their enemies drew up and retaliated by shooting blazing arrows at the straw-thatched houses and setting a number of them on fire. The French and their allies were discouraged. But Dubuisson gradually restored their resoluteness by appealing to their sense of shame, warning them of the governor's anger, and assuring them of ultimate victory. Victory, indeed, was now within their reach. Some Sacs who had been fighting with the Foxes saw in this desperate turn of events an opportunity to join their tribesmen on the side of the French. Deserting the Foxes, they escaped to the fort with a report of the pitiful state of the beleaguered camp. They declared that sixty out of eighty women and children had died of hunger and thirst in addition to those killed in battle, that the constant strife prevented the Mascoutens and Foxes from burying their dead, and that the camp had become infested with disease.[9]

This description proved accurate. Within a few days the Mascoutens and Foxes again called from their palisade for another parley. Again Dubuisson told them they were free to come. Again Pemoussa appeared at the gate of the fort. This time he was naked. Green paint covered his entire body. Wampum belts circled his waist and hung from his shoulders. A crown of wampum beads adorned his head. With him were seven women who, painted and adorned with wampum, were meant as a peace-offering. Behind them were three principal chiefs rattling gourds and wailing to the gods for help and pity. Pemoussa again addressed the assembled chiefs and officers; Dubuisson again left judgment to his Indian allies. This time their appeal was met with a fierce silence. Only Dubuisson, by his presence, saved them from death.[10]

They retired from the fort in despair, but resumed firing with intensified fury. They waited only for an opportunity to escape from their camp. At last, on the nineteenth day of the siege, under cover of a dark and rainy night, those who had strength enough to move stole past their sleeping enemies to Grosse Pointe, a headland projecting into the river opposite the end of Isle au Cochon, about five miles above Detroit. Here, knowing that they would be pursued, they barricaded themselves behind felled trees.

Sieur de Vincennes rushed toward the barricade with a group of Indians and a few Frenchmen. Its defenders fired on them, killing or wounding twenty of them. Undeterred, Vincennes had his men raise wigwams on the spot and, supplying them with axes, mattocks, and two swivels, had them build a wall of logs opposite the barricade. From it they hit the enemy with a close and deadly fire. The Mascoutens and Foxes fought for four days and then, utterly exhausted, surrendered.

The French allowed their allies to adopt or enslave the women and children. The men were massacred.[11]

Yet the rest of the tribe remained strong and troublesome. Less than two years later they attacked the Illinois, killing or carrying away seventy-seven of them. Again in 1716 they unleashed their fury in the same place. Again the French parleyed with them. Again, in the face of threats, they forswore the warpath. Again they broke their promises. Nearly all of the tribes in the Middle Valley were their hereditary enemies, and at the least provocation they sought revenge for ancient wrongs. Encouraged by the English and Dutch, many tribes brought their furs to Albany instead of trading with the French at Montreal. Alarmed at the possible ruin of the fur trade with the tribes of the Middle Valley, the French governor, Philippe Rigualt, Marquis de Vaudreuil, declared the necessity of keeping them peaceful and of destroying their enemies. "They are the common enemies of all the Western tribes," he wrote. "They have lately murdered three Frenchmen and five Hurons at Detroit. The Hurons ask for our help against them, and we must give it, or all the tribes will despise us."[12]

He asked François la Porte, Sieur de Louvigny, formerly commander at Michilimackinac, to gather a force of friendly tribes and to march against the chief village of the Foxes, about thirty miles from the mouth of the Fox river. He was to attack them if they stood their ground; if they did not he was to destroy their ripening corn, burn their wigwams, and encamp there for the winter in order to harass them as they roamed the woods in search of game.

Illness and the tardiness of his allies prevented Louvigny from pursuing the campaign until May, 1716. Then he marched with two hundred and twenty-five Frenchmen from Montreal to Detroit, where he augmented this force with another two hundred Frenchmen and many more Indian allies. With this army Louvigny attacked the Fox braves who stood their ground behind a palisade of oak. This fortress was so strong that he could not penetrate it with two cannon and a mortar. He tried to gain it by regular approaches. Protected by his artillery and eight hundred French and Indians, he dug trenches seventy yards from the palisade on the first night. On the second night he advanced to within sixty feet of it, and on the third night to within twenty-three yards. There he planned to blow it up.[13]

The Fox tribe, including the women, numbered about three thousand. They offered furious resistance; but soon, learning of the planned explosion, and unable to resist the underground approaches of their enemies, they asked for a parley. They admitted defeat and accepted Louvigny's demands to make peace with the neighboring tribes, to give up their prisoners, and to pay the cost of the campaign in furs. Pending fulfillment of their promises, they agreed to surrender six of their chiefs or the sons of their chiefs as hostages. Louvigny and his men returned in triumph to Montreal.[14]

The Foxes remained quiet for several years. Then, in 1722, Oushala, the Fox war chief, made war on the Illinois, who had burned his nephew alive. He drove them to the top of the rock on which La Salle had built Fort St. Louis. The French regarded the attack as unpardonable. Vaudreuil requested advice from the French minister, who ordered him to destroy the offending tribe. "His Majesty," wrote the minister, "will recompense The Officer who shall Reduce the Renards to submission, —or rather, who will destroy them,—as His Majesty expressly desired this."[15]

Despite this order, Vaudreuil decided to send an emissary, Marchand de Lignery, to Green Bay to make another attempt to persuade Oushala to remain at peace with his neighbors. Lignery told him that the king wished him to stop attacking the Illinois and that a great misfortune would befall him and his people if they continued in their warlike ways. Oushala replied that the Illinois had attacked his people too often to permit any thought of peace, but that a French officer might be sent to his village to help his braves restrain themselves.[16]

In 1726 Charles de la Boische, Marquis de Beauharnois, succeeded Vaudreuil as governor of Canada. Because of his dignity, charm, and love of ceremony, many historians have believed that he was an illegitimate son of Louis XIV. He had remarkably good judgment and an aptitude for administrative duties rare in the government of New France. In conformity with orders from France, he commanded that a fort be built at the headwaters of the Mississippi River to prevent the Foxes from obtaining possible asylum with their allies, the Sioux, in case they were driven from their homes in western Wisconsin. Because such an expedition had to pass through Fox territory, the governor sent Lignery to arrange a temporary truce with them. In this mission Lignery was successful. On June 7, 1726, he gained their consent to come to a conference, either at Chicago or at Le Rocher on the Illinois River, with the French commander and the Illinois. Beauharnois then obtained the financial support of the merchants of New France, who were eager to extend their fur trade to the vast territory of the Sioux and even beyond. They agreed to build a "fort of stakes, a chapel, a house for the commanding officer, and one for the missionaries."[17] In return he granted them a complete monopoly of the trade in the Sioux country for at least three years. During this ensuing period they agreed to send supplies to the proposed fort for the commander, for his second in command, and for the missionaries. They also agreed to buy at Michilimackinac three of four extra canoes to transport the supplies over the rapids and shallows of the Fox-Wisconsin waterway.[18]

The expedition left Montreal on June 16, 1727, under the command of René Boucher, Sieur de la Perrière, who had served in the French and Indian raid of 1708, which had resulted in the sacking of Haverhill, Massachusetts. He had visited the Sioux country with Louvigny in 1715 and had been promoted to the rank of captain for his gallantry. The expedition sailed up the Ottawa River with its numerous portages, across the Mattawan Portage to Green Bay, then to the fort at Michilimackinac, emporium of the western fur trade. There La Perrière stayed nine days buying new canoes, repacking goods, meeting old friends, and making new ones. On August 1 he and his men departed for their destination on the Mississippi, fortifying themselves "against the pretended extreme difficulties of securing passage through the country of the Renards."[19]

A week later they arrived at the log fort known as La Baye, on the present site of Green Bay, Wisconsin. Its commander[20] received them graciously and assured them that they would encounter no impediment in traveling through the Fox country. Accompanied by Pierre Reaume, official interpreter at the Green Bay post, and Father Jean Chardon, the post missionary, they advanced along the Fox River to Doty Island, Winnebago territory for more than two centuries, where they received a friendly welcome. The travelers then crossed the northern end of Lake Winnebago, entered the upper Fox River, and advanced to the first Fox village, at the present site of Oakwood in the city of Oshkosh, Wisconsin. As soon as the Frenchmen arrived the Fox chiefs with their peace calumets ran down to the river bank. A council was arranged in which Reaume and Father Chardon placated "these cut-throats and assassins." Their purpose accomplished, the interpreter and the missionary returned to Green Bay. The expedition, having passed its initial danger, continued to the portage of the Wisconsin, and on to the Wisconsin River. Finally, early in September, they reached the Father of Waters, which Father Louis Ignatius Guignas, one of the missionaries of the expedition, described:

> This beautiful river is spread out between two chains of high mountains, barren and very sterile, regularly distant from each other one league, three quarters of a league, or half a league where it is the narrowest. Its center is occupied by a chain of islands well wooded, so that in looking at it from the top of the heights, one would imagine that one was looking at an endless valley watered on right and left by two immense rivers. Sometimes also one does not see any river, for these islands are overflowed every year and are suitable for raising rice.[21]

At noon on September 17, they reached Lake Pepin, and began to build a fort on a low point jutting out from the water in the middle of the southern shore. The surrounding forest provided excellent firewood. "The day after landing," wrote Father Guignas, "axes were applied to the trees and four days later the fort was entirely finished. It is a plot of ground a hundred feet square surrounded by stakes twelve feet high with two bastions." Within the palisade stood the commander's and missionaries' houses and the chapel. Outside the fort each man built himself a house which, together with a blacksmith's shop and a warehouse for goods, formed the nucleus of a village. "Before the end of October," wrote Guignas, "all the houses were finished, and furnished; and everyone found himself lodged peacefully in his own home. Nothing was thought of then but to go and reconnoiter the neighboring districts and rivers, to see those herds of fallow-deer of all species of which they tell such tales in Canada. They must have disappeared or have greatly diminished since the time these former travelers left the country. They are no longer in such great numbers, and it is hard to kill any."[22]

The monks called their chapel the Mission of St. Michael the Archangel. They did not, however, confine themselves to preaching the gospel to the neighboring Indians. With the aid of a quadrant, a telescope, and several other instruments which Beauharnois had given them before they left Montreal, they studied the geography and the natural conditions of the region.[23]

La Perrière christened the little post Fort Beauharnois in honor of the governor of New France. On November 4, the governor's saint day, the missionaries celebrated high mass for him. That evening La Perrière planned a fireworks celebration which was postponed because of rain. Finally, on November 14, all was ready: "some very fine rockets were fired off," while the air resounded with a hundred shouts of "Long Live the King," and "Long Live Charles de Beauharnois." Some friendly Sioux around the post brought wine, which Father Guignas declared "most excellent, [though] his sense of patriotism induced him to add that there are no finer wines here than in Canada." The fireworks terrified the Indians. "When these poor people saw the fireworks in the air and the stars falling from heaven," wrote Guignas, "women and children took to flight, and the most courageous of the men cried for mercy, and urgently asked that the astonishing play of this terrible medicine should be made to cease."[24]

La Perrière was not destined to remain long at his post. In April the fort was flooded with three feet of melted snow. The water and the cold weather affected the commander's health seriously, and he was forced to leave his command to his nephew, Pierre Boucherville, and to return with one of the missionaries to Montreal. He arrived there too ill to report to the governor, who had to obtain information of conditions at the fort from the missionary. This was of vital importance to the governor; the Foxes had broken their truce and had massacred both French soldiers and their Indian allies in the Illinois country. Resolving to destroy them, Beauharnois ordered his old emissary, Lignery, to attack their village on the Fox River. In June, 1728, Lignery gathered five hundred Frenchmen and about a thousand Indians in a flotilla of birch canoes and departed on his mission. Paddling up the Fox River, they reached a Winnebago village. From there they followed the stream, "a ribbon of lazy water twisting in a vague, perplexing way through the broad marsh of wild rice and flags," until they saw the chief village of the Foxes standing on a little hill. Lignery had hoped to surprise them, but they had seen him coming and most of them had fled. His men found only three squaws and an old man. He gave them to his Indian allies,

289

who enslaved the women and burned the old man at a slow fire. Lignery had to content himself with burning the village and destroying their crops of maize, peas, beans, and squashes. Then he returned with his force to Mackinac.[25]

Since the surrounding country now swarmed with fugitive Foxes intent on wreaking vengeance on every white man who crossed their path, Lignery sent seven of his men overland to warn Boucherville that Fort Beauharnois might be besieged. With the seven men he sent two Menominees as guides. The fort commander quickly recognized the danger. Since the Indians had, in the words of the Menominee messengers, "Renard hearts," Boucherville and most of his men resolved to escape as expeditiously as possible. The rest, under an intrepid officer named Sieur de la Jémerais, determined to stay and hold the fort for another year.[26]

Meanwhile Boucherville, his cousins the Montbruns, Father Guignas, and eight other men paddled in three canoes down the Mississippi, hoping to pass the Foxes unobserved. But one foggy morning they saw, just below the mouth of the Rock River, a group of Kickapoos and Mascoutens—allies of the Foxes—running along the river bank. Another group approached them in canoes and soon took them prisoners. At first the Indians intended to turn them over to the Foxes, who would either have burned them or kept them for a profitable ransom. The Montbruns, however, escaped. This alarmed their captors, who feared that French soldiers might be summoned. The Indians therefore agreed to make peace with the white men. They escorted Boucherville and his comrades to Peoria and permitted them to communicate with the officers in the Illinois country. Eventually they returned to Montreal.[27] The prospects for a profitable trade with the Sioux soon faded. Sometime in 1729 La Jémerais abandoned Fort Beauharnois, which the Sioux probably burned to the ground.[28]

The French authorities now had no recourse but to turn the neighboring tribes loose on the victorious Foxes and their allies. Gradually they wore away the Fox powers of resistance by harassing them and cutting down any stragglers.

In 1730 Nicolas Coulon, Sieur de Villiers, commander of the fort on the St. Joseph and father of Coulon de Villiers who twenty-four years later defeated George Washington at Fort Necessity, led a formidable force of French and Indian allies against the Foxes near Le Rocher, in the Illinois country, and besieged them for twenty-nine days in a grove they had surrounded with a stockade. Attempting to desert the stockade during a storm at night, they were detected and many were slaughtered. When only fifty or sixty of them remained—twenty men and thirty or forty women and children—they came out and cast themselves at Villier's mercy. The French commander spared their lives when they agreed to submit to the orders of the French authorities in Canada. Sometime later, while Coulon was on his way to command the fort at La Baye, he learned that some Foxes had taken refuge in a Sac village. Incautiously going to the village with one of his sons, he demanded that the Sacs give up their guests. The Sacs refused and asked him to withdraw. When he tried by force to enter a cabin, one of the Indians approached with uplifted tomahawk while three others fired at him. One of the bullets killed his son. Villiers fired several times into the crowd of Indians, but was killed with rifle shot.[29]

This incident proved significant in the history of the Mississippi Valley frontier. The Sacs, while frequently sympathizing with and secretly aiding their kinsmen, had up to this time remained ostensibly allied to the French. But now, afraid of being unable to answer for the death of so prominent a French official, they united with the Foxes. Henceforth the two tribes acted as one nation. They withdrew from their old residence at Green Bay and moved to the land of the Iowas across the Mississippi. There they continued to harass the French fur traders, to cut off the French Indians, and to pursue and attack the timid Illinois to the very gates of French posts. When the French retaliated, the Sacs and Foxes took refuge across the Wapsipinicon River, which the French called *La Pomme de Cigne*, meaning Swan-Apple, an edible root that grew plentifully on its banks.[30]

In August, 1734, Beauharnois sent Captain Nicolas Joseph de Noyelles with eighty Frenchmen and about one hundred and thirty Indian allies to punish the Sacs and Foxes in their new homes. On his way he stopped at Detroit and at the Ouiatanon village, augmenting his force with about a hundred Hurons and Potawatomies. Near the French fort on the St. Joseph he enlisted forty Kickapoos, who proved invaluable as guides "because none of our savages knew what part of the Country They were in." They also captured a Fox and five Sacs, who informed them that their people had deserted *La Pomme de Cigne* for the *Sans Fourche* (meaning Without a Fork), a name often applied to the Des Moines. Undaunted, Noyelles led his force over the prairies, crossing the Cedar, the Iowa, and the Skunk rivers on improvised rafts in the dead of winter. By this time his Kickapoo guides, weary of the expedition, had deserted him along with a few Frenchmen. The rest of them doggedly pursued their aim, eating one skimpy meal a day. Their fortitude was rewarded when, at last, they arrived before a village of fifty-five cabins in which the Sacs and Foxes had entrenched themselves. Though Noyelles and his men were greatly outnumbered, they fought with such fury that they forced their enemies to retreat to a fort built by the women and children while the men were fighting. During the battle, which began on April 19, 1735, and which lasted four days, the French and their Indian allies had nothing to eat save twelve dogs and a horse that was killed at night near the besieged fort. Several soldiers ate their moccasins. These desperate circumstances forced Noyelles to send the Sacs a message promising to forgive them if they would agree to abandon the Foxes and return to their old homes on Green Bay. They replied that their great losses in the recent battle prevented them from following him. The Sacs requested, however, that he assure the governor of New France that they would return to their old villages as soon as they could.[31] They never kept their promise. The battle proved nothing save the endurance and intrepidity of the French.

Again, two years later, the French authorities of Canada felt constrained to send another expedition against the Sacs and Foxes to separate them and to keep them from molesting the Illinois. The leader of the new expedition was Pierre Paul, Sieur de Marin, who built a fort at Magill's Slough, which is on the Iowa side of the Mississippi below the mouth of the Wisconsin. Though he claimed that he had established peace among the two tribes he proved to be an unreliable reporter; he had achieved only a short truce. Within a few months the Sacs and Foxes again began to molest the Illinois; eventually they drove them out of the region, perhaps almost annihilating them. The victors made themselves masters of the Mississippi Valley from the Wisconsin down to the Illinois. Jointly they claimed the region on both sides of the Mississippi from the Wisconsin and the Upper Iowa to the Illinois and the Missouri. The principal village of the Foxes, Musquakinuk, stood on the Iowa side of the river, near the present site of Davenport. The principal village of the Sacs, Saukenuk, lay on the Illinois side, above the mouth of the Rock River.[32]

Saukenuk was the wonder of all who saw it. It had an enviable location on a point of land between the Rock River and the Mississippi. At the time of its greatest affluence, it contained about a hundred lodges; its surrounding fields of blue grass furnished ample pasturage for their horses; the two rivers teemed with fish; and a fertile prairie that ran parallel with the Father of Waters yielded several hundred acres of corn. The streets of the village, though seldom straight, contained open spaces for assemblies and games. The houses, which were often spacious, sometimes measuring one hundred feet long by forty feet wide, rested on poles tied with thongs and roofs made of elm bark. The largest buildings, which they called *hodensotes,* were divided into apartments which they used in common as storerooms and fireplaces. For tribal councils and public discussions they used other dwellings in which their chief men debated all questions relating to the public weal. Running the full length of each lodge was a long bench on which their women spread blankets and skins. Between each bench was an open space on which they built fires and prepared their food. Since the lodges were occupied only in summer, they had no chimney. Smoke escaped either through the roof or out of the doors. Sometimes several lodges were enclosed by fences made of poles draped with melon vines. The entire village presented a neatness and orderliness rare among Indian habitations.[33]

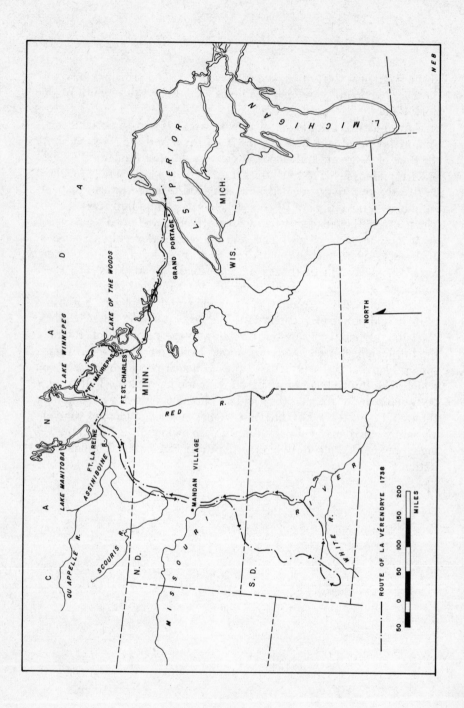

19

La Vérendrye and His Sons:
The Search for the Western Sea

ONE OF THE CHIEF MOTIVES OF THE FRENCH EXPLORERS IN THE FIRST PART of the eighteenth century was the search for a passage or channel from the Atlantic to the Western Sea, as they called the Pacific Ocean. In this endeavor they followed the Spaniards who, since the sixteenth century, had searched in Central America for the mythical Strait of Anian, which purportedly connected the Pacific with another sea to the north. At first French explorers supposed that the passage lay somewhere above Montreal; but it receded westward as they descended the St. Lawrence and its tributary the Ottawa, and it receded again as they advanced to Lake Superior. Hitherto they had entertained great hopes of eventually overtaking it, for their search had been along broad, sea-like waterways; but now these lay behind them, and they found that they stood on the threshold, not of a great sea but of a great plain—an ocean of waving grass.

The English in Canada, too, sought the Strait of Anian or the Northwest Passage, as they sometimes called it, to the "Western Sea." Their route lay farther north through Hudson Bay. For many decades their Hudson Bay Company, in the interest of establishing trade with oriental countries, made innumerable efforts to beat their French competitors to the prize. But during the War of the Spanish Succession the French subjected the company to so many depredations that they prevented it from regaining its former stability and affluence until some years after the Treaty of Utrecht in 1713. At this time the dominant figure of the

Hudson Bay region was its governor, Captain James Knight, who filled the last years of his colorful life with hopes and plans and excursions in his resolve to expand the company and to discover the coveted Northwest Passage.[1] The French were resolved to meet the challenge with equal energy.

Among the French explorers who fell under the spell of the Western Sea and who were determined to forestall England in reaching it was Pierre Gaultier de Varennes, Sieur de la Vérendrye. Like so many fascinating characters in the history of the American frontier, he is unknown to most Americans. Canadians better appreciate his unflinching courage and his magnificent patience in the face of fraud, calumny, and misrepresentation. Rebuked and censured by the government, cheated by merchants, hounded by his creditors, and gouged by his partners, he was a man without a chance. Yet he succeeded in building new forts, in establishing the system of trade which Canadians adopted for nearly a century, and in opening up a lucrative field in which future traders became wealthy.

He was born in Three Rivers, where his father was governor and where his mother's father had been governor. At twelve he joined the army as a cadet, took part in the sacking of Deerfield, in the colony of Massachusetts, and fought at Malplaquet, the decisive battle of the War of the Spanish Succession. In this battle he received four sabre wounds and one bullet wound through his body. Though he was given up for dead, his marvelous constitution pulled him through. He was rewarded for bravery with a lieutenancy, but the pay of this rank was inadequate to enable him to maintain himself and his family. So he returned to Canada, where he married Marie-Anne Dandonneau, by whom he had four sons—Jean-Baptiste, Pierre, François, and Louis-Joseph—all of whom were destined to accompany their father on his ceaseless travels.[2]

He established a little trading post on the St. Maurice, but it failed to provide him with the necessities of his growing family. Seeking more remunerative employment, he availed himself of his experience as a fur trader and obtained from Governor Beauharnois command of a trading post at Lake Nipigon, north of Lake Superior. This was the gateway to the region where he was to perform most of the great work of his life. Beyond stretched the land of conjecture, of the mysterious Western Sea, which so far had eluded the zealous searches of several of his countrymen. He never lost sight of his great aim, which he pursued with the fidelity characteristic of his undertakings in the past.

One day in 1729 he met Pako, chief of the Crees from Lake Nipigon, who with other Indians proved influential in determining the course of his immediate future. Pako told him that he had paddled with two companions on a river far toward the setting sun until he had come to a great lake. From it flowed another river down which they had traveled until it began to ebb and flow like the waters of the sea. But, fearing hostile Indians, who seemed to be lurking all around them, they had not continued to its mouth. They refrained from this even though Pako had heard that it emptied into a great salt lake or sea. Other Indians corroborated Pako's story. They told La Vérendrye that they had journeyed to a country whose people lived in fortified villages, wore armor, rode horses, and traveled in floating castles on the rivers and lakes.[3] No doubt they were alluding to the Spaniards.

Though La Vérendrye understood Indian imagination too well to accept as truth all that Pako and the others had told him, he was deeply impressed by their stories. Basically, he thought, they harmonized with his own belief of a river that flowed westward to the mysterious sea he sought. So he decided to surrender his command of the fort and to equip an expedition for the discovery of the Western Sea. Before he departed to obtain the governor's permission in person, he had Ochagach or Auchagah, an Indian from the Kaministikwia River who had consented for a few gifts to serve as his guide, draw a rough map of the region around Lake Winnipeg.

Armed with this map and others, La Vérendrye in 1730 returned to Quebec, where he reminded Governor Beauharnois that "the English have every interest in getting ahead of us, and if we allow them time they will not lose the chance of doing it." The governor was much impressed. He wrote to Louis XV's minister of marine, Jean Frédéric Phélypeaux, Count of Maurepas, urging him to adopt La Vérendrye's plans to push into the unknown west. He also enclosed the maps which he had had drawn of the Winnipeg region. Eventually Maurepas gave La Vérendrye permission to build some forts which would serve as bases for further exploration of the Western Sea. But he had no money to squander on projects which seemed to him to promise no definite return. Not one sou did he provide to defray the expenses of the proposed expedition. Instead he offered La Vérendrye a monopoly of trade which was of no use to anybody else. Undaunted, La Vérendrye went to Montreal, where on May 19, 1731, he signed, in the presence of the governor, an agreement whereby he associated himself with Jean Bouillet de la Chassaigne and other merchants in return for credit on the supplies he needed for his expedition. Being merchants first and Frenchmen second, they cared nothing for exploration; but they were willing to take a chance on the enormous prospective profits of the trade which they expected him to facilitate by building the forts they financed.[4]

In June La Vérendrye left Montreal for the west with his three oldest sons and his nephew Christophe Defrost, Sieur de la Jemeraye. This youth of twenty-three had gained invaluable experience by serving as a cadet in the Montreal militia and by wintering among the Sioux in the upper valley of the Mississippi. There he had interested himself in the customs and manners of the various tribes of the region. Traveling by way of the St. Lawrence, the Ottawa and Mattawan rivers, Lake Nipissing, and Georgian Bay, they reached the mission on the Straits of Mackinac. There they were joined by Father Charles Michel Mesaiger, a man of forty who for the past nine years had been doing apprenticeship work in the mission. La Vérendrye wrote to Maurepas, apprising him of his whereabouts and assuring him of his readiness to proceed in the following year to discover the Western Sea. Then he descended the St. Mary's River, coasted along the eastern shore of Lake Superior, turned his canoes westward, and on August 26 reached Grand Portage at the mouth of the Pigeon River. He might have pushed on to Rainy Lake, where he proposed to build the first of his western forts, had he been able to count on the support of his men; but they muttered and then mutinied at the prospect of venturing into a region which they thought was infested with monsters. Or perhaps they were acting out a deal they had made with the Montreal merchants who, wanting La Vérendrye to remain near Lake Superior to develop the fur trade, had paid them to stir up trouble to prevent him from going farther west. Whatever their design, they failed, for La Vérendrye succeeded, with Father Mesaiger's assistance, in inducing some of the mutineers to accompany one of his sons and La Jemeraye to Rainy Lake, while the rest of the party retired for the winter to the Kaministikwia River, near the present city of Fort William, Ontario.[5]

Crossing the portage to the Pigeon River and following it through the concatenation of lakes that mark the present international line, La Jemeraye eventually found himself on the western side of Rainy Lake. There he built Fort St. Pierre, named in honor of his uncle's patron saint. Then, in accordance with his uncle's program, he invited the Crees and the Assiniboins to visit him. Though they failed to appear, he was able to use his influence to promote peace by stopping several war parties of the neighboring Monsonis from attacking the Sioux. He spent the winter at Fort St. Pierre and then, probably in the early spring, returned to Lake Superior and rejoined the main party on the Kaministikwia River.[6]

Meanwhile La Vérendrye had encountered the first in a series of difficulties that plagued him for the rest of his life. He had expected the neighboring Indians to bring in furs which would have enabled him to meet his payroll and to pay for the supplies advanced to him by the Montreal merchants. They failed to appear. Yet he garnered some relief by sending out a few canoes which returned in the last days of May with a small cargo of furs. These he sent immediately to Mackinac in charge of his son Jean-Baptiste, whom he instructed to pick up some supplies which had been sent to him from Montreal and which were to be brought to Lake of the Woods. There La Vérendrye planned to build his principal post.[7]

On June 8, 1732—the first anniversary of his departure from Montreal—La Vérendrye, Father Mesaiger, and the rest of the party left in seven canoes for Fort St. Pierre. They reached the fort over two months later by traversing the intricate chain of small lakes and rivers and portages that connect Lake Superior and Rainy Lake. Here they were joined by a large group of friendly Indians who had come in fifty canoes to visit La Vérendrye and to place themselves, through him, under the protection of the Great White Father in Quebec. Eager to use them as guides, La Vérendrye soon departed for Lake of the Woods. The flotilla, as it moved downstream, assumed the aspect of a gala procession. The Indian paddlers, accompanied by their squaws and children, were clad in scanty buckskin, and the voyagers wore the usual articles of their costume: a short skirt, a red woolen cap, a blue *capote* with a hood that could be drawn over the head on cold days and thrown back on the shoulders on warm, a pair of deerskin leggings which reached from their ankles to a little above the knees and which were held up by a string tied to a belt at the waist. As they journeyed through a country covered with virgin forests of fir, pine, and oak, as they drew nearer and nearer to their destination, they sang songs that defied the daily menace of Indians who stood watching their departure or who lurked in the wilderness, waiting for an opportunity to exact from their leader the price of his hardihood in invading cherished hunting grounds:

> *En roulant ma boule roulant,*
> *En roulant ma boule.*
> *En roulant ma boule roulant,*
> *En roulant ma boule.*
>
> *Derrier' chez nous, ya-t-un étang,*
> *En roulant ma boule.*
> *Derrier' chez nous, ya-t-un étang,*
> *En roulant ma boule.*
> *Trois beaux canards s'en vont baignant,*
> *Rouli, roulant, ma boule roulant,*
> *En roulant ma boule roulant,*
> *En roulant ma boule.*
>
> *Trois beaux canards s'en vont baignant,*
> *En roulant ma boule.*
> *Le fils du roi s'en va chassant,*
> *Rouli,* etc.
>
> *Le fils du roi s'en va chassant,*
> *En roulant ma boule.*
> *Avec son grand fusil d'argent,*
> *Rouli,* etc.
>
> *Avec son grand fusil d'argent,*
> *En roulant ma boule.*
> *Visa le noir, tua le blanc,*
> *Rouli,* etc.
>
> *Visa le noir, tua le blanc,*
> *En roulant ma boule.*

O fils du roi, tu es méchant!
Rouli, etc.

. . . .

On, roll on, my ball. I roll on,
  On, roll on my ball, on!
On roll on, my ball I roll on,
  On, roll on my ball, on!

'Way back at home there is a pond,
  On, roll on my ball, on!
'Way back at home there is a pond,
  On, roll on my ball, on!
Three bonnie ducks go swimming 'round,
  Roll on, my ball, my ball I roll on.

Three bonnie ducks go swimming 'round
On, roll on my ball, on!
The prince goes off a-hunting bound,
  Roll on, etc.

The prince goes off a-hunting bound,
On, roll on my ball, on!
His gun so big with silver crown'd,
  Roll on, etc.

His gun so big with silver crown'd,
On, roll on my ball, on!
The black he saw, the white he down'd,
  Roll on, etc.

The black he saw, the white he down'd,
On, roll on my ball, on!
O prince, that was a wicked wound!
  Roll on, etc.[8]

Or they changed to the pathetic refrain of *A la claire fontaine*, which
was perhaps the most popular of their songs:

A la claire fontaine
M'en allant promener,
J'ai trouvé l'eau si belle
Que je m'y suis baigné.
> *Lui ya longtemps que je t'aime,*
> *Jamais je ne t'oublierai.*

J'ai trouvé l'eau si belle
Que je m'y suis baigné;
Sous les feuilles d'un chêne
Je me suis fait sècher.
> *Lui ya longtemps, etc.*

Sous les feuilles d'un chêne
Je me suis fait sècher;
Sur la plus haute branche
Le rossignol chantait,
> *Lui ya longtemps, etc.*

. . . .

At the clear running fountain
> Sauntering by one day,
I found it so compelling
> I bathed without delay.
Your love long since overcame me,
Ever in my heart you'll stay.

I found it so compelling
> I bathed without delay;
Under an oak tree's umbrage
> I dried the damp away.
> Your love, etc.

Under an oak tree's umbrage
> I dried the damp away.
There where the highest branch is,
Sir Nightingale sang hey!
Your love, etc.[9]

At last La Vérendrye arrived with his men at the Lake of the Woods, whence, he believed, flowed the river that was to lead him to the Western Sea. Before him spread a vast expanse of open water studded with islands whose forests of fir, pine, and oak gave the lake its descriptive name. Crossing to its western shore, he came to a small headland projecting from a bay now known as Northwest Angle, Minnesota. There he began to build Fort St. Charles, named in honor of the governor of Canada, Charles de la Boische, Marquis de Beauharnois. It stood on a rectangular piece of ground one hundred feet on each side and sixty feet on each end. Its palisade, which consisted of a double row of spruce, aspen, and oak pickets and which was reinforced by four bastions, enclosed a house for the missionary, a chapel, a house for the commander, a powder magazine, and a storehouse. All these buildings were made of logs one above another, which were caulked with clay and covered with bark to keep out rain and cold. The fort had a watchtower and two gates, one facing the lake on the north and the other facing the neighboring forest on the south.[10]

To stave off possible famine, La Vérendrye ordered his men to sow some of the grain he had brought with him. This proved needless, for the region abounded with wild rice. It enabled La Vérendrye to save most of his grain for future planting. The lake provided them with many kinds of fish and the forest with more wild game than they needed.[11]

In March or April, 1733, when the ice on the lake broke up, La Vérendrye called a meeting of the Crees who, anxious to hear what he had to say, gathered at the fort in considerable numbers. La Vérendrye presented them with a ceremonial collar of friendship in the governor's name. Then he said that he had summoned them to tell them that their White Father in Quebec wanted them to remain at peace with their enemies, the Sioux, as well as with friendly tribes of the prairie. The Cree chief agreed to heed the governor's wish and requested that he and his people be allowed to remain at the fort during the warm months to help protect their white brothers.[12]

On May 27 La Vérendrye sent his nephew La Jemeraye to Governor Beauharnois in Quebec with a written report detailing his recent activities. Father Mesaiger, who needed medical attention, went with him. When La Jemeraye saw the governor late in September, he submitted his uncle's report and supplemented it with explanations of his own. He said that La Vérendrye planned to extend his explorations to what the Crees and the Assiniboins called the villages of the Mantannes or Mandans, which were located on both banks of the Missouri in present North Dakota. La Jemeraye, depending on information which he and his uncle had received from the Crees and particularly from the Assiniboins, described the Mandans as white men with light hair or red hair instead of the jet black scalplock of Indian tribes. They were, said La Jemeraye, a superior people with an astonishing civilization. They lived in fortified cities, raised crops, horses, and goats, hunted buffaloes, and excelled in arts and crafts. They spoke a language that resembled French, fought with swords and sabers and lances, and could not be killed because they wore armor. They lived in houses like those of the French, save that the roofs were flat and covered with earth and stones. Their country, which was flat, had a fabulous fauna that included two-headed snakes and even more "prodigious" animals. La Vérendrye pictured the Mandans as Europeans, and possibly as Frenchmen. Since their villages lay on the Missouri, which might be the river he sought to lead him to the Western Sea, he was naturally very anxious to visit them.[13]

The truth was that the Mandans, as La Vérendrye himself was later to learn, were more or less like other Indians he knew. He was not surprised. He seems to have derived his false description of them from his imperfect understanding of what the Crees and the Assiniboins told him. Or perhaps his willingness to believe what he knew could not be true deceived him. The Assiniboins, while acting as middlemen in purveying English and French goods, also visited the Pawnees, the Kiowas, perhaps the Crows, and possibly the Comanches, from whom they heard stories of the Spaniards in New Mexico. These were repeated to La Vérendrye. He knew, of course, about the Spaniards. He also knew that the Indians were inclined to exaggerate for the purpose of saving a good story. Still, in his eagerness to visit the Mandans, he seems to have been willing to believe almost anything he heard about them. The stories he heard about the Spaniards he misapplied to the Mandans, either deliberately or because of his imperfect knowledge of their language.

During his interview with the governor, La Jemeraye adverted to his uncle's financial troubles. The expedition had already cost him 43,000 livres. Now his men were clamoring for their wages and refused to go a step farther unless they were paid. To continue his work he needed about 30,000 more livres, a sum which would cover wages and supplies and which could be obtained from the king's stores. Beauharnois, who had great faith in La Vérendrye and who genuinely wished him to succeed in his exploratory efforts, transmitted his written report together with his nephew's explanations to Maurepas, minister of marine. He enclosed, too, a long letter in which he praised the explorer's courage and skill and requested the government to grant him the financial assistance necessary for his success. But the answer he received in the following year was discouraging. Maurepas had placed both the governor's report and letter before the king, who approved of the forts which La Vérendrye had established on Rainy Lake and Lake of the Woods. Nevertheless, because he was preparing for the War of the Polish Succession, he emphatically refused to finance the expedition. Those interested in it, he said, should continue to finance it, "paying their way by the profits of the trade; then, if the undertaking proved successful, he would grant rewards to those deserving them."[14]

Meanwhile La Vérendrye at Fort St. Charles had resolved that he himself must go to Quebec and Montreal to plead his case before Beauharnois and the leading merchants. Before he departed, however, he told the Crees, who were planning war against the Sioux, that if they remained peaceful until his return he would give them gifts of tobacco, guns, and kettles, which he would exchange for the skins of martens and lynxes. Then, to show his confidence in them, he entrusted his son Jean-Baptiste to their care. Presenting him, he said: "I entrust to you my eldest son who is my dearest possession; consider him as another myself; do nothing without consulting him, his words will be mine; and as he is not so accustomed to fatigue as you, though he is equally vigorous, I depend on you to take care of him on the journey."[15]

Confident that, under this arrangement, the Crees would keep peace with their neighbors, he placed another son, Pierre, in command of Fort St. Charles. Then, on May 27, 1734, he started with ten men for Canada. At the Kaministikwia River he met a party of Frenchmen under René Cartier, a prominent trader whom he sent to the Red River to establish another post. At Mackinac he met the returning La Jemeraye, whom he instructed to proceed to Fort St. Charles, supercede Pierre there, and send him to help construct the new fort on the Red River. In the middle of August he reached Montreal. Resting his main hopes on the leading merchants of that town but realizing that they did not share his enthusiasm for exploration, he resolved to meet them on their own commercial grounds. He told them that the forts he had established were located in the very heart of the fur country, and that he had engaged the Assiniboins and the Crees to bring in large quantities of beaver skin. He added that he had deflected much of the trade of the Hudson Bay region from the English to the French, and that even the forests around Kaministikwia and Winnipeg abounded with fur-bearing animals that could bring them great wealth. By dint of argument and by his undying confidence in the ultimate success of his enterprise, he persuaded them to let him have additional supplies, though he already owed them considerable sums. Then he went to Quebec, where the governor received him with customary grace but could offer him no hope of financial assistance. The governor wrote to Maurepas again, suggesting help for the explorer in his plans to visit the Mandans in the spring of the following year and to find the Western Sea. The explorer waited patiently almost a whole year for a reply. When it came it proved as negative as the last one.[16]

Early in June, 1735, La Vérendrye loaded his canoes with the new supplies the merchants had granted him and left Montreal for Fort St. Charles. With him was his son Louis-Joseph, a lad of eighteen who was to be taught to make maps and plans for the projected voyage of the coming year. Father Jean-Pierre Aulneau also joined the expedition as a replacement for the ailing chaplain, Mesaiger. Traveling by the usual route, they reached Fort St. Charles on September 6 to find it destitute of provisions. Even the annual crop of wild rice had been destroyed by heavy rains. The only pleasant news came from La Jemeraye, who had succeeded in collecting four hundred loads of beaver skins and in sending them to Montreal. His delighted uncle sent him to invite the Assiniboins to join them in the expedition to the Mandans. When he returned from this mission, which he conducted with his usual success, he went at the request of his uncle to the post which Cartier had built on the Red River and which they named Fort Maurepas in honor of the minister of marine. La Vérendrye expected to join him as soon as some merchandise arrived from Montreal. So he allowed his nephew to take along most of the supplies in the fort. But snow and cold weather prevented Sieur Daniel Legras, leader of the convoy from Montreal, from advancing beyond Kaministikwia, where he remained for the rest of the winter.[17]

While La Vérendrye awaited spring at Fort St. Charles, his son Jean-Baptiste returned from his sojourn with the Crees and from Fort Maurepas. He brought tragic news. "La Jemeraye, his nephew and chief lieutenant, whose knowledge of the western tribes was invaluable, whose enthusiasm for the great project was only second to his own, whose patience and resourcefulness had helped the expedition out of many a tight corner—La Jemeraye was dead." He had been stricken ill at Fort Maurepas. As soon as he was able to move he started back for Fort St. Charles, where he thought he would have better care. But, accompanied by his cousins, probably François and Louis-Joseph, he took a longer route by way of the Roseau River. At its mouth he suffered a relapse and died. His cousins buried him on the spot, erected a wooden cross over his grave, cached their supplies, and completed their journey to Fort St. Charles. On learning of his nephew's death La Vérendrye again postponed his projected journey to the Mandans.[18]

Tragedy soon dealt him an even more terrible blow. Since the convoy he expected from Montreal had not yet arrived and since the fort was facing starvation, he sent a group of twenty men under Jean-Baptiste to hurry forward the supplies which were most urgently needed. Early in June, 1736, Jean-Baptiste and his men, including Father Aulneau, crossed the lake and reached an island now called Oak Point, a long, narrow peninsula guarding the entrance to the Rainy River. The details of what happened after they reached this island will perhaps never be known. Somehow the group was surprised by the Sioux and all were massacred.[19]

On June 8, three days after the tragedy, Sieur Legras arrived with the convoy from Kaministikwia over the same route as that followed by Jean-Baptiste and his companions. Seeing the canoes approach, La Vérendrye rushed down to meet them, and to ask Legras if he had met Jean-Baptiste and his men. Legras had seen nothing of them. Greatly alarmed, La Vérendrye sent Legras with nine men, including a sergeant, back to the mouth of the river to search for the missing men. A few days later he returned reporting that all of them had been slain and that he had found their bodies on what is now known as Massacre Island. They were lying in a circle on the beach, their heads severed from their bodies and wrapped in beaver skins. Jean-Baptiste was stretched on the ground, his back hacked with a knife, his headless trunk and legs and arms "decorated derisively with garters and bracelets of porcupine quills." Father Aulneau had been struck down by an arrow while he was in a kneeling position.[20]

For some time La Vérendrye was at a loss to understand why the Sioux had made this attack. Gradually, however, he learned that during his absence from the fort a party of Sioux had visited it and that some Crees inside of it had fired at them. "Who fire on us?" demanded the indignant Sioux. The Crees with grim humor replied, "The French." The Sioux withdrew, vowing vengeance on the treacherous Frenchmen. They soon found the opportunity they sought. The distraught explorer had the bodies of his son and of Father Aulneau, together with those of the others in the party, brought back to Fort St. Charles, where he gave them proper burial in the chapel.[21]

Again he had to delay his voyage to the Mandans. More than a year was to pass before he recovered sufficiently from his blows to resume his exploratory ventures. His best biographer, Nellis M. Crouse, sums up his position in this manner:

> His forces were disorganized; and the death of his eldest son, coming as it did just after that of his nephew, left him with only his younger sons, youths barely out of their 'teens, with whom to undertake the work of discovery. Nevertheless, he attacked the problem with his customary vigor. Being shorthanded in the midst of a country teeming with enemies, whose attacks might be expected at any moment, he decided to make his post strong enough to be defended by a small garrison. He does not tell us just what alterations were made, but he says that he had it "rebuilt and put in such a condition that four men could defend it against a hundred.[22]

Meanwhile, he never lost sight of his main aim of finding a passage to the Western Sea. To gain from the Crees and the Assiniboins more knowledge of the Mandan country and to enlist their support in his future plans, he journeyed to Fort Maurepas. There, on March 4, 1737, he held a council with the representatives of these tribes. They generously offered him all the guides he needed for his projected journey. But now, when his opportunity seemed to have arrived, his men, though tough and experienced *coureurs de bois* and *voyageurs* who had spent much of their lives among savages in the wilderness, said they were afraid to accompany him! How could he explain this obstacle to the governor? And how could the governor explain it to the minister, who now would be strengthened in his suspicions that La Vérendrye was more interested in furs than in discovery? Returning to his Indian friends, he declined their offer of guides, but he was too ashamed to admit his real reason for so doing. He said that the season was too far gone, though it was barely spring.[23]

Because he had failed even to start for the Mandan country, he felt that he owed Governor Beauharnois some explanation in person. Placing his son Louis-Joseph in command of Fort St. Charles, he departed for Montreal and Quebec. Before he left he sent messages to the chiefs of friendly tribes. He requested them to clear his route to Lake Superior of possible Sioux warring parties and advised them to keep peace among themselves. He knew that an attack on the Sioux would precipitate a general war among the regional tribes. He knew that such a war might result in the destruction of his forts and in the ruin of the fur trade and, in consequence, of his plans for the discovery of the Western Sea. The Indians promised to abide by his wishes.[24]

This time La Vérendrye took with him fourteen canoes laden with valuable furs, which went some way to satisfy his creditors in Montreal. But in Quebec he received from Beauharnois a cold welcome, which he may have expected. After all, six years had passed since he had departed for the west. He had made many promises and plans to visit the Mandans, but he had actually advanced no farther than Lake Winnepeg! Beauharnois, who understood his financial and geographical problems much better than did Maurepas, had sympathized with him. But now he felt constrained to reprimand him, perhaps to appease Maurepas. For earlier in the year he had received from the minister a message expressing displeasure at the recent massacre of Jean-Baptiste and his men. "However that may be," Maurepas had written, "all that has come to my knowledge as to the causes of that misadventure confirms the suspicions I have always entertained, and which I have not concealed from you, that the beaver trade has more to do than anything else with the Sieur de la Vérendrye's Western Sea expedition."[25]

In view of this message the governor saw fit to blame the explorer for leaving his post, warning him that he would not be allowed to return to it if he left again. La Vérendrye promised him that he would visit the Mandans in the winter of the following year. "I accepted his excuses for the moment," wrote the governor to Maurepas, "but gave him to understand not only that I would bring him back, but that he would lose my confidence entirely if he did not promptly accomplish what was expected of his zeal."[26]

This reprimand spurred the explorer to action. "With Beauharnois' threats still ringing in his ears," says Crouse, "he realized that nothing must hinder him this time, as this might well be his last chance." Believing that his immediate problem was to maintain peace among the tribes so that they would not hinder his enterprise, he determined to return to Fort St. Charles with enough merchandise to buy their loyalty. So he signed with two leading merchants of Montreal contracts by which he obtained more than 10,000 livres in merchandise. With these supplies loaded in his canoes, he left Montreal on June 18, 1738, and arrived at Mackinac in the following month. There he met Charles Nolan, Sieur de Lamarque, an enterprising trader who in the previous year had befriended him by supplying his posts. Lamarque accepted La Vérendrye's offer to serve as his lieutenant in his enterprise. Promising to rejoin him at Fort St. Charles, Lamarque for the present remained in Mackinac to collect supplies. La Vérendrye continued to Fort St. Charles, placed it under Pierre and picked up François and Louis-Joseph. Leaving word for Lamarque to join him on the Assiniboine, he continued with his men to Fort Maurepas, where they spent the night. Moving up the Red River to the mouth of the Assiniboine, he found a small group of Crees who gladly provided him with meat, but who, wishing to keep the profits of the French trade for themselves, grew "lugubrious about his prospects." They told him that the river was low and that it would ruin his canoes. They said that the Assiniboins were a people who, having low intelligence, had never learned how to kill beavers and who dressed in crude buffalo skins, "outlandish garments which were not what the French wanted anyway."[27]

Paying only politeness to their talk, La Vérendrye pushed up the Assiniboine, which no other white man had seen until that time. He found it a wide, meandering river with a strong current broken here and there by sand bars. Low in water, it was difficult to navigate. The explorer observed that none of the stately trees along its banks bore

310

conifers and that, therefore, they could not provide him with resin or gum to repair his bark canoes should something go wrong. When even the Assiniboins informed him that he could ascend the river no farther, he resolved to continue his journey overland. He left most of his men to follow with their canoes and set out across a stretch of prairie to the portage between the Assiniboine and Lake Manitoba. There, at or near the present site of Portage La Prairie in Manitoba, he began to build a new post which he called Fort La Reine in honor of the queen of France.[28]

Before the fort was completed La Vérendrye was heartened by the arrival of Lamarque with his brother Jean-Marie Nolan and their men. On October 16 he held a review of all his available force. He and Lamarque selected twenty of their best men and gave each of them a generous quantity of powder and balls, an axe and a kettle, and two fathoms of tobacco. They also enlisted a group of Indians, increasing the exploratory party to fifty-two men.[29]

Leaving a small garrison under Sergeant Sanschagrin at the fort, they set out for the Mandan country. Within three days they arrived at a village of the Assiniboins, whose chief detained them for a day of entertainment and promised to furnish the expedition with fresh supplies. Then they pushed on to Star Mound, a part of the Pembina Mountains near Snowflake, Manitoba, about eighty miles southwest of Fort La Reine. Instead of leading La Vérendrye directly toward the first Mandan village, the guide insisted on detouring to another Assiniboin village. The inhabitants of this village performed the ceremony of placing their hands on La Vérendrye's head and weeping copiously to signify that they took him as their father and his companions as their brothers.[30]

These delays, of course, consumed much precious time. November was now almost gone. He fretted because the approaching winter had temporarily forced him to change his plans. Then he decided to pass the winter with the Mandans instead of continuing to the Western Sea, wherever it might lead him. He stepped up his rate of daily travel to about fifteen miles and arrived at the outskirts of the first Mandan village on December 1. In his camp near a small river he met a welcoming committee of Mandans. They presented him with corn in the ear and with native tobacco as symbols of friendship. If he expected them to be as white as Frenchmen, he was certainly disillusioned; for, though they may have been lighter of hair and complexion, they were just like other Indians. Hoping to impress the village with the power of the sovereign he represented, he prepared to enter it with a semblance of military display. He gave his son Louis-Joseph a flag bearing the arms of France and placed him and Jean-Marie Nolan in front of his force. Behind them the rest of his men were drawn up in marching order. He had himself lifted onto the shoulders of his tallest braves. Then he and his men moved to within a short distance of the village. There he called a halt, while he ordered those of his Assiniboins who had muskets and a few men under his son François to move forward to the line of the flag, which was four paces ahead of the main body. Still riding on the shoulders of his braves, he took his place at the head of his men and started toward the village, only to find another delegation of Mandans approaching to greet him. To his great astonishment, they were carrying a pipe and two collars he had sent them four or five years before. He raised his hand; his men fired a salute of three volleys; then, at his command, they shouldered arms and, drums beating and colors flying, marched into the village. In this military formation Pierre Gaultier de Varennes, Sieur de la Vérendrye, at four o'clock on the afternoon of December 3, 1738, triumphantly led his followers to the goal he had sought for six years.[31]

The chief of the village led him and his men to an enormous reception hall. Eager to catch a glimpse of the white leader and his men, Mandans and Assiniboins, squaws and children included, surged around them in such numbers that the reception hall was soon filled. The pushing and shoving led to so much confusion that La Vérendrye felt constrained to order his Indian followers to leave and give his white companions a chance to deposit their baggage in a place of safety. The Indians immediately obeyed him, but one of them carried off a box containing some presents which La Vérendrye had brought to distribute among his hosts on the forthcoming ceremony of welcome. The loss of the box embarrassed and angered him, for it contained, in addition to some valuable presents, a considerable sum of money. He imparted his embarrassment to the chief, who, much annoyed at this breach of hospitality, immediately ordered a thorough search for the missing box. It was not found until much later.[32]

Next day La Vérendrye addressed the Mandans and Assiniboins, giving them a small amount of powder and ball while apologizing for the paucity of this gift. Then he told his hosts that he intended to prolong his stay in their village in order to make a thorough survey of their country. They were overjoyed at this announcement, and they assured him that they would provide handsomely for him and his men. But, says John Bakeless, the chief "cast a jaundiced eye upon the horde of Assiniboins." Seeing that they were reluctant to leave the generous hospitality of his people, he resorted to the trick of telling them that he was glad to see them, for he needed them to help him defeat the Sioux, who would soon attack the village. He knew that they dreaded this tribe and that they would never consent to meet it in battle. The Assiniboins, rationalizing that they had accomplished their object of escorting La Vérendrye and his men to the Mandans, decamped hurriedly. Unfortunately for La Vérendrye, his only interpreter, a Cree who knew the Mandan dialect, became enamored of a young squaw who refused to remain with the Mandans and departed with her. This reduced the explorer to the predicament of having signs as his only means of communicating with his hosts. He could not question them with any degree of clarity and certainty in regard to the westward route of the Western Sea. He had lost the box of gifts which had been his only means of persuading the Indians to remain with him. So he decided to return to Fort La Reine without delay, leaving two men behind to devote themselves to study the Mandan dialect and thereby to relieve him in the future of the necessity of relying on native interpreters.[33]

Before he departed, however, he and Lamarque made a complete survey of the village. It stood on a hill surrounded by a protecting ditch fifteen feet deep and from fifteen to eighteen feet wide. In consisted of a hundred and thirty cabins; its streets and squares were clean and well kept; and its ramparts were broad and level. Its palisades were supported by cross pieces mortised into posts fifteen feet apart. It could be entered only by a wooden stairs which could be removed in time of danger. Observing that these fortifications were unlike those he had seen among other northern tribes, La Vérendrye persuaded himself that he had discovered a race of aborigines whose complexion seemed to indicate a mixture of black and white rather than the copper color of the Indians. He noticed that their men were big, strong, handsome

313

fellows with excellent physiques and affable dispositions. They wore no clothes save for buffalo robes carelessly thrown around their bodies. Most of the women dressed in the same manner. A few modest ones wore loin cloths over which they sometimes wore petticoats and jackets of soft buckskin. Most of the Mandans were diligent, hospitable, and clean. They were highly skilled in wicker work. They were very fond of food, especially buffalo beef and corn, which they served in a number of palatable ways. They were rarely troubled with the famines that were a perpetual menace to most northern tribes. Though buffalo beef and corn constituted their staple diet, they often varied it with antelope, deer, bear, beechnuts, squashes, and pumpkins.[34]

On December 8 La Vérendrye and Lamarque bade farewell to the chief, who expressed his regrets at their departure. They prepared to leave for Fort La Reine, but that very night La Vérendrye became violently ill and was confined to his bed for three days. Then, feeling strong enough to travel, he took his leave of the two Frenchmen who were to remain behind and set out with his men for the Assiniboin village. There he searched for and found the box of presents which the Assiniboins had stolen from him. He upbraided them for their crime and for telling him repeatedly that the Mandans were white people. They denied that they had lied to him, saying that they had not described the Mandans but a tribe much farther west. As proof of the truth of this statement one of them said that he himself had visited the region, where he had killed one of the white men, whom he described as clad in iron and riding on horseback. He had been on the point of cutting off his head, he said, when he saw other white men approaching. He threw his blanket and everything he had at them, and made his escape. Of course La Vérendrye had to take him at his word. On February 10, 1739, he and his men reached Fort La Reine. Since he had not fully recovered from his illness, his journey over the wind-swept, bitterly cold prairie sapped what vitality remained to him. "Never in my life," he wrote later, "did I endure so much misery, pain, and fatigue as on that journey." But a fortnight's rest seems to have restored his health. He spent the next six months hunting moose, collecting furs, and searching for iron deposits which, however, he failed to find.[35]

At the end of September he was delighted with the return of the two men he had left among the Mandans. They reported that they had talked with a chief who, accompanied by a large body of Indians from different tribes, had come from a distant region to trade with the Mandans. That region, the chief had told them, was inhabited by white men who, like the French, wore beards. They prayed from books to the Master of Life and sang and prayed in great houses. The chief seems to have been a Christian, for he often uttered the names of Jesus and Mary and had, since birth, worn a cross suspended from his neck. The houses of the white men, said the chief, were made of brick and had vegetable gardens on their roofs. They slept in beds covered with fine fabrics. Their courtyards were lighted with large torches rather than with candles and tapers. They protected their towns by surrounding them with palisades or walls and by ditches filled with water and crossed by drawbridges. Their forts bristled with cannon, guns, hatchets, and knives. They were expert in making well-tailored shirts embroidered with silk and colored wool. The chief offered to conduct the Frenchmen to the sea, which he said he could reach before winter; but they had no authority to undertake such an expedition.[36]

Availing himself of this promised opportunity, La Vérendrye prepared to return to the Mandans; but at the last moment he was kept at the fort by trouble between the Assiniboins and the Sioux. Instead he sent Pierre to the Mandans to join the western tribes when they returned home and to find the Western Sea. The western tribes, however, failed to appear, and Pierre returned to Fort La Reine. He brought back two horses, perhaps the first he had seen during his travels on the western plains, and some porcelain, probably in the form of tubular or oblong beads which the Mandans made from pulverized European glass. La Vérendrye sent these to Maurepas who, however, was now too deeply involved in the weightier problem of war to give much of his attention to exploration in remote parts of North America. He sent word to Beauharnois to find a young man to help the explorer in his enterprise. Beauharnois protested in La Vérendrye's behalf, but Maurepas was adamant. So, in 1743, the governor appointed Nicolas de Noyelles, the veteran of the Fox wars, as commander of the forts which La Vérendrye had built. Humiliated, deeply in debt, and in poor health, La Vérendrye resigned his post.[37]

Meanwhile his sons, Louis-Joseph and François, had made another attempt to reach the Western Sea. Starting out from Fort La Reine in

April, 1742, they journeyed for the rest of the year in haphazard manner through primitive North Dakota, eastern Montana, and northeastern Wyoming. They visited the Cheyennes, the Arikaras, the Crows, and the Snakes or Shoshones. On January 1, 1743, they arrived at the Black Hills of South Dakota, though they persuaded themselves that they had reached mountains that rimmed the Western Sea. Here a party of Cheyenne guides decided to turn back on the grounds that their Snake enemies were about to attack their women and children at an unguarded camp. Louis-Joseph and François, having lost their compass and having wandered unintelligibly for months, could do nothing but return with their guides. Since they kept an irregular, unclear, and sketchy journal of their itinerary, how far they had traveled will always remain a mystery. On March 19 they reached a village of the Arikaras near the Teton River which flows into the Missouri opposite Pierre, South Dakota. There on March 30 Louis-Joseph buried a tablet on a hill overlooking the river. The tablet was made of lead and it bore the arms and inscriptions of his king. Nearly one hundred and seventy years later, on February 16, 1913, a schoolgirl named Hattie May Foster saw a corner of this plate sticking out of the ground, kicked it loose, and picked it up. It read:

ANNO XXVI REGNI LUDOVICI XV PROREGE
ILLUSTRISSIMO DOMINO DOMINO MARCHIONE
DE BEAUHARNOIS MDCCXXXXI
PETRUS GAULTIER DE LAVERENDRIE POSUIT

The plate, of course, was made to commemorate some earlier event or occasion. It was not deposited by Pierre Gaultier de la Vérendrye and not in the year 1741, but it was the only plate his two sons had, and they made what use they could of it.[38]

In July, 1743, they returned to Fort La Reine, where their father greeted them with great delight. A little later La Vérendrye went down to Quebec. Governor Beauharnois still backed him up in a letter to Maurepas. Emphasizing that the impoverished explorer had served his country for six years, had spent thirty-two years in Canada, and had suffered nine wounds, he asked the minister to promote him from a lieutenancy to a captaincy of a company of Canadian troops. In the following year, when he was sixty years old, this mark of appreciation for his great services was bestowed on him. Four years later he received his crowning reward: the Cross of the Order of St. Louis. He was destined to enjoy it only a few months. In the fall of 1749 he prepared to make another attempt to find the Western Sea, the discovery of which he had first dreamed twenty years before at Lake Nipigon. But that winter he died. His sons, who knew almost as much of the northern country as their father, were not permitted to succeed him.[39]

20

Ste. Genevieve—Old and New

In 1719, WHILE BOURGMOND WAS LIVING AMONG THE MISSOURIS, THE
Mississippi Company continued in its ceaseless endeavor to locate mines
of precious metals. As part of this effort it appointed one of its stockholders, Philippe François Renault, a wealthy banker in Paris, director
of the mines in Louisiana. His subsequent mining activities in the
Illinois country are related to the founding of Ste. Genevieve, the
earliest permanent settlement in present Missouri.[1]

Renault sailed from France with two hundred miners and laborers
and everything he needed to carry on his mining operations. For the
furnaces he even took bricks with his name stamped on each one of
them! In Santo Domingo, which was then a French colony, he purchased
five hundred Guinea Negroes to work the mines he expected to find.
Arriving in New Orleans, he ascended the Mississippi in canoes to the
Illinois country where, somewhere between Kaskaskia and Fort de
Chartres, he established his headquarters. From Boisbriant and Antoine
de la Loire Ursins, principal commissary of the Mississippi Company,
Renault received a number of land grants on either side of the Mississippi. One of these was situated north of Fort de Chartres. There Renault established St. Philippe, a village named in honor of his patron
saint. Another was known as Mine La Motte in honor of La Motte
Cadillac, governor of Louisiana who made a journey to Missouri in
search of silver. It was situated at Renault's Fork of the Big River, which
is a tributary of the Meramec. Renault, too, sought silver, but his
sanguine hopes nearly always ended in disappointment. After spending
large sums of money and twenty years of valuable time, he had to

319

content himself with the gifts of the aforementioned wild lands and with dull lead instead of glittering ores.[2]

Historians have repeatedly stated that Ste. Genevieve originated as a shipping base of lead mines in its adjacent hills. This theory is based on circumstantial rather than documentary evidence. Some of the early settlers of the Illinois country, encouraged by Renault's mining activities, conducted operations of their own across the river from Kaskaskia. Since the ore lay close to the surface, it was easily mined. While they retained their homes in Kaskaskia and other places, they spent much of their time mining and hunting in Missouri. Then, laden with ore or game or both, they returned to their homes. Some of them built a few cabins on the west bank of the river in which they found shelter and rest during their protracted stay. Eventually a few miners and hunters decided, perhaps for reasons of convenience, to move with their families to these cabins, which became the nucleus of a village later called Ste. Genevieve.[3]

The date of its establishment has always been controversial. Historians differ on the subject in accordance with how they choose to interpret the scanty information available to them. Some say 1732, some 1735, some 1749, and some 1752. One of the best scholars on the subject, Garraghan, states that the village began its existence around 1730 in the Big Field—*le grand champ*—three miles or so below the present town of Ste. Genevieve. Francis Joseph Yealy found that in 1732 the village already had a church whose patron saint was St. Joachim. A much earlier piece of information seems to support these two scholars. "In 1881," wrote Houck, "an old stone well, standing like a chimney or tower, the last vestige of the old village, was discovered accidentally amid trees and brush, at a point where the river bank had recently caved. On one of the stones at the top of this well were found, distinctly cut, the figures '1732.' It is certain that when this well was dug and walled up this place was on the outskirts of the old village, and that the village itself must have been established before the date carved on this stone." In 1767 Captain Philip Pittman of the English army visited Ste. Genevieve and wrote this interesting account of the rising village:

The first settlers of the village removed about twenty-eight years ago from [Kaskaskia]: the goodness of the soil and the plentiful harvest they reaped made them perfectly satisfied with the place they had chosen. The situation of the village is very convenient, being within one league of the salt spring, which is for the general use of the French subjects, and several persons belonging to the village have works there, and made great quantities of salt for the supply of the Indians, hunters, and other settlements. A lead mine, which supplies the whole country with shot, is about fifteen leagues distant. The communication of this village with [Kaskaskia] is very short and easy, it being only to cross the Mississippi, which is about three quarters of a mile broad at this place, and then there is a portage of two miles distant, to [Kaskaskia].[4]

The village's first settler was perhaps Jean Baptiste La Rose, who was designated its leading citizen in a census of 1752. He had a wife, three sons old enough to bear arms, two small daughters, one *volontair*, meaning perhaps a hired hand or an indentured servant, one Negro, six oxen, five cows, seven bulls, six jennets, eight horses, three mares, fifty hogs, five rifles, three livres of powder, seven livres of lead and shot, and seven arpents of land valued at one hundred livres. The title to his estate, if and when it is found, should contain a date or a reference helpful in ascertaining the old village's origin. La Rose later moved to the new village, where he died at the evergreen age of one hundred and three.[5]

The old village, which stood on flat and swampy ground, was often flooded. But its surrounding fields and meadows were very fertile, producing a great variety of crops. The proud new village of St. Louis, founded in 1764, bought all of its flour from Ste. Genevieve, whose inhabitants dubbed it *Pain Court*, meaning short of bread. The inhabitants of St. Louis retorted by nicknaming Ste. Genevieve *Misère*, meaning misery or wretchedness—words suggestive of bad living conditions, including the ever-present danger of inundation.[6]

The floods had, indeed, compelled some of the inhabitants to think of moving away. And in 1778, when a very bad flood almost destroyed his house, Joseph Coulture gathered what of his belongings he could rescue and moved with his family to nearby rising ground between the north and south forks of Gabouri Creek. There he started present Ste. Genevieve. Two years later the river bank caved rapidly in front of the old village, undermining a number of cabins and driving its occupants to the safety of the new village. There they joined some families from

321

Kaskaskia in building new homes. Then, in 1785, came *l'année des grandes eaux*, the year of the big flood. Though it is generally accepted as the year in which the new village was founded, it brought no great rush of land transfers. Nevertheless, the water of the old village was so high that it covered many of the log cabins. During the flood a trader arrived in a keelboat. By standing on the roof of a house in the Big Field he was able to tie his boat to the stone chimney of an adjacent house. Despite such a flood some persons were so attached to the old village that they remained in it as long as they could. In 1796 Collot found some traders living in the few dilapidated huts that were still standing. Eventually these too were washed away; and the last vestiges of the old village disappeared.[7]

The new village grew and prospered. Its inhabitants were French, but their government was Spanish. In 1762, by the secret Treaty of Fontainebleau, France had ceded to Spain the Isle of Orleans and that part of Louisiana lying west of the Mississippi. Early in the following year France, by the Treaty of Paris which ended the French and Indian War, ceded to Great Britain the rest of her possessions in North America save a few West Indian islands and two fishing posts in the Gulf of St. Lawrence. Hitherto France had spent 800,000 livres a year on the colony without realizing any appreciable returns. Old and infirm, Bienville had retired in 1743, and none of his immediate successors could equal him in physical vigor and administrative gifts. The military reverses which France suffered in the French and Indian War only intensified her financial troubles. Toward the end of the conflict she realized that she would lose Canada to England. She realized, too, that Louisiana, wedged in between the English and the Spaniards, would be difficult to defend. So she offered Louisiana to Spain. At first Spain was not interested in acquiring the colony; but when, in 1762, she declared war on England and in consequence lost Havana, she resolved to regain that important city so that she might exchange it for Florida. In that case Louisiana, though expensive, might prove a valuable colony in protecting the Spanish possessions of Texas and Mexico from possible English aggression. But Spain was in no hurry to increase her financial burden by taking immediate possession of Louisiana. She let France govern the colony for four more years. Not until 1766 did she send her first governor to New Orleans.

Under Spanish rule Ste. Genevieve thrived. While the Scotch-Irish and Germans were establishing settlements in the Appalachian frontier, the Spaniards were developing towns along the west bank of the Mississippi. This river and its tributaries served as a binding force which drew the two economically isolated frontiers together. And the settlements on the Mississippi attracted emigrants from the Appalachian frontier to the Mississippi Valley frontier, where, at the mouth of many large rivers, they hoped to find either excitement in a new country or better opportunities or ampler living space. After the French and Indian War many Frenchmen in the villages east of the Mississippi, finding English rule unacceptable, migrated across the river to Ste. Genevieve. And after the American Revolution many Americans moved to the same region, intensifying its industrialization, even though it continued to derive much of its support from agriculture.[8]

The town profited greatly as the heart of the lead mining region. During the French regime its mines, lacking men, capital, and efficient technical equipment, produced barely enough to meet the small wants of Frenchmen and Indians. But during the Spanish regime, when the town was revitalized by increased and aggressive migration, it became fairly prosperous and therefore important as a shipping center for lead, salt, and the abundant crops produced in its fertile common fields. It was also the center of the Spanish settlements in Upper Louisiana, while it commanded considerable importance as a strategic position and as an Indian trading post.[9]

Another factor that contributed to the town's development was Spain's land policy. Hitherto she had encouraged revolution among disgruntled American frontiersmen in the hope that they would establish buffer states between her possessions and the United States. But at the end of 1788 her position in Europe and in America became so unsure that she drastically changed her foreign policy by seeking American friendship. Heretofore she had almost brought economic ruin to American frontiersmen by refusing them permission to navigate the Lower Mississippi, where she controlled both banks. Now, by paying a 15 percent duty, Americans could ship their goods through New Orleans. Indeed, they could escape the duty by migrating to Louisiana, where they were promised free land, equal trading privileges, and the right to sell their produce at high prices in the royal warehouses. By this unaccustomed liberalism Spain hoped to strengthen her weak colonies with a wealthy and loyal population. Her officials at her command sent out to the western settlements of the United States circulars detailing the advantages that Americans would enjoy by migrating to Spanish territory. She even increased her inducements to accelerate the flow of migration. In return for their oath of allegiance to the Spanish Crown and to the Roman Catholic Church she offered Americans commercial privileges and even large grants of land. She soon realized the results she desired. During the Spanish regime the population of Upper Louisiana increased tenfold; before it ended in 1800 most of those who swelled the numbers in the census reports were Americans.[10]

The Spanish authorities built in Ste. Genevieve a fort which was located on a hill at the lower end of the village. It was garrisoned by a small detachment of the stationary regiment of Louisiana. A singular transaction relative to its construction shows the dishonesty of the governor of the province as well as the integrity of the commander of the Ste. Genevieve district. When the fort was completed the commander visited the governor and presented him with a bill for $421. The governor examined the account and then told the commander that it was incorrect. The commander retired, examined the account, and returned with it to the governor, who again told him that it was incorrect. Adding that a figure or two had been omitted, he advised him to reexamine the account with a friend. The friend whom the commander consulted looked at the account and burst out in a loud laugh. Then he added an "0" to the sum already stated. Once more the commander went to the governor; once more the governor told him that the account was incorrect. The commander's amazement turned to astonishment when his consulting friend added another "0" to the last sum, making it, this time, $42,100! Now the governor graciously received the account and assigned a small portion of it to the commander to defray the expenses involved in building the fort. About 1794 a new company of troops augmented the company of militia which had been stationed in Ste. Genevieve since the beginning of the Spanish regime.[11]

In 1793 Governor Carondelet founded a new village on a hill about two and a half miles from the old village of Ste. Genevieve. He called it New Bourbon to place it, he said, "under especial protection of the august sovereign who governs Spain, and also that the descendents of the new colonists may imitate the fidelity and firmness of their fathers toward their king." The authorities intended to establish in the village a number of French royalist families, especially from Gallipolis, in present Ohio; but few of them cared to leave their homes, which they had recently built, to migrate to remote Missouri. Most of the town's few hundred residents were salt makers who made a distinct contribution to the economic development of the Ste. Genevieve district. Equally impressive was its grain production, which provisioned not only New Orleans but also St. Louis and other settlements along the river. It also excelled in dairy products, tallow, bear's grease, meat, brandy, whiskey made of rye and Indian corn, and red and white wine.[12]

But the district of Ste. Genevieve derived most of its wealth from its lead mines. Enterprising Americans who found that Spain placed no restrictions on her mineral lands were quick to avail themselves of this opportunity to take them up and settle on them. The richest mine in the district was Mine à Breton near the present site of Potosi in Washington County. Its discoverer was a Breton named François Azor who while hunting in that region around 1773 found ore lying on the surface of the ground. A man of robust constitution, he lived to the extraordinary age of one hundred and eleven, but his longevity proved no guarantee to great wealth, for he received as compensation for his discovery only a grant of four arpents or about four acres.

In 1798 Moses Austin, a native of Durham, Connecticut, and a former merchant and miner in Richmond, Virginia, obtained a grant to the Mine à Breton and its environs and, within a decade, completely revolutionized the lead industry. As soon as he had taken the oath of allegiance and had become a Spanish subject, he plunged into work on his mine, building a shaft eighty feet deep with drifts extending from it for a considerable distance in several directions. He completed the furnace house and, in the following year, a reverberatory furnace, a sawmill, a blacksmith's shop, a shot factory, other out buildings, and a residence, Durham Hall, which became the nucleus of a settlement. His influence changed the mining methods of Upper Louisiana. Before his arrival the ore was dug only in shallow pits seldom more than ten feet deep. And the mine was being worked only during the summer months by parties of miners from Ste. Genevieve. By 1804 Austin's miners were working from the middle of August to the middle of December. At that time he was employing some forty or fifty workmen, including miners, smelters, woodcutters, carters, and others. He paid them an average wage of $43 a month, and produced annually five hundred and fifty or six hundred thousand pounds of lead valued at $35,500. These figures reveal an astonishing expansion of the industry from 1775, when Widow Gadobert's diggings at the Caster Mines—the largest in the region—produced only two hundred and thirteen pigs of lead worth $718 and when her expenses for wages, furnace, tools, and victuals were only $588. At that time the Caster Mines were supplying the whole region with shot. The industry by its expansion in the next three decades was able to extend its trade in lead and shot to such faraway places as Mackinac, Kentucky, and Havana.[13]

In the last decade of the Spanish regime the river was alive with traffic. Every day several ferryboats transported Americans from the east bank to Ste. Genevieve, where they traded chiefly through barter. Since imports always exceeded exports, Spain saw fit to mint dollars with which she paid her officials and her troops and which were preferred not only by the old villagers but by the American settlers. Though many contracts of the period stipulated that debts should be paid in silver, the government did not insist on specie as legal tender, and payments at public sales could be made in lead and peltry. Ste. Genevieve could boast of many merchants and tradesmen who dealt in large quantities of goods of all kinds from New Orleans, Kentucky, Vincennes, Pittsburgh, Philadelphia, and even Canada and Europe. Its trade with business houses in New Orleans was so extensive that each required a special agent to represent them. It was a frontier town only by location: its traditional character and its close contact with New Orleans gave it the air of a miniature Montreal or Quebec. It had a larger cultivated ruling class than that of any other frontier town of its size. It grew steadily in economic importance until the Louisiana Purchase determined the rapid development of St. Louis and other towns. But in its palmiest days Ste. Genevieve contributed more than its share to the economic growth of the Mississippi Valley.

21

St. Louis and Other Early
Settlements

In 1762, WHILE FRANCE AND SPAIN MANOEUVRED OVER THE TITLE AND
occupation of Louisiana, Governor Kerlérec granted to Maxent,
Laclede and Company of New Orleans, or the Louisiana Fur Company,
as it was generally known, a charter which conferred the privilege of
trading with Indian tribes from the mouth of the Missouri to the Minnesota for a term of eight years. In the following year Kerlérec's successor, Abbadie, confirmed the charter. Whereupon the company organized
an expedition to carry out its intended purposes. The expedition was
placed under the leadership of a junior member of the firm, Pierre
Laclede Liguest, whose bravery, sagacity, and love of adventure were
qualifications essential to the success of his mission. It seems to have
been motivated as much by his dislike of New Orleans as by the ideal-
istic picture he had formed of Missouri. New Orleans had never ap-
pealed to him; its overflows, low altitude, and swampy terrain had, he
believed, engendered many of the diseases that had vitiated the colony
and deterred its progress. Furthermore, New Orleans was too far from
Missouri, which he believed as free from disagreeable climate as it was
replete with wealth. Its chief allurements were its mineral resources and
its potential fur trade, for which his company had been organized. But
his primary purpose was to establish a settlement which would enjoy
access to every part of the great valley and which would become its
emporium of trade. He thought the settlement should be built somewhere between the Ohio and the Missouri—a region blessed with in-

numerable advantages. The Mississippi flowed from north to south while its tributaries extended far into the northeast and the northwest. The Middle Valley was, therefore, the central point of the greatest river system of the world. It would collect products representing a great variation of temperature and climate: rye, barley, and wheat from the north; livestock from the west and southwest; lead and iron from Illinois and Missouri; cotton from the south; and timber, together with some of the aforementioned products, from the Middle Valley itself. A settlement built in this region would, if its site were carefully chosen, hold the promise of developing into one of the finest cities in America.[1]

On August 3 Laclede left New Orleans with a small number of men, including trappers, mechanics, and hunters, and his family. His poorly constructed and heavily laden pirogues made slow progress against the impetuous current of the great river. Three full months slipped away before they reached Ste. Genevieve. There Laclede could find no house large enough to contain his merchandise or even a portion of it. Learning of his embarrassment, Neyon de Villiers, commander of Fort de Chartres, sent an officer to offer him a place for his goods until the English should come to take possession of the region east of the Mississippi in accordance with the Treaty of Paris, which had ended the French and Indian War. Necessity forced him to accept Villiers's generous offer. Leaving Ste. Genevieve, he crossed the river to Fort de Chartres, disembarked his goods, his family, and his followers, and prepared to search for a suitable site of the settlement he planned to build.[2]

During December he and Auguste Chouteau, a lad of thirteen who had won his confidence and whom he promoted to tasks usually assigned to much older persons, prospected the region as far north as the mouth of the Missouri and even up that river for a considerable distance. They carefully observed the landscape as they advanced. "Much of this favored locality," wrote Houck, "was gently rolling upland, sweeping far away to the horizon, alternately prairie and open woodland, covered with a high and luxuriant growth of grass, on which herds of deer and buffalo then grazed in peace and plenty." Along the river banks they came now and then to perpendicular cliffs which separated the uplands from the bottoms, "but at other places gradually and almost imperceptibly the uplands descended to the lowlands, and these were covered with noble and towering forests. From many hillsides gurgling springs broke forth, and in clear and limpid streams meandered through little valleys to larger branches, into creeks and into the great rivers almost surrounding this delightful and pleasant land."[3] In the heart of this region, about seventeen miles south of the junction of the Missouri and Mississippi rivers, Laclede found the location he desired. Marking some trees so that the spot could be identified in the future, he said to Chouteau: "You will come here as soon as navigation opens, and will cause this place to be cleared, in order to form our settlement after the plan that I shall give you." They returned to Fort de Chartres, where they spent much of the winter planning and mapping the projected settlement. Early in February, 1764, when the ice on the river thawed, Laclede sent Chouteau with thirty men, nearly all of whom were mechanics, to the designated place. "You will proceed and land at the place where we marked the trees; you will commence to have the place cleared, and build a large shed to contain the provisions and the tools, and some small cabins, to lodge the men. I give you two men on whom you can depend, who will aid you very much; and I will rejoin you before long." In accordance with these orders, Chouteau and his men erected on a block on which Barnum's Hotel later stood the first humble buildings of what was destined to become the greatest city in the Mississippi Valley. Early in April Laclede joined them and selected a spot on which he planned to build his residence. He named the settlement St. Louis in honor of Louis IX, whom Pope Boniface VIII had canonized in 1297 and who was the patron saint of Louis XV, the reigning monarch of France.[4]

Laclede daily expected the arrival of English troops in Fort de Chartres, where his supplies, most of his followers, and his family still remained. He was about to cross the river to transport them to St. Louis when, on October 10, he was detained by the arrival of one hundred and fifty Missouri warriors with several hundred women and children. The original purpose of their visit was to beg for food, but they were so delighted with the hospitality they received that they declared their intention of staying and forming a village around the house which Chouteau and his men were building for their leader. In his endeavor to rid himself of his unwelcome guests, who had an aversion to hard work, Laclede employed the women and children in digging the cellar for his house and in carrying out the dirt in wooden platters and in baskets on their heads. But the warriors would not work at all; instead they stole everything they could lay their hands on, until Laclede, his patience exhausted, peremptorily ordered them away. They hastened to reply that they were worthy of pity—like ducks and bustards seeking an easy life and open water in which they could rest. Laclede listened to them in silence; then, on the following day, he said to them:

> You told me, yesterday, that you were like ducks and bustards [seeking] for an easy living. . . . I . . . say, that if you followed the example of ducks and bustards in settling yourselves, you followed bad guides, who have no foresight; because if they had any, they would not put themselves into open water, so that the eagles and birds of prey could discover them easily, which would never happen to them if they were in a woody place, and covered with brush. You Missouris, you will be eaten by eagles; but these men who have waged war against you for a long time past, who are in great numbers against you, who are few, will kill your warriors, because they will offer resistance, and will make your women and children slaves. Behold what will happen to you, for wishing to follow, as you say, the course of ducks and bustards, rather than the advice of men of experience. You women, who are here present, and who listen to me, go, tenderly caress your children—give them food in plenty; also, to your aged parents—press them closely in your arms,—lavish upon them all the evidences of the tenderest affection, until the fatal moment which shall separate you from them—and that moment is not far distant, if your men persist in their intention to settle here. I warn you, as a good Father, that there are six or seven hundred warriors at Fort de Chartres, who are there to make war against the English,—which occupies them fully at the moment, for they turn all their attention below Fort Chartres, from whence they expect the English,—but if they learn you are here, beyond the least doubt, they will come to destroy you. See now, warriors, if it be not prudent on your part to leave here at once, rather than to remain to be massacred, your wives and children torn to pieces, and their limbs thrown to dogs and to birds of prey. Recollect, I speak to you as a good Father; reflect well upon what I have just told you, and give me your answer this evening. I cannot give you any longer time, for I must return to Fort de Chartres.[5]

That evening their spokesman told Laclede that they had opened their ears to his discourse and that they would follow his advice in all things. He begged him to provide the women and children with food and some of the men with powder and balls so that they could hunt during the return journey up the Missouri to their villages. Having little to give them,

Laclede allowed them to stay in St. Louis for another day, while he sent to Cahokia for corn. As soon as it arrived he gave them a large quantity of it, together with some powder, balls, knives, and some cloth. Next morning the Indians silently departed from the village.[6]

A few days later Laclede returned to Fort de Chartres. As soon as he brought word that the Indians were gone, those inhabitants of Cahokia who had planned to settle in St. Louis repaired to that village and began to build their houses. Laclede followed them with his family and supplies. By the end of the year the village had a population of forty. In the following year additional settlers arrived from Fort de Chartres, Kaskaskia, Cahokia, and even Ste. Genevieve. Most of them were Frenchmen or Canadians who disliked English rule and who preferred to abandon their homes rather than become the subjects of a foreign and Protestant king. In June, 1764, Neyon de Villiers, the last French commander of the Illinois country, withdrew to New Orleans just before the arrival of English troops. Many French families from Fort de Chartres, St. Philippe, and Prairie du Rocher went with him, while others, erroneously believing that the west bank of the Mississippi was still a part of the French empire, migrated to St. Louis.[7]

Imagine their chagrin when they learned that it had been ceded to Spain by the secret Treaty of Fontainebleau. They denounced, sometimes in violent outbursts, "the dastardly impolicy of the French monarch who had, by his inglorious act of surrender, alienated loyal subjects and relinquished a magnificent empire." But Spain, fearing armed resistance to her authority, humored her new subjects by adopting amicable measures and by deferring the exercise of her sovereignty. For many months she organized no civil government of her own in St. Louis. Its inhabitants seemed bound to each other by ties of personal friendship and common interests. Though the authorities had made no grant of land to Maxent, Laclede and Company, Laclede felt obliged to assign pieces of ground to his followers and to those who wished to settle at his post. Yet he wisely refrained from exercising civil authority in the village. Instead he invited Louis St. Ange de Bellarive, whom Neyon de Villiers had placed in command of Fort de Chartres, to transfer his seat of government to St. Louis rather than to Ste. Genevieve. St. Ange was, indeed, the only legally constituted authority of the region. As successor to Villiers "he held jurisdiction not only over the territory on the east, but also on the west bank of the Mississippi, practically as far as the domains of France extended—to the Rocky mountains and the Pacific." This explains why Laclede had threatened to call in the troops of the fort when the Missouris declared their intention of settling in St. Louis. St. Ange accepted Laclede's invitation. As soon as English troops, commanded by Captain Thomas Stirling, arrived to assume control of the Illinois country, St. Ange surrendered Fort de Chartres to him. The Frenchman retired with his officers and men and military stores across the river to the territory still under his jurisdiction. Though it had been ceded to Spain, he was its only embodiment of legal authority until its new sovereign should send his own officers to supercede him. Continuing the procedure he had established at Fort de Chartres, St. Ange associated himself with Joseph Lefebvre Des Bruisseau who, as royal notary and attorney, had been in charge of all land grants issued to settlers. This same service he performed with marked ability in St. Louis. When he died in 1767 he was succeeded by Joseph Labuscière.[8]

Early in March, 1766, Antonio de Ulloa, the first governor of Spanish Louisiana, arrived in New Orleans. He desired to win over the unfriendly colonists with a generous policy. To St. Louis he sent a company of forty-four men under Captain Francisco Rui y Morales "to keep for His Majesty the royal dominion which belongs to him, and at the same time keep up the friendship and good will of the savages." He was instructed to treat the settlers "with a great deal of prudence, good judgment, and consideration."[9] His primary task, however, was to build two forts, one on the south bank and the other on the north bank of the Missouri, for the purpose of defeating any possible attempt on the part of the English to ascend that river and establish settlements on it. Rui perhaps construed his instructions to mean that he was in no way to question or interfere with civil government, which remained under St. Ange's jurisdiction. Though he went through the formality of taking possession of Upper Louisiana, he never ventured to assume any civil authority. Finding that the village could provide no quarters for his men and that its inhabitants regarded them with much annoyance and even dissatisfaction, he prudently took them to the south bank of the Missouri fourteen miles away. There, on a rocky bluff, he began to build the first of the two forts. He named it Prince Carlos of the Asturias in honor of the heir apparent to the Spanish throne. He also began the second fort, which he named in honor of Charles III, but historians doubt that he ever completed it.[10] He seems to have spent more time in St. Louis than at the forts. But even his stay in Upper Louisiana was not long. In New Orleans Governor Ulloa proved pitifully inept in his efforts to acquaint the colonists with Spain's benevolent intentions toward them. He soon alienated the Supreme Council, which was composed of Frenchmen who opposed Spanish rule. Spain, in pursuance of her policy to win over the reluctant colonists with amicable measures, had refused to send Ulloa a strong force to enable him to enforce his decrees. Intrigue and agitation soon fanned the smouldering discontent into open rebellion. Then, in 1768, came the last straw: Ulloa, following instructions from home, ordered the colonists to use only Spanish ships in their commerce. The leaders of the rebellion drew up a petition demanding Ulloa's recall, restoration of their former privileges, and freedom of trade. Informed that his life was in danger, the governor gathered his family and official papers and sailed away to the safety of Havana.

His departure was the signal for demonstrations of joy. The whole population thronged into the streets, shouting, "Long live Louis XV! Down with Spain!" The Supreme Council sent one of its members to France with a memorial asking the government to retract the cession. The memorial was ignored. When word of the insurrection reached Madrid, Charles III resolved to avenge the insult to his country by suppressing the revolt and firmly establishing Spanish control. To this end he sent General Alejandro O'Reilly to New Orleans with a large fleet carrying over two thousand crack troops. The colonists, seeing the hopelessness of resistance, submitted to him without resorting to bloodshed. The general then determined to teach them by a rigorous and unforgettable example the dangers of disobedience to imperial authority. He sentenced some of the foremost leaders of the rebellion to death and some to life imprisonment in the dungeons of Cuba. This done, he turned his attention to restoring peace and order. He revived commerce and trade, abolished Indian slavery, sent the bulk of his army to Havana, and entrusted the defense of the colony to thirteen companies of native Louisianians. Having thus placated the French Creoles, he himself departed for Spain. He left the colony in charge of Luis de Unzaga y Amérzaga, a mild and indulgent man who easily reconciled it to Spanish rule by a wise and benevolent administration that lasted seven years.

Before he returned to Spain, O'Reilly appointed Pedro José de Piernas lieutenant-general and sent him to St. Louis with two companies of the Louisiana Regiment to take possession of Upper Louisiana. The people, intimidated by O'Reilly's stern discipline, accepted Piernas without any show of resistance. St. Ange quietly surrendered his authority to him. Piernas was vested with almost despotic powers. He was military commander of the entire province, chief administrator of justice and defense, and he had the authority to make land grants whenever and wherever he wished within the bounds of his jurisdiction. Yet he managed his office with rare tact. By his joviality, his generosity, and his marriage to Felicité Robineau de Pontneuf, a Frenchwoman of New Orleans, he easily won the confidence of the people. Instead of assuming immediate charge of his official duties, he went to live quietly with Laclede, spent several months ingratiating himself with new settlers, and familiarized himself with the powers of his office. He confirmed all the land titles which St. Ange had granted and rewarded him for his services by conferring on him the rank of captain of infantry. He filled minor offices with Frenchmen. He did all in his power to expand the fur trade, and he granted land titles gratuitously, thereby attracting to the village a large number of settlers from Canada and Lower Louisiana. He built the first Catholic church in St. Louis. It was made of logs, not after the fashion of American cabins with logs piled on each other horizontally but of flattened logs set perpendicularly in the earth and the chinks between them filled with mortar or more commonly with clay. It was completed in June, 1770, when Father Pierre Gibault of Kaskaskia dedicated it amid joyous ceremonies. Thereafter the village grew rapidly. By 1773 it had a population of seven hundred living in over a hundred houses made of wood or stone.[11]

By this time another village had come into existence on the mouth of the Rivière des Pères, about six miles below St. Louis and probably on the original site of the Jesuit missionary settlement. Its founder was Clement Delor de Treget, a native of Quercy, Cahors, in southern France, who had come to the place with his wife in 1767 and who, charmed by its natural beauty, its gently rolling hills, and its diversified landscape of prairie and woodland, resolved to make it his home. As soon as he received a grant from St. Ange he erected a stone house which formed the nucleus of the village. It had a number of names: Delor's Village, Catalan's Prairie, in honor of Louis Catalan, one of its first settlers, Louisbourg, and, eventually, Carondelet, after the governor of Louisiana. The people of St. Louis nicknamed it *Vide Poche,* meaning

Empty Pocket, perhaps because its twenty inhabitants, being farmers, were never overburdened with wealth. Seeing them approach for a visit, their more affluent kinsfolk in St. Louis would exclaim: *"Violà les poches vides qui viennent,"* "Here come the empty pockets." So, perhaps for lack of another name, the village was often called Vide Poche until 1793, when Carondelet, doubtless frowning on this undignified epithet, renamed it in honor of himself.[12]

In 1769 still another settlement, Les Petites Côtes or St. Charles, as it was called after 1804, was started on the north bank of the Missouri, about twenty-one miles above its junction with the Mississippi and the same distance from St. Louis. It was the largest settlement in the district of St. Charles, which embraced all the limits of Spanish territory north of the Missouri. Its probable founder, Louis Blanchette, known as *le Chasseur* or the Hunter, called it Les Petites Côtes, meaning, The Little Hills, because it was located at the foot of a range of small hills which, however, were sufficiently high to protect it from the overflows of the Missouri. Legend says that Blanchette while hunting in the region of 1758 formed a liaison with a Pawnee or an Osage woman who later was baptized Angelique and who bore him several children, including a set of twins. And legend adds that four years later he met the famous chief of the Dakotas, Bernard Guillet, a Frenchman from Marseilles, who invited him to make his home in the region. Blanchette agreed. He returned to his native post east of the Mississippi, collected and organized his followers and friends, and led them in a flotilla of canoes to his new discovery. The first settlers were French-Canadians who sought the protection of the Spanish government against incessant Indian attacks in Michigan, Indiana, and Illinois. Because the settlement was established without the sanction of the governor of Louisiana, it was not officially recognized for a number of years. But its salubrious climate, fertile soil, and invaluable timberlands assured it a steady growth. The soil of its two common fields, which were lowlands known as Crooked Swamps, consisted of yellowish loam, loess, and some sand necessary in raising the very popular variety of corn of St. Charles White.[13]

Toward the close of the Spanish regime St. Charles counted a population of four hundred and fifty living in about one hundred small and badly constructed houses strung out in a single street which ran parallel with the river. Most of its inhabitants were miserably poor, illiterate,

335

and sometimes "excessively lazy," though they were polite, hospitable, and by no means lacking in native intelligence. They lived in perfect harmony with one another, placing their entire confidence in their pastor while yielding passive obedience in "their temporal master and commandant." They farmed only to the extent of maintaining small gardens in which they raised scarcely enough vegetables to keep themselves from starving during the winter months. The young men disdained all agricultural pursuits in favor of hunting or of engaging themselves "as hirelings to such persons as possess sufficient capital to extend this traffic to the natives of the interior parts of the country." During these voyages they were often absent from their families for six, twelve, or eighteen months. They were nearly always subject to severe and incessant labor, exposed to the ferocity of Indian attacks and the vicissitudes of weather and climate, and dependent on chance or accident for food, clothes, or relief in the event of illness.[14]

In 1775 Piernas was assigned to new duties. He was succeeded as lieutenant-governor in Upper Louisiana by Francisco Cruzat, a lieutenant-colonel of the stationary Regiment of Louisiana. A mild and agreeable gentleman, he tried to conduct his administration along the healthful channels of his predecessor. "The French," wrote Waterhouse, "could not help liking a magistrate so friendly to their pleasures and interests." Ironically, the very qualities that won him the love of the people brought him the sharp disapprobation of his superiors. In his aim to be all things to all men, he failed to curb the efforts of fur traders to evade the prohibitive duties which Spain, in her resentment over the loss of Florida to Great Britain, had imposed on British goods.[15] In 1778 he was replaced by Fernando de Leyba.

The new magistrate was a man with keen insight into the principles of law. The impartiality with which he dispensed justice is unmistakable evidence of his high qualities. Yet most of the early historians of Missouri covered him with obloquy. In Waterhouse's opinion he was "singularly deficient in the qualities which command political success," devoid of tact and discretion, and "reputedly penurious and intemperate." But those who have examined his letters and official documents unhesitatingly declare him a man of clear intelligence, business acumen, and sound judgment. How are these opposing views explained? The truth seems to be that Leyba strictly enforced colonial laws which his more

336

lenient predecessor had generally ignored. He incurred the hatred of traders, for example, by prosecuting those among them who evaded the Spanish trade laws and regulations regarding the importation of British goods. In their endeavor to have him removed from office they magnified his faults and spread rumors of his incompetence, stinginess, and drunkenness. These were so prevalent that early historians mistook them for truths. Even the usually unbiased Frederic L. Billon admitted that he had imbibed the prejudices of his fellow annalists. But, he added, "after I had become familiar with his decisions on cases brought before him, and read his impartial and apparently just decisions in most of these cases, I became convinced that he had been a much vilified and abused man and grossly misrepresented." The charge of his drunkenness, however, was not always without foundation. During his short but difficult administration he suffered much personal bereavement. His young wife died, leaving two little daughters to the care of strangers in a strange land. He sometimes depended too heavily on the bottle in his endeavor to escape reality.[16]

Laclede, the one man who might have tempered Leyba's administration with cautious wisdom, was no longer alive. Stricken with either malaria or yellow fever as he journeyed from New Orleans toward St. Louis, he died at Arkansas Post just three days after Leyba assumed office. He was buried in the wilderness on the south bank of the Arkansas River. His resting place was obliterated before it could be commemorated. It matters little. His true monument was the great city he founded by his courage, imagination, and tenacity of purpose. He left considerable property, but in auction it brought far less than its value. For three thousand dollars his young friend Auguste Chouteau bought "the whole block which in later years became successively the site of the Chouteau mansion and of Barnum's Hotel." But since few persons in the colony had enough money to offer any active competition, "the greater part of his estate passed into the hands of Antoine Maxent for a fraction of its real worth."[17]

Leyba had scarcely begun his administration when the American Revolution, hitherto as remote to the inhabitants of St. Louis as though it were being fought on another planet, suddenly moved next door to the Illinois country across the great river. There George Rogers Clark undertook the conquest of the British posts in behalf of his native Virginia. But Patrick Henry, governor of Virginia, was not content with

337

this one plan in his resolve to harass and attack the British. Long before he agreed to support Clark's campaign he had begun to negotiate with Bernardo Gálvez, who in 1777 had succeeded Unzaga as governor of Louisiana, for arms, ammunition, and supplies. Though Spain was not yet a participant in the American Revolution, some of her officials in America sympathized with the American cause. Through Oliver Pollock, a wealthy merchant who was serving the Continental Congress as a member of its Commercial Committee, and through his agent, James Willing, who seized and confiscated English ships on the Mississippi and Ohio rivers, Gálvez sent the solicited assistance to Americans fighting on the frontiers of Pennsylvania and Virginia. Willing was so successful with his venture on the Mississippi that by the end of 1778 "the British flag had been completely excluded from that river."[18]

By this time George Rogers Clark had taken the ungarrisoned villages of Kaskaskia, Cahokia, and Vincennes whose inhabitants had received him as a deliverer. Always hostile to the English, they had welcomed the opportunity to provide the Americans with food and supplies. Clark could count, too, on the friendship of the scattered villages across the river. Before he began his campaign he had visited Leyba in St. Louis. The two men liked each other and became fast friends. Clark had never seen a Spanish gentleman and had entertained the frontier fallacy that Spaniards in general were haughty and formal. He was greatly surprised to find Leyba democratic and more gracious and hospitable than his fellow Virginians. Leyba offered him all the force he could raise in case of an Indian attack from the British post at Detroit.[19]

On June 21, 1779, Spain entered the American Revolution as an ally of France. The powerful arguments which Patrick Henry had addressed to one of her high officials at least partially determined her course of action:

> We are well acquainted, . . . with the Honour, Spirit, and Generosity of the Spanish nation, and should therefore glory in an intimate Connection with it—For I suppose, I need not inform your Excellency, that these States are now free and Independent, capable of forming Alliances and of making Treaties. I think the Connection might be mutually beneficial, for independent of the Beef, Pork, live Stock Flour, Staves, Shingles, and several other articles with which we could supply your Islands, we have vast quantities of Skins, Furs, Hemp and Flax, which we could, by an easy

inland navigation bring down the Mississippi to New Orleans from our back Country, in exchange for your Woolens, Linens, Wines, Military Stores etc., and were you once restored to the Possessions you held in the Floridas (which I sincerely wish to see, & which I make no Doubt these States would cheerfully contribute to accomplish) the advantages to us both in a Commercial View would be greatly increased. The English, indeed insinuate that it would be impolitic in your nation to assist us in our present Situation; but you are too wise not to perceive how much it is in their Interest that you should be imposed upon by this Doctrine & how much more formidable they must be to you with the Assistance of America than without it; and you must be too well acquainted with the Nature of our States to entertain any Jealousy of their becoming your Rivals in Trade, or, over-stocked as they are with vast tracts of Land, that they should ever think of extending their Territory.[20]

Gálvez had received word of hostilities between his country and England before they were officially declared. He was anxious to secure the territory which England had acquired from France east of the Mississippi at the end of the French and Indian War. On his own authority he marched against the British posts in the Lower Mississippi Valley. He easily captured Fort Manchac, Baton Rouge, and Natchez. Returning to New Orleans, he gathered an army of over seven hundred and fifty men with whom he sailed in twelve boats to Mobile. There they stormed Fort Charlotte and, by destroying its parapet and embrasures, forced it to surrender. He then turned his attention to Pensacola, his chief objective. With reinforcements and heavy artillery obtained in Havana he was able to storm Fort George so effectively that its commander, John Campbell, hurriedly raised a white flag. The fall of Pensacola yielded all of West Florida to Spain.

Great Britain replied to these attacks on her domain with a comprehensive plan for the conquest of the entire Mississippi Valley. It entailed four simultaneous campaigns. The first was to strike against the Spaniards in St. Louis and the Americans in Cahokia. The second was to conquer the plains between the Wabash and the Mississippi. The third was to "amuse" Clark in the fort he had built at the falls of the Ohio, then surprise the settlements in central Kentucky. The last and most formidable was to come by sea, conquer Louisiana, and unite with the forces up the Mississippi.

General Frederick Haldimand, governor of Canada, entrusted the first three of these campaigns to Major Patrick Sinclair, lieutenant-governor at Mackinac. As leader of the campaign against Cahokia and St. Louis, Sinclair chose Captain Emanual Hesse, a fur trader who had once served as an officer in the Royal American Regiment, perhaps from Pennsylvania. At Sinclair's orders Hesse journeyed from Mackinac to the portage between the Fox and Wisconsin rivers. There, through the influence of two Frenchmen, Joseph Calvé and Jean Marie Ducharme, who were partners in the fur trade, he collected about seven hundred and fifty tribesmen, including Winnebagoes, Menominees, Sacs, Foxes, and Puants. Ducharme himself would have been delighted to lead these Indians against St. Louis. In 1773 he had as a British subject engaged in illicit trade, had evaded the Spanish garrison at the mouth of the Missouri, and had carried his furs up that river to a place now known as Loutre Island where he established headquarters. But the authorities had found him and had confiscated his furs. Enraged, he had journeyed to Mackinac and had been spending much of his time in unremitting efforts to arouse the Indians of the region to hostilities against the Spanish authorities across the Mississippi. His crafty appeals to their cupidity and warlike inclinations were successful. In return for promises of pay and prospects of plunder they agreed to fight for the British. Sinclair in a letter to Haldimand declared that he had incited the northern tribes by offering them an opportunity to fall on the Illinois tribes, their ancient enemies. To "All the Traders who will secure the Posts on the Spanish side of the Mississippi during the next winter" he said he had promised "the exclusive trade of the Missouri During that time." About twenty Canadian traders and their servants joined him. He also gained the support of Matchikuis, great chief of the Ottawas, by conferring on him the title of general, permitting him to wear a scarlet coat with epaulets like that of any regularly commissioned British officer, and giving him command of all the Indians in Hesse's army.[21]

On May 2, 1780, Hesse led his men toward Cahokia, five hundred miles away. He was so sure of success that he had designated the persons whom he planned to place in command at Cahokia and St. Louis once he had captured these posts. Already luck seemed to be on his side. In the previous month thirty-six of his Menominees had captured an armed trading vessel which contained twelve men and which perhaps belonged to Charles Gratiot, a resident of Cahokia who sympathized with the Americans under Clark. About the same time near Galena, Illinois, some of Hesse's men captured "seventeen Spanish & Rebel Prisoners, & stopp'd Fifty Tonns of Lead ore" and obtained from them "a good supply of Provisions."[22]

On May 24 Hesse reached the outskirts of Cahokia and made preparations to capture that village. Its inhabitants as well as those of St. Louis, however, had been aware of his intentions since March. They had addressed an appeal for help to Clark and had sent Gratiot to deliver it. Clark at that time was at the "Iron Banks," about five miles below the mouth of the Ohio, where he had been building Fort Jefferson, named in honor of Thomas Jefferson who had succeeded Patrick Henry as governor of Virginia. "We are on the eve of being attacked," said the appeal, "by considerable parties of savages, and cannot work at the cultivation of our grounds if we have not prompt succor. For this reason we take the liberty of addressing you, having confidence in the kindness and affection you have always manifested for us."[23] With a small body of troops Clark immediately set out for Cahokia. At the mouth of the Ohio he received two more messages, one from Leyba and the other from one of his own officers, Colonel John Montgomery, urging his presence. He arrived in the village a day before Hesse's Indians and traders began to attack it. Overawed by news of his arrival, they withdrew after firing a few random shots.[24]

By this time Leyba had received fresh evidence of an impending attack on St. Louis. An old man named Quenelle had, a few days before, paddled over to the mouth of Cahokia Creek to fish. On one of its banks he saw Ducharme, who asked him to come ashore to receive some important information. Quenelle refused, and for good reasons: he remembered the circumstances under which Ducharme had left St. Louis and he had heard rumors of his contemplated attack on that village. Now he could see Indians glaring at him from behind some bushes. "No," said Quenelle, "your request is not intended for my benefit, or the gratification of your friendly feelings. Though I am old and bald, yet I value my scalp too highly to trust myself with you." So saying, he returned to St. Louis and informed Leyba of what had occurred. Leyba made little of the incident. He took no added precautions for the public defense, perhaps because he believed that those he had already taken were adequate. He had ordered entrenchments and had manned them with twenty-nine regulars and two hundred and eighty-one villagers, had requested neighboring villages to send him assistance, had erected

341

a tower at one end of the village and placed five cannon on it, had sent out scouts, and had stationed cavalrymen to act as a picket guard.[25]

The villagers spent May 25, Corpus Christi Day, in religious devotions and social festivities. They attended mass and, in the afternoon, went to the fields to pick strawberries and flowers and to make merry in picnic fashion. Their village would easily have fallen had it been attacked on that day. Unguarded, they would have been massacred. But the Indians, suspecting that many villagers might remain in their homes, spent the day lurking in the woods near present East St. Louis, Illinois. They were confident, however, that on the next day most of the able-bodied men would return to tend to their crops and that, by making a detour, they could surprise them and deprive the village of its strongest defenders. So, about one o'clock in the afternoon of May 26, they crossed the river about fourteen miles north of the village and swarmed toward it. The picket guard, seeing them approaching, rushed through the streets crying, "To arms! To arms!" An alarm gun from the tower replied with a warning to the men in the fields and to the women and children who were picking strawberries and flowers. The booming of cannon mingled with the cries and yells of women and children who had taken refuge in Leyba's house, which Lieutenant Silvio Francisco Cartabona was prepared to defend with twenty men. All this disappointed the attackers in their expectation of surprising most of the men at their work. They began to attack the village at its northern gate, where they expected to meet no resistance; but they were repulsed by the militia. This convinced them that they could not hope to reduce the alerted and armed village. They therefore vented their fury on the farmers they found working in the fields, killing twenty-two and capturing seventy, according to a Spanish report.[26] All of them would probably have escaped had they fled toward the southern gate; but the greater part of them took the road leading to the nearer northern gate, thereby exposing themselves to the enemy.

Tales of a good many incidents of the event have come down to us, but all of them are legendary. They may or may not be true. A man named Chancellier with his wife, two daughters, and an American named Kennedy went to pick strawberries in a cart drawn by two horses. When they saw the Indians they fled in the cart toward the village. The two men placed the women between themselves to protect

342

them. Kennedy, who is said to be the first American in what later became the state of Missouri, was mortally wounded. He was about to fall out of the cart when Chancellier pushed him into its bed, exclaiming, "They shan't have the scalp of my American!" He had hardly uttered these words when he was struck by two bullets which broke his arm in as many places above his elbow. His wife was wounded through the middle of her hand, his oldest daughter was shot through the shoulder just above her breasts, and his other daughter was struck in the forehead, though the bullet glanced aside and merely stunned her. The moment Chancellier arrived at the gate of the village his horses collapsed and died either from fatigue or from wounds, but his family was saved.[27]

Another legend tells of a man named Belhomme who was wounded in the thigh but who managed to crawl to a pond opposite a mill. There, as soon as the Indians were gone, he began to call for help. Finding this of no avail, he fired his gun until he spent all of his ammunition. The villagers heard his signal of distress but ignored it from fear of the Indians. Later they found Belhomme dead either from hunger or from loss of blood.[28]

Another villager, Julien Roy, is said to have found that an Indian was pursuing him and gaining on him with every step. In his desperation to save himself he turned, took dead aim, and fired at the Indian's head, shattering his jaw. As soon as the Indian fell, Roy rushed up to him and dressed his wound. Thereupon the grateful Indian guided him through the ranks of the attackers to the village.[29]

Before dusk Hesse and his men retired across the Mississippi with their prisoners. For the next three years the prisoners were subjected to menial labor and all kinds of indignities. They received barely enough food to keep alive. The Treaty of Paris, which ended the American Revolution, freed them from their miserable custody. They returned to their homes, "which the hardships of their bondage had doubly endeared to them."[30]

In a letter to Haldimand, Sinclair attributed Hesse's retreat to the treachery of Calvé and Ducharme, to the timidity of the Canadian traders, and to the want of secrecy whereby the Spaniards had received timely notice of the projected attack. He said that the Winnebagoes "would have stormed the Spanish Lines" if the Sacs and Foxes "under

343

their treacherous leader Monsr Calvé had not fallen back so early, as to give them but too well grounded suspicions that they were between two Fires. A Monsr Ducharme & others who traded in the country of the Sacks kept pace with Monsr Calvé in his perfidy. They had long shared the Profits arising from the Lead Mines & from a commerce with the Illinois." But he declared that the attack, "though unsuccessful, . . . from misconduct & unsupported," had its "good consequences." Many of the Indians "are entered & many are rivited in our interest. The Traders who would not assist in extending their Commerce cannot complain of its being circumscribed to necessary bounds, and the Indians who received a profusion of Presents without Distinction will now be Discriminated." His figures of Hesse's losses are at variance with those given in a Spanish report issued by Martín Navarro, intendant of Louisiana. The Winnebagoes, wrote Sinclair, were the only sufferers with one of their chiefs and three of their men wounded. He gave the losses of the enemy as sixty-eight killed and "eighteen Blacks & white people made Prisoners," including "several good Artificers." In addition, "many Hundreds of Cattle were destroyed & Forty three Scalps . . . brought in. There is no doubt can remain from the con current testimony of the Prisoners, that the enemy received Intelligence of the meditated attack. . . ."[31]

In giving reasons for the precipitate retreat of Hesse's men from St. Louis, Sinclair deliberately overlooked the very important factor of Clark's sudden appearance at Cahokia. We have seen that the English were mistaken in assuming that he was beyond striking distance. His presence in Cahokia not only overawed its Indian attackers but dampened their fighting ardor in St. Louis and made them prone to retreat at the first show of resistance. Had England succeeded she would have acquired the territory west of the Mississippi, just as she had planned, and she would have then possessed all of the Mississippi Valley save perhaps New Orleans. But Clark was also responsible for discouraging any new attack on St. Louis. Hesse's troops retreated rapidly in two divisions—one by the Mississippi and the other directly across the region to Mackinac. Clark at once organized a force of three hundred and fifty men, including regulars, French volunteers from around Cahokia, and Spaniards from St. Louis. He sent them under Colonel Montgomery against the Sacs and Foxes on the Rock River. Montgomery and his men traveled in boats as far as Peoria, Illinois, and thence marched overland to their destination. When he found the villages deserted he burned them to the ground and, having used his supplies, returned to his boats. On his way home he and his men had to eat their horses to keep themselves from starving. Though his campaign can hardly be called a success, it insured St. Louis against molestation by the Indians, at least for the immediate future. Later, says James A. James, Clark "claimed for himself and his men the honor of having saved St. Louis and the rest of Louisiana for the Spaniards."[32] No doubt he had changed the course of the American Revolution.

Of the three campaigns which Sinclair had planned against the Americans and the Spaniards, only the third, under intrepid Captain Henry Bird, achieved any measure of success. With seven hundred men he set out in boats to attack the fort at the Falls of the Ohio before Clark could reach it. Bird arrived within a hundred miles of his goal where he and his men heard a rumor that the dreaded American leader was already there. They were so terrified that they persuaded him to lead them instead to central Kentucky, where they attacked several settlements and forced their inhabitants to surrender. Though Bird had promised the settlers that their lives would be spared, his warriors mistreated or murdered some of them and killed nearly all of their cattle. Seeing the uselessness of trying to restrain them, Bird decided to return with three hundred prisoners to Detroit. He had to march the women and children twenty miles over high mountains in order to get them as quickly as possible to safety. Even so, the Indians murdered half of the prisoners before they reached Detroit.

Charles III of Spain was very pleased with the vigorous defense made by Leyba and Cartabona in repulsing Hesse's men. In proof of his gratitude he conferred on Leyba the rank of lieutenant-colonel and on Cartabona that of captain. Leyba died before the promotion could reach him. The cause of his death, which occurred late in June, 1780, is unknown. Some historians have suggested that dissipation and remorse over the death of his wife led him to take poison. Certain facts, however, seem to indicate that he died of protracted illness. At the end of May, when St. Louis was attacked, he was so ill he had to be carried from his house to the tower in a wheelbarrow. By early June he was too weak to sign officials documents. Feeling that his end was near, he summoned Cartabona, who was commanding the garrison at Ste. Genevieve, and placed him in charge of the government *ad interim,* that is, until a new lieutenant-governor should be sent to St. Louis to succeed him. Leyba was interred in the village church beside the body of his wife, who had passed away in the previous September.[33]

Leyba's successor was Francisco Cruzat, who has the distinction of being the only lieutenant-governor of Upper Louisiana to serve a second term under Spanish rule. In appointing him, Governor Gálvez recognized his ability and great popularity and overlooked his tolerance of illicit trade which had resulted in his removal over two years before. But this time he received instructions which were more specific than those of his first term. He was "to cause the dominion and government of His Majesty to be loved and respected; to administer justice promptly, impartially, and in accordance with law; and to protect and increase trade as much as possible." He was also instructed to give his "whole attention to the conservation of [St. Louis], applying all the means possible for its defense, in order to strain and repel the raids and designs of the enemy, both of the British Nation and of . . . Indians, who shall attempt to destroy the settlements of his jurisdiction."[34]

Cruzat left New Orleans late in July and arrived in St. Louis in fifty-nine days, shortening by a full month the usual time for such a voyage. On September 24 he took over the duties of the government from Cartabona and immediately plunged into his work. Informed repeatedly of British activities among the Indians and of their preparations for another attack on St. Louis and other Spanish villages, Cruzat proceeded to improve his defenses almost immediately after assuming office. Around St. Louis he built a stockade eighteen feet high and six inches thick, "leaving open the part [facing] the river which is naturally fortified." He mounted, too, many small cannon, though his troops and militia remained small in number. "When I do not succeed in holding the country," he wrote to Gálvez, "I shall have at least the satisfaction of defending it to the last drop of my blood, since I confide the valor and happiness of those who accompany me and follow my example and sacrifice their lives even to losing them in defense, honor and Glory to the arms of our Catholic Sovereign."[35]

At about the same time he planned to frustrate any immediate attack on St. Louis by striking at the nearest British post. This was Fort St. Joseph, a repository of war supplies located at the present site of Niles, in Berrien County, Michigan. Late in December Blackbird, a chief

346

of the Milwaukees, brought word to Cruzat that a force of sixteen men under a half-breed named Jean Baptiste Hamelin recently had marched with pack-horses from Cahokia against the fort. The force had captured the fort, seized sixty bales of goods, and hurried off toward Chicago while its Potawatomie defenders were absent on a hunt. But the report said that they had been overtaken and routed at a place called Petite Fort, near the Calumet River. Blackbird urged Cruzat to make an expedition against the fort, and the magistrate, having long contemplated such a move, agreed. The fort was a village of fifteen houses occupied by forty-eight persons, most of whom were French or half-breeds. It was garrisoned by seventeen men whose primary duty was to gather all sorts of merchandise which they traded for maize and other supplies they needed to provision another expedition against St. Louis.

Before 1932, historians of the American frontier generally misinterpreted Cruzat's reasons for undertaking his expedition. This is because they allowed themselves to be misled by an article in the *Gaceta de Madrid* for March 12, 1782, which stated that Fort St. Joseph had been occupied in the name of His Catholic Majesty and that his flag "was displayed there during the whole time." During the negotiations preceding the treaty which ended the American Revolution, Spanish diplomats used the expedition to support their claims to the territory east of the Mississippi. They stated that it had been undertaken in accordance with directions from Madrid. Historians generally accepted this diplomatic interpretation until it was proved false by a letter which Lawrence Kinniard discovered in the Bancroft Library at the University of California. In this letter, dated January 10, 1781, Cruzat gives Gálvez the true motives of his expedition, which he undertook entirely on his own responsibility. To refuse Blackbird's solicitation, he wrote, would have demonstrated to the Indians "our weakness and to make evident to them our inadequate forces; and perhaps, if they had learned of these facts, it might be sufficient reason for them to change sides, notwithstanding the evident signs of friendship which they had given us." To seize the fort, its English commissioners, and its merchandise and provisions, he added, would have the effect of terrorizing the surrounding tribes. "It would take from them the men who are exciting them to evil acts, and would deprive them of powder and merchandise given to them by the English for hunting and making war upon us." And this, he was confident, would bring about "both the destruction of the fort and the supply of provisions in it; and even though the English might not be prevented entirely from carrying out their intentions, it would cut off their resources in part and lessen their hopes of having in that place a store of provisions with which to supply those who may attempt to come by that way to attack us this spring."[36]

The expedition, which left St. Louis on January 2, 1781, consisted of sixty-five militiamen and about sixty soldiers under Eugenio Pourée, a lieutenant of militia experienced in frontier warfare and in conducting expeditions. Through cold, snow, and ice they journeyed in pirogues to the mouth of the Illinois and up that river to the vicinity of Peoria, where they picked up a French trader named Malliet with a few of his men. Continuing over two hundred miles upstream, to a place which Cruzat called Los Pes, they found the river covered with ice. Forced to complete his expedition overland, Pourée cached his pirogues and distributed to each of his men all the food and ammunition that could be carried. On five horses which he bought from some Indians, Pourée loaded the ammunition and the merchandise he thought necessary to pacify or win over tribes which should prove hostile. Suffering "all the cold, danger, and hunger that can be imagined," they continued for twenty more days to within six miles of Fort St. Joseph, where they camped for the night. Pourée sent a "very intelligent and trustworthy" young Potawatomie named Lajes to win over those of his own tribe, totaling about two hundred, who were supporting the English and guarding the traders. Lajes was to persuade them to use their influence to see that neutral or peaceful Indians remained quiet in their huts. He told them that, though they had recently attacked the Spaniards and their French allies, Pourée wished them no harm. Assured of humane treatment and promised half of the booty that should be taken, they consented to his request. Lajes then reported to Pourée, who immediately took the precaution to attack the Potawatomies should they fail to keep their agreement.

Early next morning, February 12, he led all of his men across the frozen river to the fort, which he seized before its garrison could take up arms. Eight men surrendered. They would have been scalped by the Potawatomies had they not been placed under heavy guard. Pourée hastened to divert his newly won friends from their murderous intent by distributing to them the booty his representative had promised them.

348

To his own soldiers he allowed nothing. True to his instructions, he burned or scattered all the food and supplies he found, including three hundred sacks of corn and a quantity of tallow. He hauled down the English flag and hoisted the banner of Ferdinand and Isabella. But he stayed at the fort only twenty-four hours. Then he made Lajes a chief in recognition of his services and turned with his men and his prisoners toward St. Louis, which they reached on March 6. None of the members of his expedition had been killed or wounded and only two traders, who tried to escape, had been captured and killed by the Indians. Cruzat was of course delighted with the success of the expedition. Later he wrote to Esteban Miró, governor of Louisiana, giving him a detailed account of the episode and attributing its success to the "ability, wisdom, and courage" of its leader, whom he recommended for promotion.[37]

During the last two years of the American Revolution, Cruzat spared no effort to maintain peace with the Indians and to gain their allegiance to Spain. He countered the English policy of seducing them with gifts by a similar one of his own. In his endeavor to keep the expenses of the crown at a minimum, he contracted for the gifts with Antoine Maxent in New Orleans; but that merchant, for reasons known only to himself, was unable to send him adequate quantities of them. Cruzat could not obtain them from traders or Americans. "The traders," says Nasatir, "were not making good trades and they did not care to sell to the government; while the Americans, themselves having barely enough, could not give anything to the Indians." So Cruzat had to buy gifts from merchants in St. Louis which in a few months cost the Crown nearly 25,000 pesos.[38]

Cruzat sent able men to persuade wavering tribes or those under British jurisdiction to change their allegiance. To counter the influence of the British agent Augustine Roque among the Sioux, he sent Pierre Dorion, who had been a trader to that tribe and who in May, 1780, had pledged his allegiance to George Rogers Clark. Meeting the Sioux above Prairie du Chien, Dorion succeeded in bringing all of their chiefs save one into the Spanish fold. In July he returned to St. Louis accompanied by six of the Sioux chiefs, who assured Cruzat that they had given up their friendship for the English and requested him to take them into an alliance with His Catholic Majesty. Careful to keep their faith, Cruzat granted their request to allow Dorion to return to their villages with more goods. In return they promised that if Roque or any other British trader visited their villages they would refuse to trade with him and would tell him that they had "a Spanish, not an English heart."[39]

By the Treaty of Paris, which ended the American Revolution, the British possessions east of the Mississippi, south of Canada, and north of Florida became the United States. Spain had never felt any of the sympathy which some of her officials in America had shown toward the American cause. The American Revolution had simply provided her with a golden opportunity to side with France in her determination to crush England and to recover Florida, Minorca, and the Strait of Gibraltar. Though Minorca and the Strait of Gibraltar were irretrievably lost to her, she did recover Florida. This gave her control of the Bahama Channel and the Mississippi River, and made the Gulf of Mexico a Spanish lake. Yet her position in America was less secure than it had been before the war. She found herself, says Arthur Preston Whitaker, "face to face with the first independent power of the New World, a power possessing a numerous and energetic population animated by the British urge to expansion and liberated from that intimate participation in the European state system which had so often checked England's spoliation of Spain."[40] She regarded her new neighbor as a kind of pygmy who, if properly fed, might grow into a giant with an appetite for Louisiana. To safeguard that possession as well as New Spain and the West Indies, Spain claimed the territory between the Cumberland River and the Gulf of Mexico. When she failed to obtain it, she declared her exclusive right to the navigation of the Mississippi. In so doing she ignored that section of the Treaty of Paris which provided that "the navigation of the river Mississippi, from its source to the ocean, shall remain forever free and open to . . . the citizens of the United States." Since she had played no part in forming the treaty, she had no right to question, let alone oppose, its stipulations regarding navigation of the Mississippi.

To American frontiersmen settling in ever increasing numbers in the Mississippi Valley, unrestricted use of the river, which the Treaty of Paris confirmed, was of vital importance. Only by way of the Mississippi could their products be sent to New Orleans, where they could be reshipped by way of the Gulf of Mexico to various Atlantic ports. The frontiersmen had always regarded Spanish control of New Orleans with considerable chagrin; when this control was extended to Florida as well, they became generally alarmed. For Spain now controlled not only the mouth of the Mississippi but also the ports and harbors along the coast of Florida. Thus, if she chose, she could bar American trade by way of Pensacola and Mobile. And at Natchez, between St. Louis and New Orleans, she established a custom house whose officials stopped every American boat that requested passage down the river. Though the Spanish officials usually threatened to confiscate each boat, they seldom did so; but they subjected its captain or owner to the payment of heavy tolls and frequently annoyed and delayed him in many ways. "Besides the inconveniences and losses suffered at the hands of the rapacious Spaniards," says Ogg, "there was always the consciousness, so utterly repugnant to the freedom-loving Westerner, that his trade, his gains, indeed, his very livelihood, were entirely at the mercy of a Bourbon king and his emissaries."[41]

In 1785 Spain sent Diego Gardoqui to New York to buy from the United States acquiescence to Spain's exclusive navigation of the Mississippi as far as she owned both banks. In return he was instructed to concede the privilege of trading with Spain and the Canary Islands and to recognize American claims to the thirty-first parallel as the boundary between the United States and the Spanish colony of West Florida. At the same time, however, he was to try to alienate frontiersmen from the United States by encouraging them to settle in Spanish territory, offering them freedom of trade, land grants, and even religious toleration. Though his insistence in closing the Mississippi aroused the indignation of frontiersmen, it caused hardly a murmur in the eastern states, which, in Gardoqui's opinion, could ask for no greater favor than a trade that would bring Spanish gold and silver into their ports. They urged a commercial treaty with Spain, "even if such a course should involve a sacrifice of the trading rights on the Mississippi." Eventually the eastern states were influential in getting their way. John Jay, secretary of state, advised Congress to agree to the closing of the Mississippi for a period of twenty-five years. "Spain," he said, "now excludes us from that navigation and with a strong hand holds it against us. She will not yield it peaceably, and therefore we can only acquire it by war. Now as we are not prepared for a war with any power; as many of the states would be little inclined to a war with Spain for that object at this day; and as such a war would for those and a variety of obvious reasons be inex-

351

pedient,—it follows that Spain will, for a long space of time yet to come, exclude us from that navigation." Why not, therefore, forego navigation of the Mississippi in order to secure commercial concessions which Spain now offered and which the new nation greatly needed? Eventually, said Jay, the United States could renew its claim to free navigation of the river with even better reasons than at present. His arguments precipitated long and bitter debates, but in the end they prevailed.[42]

So matters stood until December, 1788, when, we will recall, Spain saw the wisdom of changing her American policy. While she faced increasingly grave problems at home she began to realize the failure of her policies in regard to the United States. By closing the Mississippi to frontiersmen she had only incurred their wrath; she was afraid that their resentment might lead them to invade her possessions, as many rumors and reports indicated. To protect Louisiana and West Florida—her first and foremost consideration—she decided to mollify the frontiersmen by allowing them navigation of the Mississippi on payment of a 15% duty and by inviting them to settle in Spanish territory. The colony of Louisiana could never hope to realize any considerable economic progress as long as its population remained sparse. Why not draw from neighboring Kentucky and Tennessee immigrants who regarded their settlements there as temporary and who wished to move across the river or nearer to its mouth? As individuals, frontiersmen had never seemed formidable to Spain. She rationalized that they were unruly from lack of an established government, dangerous from lack of a market. Very well, Spain was now willing to give them both, hoping in return to gain the protection of her possessions and, at the same time, a vital and loyal population. She had heard that most of the frontiersmen were German, Scotch-Irish, and French—persons of foreign extraction who, dispossessed in Europe, had no tie of sentiment to any country and who, therefore, would become obedient Spanish subjects. But Thomas Jefferson knew them better. When he heard of Spain's change of policy, he wrote gleefully: "I wish a hundred thousand of our citizens would accept the inivitation. It will be the means of delivering to us peacefully what may otherwise cost us in war."[43]

Among the first Americans to apply for a concession in Louisiana was George Morgan, a native of New Jersey, a graduate of Princeton, and a colonel in the Revolutionary War. In his younger days he had traded with the Indians of Kaskaskia as a partner of the Philadelphia firm of

Baynton, his father-in-law, and Wharton. Later he had lost heavily in land speculation and was eager to recoup his fortune. While in New York he entered into negotiations with Gardoqui, proposing to establish a colony near the mouth of the Ohio and in territory within the present state of Missouri. Gardoqui assured him of a concession of 15,000,000 acres of land extending along the Mississippi for three hundred miles from the mouth of the St. Francis River to what is now Perry County, Missouri. Morgan agreed to accept the concession under cetrain conditions, including guarantees of self-government for his settlers and of exemption from practically all taxation. Gardoqui then authorized him to examine the territory which was to be granted to him and to advertise it among the frontiersmen as he journeyed westward. In Pennsylvania he selected about seventy farmers, artisans, tradesmen, and sons of German immigrants, gathered them at Pittsburgh, and in January, 1789, took them down the Ohio River in four armed boats. Reaching the mouth of the Ohio in February and finding the Mississippi frozen, he left his followers at a camp of friendly Indians and tramped overland to Kaskaskia, where he hired a horse and carriage to take him to St. Louis. There he was cordially received by Manuel Pérez, who had succeeded Cruzat as lieutenant-governor two years before. The magistrate furnished him with horses, guides, and provisions for his exploratory journey into the interior of Louisiana. Eventually Morgan selected as the site of the capital of his settlement a place known as L'Anse à la Graise, meaning "the greasy bend," so named because fur traders often stored up great quantities of bear meat for the use of the garrisons and of the French and Spanish voyagers up and down the Mississippi. He named it New Madrid and moved his followers to it.[44]

The settlement was to be a frontier Utopia. It was to have wide streets and sidewalks, fragrant groves and orchards, and park highways. It would also have schools and churches of every denomination, for Gardoqui had promised Morgan that he would grant his followers, and even those who came after them, the special dispensation of religious toleration. No white hunters were to be allowed to live in New Madrid, which was to thrive on agriculture and commerce alone. The wild animals of the surrounding forest were to be reserved for the neighboring tribes.[45]

But Morgan's grandiose plans miscarried at the very beginning. Before he could proceed with them, he had to obtain Governor Miró's

353

approval, and for this reason he went to New Orleans. The governor frowned on the whole project. Not only was he averse to peopling Louisiana with Protestants but he had formed with James Wilkinson a scheme or conspiracy. Wilkinson, that unscrupulous adventurer, had agreed to keep Kentucky, where he resided, from joining the Union, and to convert it into a buffer state between the United States and the Spanish possessions. In return he was to have the privilege of using the Mississippi to trade in Kentucky products with royal warehouses in New Orleans. Therefore, Wilkinson was thunderstruck when, in the fall of 1789, he learned that Spain's new policy permitted Kentuckians to ship their goods through New Orleans. A more severe blow to his scheme was the word from New York that Gardoqui had granted Morgan a concession in Missouri. The establishment of such a colony meant the ruin of Wilkinson's monopoly, since Kentuckians could dispose of their products in nearer New Madrid, where they would be detained until they could be taken to market in New Orleans. Greatly alarmed, Wilkinson hurried southward to confer with Miró. He was relieved to learn that the governor had recently seen Morgan and had, for obvious reasons, disparaged his project. Thereupon Morgan had abandoned it and had returned to his estate in western Pennsylvania. His followers, however, remained in New Madrid and others later joined them, thanks to his campaign of publicity. By the end of the century New Madrid "had become a gateway to all commerce between the Gulf of Mexico and the region between the Allegheny Mountains and the Mississippi."[46]

Though Spain's generous policy made New Madrid possible, it was otherwise unsuccessful in attracting large numbers of Americans to Louisiana. Much more effective was the Great Ordinance of July 13, 1787, which, by prohibiting slavery for the Northwest Territory, drove a number of slave owners to Missouri and deflected to it the frontiersmen who had been migrating from Kentucky into the region north of the Ohio. Just what percentage of immigration was affected by the ordinance would be difficult to determine, since the prohibition of slavery was not always enforced and since climate and agricultural conditions in the Northwest Territory were less favorable to Negro slavery than those in Missouri. Cape Girardeau, which was founded in 1793 on the site of an old trading post and which was predominantly American, may owe its origin to the Northwest Ordinance. Its founder,

Louis Lorimier, a French trader in the Spanish service, became commander of the village and held that position for ten years.

On October 1, 1800, Spanish rule in Louisiana ended. The Treaty of San Ildefonso returned the colony to France. It had remained French despite a generation of mild Spanish government. Its first settlements were French, its population was largely French, its manners and customs were French. A fairly large percent of the people in the new village of New Madrid was French. It seems that the French population in the five districts which Spain had created in Upper Louisiana "varied inversely and almost according to a geometric ratio." The French collected in villages, forming social units on either the Mississippi or the Missouri rivers. Wherever they migrated they extended an element of the future state of Missouri. But the American settlers were quite different. They scattered and lived on isolated farms, making the family and sometimes the individual himself the social unit and forming their own government. Though geography may not have engendered these tendencies, it certainly "afforded the means by which the French and American traits may be contrasted."

For reasons which need not detain us here, France failed to acquire actual possession of Louisiana from Spain. Soon after the Treaty of San Ildefonso, Napoleon sent Pierre Clement de Laussat to New Orleans to make arrangements for the transfer of Louisiana to France. But Laussat did not assume authority until November 30, 1803—seven months after Napoleon had sold the colony to the United States for $15,000,000. Furthermore, Upper Louisiana was not formally transferred until March 4, 1804. Captain Amos Stoddard, an American, acted as the agent of the French government. He had come to St. Louis under orders from Laussat to take possession of Upper Louisiana for France. Amid pomp and circumstance he lowered the Spanish flag and raised the French flag in its stead. On the same day another ceremony marked the transfer of Upper Louisiana from France to the United States. Stoddard had not only been commissioned to transfer the colony from Spain to France but also had been authorized to declare the formal transfer of the same territory from France to the United States. So he raised the French flag, lowered it, and ran up the Stars and Stripes in its place. Louisiana had become American.

22

Creole Society

AT THE CLOSE OF ITS COLONIAL PERIOD LOUISIANA WAS AN UNKNOWN
land save for belts along the western bank of the Mississippi, along a
part of the Missouri, and along a few smaller rivers. It had no exact
boundaries. It sprawled its immense mass roughly from the Mississippi
to the Rockies, from British Canada to the Gulf of Mexico. "Its northeastern limit," wrote Walter Robinson Smith, "was muffled in the ignorance that hid the source of the Mississippi; its southeastern boundary
was concealed in the sinuous diplomacy that enveloped the mouth of
the river. The southern boundary was the Gulf of Mexico but just how
much of the coast was included no one can say. The western limit sank
away into the unknown prairies toward the Pacific while its northward
projection remained to be outlined."[1] The area of the colony exceeded
that of the original thirteen states or that of Great Britain, Germany,
France, Spain, Portugal, and Italy combined. Tales of its fabulous
resources fell far short of the truth; but Thomas Jefferson—that avid
collector of tales and traditions of hunters and trappers along the Upper
Mississippi—believed them and wrote them down in a lengthy report
in his determination to dispel the cynicism and the bubbling ridicule
of his Federalist opponents. It told of Indians of gigantic size, tall bluffs
faced with precious stones, and a huge mountain of pure rock-salt towering above the earth. "There exists," wrote Jefferson, "about one thousand
miles up the Missouri, and not far from that river, *a salt mountain.* The
existence of such a mountain might well be questioned, were it not for
the testimony of several respectable and enterprising traders who have
visited it, and who have exhibited several bushels of the salt to the

357

curiosity of the people of St. Louis, where it still remains. . . . This mountain is said to be one hundred and eighty miles long, and forty-five feet in width, composed of solid rock salt, without any trees, or even shrubs on it."[2]

The colony had a population of forty-two thousand. Six thousand lived north of New Madrid and two thousand between that town and the Arkansas River, leaving thirty-four thousand between the river and the Gulf. John Bach McMaster stated that three-fourths of the population and seven-eighths of the wealth were to be found below Pointe Coupée, fifty miles south of the mouth of the Red River. The colony's largest city was New Orleans which had a population of between eight and ten thousand. The second largest city, St. Louis, had a population just below one thousand. To Spain the colony had never been a profitable investment. "I think I may safely come to the conclusion," wrote Charles Gayarré, "that the ordinary and extraordinary expenses incurred by Spain in relation to Louisiana, over and *above* the small revenue she derived from that colony, may, without exaggeration, be put down at about fifteen millions of dollars, from the 5th of March, 1766, when Ulloa landed at New Orleans, to the 30th of November, 1803, when the retrocession to France took place."[3] So Spain, in her endeavor to maintain Louisiana as a barrier against possible English or, later, American aggression toward her more valuable southernly possessions, spent on that colony in four decades of hazardous tenure as much as it cost the United States to secure full, complete, and permanent possession.

The people of Louisiana, and especially those of New Orleans, were heterogeneous. Josiah Quincy called them "Anglo-Hispano-Gallo-Americans." By far the most numerous were the Creoles. Contrary to a prevailing misconception, they were not persons of mixed Caucasian and Negro blood but were pure white persons born in the New World of French or Spanish blood or of both. The origin of the word creole is obscure; it may be derived from *criadillo,* diminutive of *criado,* meaning one educated, instructed, or bred up, from *criar,* to create, nurse, or instruct. According to Amos Stoddard, who knew them well, the Creoles were usually small in stature, though they were remarkably well proportioned, supple, and active. Their complexions were somewhat sallow, suggesting a sickly aspect; but their diet, which consisted largely of vegetables, kept them in excellent health. Their eyes, usually dark and

358

piercing, remained undimmed longer than those of most other people. They were strangers to such chronic ailments as gout, gravel, and stone in the bladder. Stoddard observed that the hair of old people in New Orleans retained its dark brown color while that of old people in St. Louis commonly became grey. The complexions of Creole women were generally much fairer than those of Creole men. When they were young they were usually pretty or attractive, but after they reached thirty-five or forty they became wrinkled and withered.[4]

But though the Creoles were generally free of chronic ailments they sometimes suffered greatly from epidemics of yellow fever, malaria, tuberculosis, and smallpox. The eminent traveler Henry Marie Brackenridge wrote an opinionated account of the climate in the Mississippi Valley and of its effect on the people:

There is no doubt, but that, as in other parts of the western country, which have not been properly put under cultivation, autumnal fevers will prevail. The vicinity of the lakes has not been remarked as more unhealthy than at a distance: convenience generally induces the settlers to choose this situation. It is a prevailing notion, that to be sick the first summer, is what every settler must expect. This is not generally true. In some parts of the territory, the district of New Madrid, and immediately on the Mississippi, this *seasoning* is severely paid: but in other parts of the territory, I can say with confidence, that not more than one tenth undergo it, and that in a slight degree. From the first of August to the last of September, is considered the most unhealthy. Much depends upon the care which the settler takes in avoiding whatever may tend to produce sickness. The scorching heat of the sun is universally agreed to be unfavorable to health. Night dews and exhalations are not less so. . . . The mephitic exhalations from putrid vegetables, and from enormous masses of putrifying trees, in the new clearings, also contribute to this insalubrity.

He believed that the "rich and massy" leaves of the corn in the fields surrounding the settlements prevented the sun from drying up "unwholesome damps."[5]

Despite forty years of Spanish rule, the language, the social customs, the religious institutions, and the political practices of the colony remained French. Most of the Spaniards in it were officials. Many Americans crossed the Mississippi, but few of them were permanent settlers;

359

they were usually traders who came and went with the seasons. The Creoles regarded them as dashing, swaggering, boisterous folk who often quarreled with Spanish tax officials. They found that the Americans threatened all manner of dire consequences if their precious cargoes of pork or ham or grain or whiskey were in any way molested. They found them, too, cold and phlegmatic, deliberately forming plans and sedulously pursuing them to some materialistic goal. Fun-loving and gregarious, they naturally thought Americans were grasping, strangely taciturn, and withdrawn. They called them "Bostonais" or "long knives" and trusted them far less than they did the Indians, with whom they had usually lived in peace and friendship. Since they disliked Americans, especially those in New Orleans, they regarded the purchase of Louisiana by the United States in 1803 with badly concealed chagrin.[6]

Most of the American frontiersmen were descendents of those Germans and Scotch-Irish who, in the previous generation, had migrated to America to escape from religious, social, and economic persecution. Since they and their descendents had no ties in Europe, they were free to establish in the Appalachian frontier, where they first settled, the social order which we call American democracy. The Creoles, on the contrary, had escaped from nothing. They still turned fondly toward their homeland, France, or *la patrie*, as they called it. Collot found those of St. Louis "less degenerate than the race which dwells on the American side; we found among them that sentiment of attachment to their country which characterises the French nation; they appeared to be excellent patriots, whose lives and fortunes are devoted to France; families of laborers in easy circumstances, and prosperous merchants."[7]

Yet their new pattern of living modified somewhat the traits which they had acquired from their ancestors and which set them sharply apart from the Scotch-Irish and Germans. The gentle, easy life they led in their villages gave a certain softness and mildness to their language as well as to their manners. They became less fiery, less impatient, less adventuresome than Frenchmen in Europe. While they retained much of their gaiety and fondness for amusement they assumed some of the gravity of Spaniards. Few objects could urge them to enterprises or could call forth their energies. The necessities of life were always within their reach; beggary was unknown among them. The great majority of them cared nothing for knowledge and never bothered to pursue it with any degree of intensity. They were as ignorant of politics as children are of life and manners. Peaceably disposed, genial, courteous, and somewhat indolent, they were poorly equipped for the exigencies of frontier life. Unlike the Scotch-Irish and Germans, they were loath to settle on isolated farms. Instead they located in compact villages so that they could indulge in an endless interchange of visits with their neighbors. Visit and talk were so essential to French frontiersmen that in Canada and Louisiana they always settled in groups. They felt sorry for the "odd" or "remote" neighbor who "lived in the woods like a bear, a league from any house, with nobody to talk to."[8]

But in money matters they had a strict sense of honesty which bound them as fully as would have a legal document. The grasping Scotch-Irish failed to understand them and sometimes blamed their occasional business failures on their lack of business sense and to their indolence. In reality it was their sense of honor that sometimes made them dupes of the Scotch-Irish, who were far less scrupulous than they in money matters. The truth is that the Creoles showed very sound business judgment in their trade with the Indians, in their sale of furs, and in their choice of property.

Along with their sense of honor they prided themselves on their courtesy and politeness in dealing with everybody. "Certain things like raiment or clothes," wrote Berthold, "could be removed, changed, but politeness was like the skin, one could neither do without it nor shed it, and this courtesy bequeathed to their descendents remained long one of their distinctive characteristics, even that of the slaves born in those families."[9]

In their relations with the Indians they proved vastly superior to the Scotch-Irish and the Germans. While the American frontiersman was in the process of exterminating the Indian and establishing a uniform type of civilization from Maine to California, the Frenchman, eager to win his good will, met him more than halfway. He studied his language, flattered his prejudices, and refrained from ruffling his dignity or insulting his ancient customs. The Anglo-American thought: "How shall I make that damned redskin respect me?" The Frenchmen thought: "How shall I win the Indian's heart?" Since the days of Champlain the actuating policy of the French government toward the Indians had been much more humane than that of the English government. The character which Richelieu granted to the company of the Hundred Associates stipulated that any Indian who had been received within the Catholic Church had a perfect right to live in France and enjoy the privileges of citizenship without any letter of naturalization.[10] The French, moreover, were much more successful than the English in supplying the Indians, even the remotest tribes, with merchandise. The Indians repaid this thoughtfulness with respect for Frenchmen in general. Seldom did a Frenchman meet with foul play at their hands. And the French in apprehending an Indian for some crime took the greatest care to impress his tribe that his sentence of punishment was fully justified. The Americans, on the contrary, hardly ever bothered themselves in this respect.[11]

In dealing with Negroes, however, the French often invoked the Black Code which in some cases provided for very severe punishment. In 1742 a slave in New Orleans was found guilty of striking a soldier. He was whipped every week day and on Sundays by the public executioner, his right ear was cut off, and he was forced to carry a six-pound ball around his leg for the rest of his life. Sometimes slaves who had been manumitted were returned to slavery for failing to pay their debts.[12]

Far removed from cities of trade and fashion, most of the Creoles adopted their own fashions of dress. That of the laboring class was very plain and simple, but that of affluent merchants was often foppish or luxurious. The man of small means usually wore a *capote*, which was a blanket coat of coarse cloth with an attached cape that he could draw over his head in cold or in rainy weather. Men and women of this class wore blue handkerchiefs on their heads in the place of hats and moccasins or Indian sandals in the place of shoes. In summer many of them went barefoot. Some men of means dressed no better than did peasants. Though Vital Beauvais, with whom Brackenridge lived, was perhaps the wealthiest man not only in Ste. Genevieve but in Upper Louisiana, he went about "with a blue handkerchief on his head, one corner thereof descending behind and partly covering the eel skin which bound his hair, and a check shirt, coarse linen pantaloons on his hips, and the Indian sandal or moccasin, the only covering to the feet worn by both sexes." In winter men kept themselves warm in buckskin suits; in summer they wore only shirts and pantaloons of coarse blue cloth. Blue was either the most favored or the most accessible color.[13]

362

On festive occasions the women were tastefully and neatly attired. Their hats were wreathed with bright-colored ribbons and sometimes with artificial flowers. Their moccasins were lighter than those of the men, heavily fringed, and ornamented with beads and brightly painted porcupine quills. Each wore a fichu at her throat and a skirt that was voluminous over many petticoats.[14]

The well-to-do or rich Creoles generally tried to keep up with the French fashions from New Orleans and Paris. Indeed, they adopted these fashions with singular avidity to the full size of their pocketbooks. Considering that they lived deep in the surrounding wilderness, some of them accumulated an astonishing number of accessories: French soap, ribbons for their queues, razors, watches, rings, walking sticks and *cannes à épées,* swords and belts, snuff boxes of silver and inlaid woods, tassels, and fringed handkerchiefs.[15] When Jacques Louis Lambert, a rich merchant and militia officer, died in December, 1771, the inventory of his personal property showed that he owned a regimental coat and vest worth two hundred livres, gold button, silver snuffbox, twenty-two shirts, twelve night caps, thirty handkerchiefs, six drawers, two umbrellas, and eight pairs of breeches.[16] In the following year another rich merchant and mine owner of Ste. Genevieve, Sieur Gadobert, was forced to leave his home, his wife, and most of his property, perhaps because of some shady business deal. He must have taken his best clothes with him. But even what he left behind or discarded would have aroused the envy of a Beau Brummel:

Included in the somewhat damaged remnants of Gadobert's wardrobe are seven jackets *(vestes)* of drugget *(drouguet),* a fabric defined in a contemporary dictionary as "a kind of stuff." Whatever "stuff" may have meant at that time was apparently so well known that this same dictionary felt it unnecessary to include a separate definition for it. Gadobert also had other jackets of *basin* (a form of dimity, then a heavy twilled cotton), of embroidered white cloth, two of yellow cloth, and an old green velvet jacket lined with red serge, which was probably *sergé,* a checked or diapered dimity. His waistcoats *(gilets)* include two each of gray drugget, crimson cut velvet, and of apple green, and gray cloth. Nine pairs of breeches were discarded, possibly because most of them were badly worn, but these were of black silk, black drugget, serge (or *sergé?),* gray velvet, and some workaday ones of ticking *(gingas),* and of a heavy

363

cotton. Other pairs, with fabrics unnamed, were yellow and olive-colored. His *habits* (if we can translate them as coats), included one chestnut colored, another of flannel lined with serge *(sergé?)*, and one of *camelot* lined with linen. He also had a supply of short coats *(mantelets)*, some of striped *Callemande (calmande, calamanco,* etc., the popular woolen fabric woven in Flanders, which was glossy on the surface, with a satin twill checkered in the warp, so that the checks are seen only on one side). Others were of unlined flannel, and printed cotton lined with serge *(sergé?)*. Gadobert's stockings *(bas)* were iron-gray silk, black wool, and some eighteen colored gray. Fifteen shirts of unbleached Beaufort linen were included, as well as a red wool hat *(bonnet)*, two pairs of half-worn boots, and nine pairs of white leather gloves.[17]

Even these discarded articles present considerable expenditures. The prices of imported fabrics and clothing were generally high in New Orleans, but they were higher in Upper Louisiana. N. M. M. Surrey, who made a thorough study of commerce in Louisiana during the French regime, listed the prices of a number of articles that could be purchased from merchants in New Orleans in 1762: "an ell of cloth for a man's coat, 250 livres, with a lining of silk, 150 livres additional; a beaver hat, 400 livres, with a band of gold 250 livres extra; a hat half beaver, 250 livres; a pair of silk stockings, 150 livres; a purse, 25 livres; an ell of cloth for a shirt, 60 livres, the same amount of batiste, 120 livres, and of muslin, 200 livres; powder for the face and hair, 15 livres a pound. Imported soap in 1762 sold at 25 livres a pound, while at the same period the domestic article brought from 2 to 6 livres a brick."[18] All of the fabrics used in the colony were imported. The spinning wheel and the loom seem to have been unknown to the Creoles until Americans introduced them at the end of the colonial period.[19] But the prices of wearing apparel were not always as high as those listed by Surrey. After Pinckney's Treaty in 1795, which opened the navigation of the Mississippi to the United States, French, Spanish, and American merchandise was brought to the French settlements along the Mississippi Valley in increasing quantities.

The Creoles lived in houses either of stone or of timber. Usually they were designed to meet the climate and circumstances of a particular region. Many of those in St. Louis were built of stone from the river bluff while most of those in Ste. Genevieve and New Madrid were made of timber from the surrounding forest. Those in New Orleans were generally much larger, more richly designed, and contained a variety of furniture seldom seen in Upper Louisiana. The houses ranged in size from low, single-room dwellings to two-and-a-half story mansions. They were built in five styles. The *maison de poteaux en terre*, meaning, "house with posts in the earth," resembled a palisade of square cedar timbers set upright in the ground and fastened together only at the top. A cruder and less durable structure was the *maison de pieux en terre*, built of rounded posts and often seen in Ste. Genevieve. More popular was the *maison de poteaux sur solle*, or "house of posts on a sill." This was a large frame structure with massive timbers closely spaced and supported on a stone foundation or, in New Orleans, on wooden blocks designed to keep it away from the dampness of the ground. The stone house or *maison de pierre* was introduced into Upper Louisiana from France and Canada. The *maison de pieces sur pieces*, that is, "the house of timbers on timbers," resembled the horizontal log cabin so popular among American frontiersmen. The Creoles, however, disliked this style and used it mainly in building their outhouses.[20]

Nearly every house, regardless of its size or style, was equipped with a gallery either all around or in front and sides or only in front. The choice depended on the affluence or the taste of its owner. The gallery was an adoption from the French West Indies. Usually whitewashed, it deflected some of the heat of the sun and afforded a measure of sanitation. It protected against rain and offered many pleasant hours in the open during the summer months. It was usually four to eight feet wide, floored, and furnished.[21] The roofs of the houses were usually composed of massive Norman trusses made very steep to shed water from the clapboards or shingles, which formed the thatching. Sometimes gables were substituted for the purpose of allowing window light in the rooms.[22]

The number of rooms in a house depended on its size. The houses of impoverished Creoles were usually one-room structures from fifteen to twenty feet square serving as parlor, bedroom, dining room, and kitchen. A few of the larger houses contained three rooms, each with a fireplace, a ceiling eight to ten feet high, and a floor of hewn puncheons. Here and there were a few stone houses of richer men. Each of these contained as many as five rooms—a large one in the center, and, opening into it, two small ones on each side. The vertical walls were plastered and white-washed, but the ceilings were left open, showing the massive beams or flooring of the attic. Shutters, which the French called *contravents,* literally, "against the wind," protected doors and windows on the outside. Some of the early houses were equipped with mantelpieces such as those found in houses of colonial Virginia and South Carolina. Glass, which was very expensive because it had to be imported from Europe, was used only in the best homes. The Lorraine-Lisa house in St. Louis, which was built before 1799, had double glazed French doors. But the windows in most of the houses were of paper that owed its translucence to a generous supply of hog's lard or bear's oil. "The more pretentious houses," wrote Van Ravenswaay, "had a certain elegance, even though it was an elegance distinct and individual to that time and place. The whitewashed walls and high ceilings with their dark beams, the cavernous fireplaces spanned by chamfered beams, the glistening but almost bare floors, and the unfamiliar bulk and restrained lines of their furniture, represented a stepping back in time and taste to visitors from the Eastern seaboard and Europe, which all the gay fabrics, the silver, pewter, and other decorative objects, could not completely relieve."[23]

Brackenridge, who lived with the Beauvais family while he attended school in Ste. Genevieve, wrote this intimate description of their house:

The house of Mr. Beauvais was a long, low building, with a porch or shed in front and another in the rear; the chimney occupied the center, dividing the house into two parts, with each a fireplace. One of these served for dining-room, parlor, and principal bed-chamber; the other was the kitchen; and each had a small room taken off at the end for private chambers or cabinets. There was no loft or garret, a pair of stairs being a rare thing in the village. The furniture, excepting the beds and the looking-glass, was of the most common kind, consisting of an armoire, a rough table or two, and some coarse chairs. The yard was inclosed with cedar pickets, eight or ten inches in diameter and seven feet high, placed upright, sharpened at the top, in the manner of a stockade fort. In front the yard was narrow, but in the rear quite spacious, and containing the barn and stables, the negro quarters, and all the necessary offices of a farm-yard. Beyond this there was a spacious garden inclosed with pickets in the same manner with the yard. It was, indeed, a garden—in which the greatest variety and the finest vegetables were cultivated, intermingled with flowers and shrubs: on one side of it there was a small orchard containing a variety of the choicest fruits. The substantial and permanent character of these inclosures is in singular contrast with the slight and temporary fences and palings of the Americans.

The house was a ponderous wooden frame which, instead of being weather-boarded, was filled in with clay and then whitewashed.[24]

The furniture of the Creoles was usually inferior to that of Americans living in the large towns along the Atlantic coast. "It is usually fabricated," wrote Stoddard, "by the artizans of the country, and is rough and misshapen," though it was highly polished. The floors were "waxed and smooth and bright as a mahogany dining table."[25] They were bare save for deerskins or bearskins or both. The chief piece of furniture in a Creole household seems to have been *un grand bois de lit* or large wooden bed. One of the finer types was decorated and dressed ornately with a canopy and side-curtains, equipped with a mattress and pillows stuffed with feathers or with Spanish moss, and covered with a deerskin or with a heavy linen sheet or, for chilly nights, with a buffalo robe. In summer the bed wore a *moustifiquaire* of linen, lawn, or dimity which protected its occupant or occupants from mosquitoes. Children usually slept in cots.[26]

The lack of closets made *armoires* or wardrobes necessary. The ordinary ones were built of poplar or pine, especially in the region of Ste. Genevieve, where these woods were plentiful. Some of the finer wardrobes, made of walnut or cherry or both, had two doors which were handsomely carved or molded with diamond-shaped designs or escutcheons. These opened on brass hinges imported from France. One of the surviving armoires of the affluent Chouteau home "had *bombé* front and sides, together with carved details and the curious French claw-and-ball feet." Another had diamond panelling in the style of Louis XIII which was very popular with Canadian makers. Still another, which belonged to Charles Delassus, last Spanish governor of Upper Louisiana, was probably built in New Orleans in the last decade of the eighteenth century. Van Ravenswaay describes it as built "of handsomely grained West-Indian mahogany, seven feet two inches high, and five feet seven inches wide. The door panels are plain and the only ornamentation is found in the skirt and the somewhat inadequate feet."[27]

Tables were built in a wide variety of sizes and styles for many different uses. Some of them could be folded, some could be extended, some were with or without drawers, some were detachable and could be stored away, and some had a small shelf for books. One style resembled a bureau. On one of its sides it had a drawer which served as a writing desk.[28]

The Creoles were very fond of mirrors, perhaps because on the frontier these were regarded as symbols of luxury and refinement. Every home, rich or poor, had three, four, five, or more of them in a wide variety of shapes, sizes and styles. They were gilded, framed in wood, carved, plain, copper, silver, square, round, or oval. Some were mounted on paper for the Indian trade. Much less in demand were chairs which, though common and inexpensive, were found only in the better homes. In poorer homes chests and benches were used in place of chairs. The most popular type of chair was in the French-Canadian style, which had square posts, two narrow slats, and woven bark or rawhide seats. At mealtime the head of an affluent family would occupy his *fauteuil* or armchair while his wife and children sat in ordinary *chaises* around a table covered with embroidered linen and lighted with candles in silver or copper holders. The meal was by no means coarse or disagreeable. On the contrary, says Dorrance, it offered one explanation for the presence of the Creoles in a strange land:

Garden and orchards provided the vegetables, the salads, the fruits so necessary to the French; game might be had for the shooting; a good wine could be made of the wild grape; wheat bread was plentiful enough that breads of cornmeal were thought fit only for the *voyageurs;* maple sugar was made after the Indian fashion and was used, with wild bee honey, to sweeten coffee (or a substitute made of rye). For the winter fruits were dried, and corn (for a soup still called *'tsit blé*); meat had been salted or *bouncannée* [smoked]; rabbits, squirrels, 'possums, turkeys and certain other birds might still be had; nuts had been stored; *taffia* [liquor made of molasses] and wine were still on tap, so that it was an indolent man who could not provide in any season a merry and sustaining meal.[29]

Well-to-do Creole families, indeed, were no strangers to madeira, wines of better brands, liquors, vinegar and olive oil, cheeses, mustard, chocolate, preserved fruits, and cigars from Havana.

The preparation of food was an art with the Creoles, as it is with Frenchmen everywhere. The table was provided with a far different fare than that of most American frontiersmen. The Creoles made great uses of vegetables and prepared them in many wholesome and palatable ways. Instead of roasts and fried meats they made soups and fricassees and gumbos, which they may have derived from their Negro slaves. Festal tables often groaned under gargantuan quantities of such favorite Creole dishes and drink as frog legs, bouillabaisse, poulet Creole, Creole gumbo, pralines, absinthe, and orange wine.[30]

By their French heritage the Creoles enriched American speech with many picturesque words. These include bayou, levee, crevasse, depot, chute, bureau, picayune, and *lagniappe,* which refers to a little extra something, perhaps a yam, a flower, or a fig that merchants added to purchases as their way of thanking their customers. The daily speech of Missouri frontiersmen included such words as prairie, pirogue, voyageur, coureur de bois, cache, portage, batteau, and rapids—all of which they borrowed from French traders, explorers, and settlers of the region.[31]

The French policy of trade was monopolistic from its inception. It entailed a succession of colonizing companies including the Company of New France or the Hundred Associates, as it was better known, the Community of Habitants, which was the first public enterprise formed in Canada that was composed of Canadians, and the West Indian Company, which was established in 1664, shortly after Canada became a royal colony. Most of the explorers and traders from Nicolet to La Vérendrye were agents of one or another of these companies. Because of delay, indecision, greed, fraudulence, mismanagement, and recurring Iroquois wars, none of them was entirely successful in its endeavor to establish a French mercantile empire. We have seen that John Law's powerful Mississippi Company, founded in 1717, fell far short of achieving its aims. The fur trade as it pertains to the French period of the Mississippi Valley has been treated in previous chapters. Here we need to describe only the missionary, the *bourgeois,* the *partisan,* the *mangeur de lard,* the *hivernant,* and the *voyageur*—each of whom gave the fur trade meaning and movement and formed a colorful unit of French colonial society.

Among these scouts of civilization a place of honor must be accorded to the Jesuit, that black-robed missionary of the American frontier who gladly risked his life to follow the trader and introduce the Indian to Christianity. Both were interested in the savage—one sought him for his peltries, the other for the salvation of his soul. Though the Jesuit was no trader, he was permitted to trade "moderately" and "quietly." This, however, had not always been the case. Louis XIV, says Parkman, "forbade the Jesuits and other ecclesiastics in Canada to carry on trade."[32] But the missionaries had never liked this regulation. Father Le Jeune, superior of missions, tells us that some of them complained because they were forbidden "to even look at, from the corner of our eyes, or touch with the ends of our fingers, the skins of any of the animals." They regarded peltry not only as the best and most useful article on the frontier but also as a coin of rare value. So, heedless of royal command, they never scrupled to barter a pelt or two for whatever they needed. They even sent some elk skins to their fellow missionaries among the Hurons. Father Crépieul held that missionaries could hunt hares and martens with absolute propriety when it was necessary and when it constituted a diversion—provided they did not overdo it. And Father Vimont obtained from Des Chastelet, commissary of furs in Montreal, a consent that the prohibition of trade with the Indians should not apply to the Jesuits—if they carried it on "quietly."[33]

Not that the Jesuits were in any way averse to the trade; indeed, they helped to make it possible and profitable. By their kindness to the Indians they made them well disposed toward the French traders. Though they sometimes failed in their main objective of converting the Indians to Christianity, they nearly always performed invaluable service for the trade. Father Carheil, missionary at Mackinac, wrote to Louis Hector de Callieres, governor of Canada, that he wished "the good of both Religion and the Trade, which you are obliged to keep in accord one with the other, without Ever separating one from the other,—so that Trade may Never interfere with Religion, which must ever be the foremost and most essential of all our Interests."[34] The missionaries, as we have seen in earlier chapters, left us some of the most interesting and accurate accounts of the fur trade. The trading posts with their lawlessness, lewdness, drunken brawls, and illicit trade are nowhere as vividly portrayed, and as vehemently denounced, as in the relations of the Jesuits.

In 1670 Great Britain established a post on Hudson Bay, thereby precipitating with France a duel for empire that was to last nearly a century. At the same time the French government was obliged to adopt a more aggressive policy in its endeavor to protect the trade against English encroachment and to arrest French lawless adventurers. It required traders to have *congés* or licenses, and at first it issued only twenty-five of them in a year. Later it modified its policy to meet the demands of a rapidly growing trade. Each license specified the number of canoes which its holder could take on his expedition, his route, and the number of his employees or *engagés*. It also described their duties to prevent unlicensed men from joining the expedition. The licensed trader was required to carry in each of his canoes a specified amount of merchandise from the king to the commander of a fort, to a missionary, or to an interpreter. The license placed the employees under contract with the voyageur, who agreed to make his journey and return for a specified amount in peltries.[35]

Each trading post had a manager or *bourgeois,* as the French called him, who conducted his business with almost military discipline and usually with great ability. His authority was absolute. He usually dined alone and held himself aloof from his employees, who "would no sooner presume unbidden to hold social intercourse with [him] than would a soldier with his regimental commander." Sometimes, indeed, he wore a uniform as embroidered and decorated as that of a field marshal. He dictated every order of business, formulated policy in regard to the tribes within the geographic limits of his post, and organized groups of trappers whom he sent out to work in designated streams. He hired hunters who supplied him and his men with fresh meat and he determined the extent of gardening around his post. He selected men to serve as messengers or agents to Indian tribes while he kept up a steady correspondence with his company in St. Louis or with his subordinates in posts subsidiary to his own. The responsibilities of the leader or *partisan* of an itinerant expedition were similar to those of the *bourgeois,* though the nature of his business was somewhat different.[36]

The most interesting and picturesque figure in the fur trade was undoubtedly the *voyageur* who, as his name implies, spent much time on lakes and rivers, though he was by no means confined to them. In time the term *voyageur* included the *mangeur de lard* or pork eater and the *hivernant* or winterer. The *mangeur de lard* was so called because, en route from Canada or New Orleans to his place of work, he was fed usually on pork, hard bread, and pea soup, but principally on pork. He was not yet inured to the voyager's harder fare of bear's grease, lard, and lyed corn. The *mangeur de lard* was a recruit or greenhorn who could be trusted only with such common labor as tending to canoes and carrying merchandise from canoes into the trading post. He was bound to the hardest kind of work for a period of five years and at wages that never permitted him to arrive at the end of his term without being in his employer's debt. Since he had no way of obtaining passage out of the country while he remained in debt, he usually stayed on or resorted to the dangerous expedient of deserting. Much easier was the lot of the *hivernant,* who was an old hand at the trade. He spent his winters at posts in the interior, exchanging trade goods for furs under the direction of a *commis* or clerk, who was in training to become a *bourgeois* and who was frequently in command of a post. The work of the clerk was perhaps the most exacting of any that pertained to the trade. He was often required to take a quantity of merchandise to some Indian village, where he resided in the lodge of a chief until he succeeded in selling all of his wares. Several clerks were usually stationed at larger posts. "The most trusted of them," wrote Chittenden, "were frequently stockholders or partners in the companies for which they were working, but ordinarily they were only salaried employes."[37]

The *voyageur* was usually a small man, about five feet six inches tall, with overdeveloped arms and shoulders that made his legs seem weak or inadequate by comparison. In a canoe always overcrowded with merchandise, his short legs were a blessing, an actual requirement of his occupation. And he more than made up in strength what he lacked in stature. He could if he wished, or if he must, paddle fifteen to eighteen hours a day for weeks on end while he and his companions, numbering from six to fourteen, lightened their labors by singing songs which included humorous jingles about their canoes, old ballads about their country and their religion, and ribald versification about their lives and their loves. He could carry merchandise twice or thrice his own weight. His pace over bumpy portages was so vigorous that any unburdened companion was left breathless in endeavoring to keep up with him. John J. Bigsby, secretary of the commission that ran the boundary line between Canada and the United States, found some extraordinary types among the *voyageurs*:

One man's face, with a large Jewish nose, seemed to have been squeezed in a vice, or to have passed through a flattening machine. It was like a cheese-cutter,—all edge. Another had one nostril bitten off. He proved the buffoon of the party. He had the extraordinary faculty of untying the strings of his face, as it were, at pleasure, when his features fell into con-fusion—into a crazed chaos almost frightful; his eye, too, lost its usual significance; but no man's countenance . . . was fuller of fun and fancies than his, when he liked. A third man had his features wrenched to the right—exceedingly little, it is true; but the effect was remarkable. He had been slapped on the face by a grisly bear. Another was a short, paunchy old man, with vast features, but no forehead—the last man I should have selected; but he was a hard-working creature, usually called "Passe-partout," because he had been everywhere, and was famous for the weight of fish he could devour at a meal. . . . Except the younger men, their faces were short, thin, quick in their expression, and mapped out in furrows, like those of the sundayless Parisians.[38]

In his language, customs, and manners the *voyageur* was as unique as a sailor or a lumberjack. He not only spoke a patois of French but he also used words and phrases of his own which were unintelligible to his employers and to those with whom he conducted business. He was usually dressed in a short shirt, a red woolen cap, deerskin moccasins without stockings, and a pair of deerskin leggings which reached from his ankles to a little above his knees and which were held up by a string tied to a belt around his waist. He left his thighs bare. With inevitable pipe in his mouth and gray bag or pouch flung over his expansive shoul-der, "he appeared," says Grace Lee Nute, "speeding over lakes, advanc-ing cautiously up narrow creeks, toiling over portages, cracking his whip over the heads of his dogs, laughing down rapids, fiddling in log forts, and singing wherever he was."[39]

His entire existence was bound up in his canoe, that "frail basket" which the Chippewas and other Algonkin tribes of the north had taught him how to fashion, which he could carry on his shoulders, and which "was his carriage by day, his house by night, the topic of half his con-versation, and the object of his pride."[40] He made it distinctly his own by painting it in gay colors, usually red and green, and by festooning it with a horse or Indian head or the antlers of a moose or deer. On such rivers as the St. Lawrence, the Mississippi, and the Missouri he used the largest of canoes, known as *canot de maître*, which was between thirty-five and forty feet long and which could carry about three thousand pounds of merchandise. The men in the center of the canoe, known as *milieux* or middlemen, used a paddle about two feet long and three inches wide; but the steersman or *gouvernail* who stood at the stern and the bowsmen or foremen used longer paddles, especially in running rapids or leaping over small falls. Most of the paddles were made of red cedar and had blades painted red or decorated in red and black.[41]

He planned his voyage with infinite care. The merchandise he loaded on his canoes for the Indian trade included guns and ammunition packed conveniently in boxes, intoxicating beverages usually in small kegs, blankets, colored cloths, calico, strouds, beads, handkerchiefs, ribbons, sleigh-bells, looking-glasses, combs, knives, scissors, tobacco, and toys. On the eve of his departure, after he had checked and rechecked his cargo, he repaired to the nearest church, where he implored St. Anne, patron saint of voyagers, for protection and help against the possible evils and hardships of the journey he was about to undertake.[42]

Then, bidding his family and friends farewell, he started on his hazardous journey. If it began at Montreal it usually took the main waterway of New France to the Indian tribes: along the St. Lawrence to its junction with the Ottawa and up that river to the Mattawa, Lake Nipissing, the French River, and Georgian Bay. On this route the *voyageurs* crossed no less than eighteen portages. They also encountered almost as many obstructions or *décharges*, over which they were obliged to tow by means of ropes or cables their canoes and sometimes even a part of their merchandise. They portaged their merchandise by using a kind of harness known as tump-lines, which consisted of a leather collar to which several narrow straps were attached. Tying these around each end of a bale, the *voyageur* swung it onto his back. Then he brought the collar over his head, placed it on his forehead, and inclined a little forward so that his burden would rest more securely. Then, with the ease of a man lifting a small child onto his shoulders, he swung another bale on top of the first.[43]

When the *voyageurs* passed from the St. Lawrence into the Ottawa, and again when they passed into the Mattawa, they pulled off their caps and prayed. At Lake Nipissing, amid shouts of joy, they threw away their setting poles which had helped their paddles control their canoes, again pulled off their caps, and again prayed to *le bon Dieu* for protecting them against the swift streams they had just passed. When they arrived at Sault Ste. Marie or some other falls they caught sight of wooden crosses which marked the watery graves of *voyageurs* who had been caught in its treacherous swirl or eddies. Again their caps came off; again they prayed—this time lugubriously and long.[44]

Every night they camped, usually under trees near the bank of a river or on the shore of a lake, made a fire, and cooked their *souper* or evening meal, which often consisted of a quart of lyed corn, some wild rice, and an ounce or two of bear's grease for each man. The voyager's monthly allowance seldom exceeded a bushel of corn and two pounds of fat or grease. Usually he was told he must not consume more than a quart of corn and a half pint of bear's grease, oil, or fat at a meal. Sometimes, when his food gave out, he was forced to live entirely on wild rice; and sometimes, when he was lost or when he failed to find an Indian camp, he faced starvation. Perrault tells us that he once lent three fawn skins of rice to a *voyageur* who was reduced to eating moss from pine trees. Alexander Henry, who in the latter part of the eighteenth century wrote an excellent account of his travels, once came on a sole survivor of a voyage who, because his provisions had given out, was forced to feed on his dead companions. On reaching wintering ground the *voyageur* began to build a fort, unless, of course, one already existed. The kind of life he led there has been suggested in many pages of this volume. The spring was usually the time for a return trip home.

NOTES

Chapter 1

1. James H. Baker, "The Sources of the Mississippi," in *Collections of the Minnesota Historical Society*, VI (1887), 1–27; W. J. Petersen, "Veritas Caput: Itasca," in *Minnesota History*, XVIII, 180–85; Philip P. Mason, ed., *Schoolcraft's Expedition to Lake Itasca*, pp. 34–39.
2. W. J. Petersen, *Steamboating on the Upper Mississippi*, pp. 22, 23.
3. Lyle Saxon, *Father Mississippi*, pp. 68–70.
4. Grace Lee Nute, *Lake Superior*, p. 331.
5. *Ibid.*, pp. 335–36. *See also* J. G. Kohl, *Kitchi-Gami*, p. 87.
6. Mentor L. Williams, ed., *Schoolcraft's Indian Legends*, p. 81.
7. J. C. Beltrami, *A Pilgrimage in America*, pp. 130, 179.
8. Mark Twain, *Life on the Mississippi*, pp. 473–74.
9. Walter Havighurst, *Upper Mississippi*, p. 9.
10. Frank E. Williams, "The Geography of the Mississippi Valley," in *The Annals* of American Academy of Political and Social Science, CXXXV (1928), p. 11.
11. Twain, p. 153; J. W. Foster, *The Mississippi Valley*, pp. 5–13.
12. Twain, p. 3.
13. *Ibid.*, p. 154.
14. *Ibid.*, p. 156.
15. Hodding Carter, *Lower Mississippi*, p. 5.

Chapter 2

1. William Watts Folwell, *A History of Minnesota*, I, 80–82; N. H. Winchell, *The Aborigines of Minnesota*, pp. 67, 69.
2. Walter S. Campbell, "The Plains Indian in Literature—and in Life," in James F. Willard and Colin B. Goodykoontz, eds., *The Trans-Mississippi West*, p. 182.
3. *Ibid.*, pp. 183–85.
4. *Ibid.*, p. 185.
5. *Ibid.*
6. *Ibid.*, pp. 185–86.
7. *Ibid.*, pp. 186, 189.

8. Frederick Jackson Turner, *The Frontier in American History*, p. 14.

9. Everett E. Edwards, "American Indian Contributions to Civilization" in *Minnesota History*, XV (1934), 255–272.

10. Claude Charles Le Roy, Bacqueville de la Potherie, *History of the Savage People Who Are Allies of New France*, in Emma Helen Blair, ed., *The Indian Tribes of the Upper Mississippi Valley and Region of the Great Lakes*, II, 71–73.

11. Samuel William Pond, "The Dakotas or Sioux in Minnesota As They Were in 1834," in *Collections of the Minnesota Historical Society*, XII (1908), 387.

12. *Ibid.*, 387–88.

13. *Ibid.*, 353–55.

14. E. D. Neill, "Dakota Land and Dakota Life," in *Collections of the Minnesota Historical Society*, I (1872), 287–88.

15. Reginald and Gladys Laubin, *The Indian Tipi*, pp. 19–32.

16. Neill, I, 288.

17. Pond, XII, 343; Edwin Thompson Denig, *Five Indian Tribes of the Upper Missouri*, pp. 11–12.

18. *Ibid.;* Winchell, pp. 495–96.

19. *Ibid.*

20. Pond, XII, 344; Winchell, pp. 495–96.

21. *Ibid.*

22. Pond, XII, 345.

23. *Ibid.*, 347–48.

24. *Ibid.*

25. *Ibid.*, 349.

26. *Ibid.*, 350.

27. *Ibid.*

28. *Ibid.*, 351–52.

29. Mari Sandoz, *These Were the Sioux*, pp. 25–26.

30. *Ibid.*, pp. 27–33.

31. Pond, XII, 453–56.

32. *Ibid.*, 453

33. *Ibid.*, 454

34. *Ibid.*, 454–55.

35. *Ibid.*, 455.

36. Neill, I, 266.

37. James W. Lynd, "The Religion of the Dakotas," in *Collections of the Minnesota Historical Society*, II, Part II (1881), 153–154.

38. *Ibid.*, 151–52; Neill, I, 267.
39. Pond, XII, 403.
40. *Ibid.*, 403.
41. Neill, I, 268.
42. *Ibid.*, 268; Pond, XII, 404.
43. Lynd, II, 158.
44. Neill, I, 269; Pond, XII, 417–18.
45. S. R. Riggs, Lac Qui Parle, October, 1838, in *Missionary Herald,* XXXV (1839), 59–60; *Dakota Friend,* June, 1852.
46. *Ibid.*
47. Riggs, Lac Qui Parle, October, 1838, in *Missionary Herald,* XXXV (1839), 59–60.
48. S. R. Riggs, "Journal" in *Missionary Herald,* XXXVI (1840), 324.
49. Neill, I, 277–78.
50. Riggs, "Journal," Lac Qui Parle, September, 1839, in *Missionary Herald,* XXXVI (1840), 322–23.
51. Pond, XIII, 478–85.
52. James W. Lynd, "History of the Dakotas," in *Collections of the Minnesota Historical Society,* II, Part II, 145–46; L. Nydahl, "The Pipestone Quarry and the Indians" in *Minnesota History,* XXX (1931), 193–208.
53. W. J. McGee, "The Siouan Indians," in *Annual Report,* Bureau of Ethnology (1893–94), pp. 173–74; W. T. Hornaday, "The Extermination of the American Bison," in *Annual Report,* United States National Museum (1887), Part II, 373–88.
54. Mari Sandoz, *The Buffalo Hunters,* pp. ix–xii.
55. Pond, XII, 359–60.
56. *Ibid.*, 360.
57. *Ibid.*
58. *Ibid.*
59. *Ibid.*, 361.
60. *Ibid.*, 365.
61. *Ibid.*, 366.
62. *Ibid.*, 437–38.
63. *Ibid.*
64. S. R. Riggs, "Dakota Grammar, Texts, and Ethnography," in *North America Ethnology* (1881), pp. 229–32; James George Frazer, *The Native Races of America,* pp. 148–49; George A. Dorsey, "The Ponca Sun Dance," in *Publications,* Field Museum of Natural History, VII (1905), 71–88.
65. Riggs, "Dakota Grammar, etc." p. 230.

66. Dorsey, VII, 74.
67. Riggs, "Dakota Grammar," p. 232.

Chapter 3

1. William W. Warren, "History of the Ojibways," in *Collections of the Minnesota Historical Society*, V, 99.
2. Winchell, p. 582.
3. Joseph A. Gilfillan, "The Ojibways in Minnesota," in *Collections of the Minnesota Historical Society*, IX, 57–58.
4. *Ibid.*, 58.
5. *Ibid.*, 58–59.
6. Frances Densmore, *Chippewa Customs*, pp. 150–52.
7. George Catlin, *North American Indians*, II, 157–58.
8. Densmore, pp. 135–37.
9. *Ibid.*, pp. 22–23; Frederick Webb Hodge, ed., *Handbook of American Indians North of Mexico*, Part 2, p. 951.
10. Densmore, pp. 28–30; Winchell, pp. 592–96.
11. Densmore, pp. 120, 144.
12. *Ibid.*, p. 31.
13. *Ibid.*
14. Hodge, Part I, p. 277.
15. Densmore, p. 38.
16. *Ibid.*, p. 48.
17. *Ibid.*, p. 53.
18. *Ibid.*, p. 61.
19. *Ibid.*, p. 87.
20. Harold E. Driver, *Indians of North America*, pp. 420–22; W. J. Hoffman, "The Mede'Wiwin or Grand Medicine Society," in *Annual Report* (1885–86), Bureau of American Ethnology, pp. 143–300; Densmore, pp. 94–95.
21. Driver, p. 421; Densmore, pp. 93–94.
22. *Ibid.*, p. 70.
23. *Ibid.*, pp. 70–72.
24. *Ibid.*, p. 71.
25. Charles Hamilton, ed., *Cry of the Thunderbird*, pp. 12–13.
26. *Ibid.*, p. 13.
27. William Jones, *Ojibwa Texts*, Part II, p. 289.

28. *Ibid.*, p. 337.
29. Densmore, p. 98.
30. *Ibid.*, pp. 103, 104–05.
31. *Ibid.*
32. *Ibid.*, p. 106.

Chapter 4

1. John R. Swanton, *The Indian Tribes of North America,* pp. 266–68; Hodge, Part I, 612–13.
2. John Ely Briggs, "The Sacs and Foxes," in *The Palimpsest,* IX (1928), 45.
3. Swanton, *Indian Tribes,* pp. 251–52; Horace M. Rebok, "The Last of the Mus-Qua-Kies," in *Iowa Historical Record,* XVII (1901), No. 3, 307.
4. *Ibid.,* 314; William T. Hagan, *The Sac and Fox Indians,* pp. 6–7.
5. Thomas Forsyth, "Account of the Manners and Customs of the Sauks and Fox Nations of Indians . . ." in Blair, ed., II, 187; Hagan, p. 7.
6. Briggs, IX, 46–47.
7. Forsyth, II, 217 n.
8. Morrell Marston, "Letter to Reverend Dr. Jedidiah Morse," in Blair, ed., II, 164.
9. *Ibid.,* 165.
10. *Ibid.*
11. *Ibid.*
12. Forsyth, II, 214.
13. *Ibid.*
14. Cutting Marsh, "Documents Relating to the Stockbridge Mission," in *Collections of the State Historical Society of Wisconsin,* XV (1900), 147.
15. *Ibid.,* 148.
16. Forsyth, II, 215.
17. *Ibid.,* 195–96.
18. *Ibid.,* 196–97.
19. *Ibid.,* 206–07.
20. *Ibid.,* 208–09.
21. *Ibid.*
22. *Ibid.,* 222.
23. *Ibid.,* 230.
24. *Ibid.,* 230–31.

25. Marsh, XV, 128–29.
26. *Ibid.*, 130–31.
27. *Ibid.*, 131–32.
28. *Ibid.*, 129.
29. *Ibid.*
30. *Ibid.*, 130.
31. *Ibid.*, 137.
32. *Ibid.*, 135.
33. *Ibid.*, 136.
34. *Ibid.*, 137–38.

Chapter 5

1. John Joseph Mathews, *Wah'Kon-Tah,* p. 345.
2. Catlin, II, 46.
3. Thomas Nuttall, *Journal of Travels into the Arkansa Territory,* p. 249.
4. *Ibid.*, p. 250.
5. John Joseph Mathews, *The Osages,* pp. 10–11.
6. *Ibid.*, p. 21; Francis La Flesche, "The Osage Tribe" in *Annual Report* (36th), Bureau of American Ethnology, pp. 48–49.
7. Mathews, *Osage,* p. 10.
8. La Flesche, pp. 59–60.
9. *Ibid.*, pp. 60–61.
10. *Ibid.*, p. 61.
11. *Ibid.*
12. *Ibid.*, pp. 68–69.
13. Mathews, *The Osages,* pp. 64–74.
14. La Flesche, "The Osage Tribe," p. 72.
15. Mathews, *The Osages,* p. 54.
16. *Ibid.*, pp. 54–55.
17. *Ibid.*, p. 54.
18. La Flesche, "The Osage Tribe, pp. 71, 88, 90.
19. *Ibid.*, p. 91.
20. Francis La Flesche, "War Ceremony and Peace Ceremony of the Osage Indians," in *Bulletin 101,* Bureau of American Ethnology, pp. 3–21.
21. *Ibid.*, pp. 29–30.
22. *Ibid.*, pp. 78–79.
23. *Ibid.*, pp. 79–81.

Chapter 6

1. Muriel H. Wright, *A Guide to the Indian Tribes of Oklahoma*, pp. 218–19; Hodge, Part II, p. 334.

2. Garcilaso de la Vega, *The Florida of the Inca*, pp. 436–37; John Anthony Caruso, *The Southern Frontier*, p. 48.

3. See McGee, p. 193, and George E. Hyde, *Indians of the Woodlands*, p. 156.

4. Claude Dablon, "Relation of the Voyages, Discoveries, and Death of Father . . . Marquette, . . ." in John Gilmary Shea, ed., *Discovery and Exploration of the Mississippi Valley*, pp. 46–47.

5. *Ibid.*, pp. 48–49.

6. *Ibid.*, p. 49.

7. *Ibid.*, p. 50.

8. Zenobius Membré, "Narrative," *ibid.*, pp. 169–170.

9. Hyde, pp. 173–74.

10. [Jacques] Gravier, "Journal," in John Gilmary Shea, ed., *Early Voyages Up and Down the Mississippi*, p. 130.

11. Bernard de La Harpe, *Journal Historique de l'Établisse-ment des Français à La Louisiane*, p. 317.

12. *Ibid.*, pp. 318–21.

13. Gravier, p. 129.

14. *Ibid.*, p. 130.

15. Jean-Bernard Bossu, *Travels in the Interior of North America, 1751–1762*, p. 61.

16. *Ibid.*, pp. 61–62.

17. Nuttall, p. 125.

18. *Ibid.*, Boyd W. Johnson, *The Arkansas Frontier*, p. 11.

19. Bossu, p. 62.

20. *Ibid.*

21. *Ibid.*, p. 63.

22. *Ibid.*, p. 64.

23. *Ibid.*, pp. 64–65.

24. *Ibid.*

25. *Ibid.*

26. *Ibid.*, p. 66.

Chapter 7

1. William B. Glover, "A History of the Caddo Indians," in *Louisiana Historical Quarterly*, XVIII (1935), 875.

2. M. B. Harrington, *Certain Caddo Sites in Arkansas*, pp. 140–41.

3. Glover, XVIII, 879; *American State Papers, Indian Affairs*, I, p. 721.

4. John R. Swanton, "Source Material On the History and Ethnology of the Caddo Indians," in *Bulletin 132*, Bureau of American Ethnology, pp. 15–16. Hereinafter cited as Swanton, "History of the Caddoes." See also Francisco Casañas de Jesus Maria, "Description of the Tejas or Asinai Indians," in *Southwestern Historical Quarterly*, XXX (1927), 208.

5. Isidro Felis de Espinosa, "Description of the Tejas or Asinai Indians," *ibid.*, XXXI (1927), 152

6. *Ibid.*, 175.

7. *Ibid.*

8. Juan Antonio Padilla, "Report on the Barbarous Indians of the Province of Texas," in *Southwestern Historical Quarterly*, XXIII (1919), 47–52.

9. Anastasius Douay, "Narrative of La Salle's Attempt to Ascend the Mississippi in 1687," in Shea, ed., *Discovery and Exploration*, pp. 217–220; Pierre Margry, ed., *Découvertes et Établissements des Français dans l'Ouest et dans le Sud de l'Amérique Septentrionale*, III, 345.

10. Gaspar José de Solís, "Diary of a Visit of Inspection of the Texas Mission . . ." in *Southwestern Historical Quarterly*, XXXV (1931), 70.

11. Juan Agustín de Morfi, *Excerpts From the Memorias for the History of the Province of Texas*, pp. 36–37; Espinosa, XXXI, 164.

12. Elsie Clews Parsons, "Notes on the Caddo," in *Memoirs of the American Anthropological Association*, No. 57, p. 28.

13. Casañas, XXX, 283–84.

14. Morfi, pp. 44–45.

15. Casañas, XXX, 297–99; W. W. Newcomb, *The Indians of Texas*, p. 301.

16. Casañas, XXX, 216–18.

17. *Ibid.*

18. *Ibid.*

19. Espinosa, XXXI, 154–55.

20. Morfi, pp. 40–41.

21. *Ibid.*, p. 47.

22. Margry, ed., III, 363–64.

23. Espinosa, XXXI, 156–57.
24. *Ibid.*
25. Casañas, XXX, 220.
26. Margry, ed., III, 357–58.
27. Solís, XXXV, 42–43.
28. Espinosa, XXXI, 165–68.
29. *Ibid.*
30. *Ibid.*, Morfi, pp. 35–36.
31. Espinosa, XXXI, 168–69; Swanton, "History of the Caddoes," p. 222.
32. *Ibid.*
33. Espinosa, XXXI, 158–60; Newcomb, p. 309; Morfi, pp. 21–23.
34. Espinosa, XXXI, 160–62; Morfi, pp. 23–26.
35. Espinosa, XXXI, 168; Swanton, "History of the Caddoes," p. 232.
36. Robert Dabney Calhoun, "The Taënsa Indians," in *Louisiana Historical Quarterly*, XVII (1934), 411–16; Henri de Tonti, "Narrative," in Margry, ed., I, 600–02.
37. *Ibid.*
38. *Ibid.*, 603–04.
39. B. F. French, ed., *Historical Collections of Louisiana*, I, 61–62.
40. Hodge, ed., Part II, 668.
41. Membré, in Shea, ed., *Discovery and Exploration*, pp. 172, 173–74, 177.
42. F. J. Montigny in Shea, ed., *Early Voyages*, pp. 75–79.
43. Tonti in Margry, ed., I, 566–68.
44. Le Petit in *Jesuit Relations*, LXVIII, 122–25.
45. *Ibid.*
46. Iberville Journal in Margry, ed., IV, 412–17.
47. Calhoun, XVII, 670–76.

Chapter 8

1. C. W. Butterfield, *History of the Discovery of the Northwest*, p. 37; Bernard DeVoto, *The Course of Empire*, p. 89.
2. Butterfield, pp. 29–30; Paul le Jeune, "*Relation de ce qui s'est passé en la Nouvelle France, en l'année, 1636*, in *Jesuit Relations*, VIII, 173.
3. Butterfield, pp. 36, 48; Barthélemy Vimont in *Jesuit Relations*, XXIII (1642-43), 275–79.
4. Butterfield, pp. 46, 54.
5. *Ibid.*, pp. 56–57.

6. Frederic Austin Ogg, *The Opening of the Mississippi*, pp. 48–49; Vimont in *Jesuit Relations*, XXIII, 279.

7. Butterfield, pp. 65–67, 70–71.

8. *Ibid.*, pp. 71–73; Folwell, I, 6; Ogg, pp. 49–50; Vimont in *Jesuit Relations*, XXIII, 279–81.

Chapter 9

1. Ogg, pp. 51–53.

2. Blegen, *Minnesota*, pp. 38–39.

3. A. T. Adams, ed., *The Explorations of Radisson*, p. xv; Grace Lee Nute, "The Radisson Problem," in *Minnesota History*, XIII (1932), 256; Blegen, *Minnesota*, p. 36; DeVoto, p. 572.

4. Adams, ed., p. ii.

5. *Ibid.*, p. xv.

6. Peter Esprit Radisson, *Voyages*, pp. 13–14; Adams, p. i.

7. *Ibid.*, pp. 3, 39–40, 41, 42–44, 46, 48–49, 79, 82–84, 85–86.

8. Grace Lee Nute, *Caesars of the Wilderness*, p. 31; John B. Brebner, *Canada*, p. 49.

9. Nute, *Caesars of the Wilderness*, p. 24n.

10. See *ibid.*, pp. 23, 24n, 30.

11. *Ibid.*, pp. 31–32; Edward C. Gale, "The Radisson Manuscript," in *Minnesota History*, VII (1926), 340–42.

12. Radisson, pp. 20–21.

13. Nute, *Caesars of the Wilderness*, pp. 33–34.

14. Radisson, pp. 167–68.

15. *Ibid.*, pp. 150–51.

16. Stanley Vestal, *King of the Fur Traders*, p. 135; Nute, *Caesars of the Wilderness*, p. 28.

17. E. E. Rich, *Hudson's Bay Company*, I, 28.

18. Hjalmar R. Holand, "Radisson's Two Western Voyages," in *Minnesota History*, XV (1934), 174.

19. Blegen, *The Land Lies Open*, p. 21.

20. Adams, p. vii.

21. *Jesuit Relations*, XLV, 105.

22. Radisson, pp. 174–75.

23. *Ibid.*, p. 176.

24. T. J. Campbell, *Pioneer Laymen of North America*, I, 261.

25. Radisson, pp. 188–89.

26. *Ibid.*, p. 190.

27. *Ibid.*

28. Nute, *Lake Superior*, p. 51; Henry Schoolcraft, *Summary Narrative of an Exploratory Expedition to the Source of the Mississippi River in 1820*, p. 86; Vestal, pp. 156–57; Radisson, pp. 190–91.

29. *Ibid.*, p. 192.

30. *Ibid.*, p. 193.

31. *Ibid.*, pp. 194–95.

32. *Ibid.*, pp. 195–96.

33. *Ibid.*, pp. 196–97.

34. *Ibid.*, p. 198.

35. *Ibid.*, pp. 199–201; Vestal, p. 163.

36. Radisson, p. 202.

37. *Ibid.*, p. 203.

38. *Ibid.*, p. 204.

39. *Ibid.*, p. 205; Vestal, p. 168.

40. *Ibid.*, p. 169; Radisson, p. 205.

41. *Ibid.*

42. *Ibid.*, p. 206.

43. Nute, *Caesars of the Wilderness*, p. 63.

44. Vestal, pp. 173–75; Radisson, p. 207.

45. *Ibid.*, p. 209.

46. Adams, p. lix–lx; Radisson, p. 210; Vestal, p. 175.

47. *Ibid.*, p. 176.

48. Radisson, p. 213.

49. *Ibid.*, p. 215.

50. *Ibid.*

51. *Ibid.*, pp. 221–22.

52. Vestal, p. 185; Radisson, pp. 224–25.

53. Nute, *Caesars of the Wilderness*, pp. 65–67, 75; Gustave Lanctot, *A History of Canada*, I, 247–48.

Chapter 10

1. Allouez in *Jesuit Relations*, LI (1666–68), 53.

2. Dablon, *ibid.*, LV (1670–72), 207, 209.

3. Marquette to the Reverend Father Superior of the Missions, *ibid.*, LIV, 169, 171.

4. La Potherie, I, 307–16; *Collections of the State Historical Society of Wisconsin*, XIV, 32–50.

5. *Jesuit Relations*, LV, 111, 113.

6. Ogg, p. 65; Jean Delanglez, *Louis Jolliet, Vie et Voyages,* pp. 186–89.

7. John Anthony Caruso, *The Great Lakes Frontier,* p. 12; Earnest Gagnon, *Louis Jolliet,* p. 10ff.

8. Lionel Groulx, *Notre Grande Aventure,* pp. 164–68; Francis Borgia Steck, *The Marquette-Jolliet Expedition,* pp. 207–13. In the first volume of his celebrated work Margry published Abbé Renaudot's *Recit d'un ami de l'abbé de Galinée,* an unreliable document which contended that La Salle made several journeys to the Mississippi River several years before Jolliet and Marquette saw it. Jean Delanglez, *Some La Salle Journeys,* pp. 43–61, brilliantly exposes Renaudot and his followers who, by their zeal, unintentionally "transformed the great explorer into an elaborate hoaxer."

9. Margry, ed., I, 259–70.

10. Louise Phelps Kellogg, ed., *Early Narratives of the Northwest,* p. 268.

11. Caruso, *The Great Lakes Frontier,* pp. 19–20.

Chapter 11

1. Caruso, *The Great Lakes Frontier,* pp. 20–21; Joseph Wallace, *The History of Illinois and Louisiana,* pp. 78–79.

2. Frontenac to Colbert, November 14, 1674, in Francis Parkman, *La Salle and the Discovery of the Great West,* pp. 99–100n. Hereinafter cited as Parkman, *La Salle.*

3. Wallace, p. 80.

4. Parkman, *La Salle,* pp. 126–27.

5. Wallace, p. 83.

6. Edmund Robert Murphy, *Henry de Tonty: Fur Trader of the Mississippi,* pp. 1–12.

7. *Ibid.,* pp. 1–2.

8. Parkman, *La Salle,* pp. 131–43, Harold A. Innis, *The Fur Trade in Canada,* p. 49.

9. Parkman, *La Salle,* pp. 144–50; 152–63.

10. Wallace, pp. 89-90.

11. Parkman, *La Salle,* pp. 170–71.

12. *Ibid,* pp. 173–77.

13. *Ibid.,* p. 179.

14. Wallace, p. 94.

15. *Ibid.,* p. 105.

16. Parkman, *La Salle,* pp. 193–97.

17. Letters of La Salle in Margry, ed., II, 166–176.

18. *Ibid.*

19. Parkman, *La Salle*, p. 204.
20. Caruso, *The Great Lakes Frontier*, pp. 28–29; Frances Gaither, *The Fatal River*, pp. 159–60.
21. Parkman, *La Salle*, p. 211.
22. *Ibid.*, p. 213.
23. *Ibid.*, p. 214.
24. *Ibid.*, p. 215.
25. Gaither, pp. 165, 167; Parkman, *La Salle*, p. 282.
26. *Ibid.*, pp. 217–38, 292.
27. *Ibid.*, p. 233.
28. *Ibid.*, pp. 234–38.
29. See will of La Salle, Montreal, August 11, 1681, in Wallace, p. 134.
30. Letters of La Salle in Margry, ed., II, 164–203.
31. Parkman, *La Salle*, pp. 297–98.
32. Gaither, p. 177; Parkman, *La Salle*, p. 299.
33. *Ibid*, p. 306.
34. French, Part I, 48–50.
35. Ogg, p. 112.
36. Letters of La Salle in Margry, ed., II, 337, 348.
37. Wallace, pp. 148–49.
38. Louis XIV to La Barre, August 5, 1683, in Margry, ed., II, 403.
39. Paul Chesnel, *History of Cavelier de la Salle*, pp. 169–70. This work contains many errors and should be used with caution.

Chapter 12

1. Louis Hennepin, "Narrative of the Voyage To the Upper Mississippi" in Shea, ed., *Discovery and Exploration of the Mississippi Valley*, pp. 103–04, 107–08.
2. Jean Delanglez, *Hennepin's Description of Louisiana*, p. 75.
3. *Ibid.*
4. *Ibid.*, pp. 3–32.
5. *Ibid.*, p. 79.
6. Parkman, *La Salle*, pp. 243–44.
7. Hennepin, p. 118.
8. *Ibid.*, p. 114. Delanglez, *Hennepin's Description of Louisiana*, p. 97, accepts this date as certain because Hennepin "mentions several times that it took nineteen days to reach the Falls of St. Anthony."
9. Hennepin, p. 115. Delanglez, *Hennepin's Description of Louisiana*, p. 74, says sarcastically that Hennepin too often reminds his readers that he

was "on the verge of being killed." Actually, he was always fairly well treated.

10. Hennepin, p. 116.

11. *Ibid.*

12. *Ibid.*; Parkman, *La Salle*, p. 253.

13. Hennepin, pp. 117-18.

14. *Ibid.*, p. 118.

15. Parkman, *La Salle*, p. 256.

16. Hennepin, pp. 120-21.

17. *Ibid.*

18. *Ibid.*, pp. 123.

19. *Ibid.*, pp. 123–25. Delanglez, *Hennepin's Description of Louisiana*, pp. 76–77, is critical of the monk's use of "our" chasuble, for obviously it "was not the common property of Hennepin, Accault, and Auguelle." He urges historians to be careful to "find out exactly whether Hennepin means himself or the whole party. When he speaks of the *Griffon* as 'our bark,' of the expedition as 'our discoveries' or 'our undertaking,' it is not always clear that he considers himself the owner of the ship, or the leader of the expedition."

20. Parkman, *La Salle*, p. 261; Hennepin, p. 125.

21. *Ibid.*, p. 126. Hennepin's chronology is nearly always incorrect. He says that he remained with the Sioux two months, whereas later La Salle was informed that Hennepin remained with them six weeks. See Margry, ed., II, 257.

22. Hennepin, p. 130.

23. *Ibid.*, pp. 132–33.

24. *Ibid.*, pp. 133-35.

25. *Ibid.*, p. 139.

26. Duluth, "Memoir," in Kellogg, ed., *Early Narratives*, pp. 329–30; Parkman, *La Salle*, pp. 274, 275–76n, 276-78. For a discussion of the actual meeting place of Hennepin and Duluth see Delanglez, *Hennepin's Description of Louisiana*, p. 96.

27. Margry, ed., VI, 26–34; Folwell, I, 23.

28. Duluth, p. 331; Nute, *Lake Superior*, p. 30.

29. Duluth, p. 332.

30. Hennepin, p. 142.

31. Parkman, *La Salle*, pp. 279-80; Grace Lee Nute, "Father Hennepin's Later Years," in *Minnesota History*, XIX (1938), 393–98.

Chapter 13

1. Parkman, *La Salle*, pp. 345–47.

2. Henry Folmer, *Franco-Spanish Rivalry in North America*, pp. 146–47.

3. Margry, ed., III, 55.

4. Folmer, *Franco-Spanish Rivalry,* pp. 149, 150, 151–54.

5. Beaujeu to Cabart de Villemont, May 21, 1684, in Margry, ed., II, 421–23.

6. Parkman, *La Salle,* pp. 352–53; Margry, ed., II, 378.

7. Christian Le Clercq, "Account of La Salle's Attempt to Reach the Mississippi by Sea," in Shea, ed., *Discovery and Exploration of the Mississippi Valley,* p. 188.

8. Wallace, pp. 155–56.

9. See Margry, ed., II, 492.

10. Folmer, *Franco-Spanish Rivalry,* pp. 159–60.

11. Wallace, pp. 157-58.

12. Chesnel, pp. 199–200; Parkman, *La Salle,* pp. 380–82.

13. Henri Joutel, *A Journal of La Salle's Last Voyage,* p. 51.

14. Parkman, *La Salle,* p. 383.

15. Chesnel, pp. 202–03.

16. See Letters of La Salle in Margry, ed., II, 577–88.

17. Folmer, *Franco-Spanish Rivalry,* pp. 161–62.

18. Parkman, *La Salle,* pp. 391–92.

19. Herbert Eugene Bolton, "The Location of La Salle's Colony on the Gulf of Mexico, *Mississippi Valley Historical Review,* II, 91915, 178.

20. Margry, ed., III, 174; Joutel, p. 64.

21. C. W. Hackett, ed., *Historical Documents Relating to New Mexico, Vizcaya, and Approaches Thereto, to 1773,* II, 268.

22. *Ibid.,* 271.

23. Joutel, pp. 75-76.

24. *Ibid.,* p. 76.

25. Anastasius Douay, "Narrative of La Salle's Attempt to Ascend the Mississippi in 1687," in Shea, ed., *Discovery and Exploration,* pp. 198-99.

26. *Ibid.,* pp. 199–200.

27. *Ibid.,* p. 204.

28. Jean Delanglez, ed. and trans., *The Journal of Jean Cavelier,* p. 73. Hereinafter cited as Cavelier, *Journal.*

29. Douay, pp. 204–05.

30. *Ibid.,* pp. 205–06; Cavelier, *Journal,* p. 75.

31. *Ibid.*

32. Parkman, *La Salle,* p. 416.

33. *Ibid.,* p. 418.

34. *Ibid.,* p. 417; Margry, ed., III, 258.

35. Joutel, pp. 84–85.

36. Cavelier, pp. 81–82.

37. *Ibid.*, pp. 82–83.

38. *Ibid.*, pp. 97–98.

39. Parkman, *La Salle*, p. 425; Douay, p. 212.

40. *Ibid.*, p. 213.

41. Joutel, p. 103; Gaither, p. 284.

42. Tonti, "Memoir," in Kellogg, ed., *Early Narratives*, p. 319.

43. Joutel, p. 103.

44. Quoted in Wallace, p. 172.

45. Parkman, *La Salle*, p. 432.

46. Henry Bamford Parkes, *The American Experience*, p. 170.

47. Joutel, pp. 105–23.

48. Parkman, *La Salle*, pp. 447–53; Joutel, pp. 144.

49. Murphy, pp. 35–41; Margry, ed., III, 439–40, 554–58; Parkman, *La Salle*, p. 455.

50. *Ibid.*, pp. 455–58.

51. Joutel, pp. 164–70.

52. Alonso de León, "*Historia de nuevo León Con Noticias Sobre Coahuila, Tejas, y Nuevo Mexico,*" in G. Garcia and C. Pereyra, eds., *Documentos Inéditos ó Muy Raros Para la Historia de México*, XXV, 327–32; Elizabeth H. West, trans. and ed., "De León's Expedition of 1689," in Texas Historical Association *Quarterly*, VIII (1905), 289; Walter F. McCaleb, *Spanish Missions of Texas*, pp. 23-24.

53. "*Carta de Don Damien Manzaret a Don Carlos de Suguenza Sobre el Descubrimiento de la Bahai del Esperitu Santo,*" in *ibid.*, II, 253–80; León, XXV, 334.

54. Tonti, pp. 307–18.

55. *Ibid.*, pp. 318–22.

Chapter 14

1. William Edward Dunn, *Spanish and French Rivalry in the Gulf Region of the United States*, pp. 50–56.

2. Margry, ed., IV, 3–5.

3. John Anthony Caruso, *The Southern Frontier*, p. 148.

4. Rémonville Memoir in Margry, ed., IV, 19–43.

5. Ogg, pp. 173–74.

6. Pez Memoir, June 2, 1689, in I. A. Leonard, trans. and ed., *Spanish Approach to Pensacola, 1689–1693*, p. 84.

7. Folmer, *Franco-Spanish Rivalry*, pp. 193, 194, 195–96.

8. Caruso, *The Southern Frontier*, pp. 148–49.

9. Nellis M. Crouse, *Le Moyne d'Iberville, Soldier of New France*, pp. 161–62. For a detailed account of Iberville's early career see *ibid.*, pp. 1–154.

10. *Ibid.*, pp. 169–70.

11. *Ibid.*, pp. 173–74.

12. *Ibid.*

13. Margry, ed., IV, 155.

14. A. C. Albrecht, "The Origin and Settlement of Baton Rouge, Louisiana," in *Louisiana Historical Quarterly*, XXVIII (1945), 5–68.

15. Crouse, *Iberville*, p. 185.

16. *Ibid.*, pp. 186–90.

17. *Ibid.*, p. 190.

18. Caruso, *The Southern Frontier*, pp. 152–53.

19. Margry, ed., IV, 328. H. Mortimer Favrot, "Colonial Forts of Louisiana," in *Louisiana Historical Quarterly*, XXVI (1945), 725, says that the fort was named after the minister's oldest son, Jean Frédéric. This is impossible, since he was not born until 1701. See Crouse, *Iberville*, p. 193n.

20. *Ibid.*, p. 195.

21. Peter Hamilton, *Colonial Mobile*, p. 80.

22. Verner W. Crane, *The Southern Frontier*, p. 57.

23. Sauvole to Pontchartrain, Biloxi, August 4, 1701, in Dunbar Rowland and Albert Godfrey Sanders, eds., *Mississippi Provincial Archives*, II, 9–18.

24. Paul du Ru, *Journal*, pp. 7–11. Gravier, p. 152.

25. Marcel Giraud, *Histoire de La Louisiane Française*, I, 38n.

26. Maurice Ries, "The Mississippi Fort Called Fort de la Boulaye," in *Louisiana Historical Quarterly*, XIX (1936), 841.

27. Du Ru, pp. 17–20; Crouse, *Iberville*, pp. 211–13.

28. Tonti to his brother, Fort de la Boulaye, March 4, 1700, in *Mid-America*, XXI (1939), 220–235; *Jesuit Relations*, LXV, 116–18; Margry, ed., V, 354–55.

29. Crouse, *Iberville*, pp. 213–14, 216–17.

30. *Ibid.*, p. 219.

31. *Ibid.*, pp. 220–21.

32. Wallace, p. 228; Murphy, pp. 92–93.

Chapter 15

1. N. M. Miller Surrey, *The Commerce of Louisiana During the French Regime, 1699-1763*, p. 310; Margry, ed., VI, 90–92.

2. André-Joseph Pénicaut, *Narrative,* edited and translated by Richebourg Gaillard McWilliams as *Fleur de Lys and Calumet,* pp. 33–37.

3. *Ibid.,* pp. 28–39.

4. *Ibid.,* p. 40.

5. *Ibid.,* pp. 40–41.

6. Margry, ed., V, 409.

7. *Collections of the Minnesota Historical Society,* I, 322–27; Le Sueur, "Journal," in Shea, ed., *Early Voyages,* pp. 930–55.

8. Pénicaut, p. 46; Le Sueur, pp. 96–100.

9. Pénicaut, pp. 47–48; Le Sueur, pp. 101–04.

10. *Collections of the Minnesota Historical Society,* I, 333; Le Sueur, pp. 102–04.

11. Pénicaut, p. 49.

12. Le Sueur, p. 103.

13. Pénicaut, pp. 53–59.

14. Surrey, p. 314; Margry, ed., V, 417-19.

15. Giraud, p. 46 and 46n.; Thomas Hughes, "The Site of Le Sueur's Fort L'Huillier" in *Collections of the Minnesota Historical Society,* XII, 283–85. See also Thomas Hughes, "Discovery of the Skeletons of Many Sioux Killed in War, Buried Near Fort L'Huillier," *ibid.,* 288–90.

Chapter 16

1. Gilbert J. Garraghan, *Chapters in Frontier History,* pp. 73–84.

2. *Ibid.*

3. *Ibid.,* p. 82.

4. *Ibid.,* p. 84. An illuminating study of Father Marest is John Francis Bannon, "Black-Robe Frontiersman: Gabriel Marest, S. J.," in *Bulletin,* Missouri Historical Society, X (1954), No. 3, 351–66.

5. See Gilbert J. Garraghan, "Earliest Settlements of the Illinois Country," in *Catholic Historical Review,* XV, 359, and Sister Mary Borgias Palm, *Jesuit Missions of the Illinois Country, 1763-1763,* p. 9ff.

6. James Fernando Ellis, *The Influence of Environment on the Settlement of Missouri,* pp. 1–21.

7. Membré, p. 179.

8. *Jesuit Relations,* LXVI, 225.

9. Victor Collot, *A Journey In North America,* I, 233–34.

10. Louis Houck, *A History of Missouri,* I, 32.

11. Ellis, p. 9.

12, Gravier, pp. 119-120.

13. A. P. Nasatir, ed., *Before Lewis and Clark*, I, 8–9.

14. *Ibid.*, 9–10.

15. Henri Folmer, "Etienne Veniard de Bourgmond in the Missouri Country," in *Missouri Historical Review*, XXXVI (1942), 282–83. The author confuses La Chenette with Bourgmond's Indian mistress. *See* Houck, *History of Missouri*, I, 258n. Bernard de Voto and most other historians confuse Alphonse de Tonti with Henri de Tonti in stating that the latter was temporary commander of Detroit. *See* Ida Amanda Johnson, *The Michigan Fur Trade*, p. 46.

16. Marc Villiers du Terrage, *Découverte du Missouri*, pp. 46ff.

17. Folmer, "Etienne Veniard de Bourgmond," XXXVI, 284.

18. Du Tisné to Bienville, November 22, 1719, in Margry, ed., VI, 313.

19. J. H. Scharman, *From Quebec to New Orleans*, pp. 191–92.

20. Bossu, p. 115.

21. [Antoine Simon] Le Page du Pratz, *Voyages aux Indies Occidentals*, II, 296–303.

22. Margry, ed., VI, 309–15.

23. Du Tisné to Bienville, November 22, 1719, in French, ed., pp. 151–52.

24. Diary of Valverde in A. B. Thomas, trans. and ed., *After Coronado*, p. 132.

25. A. B. Thomas, "Massacre of Villasur Expedition," in *Nebraska History*, VII (1924), No. 3, 68–71.

26. *Ibid.* *See* also "Unpublished Diary of Spanish Officer Found in the Field of Battle Gives Account of the March From Santa Fé," in *Nebraska History*, VI (1923), No. 1., 17.

27. Thomas, "Massacre of Villasur Expedition," VII, 78–79.

28. *Ibid.*, 80.

29. William E. Dunn, "Spanish Reaction Against the French Advance Toward New Mexico," in *Mississippi Valley Historical Review*, II (1915), 357.

30. *Ibid.*, 358.

31. P. F. X. Charlevoix, *Journal of a Voyage to North America*, II, 331.

Chapter 17

1. Villiers, *La Découverte du Missouri*, p. 79.

2. *Ibid.*

3. Margry, ed., VI, 388, 389ff.

4. Villiers, *La Découverte du Missouri*, pp. 88–91. Nasatir, ed., *Before Lewis and Clark*, I, 20.

5. Villiers, *La Découverte du Missouri*, pp. 80–81; Margry, VI, 388–91.

6. Houck, *History of Missouri*, I, 258.

7. Clarence W. Alvord, *The Illinois Country*, p. 156.

8. Lucian Carr, *Missouri*, p. 25n.

9. Justin Winsor, *The Mississippi Basin*, p. 141.

10. Bickford Davis, *Illustrated History of Missouri*, p. 116.

11. Villiers, *La Découverte du Missouri*, pp. 84–85. See also Garraghan, *Chapters in Frontier History*, pp. 85–93.

12. Villiers, *La Découverte du Missouri*, p. 88.

13. *Ibid.*, p. 96.

14. *Ibid.*, p. 104.

15. Gilbert J. Garraghan, "Fort Orleans of the Missoury," in *Missouri Historical Review*, XXXV (1941), 379–80; Villiers, *La Découverte du Missouri*, pp. 105ff.

16. Mathews, *The Osages*, p. 201.

17. Bourgmond's Journal in Margry, ed., VI, 398–449; M. F. Stipes, "Fort Orleans, the First French Post on the Missouri," in *Missouri Historical Review*, VIII (1914), 131.

18. Margry, ed., VI, 399–401; Stipes, VIII, 130.

19. *Ibid.*

20. Nasatir, ed., *Before Lewis and Clark*, I, 21–22; Marc Villiers du Terrage, "Le Massacre de L'Expedition du Missouri," in *Journal de la Société des Americanistes de Paris, Nouvelle Série–Tome XIII, Fasc.* II, 239–55.

21. Bossu, p. 83.

22. *Ibid.*, pp. 83–84.

23. *Ibid.*, p. 84.

24. Garraghan, "Fort Orleans," XXXV, 382.

Chapter 18

1. Dubisson to the Marquis de Vaudreuil, Detroit, June 15, 1712, in *Collections of the State Historical Society of Wisconsin*, XVI (1902), 269.

2. *Ibid.*

3. Francis Parkman, *A Half-Century of Conflict*, I, 272; *Collections of the State Historical Society of Wisconsin*, XVI, 270–71.

4. Parkman, *A Half-Century of Conflict*, I, 272-73.

5. *Collections of the State Historical Society of Wisconsin*, XVI, 274-75.

6. *Ibid.*, 275.

7. *Ibid.*, 275–76.

8. *Ibid.*, 276.

9. *Ibid.*, 277–78.

10. Parkman, *A Half-Century of Conflict*, I, 276–79.

11. *Ibid.*, pp. 284-85.

12. Ramezay and Bégon to the French Minister, September 13 and 16, 1715, in *Collections of the State Historical Society of Wisconsin*, XVI, 311–17.

13. Proceedings in French Council of Marine, March 28, 1716, *ibid.*, 338–40; Letters of Vaudreuil to Council of Marine, October 14, 1716, *ibid.*, 341–44.

14. *Ibid.*

15. Parkman, *A Half-Century of Conflict*, I, 324–25; Vaudreuil to the Minister, October 11, 1723, in *Collections of the State Historical Society of Wisconsin*, XVI, 433–39.

16. Lignery to Boisbriant, August 23, 1724, *ibid.*, 444–46.

17. Louise Phelps Kellogg, "Fort Beauharnois," in *Minnesota History*, VIII (1927), 233–36.

18. *Ibid.*, 236; "Memorandum About the Scioux," April 29, 1727, in *Collections of the State Historical Society of Wisconsin*, XVII (1906), 7–9.

19. Kellogg, "Fort Beauharnois," VIII, 237–38.

20. Not Francois Amariton, as Kellogg states, but Zacherie Robertel, Sieur La Noüe, who had succeeded him in the previous year.

21. Louis Ignatius Guignas, "Voyage Up the Mississippi" in Shea, ed., *Early Voyages*, pp. 171–72.

22. Kellogg, "Fort Beauharnois," VIII, 239–40; Guignas, pp. 172–73.

23. *Ibid.*, pp. 173–75.

24. *Ibid.*; Kellogg, "Fort Beauharnois, VIII, 240–41.

25. *Ibid.*, 241–42.

26. *See* Narrative of Boucherville in *Collections of the State Historical Society of Wisconsin*, XVII, 36–58.

27. *Ibid.*

28. Kellogg, "Fort Beauharnois," VIII, 243.

29. Parkman, *A Half-Century of Conflict*, I, 328-29; Beauharnois and Hacquart to the French minister, November 2, 1730, in *Collections of the State Historical Society of Wisconsin*, XVII, 109–113.

30. Cyrenus Cole, *A History of the People of Iowa*, p. 32.

31. *Ibid.*, p. 33; Luc François Nau in *Jesuit Relations*, LXVIII, 275–77.

32. Margry, ed., VI, 575–80; Cole, p. 33.

33. *Ibid.*, pp. 58–59. See also Peter Pond in *Collections of the State Historical Society of Wisconsin*, XVIII, 335.

Chapter 19

1. Glyndwr Williams, *The British Search for the Northwest Passage in the Eighteenth Century*, pp. xv, 1-30; Laurence J. Burpee, *The Search for the Western Sea*, I, xviii.

2. Nellis M. Crouse, *La Vérendrye, Fur Trader and Explorer*, pp. 17–33; Theodore C. Blegen, *The Land Lies Open*, p. 63.

3. Crouse, pp. 41–45; La Verendrye to Beauharnois, October 10, 1730 in Laurence J. Burpee, ed., *Journals and Letters of Pierre Gaultier de Varennes de la Vérendrye and His Sons*, pp. 43–63. Hereinafter cited as Burpee, ed., *Journals and Letters*.

4. *Ibid.*, pp. 53–54; John Bakeless, *The Eyes of Discovery*, p. 161.

5. La Vérendrye to Maurepas, Michilimackinac, August 1, 1731, in Burpee, ed., *Journals and Letters*, pp. 70–72; Crouse, *La Vérendrye*, pp. 58–59; Laurence J. Burpee, *Pathfinders of the Plains*, p. 28.

6. Crouse, pp. 60–61.

7. *Ibid.*, p. 61.

8. *Ibid.*, pp. 61–62; J. Murray Gibbon, ed., *Canadian Folk Songs: Old and New*.

9. *Ibid.*, pp. 105, 106–07.

10. Crouse, *La Vérendrye*, pp. 63–64; Blegen, *The Land Lies Open*, p. 64. See also Theodore C. Blegen, "Fort St. Charles and the Northwest Angle," in *Minnesota History*, XVIII (1937), 231–48.

11. Crouse, *La Vérendrye*, p. 64.

12. La Vérendrye to Maurepas, May 21, 1733, in Burpee, ed., *Journals and Letters*, pp. 95–102.

13. See La Vérendrye's Journal, 1733-34, *ibid.*, pp. 164–192.

14. Crouse, *La Vérendrye*, pp. 69–70; Burpee, *The Search For the Western Sea*, I, 244.

15. La Vérendrye's Journal, 1733-34, in Burpee, ed., *Journals and Letters*, pp. 178-86.

16. Beauharnois to Maurepas, October 8, 1734, *ibid.*, pp. 110–16; Harold A. Innis, *The Fur Trade in Canada*, p. 95.

17. Crouse, *La Vérendrye*, p. 102; see also Nellis M. Crouse, "The Location of Fort Maurepas," in *Canadian Historical Review*, IX (1928), 206–222.

18. Burpee, *Pathfinders,* pp. 36–37. Though often beautifully written, this work is highly romanticized and should be used with caution.

19. Burpee, *The Search for the Western Sea,* I, 247. See also Burpee, "The Lake of the Woods Tragedy," in *Proceedings and Transactions,* Royal Society of Canada, Series II, IX (1903), sec. 2, 15–28. Crouse, *La Vérendrye,* pp. 107–08.

20. *Ibid.,* p. 105.

21. Burpee, *The Search for the Western Sea,* I, 247–48; Innis, pp. 93–94, gives an economic interpretation for the massacre.

22. Crouse, *La Vérendrye,* p. 109.

23. *Ibid.,* p. 124.

24. *Ibid.,* p. 126.

25. Maurepas to Beauharnois, April 22, 1737, in Burpee, ed., *Journals and Letters,* pp. 269–70.

26. Beauharnois to Maurepas, October 1, 1738, *ibid.,* pp. 279–89.

27. Crouse, *La Vérendrye,* p. 131; Bakeless, *The Eyes of Discovery,* p. 164.

28. Crouse, *La Vérendrye,* pp. 137–38. A. S. Morton, *A History of the Canadian West to 1870-71,* p. 190, states that Fort La Reine was originally built twenty miles east of Portage La Prairie and that it was moved to the town a year after he established it. Crouse, *La Vérendrye,* p. 130, finds no record in his papers to support this theory.

29. Crouse, *La Vérendrye,* p. 139.

30. Burpee, *The Search for the Western Sea,* p. 250.

31. Crouse, *La Vérendrye,* pp. 142–46.

32. *Ibid.,* pp. 148–49; De Voto, p. 210.

33. Crouse, *La Vérendrye,* p. 151.

34. Burpee, *Pathfinders,* pp. 64–67; Bakeless, *The Eyes of Discovery,* pp. 168–69; Crouse, *La Vérendrye,* pp. 152–53.

35. Bakeless, *The Eyes of Discovery,* p. 170; Crouse, *La Vérendrye,* pp. 155–57, 160.

36. La Vérendrye's Journal in Burpee, ed., *Journals and Letters,* pp. 366–70.

37. Crouse, *La Vérendrye,* p. 192.

38. Relation of Louis-Joseph and his brother to Beauharnois, in Burpee, ed., *Journals and Letters,* pp. 406–32; Doane Robinson, "La Vérendrye's Farthest West," in *Proceedings,* State Historical Society of Wisconsin, 1913, pp. 146–50. *See* also the same author, "The Vérendrye Plate," in *Proceedings,* Mississippi Valley Historical Association, VII (1913-14), 244-53.

39. De Voto, pp. 216–17; Maurepas to Beauharnois, May 12, 1745, in Burpee, ed., *Journals and Letters,* pp. 459-61; Crouse, *La Vérendrye,* p. 209.

Chapter 20

1. Schlarman, pp. 204–05; Edwin C. McReynolds, *Missouri, A History of the Crossroads State,* pp. 16–17.
2. John E. Rothensteiner, *Earliest History of Mine La Motte,* pp. 205ff. See also Ida M. Schaaf, "The Founding of Ste. Genevieve, Missouri," in *Missouri Historical Review,* XXVII (1933), 145–46.
3. Houck, *History of Missouri,* I, 282–83; Gilbert J. Garraghan, "Some Highlights in Missouri History," in *St. Louis Catholic Historical Review,* III, 236.
4. Francis Joseph Yealy, *Sainte Genevieve, the Story of Missouri's Oldest Settlement,* pp. 11–23; Houck, *History of Missouri,* I, 338; Philip Pittman, *The Present State of the European Settlements on the Mississippi, . . .* pp. 95–96.
5. Charles E. Peterson, "Early St. Genevieve and Its Architecture," in *Missouri Historical Review,* XXXV (1941), 166–67.
6. *Missouri Historical Society Collections,* IV (1912), 166–67.
7. Peterson, XXXV, 212–13; Victor Collot, "A Journey in North America," in *Transactions,* Illinois State Historical Society, 1908, p. 294.
8. J. Manuel Espinosa, "Spanish Louisiana and the West: The Economic Significance of the Ste. Genevieve District," in *Missouri Historical Review,* XXXII (1932), 287–88.
9. *Ibid.,* 290.
10. Lawrence Kinniard, "American Penetration into Spanish Louisiana," in *New Spain and the Anglo-American West,* I, 222.
11. Houck, *History of Missouri,* I, 357–60.
12. *Ibid.,* 362–63.
13. J. Manuel Espinosa, XXXII, 294; James A. Gardner, "The Business Career of Moses Austin in Missouri, 1798-1821," in *Missouri Historical Review,* L (1956), 235–38; Ruby Swartzlow, "Early History of Lead Mining in Missouri," *ibid.,* XXVIII (1934), 184–94; E. M. Violette, *History of Missouri,* p. 45.

Chapter 21

1. Ellis, pp. 37–38; Surrey, p. 365.
2. Houck, *History of Missouri,* II, 4.

3. *Ibid.*, 5. Floyd C. Shoemaker, *Missouri and Missourians*, I, 90.

4. Auguste Chouteau, "Journal of the Founding of St. Louis," in *Missouri Historical Society Collections*, III (1911), 352.

5. *Ibid.*, 354.

6. *Ibid.*, 355–56.

7. *Ibid.*, 356–57.

8. Houck, *History of Missouri*, II, 17–18.

9. Instructions of Ulloa to Rui in *Missouri Historical Society Collections*, III, 145–52.

10. *Ibid.*, 145–69; Houck, *History of Missouri*, II, 19; *Missouri Historical Society Collections*, III, 269–74.

11. *Ibid.*, IV (1913), 176–77.

12. Houck, *History of Missouri*, II, 63–64; *Senate Executive Documents*, 26th Cong., 2nd Sess., No. 237, p. 83.

13. Jonas Viles, "Population and Extension of Settlement in Missouri Before 1804," in *Missouri Historical Review*, V (1911), 209–13; E. M. Violette, "Early Settlements in Missouri," *ibid.*, I (1906), 38–52; Ben L. Emmons, "The Founding of St. Charles and Blanchette, its Founder," *ibid.*, XVIII (1924), 507–20; Shoemaker, I, 95.

14. Reuben Gold Thwaites, ed., *Original Journal of the Lewis and Clark Expedition*, I, 18, 23–24.

15. S. Waterhouse in J. Thomas Scharf, *History of Saint Louis City and County*, I, 203–04.

16. *Ibid.*, 204; Frederic L. Billon, *Annals of St. Louis*, pp. 195–96.

17. Scharf, I, 204. Shoemaker, I, 92.

18. Theodore Calvin Pease, "The Revolution at Crisis in the West," in *Journal*, Illinois State Historical Society, XXIII (1931), 664–65; A. P. Nasatir, "The Anglo-Saxon Frontier in the Illinois Country During the American Revolution, *ibid.*, XXI (1929), 291–300; Caruso, *The Southern Frontier*, pp. 249–52.

19. James A. James, *George Rogers Clark*, p. 123; John Bakeless, *Background to Glory*, p. 112.

20. Patrick Henry to Governor of Cuba, October 18, 1777, in James A. James, "The Significance of the Attack on St. Louis," *Proceedings*, Mississippi Valley Historical Society (1908–09), p. 201.

21. Stella M. Drumm, "The British-Indian Attack on Pain Court (St. Louis)" in *Journal*, Illinois State Historical Society (1931), 642–46; Pease, XXXIII, 674–75; see also Sinclair to Haldimand, Mackinac, May 29, 1780, and same to same, July 8, 1780, in *Collections of the State Historical Society of Wisconsin*, XI (1888), 151–53, 155–57. See also Shoemaker, I, 95; and McReynolds, p. 23.

22. Pease, XXXIII, 674–75.

23. James, p. 207.

24. *Ibid.*

25. *Missouri Historical Society Collections*, IV, 179.

26. Drumm, XXXIII, 646.

27. *Missouri Historical Society Collections*, IV, 186.

28. *Ibid.*, 186–87.

29. *Ibid.*, 187.

30. Scharf, I, 209.

31. Sinclair to Haldimand, July 8, 1780, in *Collections of the State Historical Society of Wisconsin*, XI, 155–57.

32. James, pp. 207–08.

33. Billon, p. 205.

34. Instructions to Cruzat, New Orleans, July 25, 1780, in Louis Houck, *The Spanish Regime in Missouri*, I, 171–72.

35. Nasatir, "The Anglo-Saxon Frontier," XXI, 329.

36. Lawrence Kinniard, "The Spanish Expedition Against Fort St. Joseph in 1781, A New Interpretation," in *Mississippi Valley Historical Review*, II, 195–210; Nasatir, "The Anglo-Saxon Frontier," XXI, 343–48.

37. Clarence Walworth Alvord, "The Conquest of St. Joseph, Michigan, by the Spaniards in 1781," *Missouri Historical Review*, II, 195–210; Nasatir, "The Anglo-Saxon Frontier," XXI, 343–48.

38. *Ibid.*, 351.

39. *Ibid.*, 352–53.

40. Arthur Preston Whitaker, *The Spanish-American Frontier*, pp. 3–4.

41. Ogg, p. 417.

42. Quoted, *ibid.*, p. 426.

43. Quoted in Whitaker, p. 103.

44. Max Savelle, *George Morgan*, pp. 200–06, 210, 211.

45. *Ibid.*, p. 213; John Anthony Caruso, *The Appalachian Frontier*, pp. 331–32.

46. *Ibid.*, p. 331. For a description of the growth of New Madrid *see* Houck, *History of Missouri*, II, 133–35.

Chapter 22

1. Walter Robinson Smith, *Brief History of the Louisiana Territory*, pp. 74–75.

2. *American State Papers, Miscellaneous*, I, 346.

3. Charles Gayarré, *History of Louisiana, The Spanish Domination*, p. 624.

4. George W. Cable, *The Creoles of Louisiana*, p. 41n–42.

5. Henry Marie Brackenridge, *Views of Louisiana*, pp. 111–12. Brackenridge is contradicted by Peter Kalm, *Travels into North America*, III, 8–9, 32–33, who says that rheumatism and "pleurisies" were common among the Creoles. Venereal diseases were very common, and the Canadians were more susceptible to worms than were the New England colonists.

6. Charles Van Ravensswaay, "Creole Arts and Crafts of Upper Louisiana," in *Bulletin, Missouri Historical Society*, XII (1956), 214.

7. Collot, I, 247.

8. C. F. Volney, *View of the Soil and Climate of the United States of America*, p. 345.

9. Eugenie Berthold, *Glimpses of Creole Life in Old St. Louis*, pp. 7–8.

10. Schlarman, p. 334.

11. Houck, *History of Missouri*, II, 240, 242.

12. Norman W. Caldwell, *The French in the Mississippi Valley*, p. 17.

13. John W. Monett, *History of the Discovery and Settlement of the Valley of the Mississippi . . .* , I, 188–89; Ward A. Dorrance, *The Survival of French in the Old District of Sainte Genevieve*, pp. 19–20.

14. John Reynolds, *The Pioneer History of Illinois . . .* , pp. 51–52.

15. Dorrance, pp. 19–20.

16. Houck, *History of Missouri*, II, 269.

17. Ravensswaay, XII, 236–37.

18. Surrey, p. 310.

19. Dorrance, p. 27.

20. Peterson, "Early Ste. Genevieve and Its Architecture," XXXV, 217–18.

21. Dorrance, p. 15.

22. Peterson, "Early Ste. Genevieve and Its Architecture," XXXV, 219.

23. Charles E. Peterson, "French Houses of the Illinois Country, *Missouri Magazine*, X (1938), 10; Ravensswaay, XII, 222.

24. Henri M. Brackenridge, *Recollections of Persons and Places in the West*, p. 21.

25. Amos Stoddard, *Sketches, Historical and Descriptive, of Louisiana*, p. 328.

26. Ravensswaay, XII, 225.

27. *Ibid.*, 226–27.

28. *Ibid.*

29. Dorrance, pp. 18–19.

30. Clement Eaton, *A History of the Old South*, p. 196.

31. *Ibid.*, pp. 195–96.

32. Francis Parkman, *The Old Regime in Canada*, p. 329.

33. *Jesuit Relations*, XXVII, 99.

34. *Ibid.*, LXV, 245.

35. Caldwell, p. 52. In 1730 the standard price of a trip from Montreal to Mackinac was two hundred livres.

36. Hiram Martin Chittenden, *The American Fur Trade in the West*, I, 53–54.

37. John Bigsby, *Shoe and Canoe*, I, 133.

38. Grace Lee Nute, *The Voyageur*, p. 13.

39. *Ibid.*, p. 23.

40. *Ibid.*, pp. 25–26.

41. Peter Pond in *Collections of the State Historical Society of Wisconsin*, XVIII, 326.

42. Nute, *The Voyageur*, pp. 39–40.

43. *Ibid.*

44. *Ibid.*, p. 41.

Selected Bibliography

PRIMARY WORKS

Books

Adams, Arthur T., ed., *The Explorations of Pierre Esprit Radisson*. Minneapolis, 1961.
American State Papers, Indian Affairs. 2 vols. Washington, 1832–34.
American State Papers, Miscellaneous. 2 vols. Washington, 1834–35.
Bigsby, John J., *The Shoe and the Canoe*. 2 vols. London, 1850.
Billon, Frederic L., *Annals of St. Louis*. St. Louis, 1886.
Blair, Emma Helen, ed., *The Indian Tribes of the Upper Valley and Region of the Great Lakes*. 2 vols., Cleveland, 1911–12.
Bossu, Jean Bernard, *Travels in the Interior of North America*. 1751–1762. Translated and edited by Seymour Feiler. Norman, Oklahoma, 1962.
Brackenridge, Henry M., *Recollections of Persons and Places in the West*. Philadelphia, 1868.
———*Views of Louisiana*. Chicago, 1962.
Burpee, Lawrence J., ed., *Journals and Letters of Pierre Gaultier de Verennes de la Vérendrye and His Sons*. Toronto, 1927.
Catlin, George, *North American Indians*. 2 vols. Edinburgh, 1926.
Charlevoix, P. F. X., *Journal of a Voyage to North America*. Translated by Louise Phelps Kellogg. 2 vols. Chicago, 1932.
Collot, Victor, *A Journey in North America*. 2 vols. Paris, 1826.
Collections of the State Historical Society in London.
Delanglez, Jean, trans. and ed., *The Journal of Jean Cavelier*. Chicago, 1938.
Du Ru, Paul, *Journal*. Translated by Ruth L. Butler. Chicago, 1934.
French, B. F. ed., *Historical Collections of Louisiana*. New Orleans, 1852.

Hackett, C. W., ed., *Historical Documents Relating to New Mexico, Nueva Vizcaya, and Approaches Thereto, to 1773.* 2 vols., Washington, 1926.

Hamilton, Charles, ed., *The Cry of the Thunderbird.* New York, 1950.

Jones, William, *Ojibway Texts.* New York, 1919.

Joutel, Henri, *A Journal of La Salle's Last Voyage.* Edited by Darrett B. Rutman. New York, 1962.

Kalm, Peter, *Travels into North America.*

Kellogg, Louise Phelps, ed., *Early Narratives of the Northwest.* New York, 1917.

La Harpe, Bernard de, *Journal Historique de l'Établissment des Français à la Louisiane.* New Orleans, 1831.

La Vega, Garcilaso de, *The Florida of the Inca.* Translated by John Grier Varner and Jeanette Johnson Varner. Austin, Texas, 1951.

Le Page du Pratz, Antoine Simon, *Voyages aux Indies Occidentales.* Paris, 1771.

Leonard, I. A., trans. and ed., *The Spanish Approach to Pensacola, 1689–1693.* Albuquerque, New Mexico, 1939.

Margry, Pierre, ed., *Découvertes et Établissments des Français dans l'Ouest et dans le Sud d'Amérique Septentrionale, 1614–1698, memoires et documents inédits.* 6 vols. Paris, 1879.

Mason, Philip P. ed., *Schoolcraft's Expedition to Lake Itasca.* East Lansing, Michigan, 1958.

McWilliams, Richebourg Gailliard, ed. and trans., *Fleur de Lys and Calumet.* Baton Rouge, Louisiana, 1953.

Nasatir, A. P., ed., *Before Lewis and Clark.* 2 vols. St. Louis, 1952.

Nuttall, Thomas, *Journal of Travels Into the Arkansa Territory.* Cleveland, 1905.

Pénicaut, André, *Narrative, see* Richebourg Gaillard McWilliams.

Pittman, Philip, *The Present State of the European Settlements on the Mississippi.* Cleveland, 1906.

Radisson, Peter Esprit, *Voyages.* Edited by Gideon D. Scull. New York, 1943.

Rowland, Dunbar and Sanders, Albert Godfrey, eds., *Mississippi Provincial Archives.* 3 vols. Jackson, Mississippi, 1927–32.

Schoolcraft, Henry Rowe, *Summary Narrative of An Exploratory Expedition to the Sources of the Mississippi River in 1820.* Philadelphia, 1855.

Senate Executive Documents, 26th Congress, 2nd Session.

Shea, John Gilmary, ed., *Discovery and Exploration of the Mississippi Valley,* New York, 1852.

———, ed., *Early Voyages Up and Down the Mississippi.* Albany, 1861.

Stoddard, Amos, *Sketches, Historical and Descriptive, of Louisiana.* Philadelphia, 1812.

Thomas, A. B., ed. and trans., *After Coronado*. Norman, Oklahoma, 1935.
Thwaites, Reuben Gold, ed., *Jesuit Relations*. 73 vols. Cleveland, 1896–1901.
————, ed., *Original Journal of the Lewis and Clark Expedition*. 2 vols., New York, 1959.
Volney, C. F., *View of the Soil and Climate of the United States of America*. Philadelphia, 1804.
Williams, Mentor L., ed., *Schoolcraft's Indian Legends*. East Lansing, Michigan, 1956.

Articles, Journals, Newspapers and Monographs

"Carta de Don Damien Manzaret a Don Carlos de Siguenza sobre el Descubrimiento de la Bahia del Espiritu Santo." *Texas State Historical Association Quarterly*, II, 1899.
Chouteau, Auguste, "Journal of the Founding of St. Louis." Missouri Historical Society Collections, III, 1911.
Collot, Victor, "A Journey in North America," *Transactions of the Illinois State Historical Society*, 1908.
Dakota Friend. 1852.
Espinoza, Isidro Felis de, "Description of the Tejas or Asinai Indians, 1691–1722," *Southwestern Historical Quarterly*, XXXI. 1927. Translated by Mattie Austin Hatcher.
Forsyth, Thomas, "Account of the Manners and Customs of the Sauk and Fox Nations of Indians," *see* Emma Helen Blair, ed.
Leon, Alonso de, "Historia de Nuevo Leon . . ." in G. Garcia and C. Pereyra, ed., *Documents Ineditos o Muy Raros Para la Historia de Mexico*. 35 vols., Mexico City, 1905–11.
Marsh, Cutting, "Documents Relating to the Stockbridge Mission," *Collections of the State Historical Society of Wisconsin*, XV. 1900.
Marston, Morrell, "Letter to Reverend Dr. Jedidiah Morse," *see* Emma Helen Blair, ed.
Missionary Herald, 1838-1841.
Morfi, Juan Agustín de, *Excerpts From the Memorias for the History of the Province of Texas*. Appendix, prologue and notes by Fr. Frederick C. Chabot. (Privately printed, 1932.)
Neill, E.D., "Dakota Land and Dakota Life," in *Collections of the Minnesota Historical Society*, I. 1872.
Padilla, Juan Antonio, "Report of the Barbarous Indians of the Province of Texas," *Southwestern Historical Quarterly*, XXXV. 1919. Translated by Mattie Austin Hatcher.

Pond, Samuel William, "The Dakotas or Sioux in Minnesota as they were in 1834," *Collections of the Minnesota Historical Society*. XII. 1908.
Solis, Gaspar Jose de, "Diary of a Visit of Inspection to the Texas Mission," *Southwestern Historical Quarterly*, XXXV. 1931.
Tonti, Henri de, "Letters," *Mid-America*, XXI. 1939.

SECONDARY WORKS

Books

Alvord, Clarence Walforth, *The Illinois Country*. Springfield, Illinois, 1920.
Bakeless, John, *The Eyes of Discovery*. Philadelphia, 1950.
———, *Background to Glory*. Philadelphia, 1957.
Beltrami, J.C., *A Pilgrimage in America*. Chicago, 1962.
Berthold, Eugenie, *Glimpses of Creole Life in Old St. Louis*. St. Louis, 1933.
Blegen, Theodore C., *Building Minnesota*. New York, 1938.
———, *The Land Lies Open*. Minneapolis, 1949.
———, *Minnesota: A History of the State*. Minneapolis, 1963.
Brebner, J. Bartlet, *Canada: A Modern History*. Ann Arbor, Michigan, 1960.
Burpee, Lawrence J., *Pathfinders of the Great Plains*. Toronto, 1921.
———, *The Search for the Western Sea*. 2 vols. Toronto, 1935.
Butterfield, C. W., *History of the Discovery of the Northwest by John Nicolet in 1634*. Cincinnati, 1881.
Cable, George W., *The Creoles of Louisiana*. New York, 1889.
Caldwell, Norman Ward, *The French In the Mississippi Valley, 1740-1750*. Urbana, Illinois, 1941.
Campbell, T. J., *Pioneer Laymen of North America*. 2 vols. New York, 1915.
Carr, Lucian, *Missouri*. Boston, 1896.
Carter, Hodding, *Lower Mississippi*. New York, 1942.
Caruso, John Anthony, *The Appalachian Frontier*. Indianapolis and New York, 1959.
———, *The Great Lakes Frontier*. Indianapolis and New York, 1961.
———, *The Southern Frontier*. Indianapolis and New York, 1963.
Chesnel, Paul, *History of Cavelier de la Salle*. New York, 1932.
Cole, Cyrenus, *A History of the People of Iowa*. Cedar Rapids, Iowa, 1921.
Crane, Verner W., *The Southern Frontier*. Ann Arbor, Michigan, 1959.
Crouse, Nellis M., *La Vérendrye: Fur Trader and Explorer*. Ithaca, New York, 1956.

———, *Le Moyne d'Iberville, Soldier of New France.* Ithaca, New York, 1954.

Davis, Bickford, *Illustrated History of Missouri.*

Delanglez, Jean, *Hennepin's Description of Louisiana.* Chicago, 1941.

———, *Louis Jolliet, Vie et Voyages.* Montreal, 1950.

———, *Some La Salle Journeys.* Chicago, 1938.

Denig, Edwin Thompson, *Five Indian Tribes of the Upper Missouri.* Edited by John C. Ewers. Norman, Oklahoma, 1961.

De Voto, Bernard, *The Course of Empire.* Boston, 1952.

Dorrance, Ward A., *The Survival of French In the Old District of Sainte Genevieve.* Columbia, Missouri, 1935.

Driver, Harold E., *Indians of North America.* Chicago, 1961.

Dunn, William Edward, *Spanish and French Rivalry in the Gulf Region of the United States.* Austin, Texas, 1917.

Eaton, Clement, *A History of the Old South.* New York, 1949.

Ellis, James Fernando, *The Influence of Environment on the Settlement of Missouri.* St. Louis, 1929.

Folmer, Henry, *Franco-Spanish Rivalry in North America.* Glendale, California, 1953.

Folwell, William Watts, *A History of Minnesota.* 4 vols. St. Paul, 1956.

Foster, J. W., *The Mississippi Valley.* London, 1869.

Frazer, James George, *The Native Races of America.* London, 1939.

Gaither, Frances, *The Fatal River.* New York, 1931.

Garraghan, Gilbert J., *Chapters in Frontier History.* Milwaukee, 1934.

Gayarré, Charles, *History of Louisiana, The Spanish Domination.* New York, 1854.

Gibbon, J. Murray, *Canadian Folk Songs: Old and New.* New York, 1927.

Giraud, Marcel, *Histoire de Louisiane Française.* 2 vols. Paris, 1953.

Groulx, Lionel, *Notre Grande Aventure.* Montreal, 1957.

Hagan, William T., *The Sac and Fox Indians.* Norman, Oklahoma, 1958.

Hamilton, Peter, *Colonial Mobile.* Boston, 1897.

Harrington, M. B., *Certain Caddo Sites in Arkansas.* New York, 1920.

Havighurst, Walter, *Upper Mississippi.* New York, 1944.

Hodge, Frederick Webb, ed., *Handbook of American Indians North of Mexico.* 2 parts. Washington, 1910.

Hoffman, W. J., *The Mede' Wiwin or "Grand Medicine Society" of the Ojibwa.* Washington, 1891.

Houck, Louis, *The Spanish Regime in Missouri.* 2 vols. Chicago, 1910.

———, *A History of Missouri.* 2 vols. Chicago, 1908.

Hyde, George E., *Indians of the Woodlands.* Norman, Oklahoma, 1962.

Innis, Harold A., *The Fur Trade in Canada*. New Haven, 1930.

James, James A., *The Life of George Rogers Clark*. Chicago, 1928.

Johnson, Boyd W., *The Arkansas Frontier*. n.p. 1957.

Johnson, Ida Amanda, *The Michigan Fur Trade*. Lansing, Michigan, 1919.

Kohl, J. G., *Kitchi-Gami*. Minneapolis, 1956.

Lanctot, Gustave, *A History of Canada*. Cambridge, 1963.

Laubin, Reginald and Gladys, *The Indian Tipi*. Norman, Oklahoma, 1957.

Mathews, John Joseph, *The Osages*. Norman, Oklahoma, 1961.

———, *Wah'Kon-Tah*. Norman, Oklahoma, 1932.

McCaleb, Walter F., *Spanish Missions of Texas*. San Antonio, 1961.

McReynolds, Edwin C., *Missouri, A History of the Crossroads State*. Norman, Oklahoma, 1962.

Monett, John W., *History of the Discovery and Settlement of the Mississippi. . . .* 2 vols. New York, 1846.

Morton, A. S., *A History of the Canadian West to 1870-1871*.

Morton, W. L., *The Kingdom of Canada*. Toronto, 1963.

Murphy, Edmund Robert, *Henry de Tonti*. Baltimore, 1941.

Newcomb, W. W., *The Indians of Texas*. Austin, Texas, 1961.

Nute, Grace Lee, *Caesars of the Wilderness*. New York, 1943.

———, *Lake Superior*. Indianapolis, 1944.

———, *The Voyageur*. St. Paul, 1955.

Ogg, Frederic Austin, *The Opening of the Mississippi*. New York, 1904.

Palm, Mary Borgias, *Jesuit Missions of the Illinois Country*.

Parkes, Henry Bamford, *The American Experience*. New York, 1947.

Parkman, Francis, *A Half-Century of Conflict*. 2 vols. Boston, 1893.

———, *La Salle and the Discovery of the Great West*. Boston, 1919.

———, *The Old Regime in Canada*. Boston, 1891.

Petersen, William J., *Iowa: The Rivers of Her Valleys*. Iowa City, 1941.

———, *Steamboating On the Upper Mississippi: The Waterway to Iowa*. Iowa City, Iowa, 1937.

Reynolds, John, *The Pioneer History of Illinois*.

Rich, E. E., *Hudson's Bay Company*. 2 vols. New York, 1960.

Rothensteiner, John E., *Earliest History of Mine La Motte*.

Sandoz, Mari, *The Buffalo Hunters*. New York, 1954.

———, *These Were the Sioux*. New York, 1961.

Savelle, Max, *George Morgan: Colony Builder*. New York, 1932.

Saxon, Lyle, *Father Mississippi*. New York, 1927.

Scharf, J. Thomas, *History of Saint Louis City and County*. 2 vols. Philadelphia, 1883.

Schlarman, J. H., *From Quebec to New Orleans*. Belleville, Illinois, 1930.

Shoemaker, Floyd Calvin, *Missouri and Missourians.* 5 vols. Chicago, 1943.

Smith, Walter Robinson, *Brief History of the Louisiana Territory.* St. Louis, 1904.

Steck, Francis Borgia, *Jolliet-Marquette Expedition.* Quincy, Illinois, 1928.

Surrey, N. M. Miller, *The Commerce of Louisiana During the French Regime, 1699-1763.* New York, 1916.

Swanton, John R., *The Indian Tribes of North America.* Washington, 1952.

Turner, Frederick Jackson, *The Frontier in American History.* New York, 1920.

Twain, Mark, *Life on the Mississippi.* New York, 1923.

Vestel, Stanley, *King of the Fur Traders.* Boston, 1940.

Villiers du Terrage, Marc, *La Decouverte du Missouri et L'Histoire du Fort d'Orleans.* Paris, 1925.

Violette, E. M., *A History of Missouri.* n.p., 1960.

Wallace, Joseph, *The History of Illinois and Louisiana Under French Rule.* Cincinnati, 1893.

Whitaker, Arthur Preston, *The Spanish-American Frontier.* Boston, 1927.

Williams, Glyndwr, *The British Search for the Northwest Passage in the Eighteenth Century.* London, 1962.

Winchell, N. H., *The Aborigines of Minnesota.* St. Paul, 1911.

Winsor, Justin, *The Mississippi Basin.* Boston, 1895.

Wright, Muriel H., *A Guide to the Indian Tribes of Oklahoma.* Norman, Oklahoma, 1951.

Yealy, Francis Joseph, *Sainte Genevieve: The Story of Missouri's Oldest Settlement.* Sainte Genevieve, 1935.

Articles and Monographs

Albrecht, A. C., "The Origin and Settlement of Baton Rouge, Louisiana" in *Louisiana Historical Quarterly,* XXVIII (1945).

Alvord, Clarence Walworth, "The Conquest of St. Joseph, Michigan, By the Spaniards in 1781," in *Missouri Historical Review,* II (1908).

Bannon, John Francis, "Black-Robe Frontiersman: Gabriel Marest, S.J., in *Bulletin* Missouri Historical Society, X (1954).

Boston, Herbert Eugene, "The Location of La Salle's Colony On the Gulf of Mexico," in *Mississippi Valley Historical Review,* II (1915).

Briggs, John Ely, "The Sacs and Foxes" in *The Palimpsest,* IX (1928).

Burpee, Lawrence J., "The Lake of the Woods Tragedy," in *Proceedings and Transactions,* Royal Society of Canada, IX (1903).

Calhoun, Robert Dabley, "The Taënsa Indians," in *Louisiana Historical Quarterly*, XVII (1934).

Campbell, Walter S., "The Plains Indian in Literature—and in Life," in James F. Willard and Colin B. Goodykoontz, eds., *The Trans-Mississippi West*. Boulder, Colorado, 1930.

Coopwood, Bethel, "Notes on the History of La Bahía del Espíritu Santo," in *Texas Historical Association Quarterly*, II (1899).

Crouse, Nellis M., "The Location of Fort Maurepas," in *Canadian Historical Review*, IX (1928).

Densmore, Frances, *Chippewa Customs*. Washington, 1929.

Dorsey, George A., "The Ponca Sun Dance," in *Publications*, Field Museum of Natural History, VII. Chicago, 1905.

Drumm, Stella M., "The British-Indian Attack on Pain Court (St. Louis)" in *Journal of the Illinois State Historical Society*, XXIII (1931).

Dunn, William E., "Spanish Reaction Against the French Advance Toward New Mexico," in *Mississippi Valley Historical Review*, II (1915).

Edwards, Everett E., "American Indian Contribution to Civilization" in *Minnesota History* XV (1934).

Emmons, Ben L., "The Founding of St. Charles, and Blanchette, Its Founder," in *Missouri Historical Review*, XVIII (1924).

Espinosa, J. Manuel, "Spanish Louisiana and the West: The Economic Significance of the Genevieve District," in *Missouri Historical Review*, XXXII (1932).

Favrot, H. Mortimer, "Colonial Forts of Louisiana," in Louisiana *Historical Quarterly*, XXVI (1945).

Folmer, Henri, "Etienne Veniard de Bourgmond in the Missouri Country," in *Missouri Historical Review*, XXXVI (1942).

Gale, Edward C., "The Radisson Manuscript," in *Minnesota History*, VII (1926).

Gardner, James A., "The Business Career of Moses Austin in Missouri, 1798-1821," in *Missouri Historical Review*, L (1956).

Garraghan, Gilbert J., "Earliest Settlements of the Illinois Country," in *St. Louis Catholic Historical Review*, XV.

———, "Fort Orleans of the Missoury," in *Missouri Historical Review*, XXXV (1941).

———, "Some Highlights in Missouri History," in *St. Louis Catholic Historical Review*, III.

Gilfillan, Joseph A., "The Ojibways in Minnesota," in *Minnesota Historical Society Collections*, IX (1898-1900).

Glover, William B., "A History of the Caddo Indians," in *Louisiana Historical Quarterly*, XVIII (1935).

Holand, Hjalmar R., "Radisson's Two Western Voyages," in *Minnesota History*, XV (1934).

Hornaday, William T., "The Extermination of the American Bison," in *Annual Report*, United States National Museum. Washington, 1887.

James, James Alton, "The Significance of the Attack on St. Louis" in *Proceedings*, Mississippi Valley Historical Association (1908–09).

Kellogg, Louise Phelps, "Fort Beauharnois," in *Minnesota History*, VIII (1927).

Kinniard, Lawrence, "American Penetration into Spanish Louisiana," in *New Spain and the Anglo-American West*.

——, "The Spanish Expedition Against Fort St. Joseph in 1781," in *Mississippi Valley Historical Review*, II (1915).

La Flesche, Francis, "The Osage Tribe," in *Annual Report*, Bureau of American Ethnology. Washington, 1921.

——, "War Ceremony and Peace Ceremony of the Osage Indians," in *Bulletin*, Bureau of American Ethnology. Washington, 1939.

Lynd, James W., "History of the Dakotas," in *Collections of the Minnesota Historical Society*, II, Part II (1881).

——, "The Religion of the Dakotas," in *Collections of the Minnesota Historical Society*, II, Part II (1881).

McGee, W. J., "The Siouan Indians," in *Annual Report*, Bureau of American Ethnology. Washington, 1893-94.

Nasatir, A. P., "The Anglo-Saxon Frontier in the Illinois Country During the American Revolution," in *Journal of the Illinois State Historical Society*, XXI (1929).

Nute, Grace Lee, "The Radisson Problem," in *Minnesota History*, XIII (1932).

——, "Father Hennepin's Later Years," in *Minnesota History* XIX (1938).

Nydahl, Theodore L., "The Pipestone Quarry and the Indians" in *Minnesota History*, XXXI (1931).

Parsons, Elsie Clews, "Notes on the Caddo," in *Memoirs of the American Anthropological Association*, No. 57. Menasha, Wisconsin, 1941.

Pease, Theodore Calvin, "The Revolution at Crisis in the West," in *Journal of the Illinois State Historical Society*, XXIII.

Peterson, Charles E., "Early Ste. Genevieve and Its Architecture," in *Missouri Historical Review*, XXXV (1941).

413

————, "French Houses of the Illinois Country," *Missouri Magazine*, X (1938).

Rebok, Horace M., "The Last of the Mus-Qua-Kies," in *Iowa Historical Record*, XVII (1901).

Ries, Maurice, "The Mississippi Fort Called Fort de la Boulaye," in *Louisiana Historical Quarterly*, XIX (1936).

Riggs, S. R., "Dakota Grammar, Texts, and Ethnology," in *North American Ethnology* (1881).

Robinson, Doane, "La Vérendrye's Farthest West," in *Proceedings*, State Historical Society of Wisconsin (1913).

————, "The Vérendrye Plate," in *Proceedings*, Mississippi Valley Historical Association, VII (1913-14).

Schaaf, Ida M., "The Founding of Ste. Genevieve, Missouri," in *Missouri Historical Review*, XXVII (1933).

Stipes, M. F., "Fort Orleans, the First French Post on the Missouri," in *Missouri Historical Review*, VIII (1914).

Swanton, John R., "The Indians of the Southeastern United States," in *Bulletin*, Bureau of American Ethnology. Washington, 1946.

————, "Source Material on the History and Ethnology of the Caddo Indians," in *Bulletin*, Bureau of American Ethnology. Washington, 1942.

Swartzlow, Ruby, "Early History of Lead Mining in Missouri," in *Missouri Historical Review*, XXVIII (1934).

Thomas, A. B., "Massacre of Villasur Expedition," in *Nebraska History*, VII (1924).

Van Ravenswaay, Charles, "Creole Arts and Crafts of Upper Louisiana," in *Bulletin*, Missouri Historical Society, XII (1956).

Viles, Jonas, "Population and Extension of Settlement in Missouri Before 1804," in *Missouri Historical Review*, V (1911).

Villiers du Terrage, Marc, *"Le Massacre de l'Expédition du Missouri,"* in *Journal de la Société des Américanistes de Paris, Nouvelle Série, Tome XIII.*

Violette, E. M., "Early Settlements in Missouri," in *Missouri Historical Review*, I (1906).

Warren, William W., "History of the Ojibways," in *Minnesota Historical Society Collections*, V (1885).

West, Elizabeth H., "De Leon's Expedition of 1689," in *Texas Historical Association Quarterly*, VIII (1905).

Williams, Frank E., "The Geography of the Mississippi Valley," in *The Annals*, American Academy of Political and Social Science, CXXXV (1928).

414

Index

415

Chaponga, Jean Baptiste, 244
Charles II, King of England, 126,
128, 146-147, 202
Charles II, King of Spain, enlists
support of James II, 225; 227
Charles III, King of Spain, 333, 345
Charlevoix (Jesuit missionary), 266
de la Chassaigne, Jean Bouillet, 298
de Champlain, Samuel (founder of
Quebec, Governor of New
France), 116-118, 120-121, 124
Chateaubriand, François, 12
de Châteaumorant, Joubert, Marquis,
229-230
Cheyenne Indians, 316
Chicago, 347
Chicagou, Chief, 275
Chickasaw Indians, 112, 176, 234;
and slave trade, 238
"China Sea," 124
Chippewa Indians, 1-4, 13; origins,
37; and Sioux, 37-38, 43, 241;
women, 38-39, 41, 44; child
rearing, 41, 43-44, 46; cere-
monies, 45; marriage, 47; 50,
119, 135, 145, 147, 150, 197
Clark, George Rogers, 337, 338, 341;
and defense of St. Louis, 344,
345, 349
Clark, William, 55
Cody, William (Buffalo Bill), 12
Colbert, Jean-Baptiste, Marquis of
Seignelay, son of Colbert, 180
Colbert, Jean-Baptiste, Minister of
France, 149, 154, 159; and La
Salle, 161, 180
Colapissa Indians, 112, 234
Comanche Indians, 211, 258; and
Tisne, 261-262; 268-269, and

Bourgmond, 272-274; treaty
with French, 275; 304
Company of New France, *see* Hundred Associates
de Conti, Prince, 163
Cooper, James Fenimore, 12
de Cosme, Jean François Buisson,
243
coureurs de bois, 124, 150, 162, 164,
167, 198
Coxe, Dr. Daniel, grant of Carolina
by Charles II, 227, 235
Cree Indians, and Radisson, 134-
135, 145-146 and Sioux, 142,
144-145; and La Vérendrye,
297, 303-306, 308, 310
Creoles, 358-360; description, 361-
362; and Americans, 360; and
Indians, 361; and Negroes, 362;
dress, 362-364; housing, 365-
368; food, 368-369; trade, 369-
371
Crouse, Nellis M., 308
Crow Indians, 304, 316
Crozat, Antoine, 256, 258
Cruzat, Francisco, 336, 346; expedition against British, 347-349

Dablon, Father Claude, 150-152,
155-157
Dakota Indians, 335
Daumont, Simon François, Sieur de
Saint-Lusson (soldier of for-
tune), 151
Davis, Bickford, 270
Delanglez, Jean (Jesuit historian),
185-186
Delor de Treget, Clement, 334

417

Groseilliers, Sieur des, Médart Chouard, 124, 128-130; the Superior Voyage, 131; 147; and Hudson's Bay, 147

Haldimand, General Frederick, 339
Havighurst, Walter, 5
Hennepin, Father Louis (explorer with La Salle), 145, 161, 164-166, 168; biography, 183; 184-187; prisoner of Sioux, 187-196; with Duluth, 196-199; 228
Henry, Alexander, 375
Hesse, Captain Emanual, 340
Hiawatha, 2-3, 11, 29, 39-40
Holand, Hjalmar R., 130
Houck, Louis, 253, 270, 328
Houma Indians, 112, 231-233, 238
Hudson Bay, 128, 131, 371
Hudson's Bay Company, founding of, 147; 295
Hundred Associates, The (Company of New France), 116-118, 123, 362, 369
Huron, Lake, 117-118
Huron Indians, 118-121; and fur trade, 123-124, 147; and Iroquois, 123-124; and Radisson, 126-127, 129; and Ottawas, 139; and Sioux, 151, 154; and Foxes, 279; and Detroit, 279-285; and French, 291
Hyde, George E., 87

Iberville, Pierre Lemoyne, Sieur de, 220, 228-233, 236-238; and Indians, 238, 251
Illinois Indians, 83, 84, 120; and Marquette and Jolliet, 156, 157; and Iroquois, 156, 165; and La Salle, 165, 173; massacred by Iroquois, 170-171; and Sioux, 188; and Le Sueur, 243; defense of Detroit, 281-285
Iroquois Indians, 2, 123-124; and French, 128, 220, 279; and Nicolet, 117; and Radisson, 127, 132; and fur trade, 131; and La Salle, 160, 173, 179; and Frontenac, 160; massacre of Illinois, 170-171; and de Tonti, 180
Itaska, Lake, 1-2

Jay, John, 351
Jefferson, Thomas, 352, 357
Jesuits, 124, 128, 131, 132, 149-150, 154, 167, 217, 238, 251, 334, 370
Jolliet, Louis, 6, 152, 159, 154-157, 161
Joutel, Henri, 93, 95, 97, 206-209, 213, 215-220

Kansas Indians, origins, 69; and Bourgmond, 258, 272-274
Kaskaskia, 252, 319, 320, 322, 331, 338, 352
Keokuk, Algonkian chief, 60
Kickapoo Indians, 14, 174; and French, 291
King Philip's War, 173
Kinniard, Lawrence, 347
Kiowa Indians, 304
Knight, Captain James, 296

La Chesnaye, Aubert de, 180
Laclede Liguest, Pierre, 327-328, 331, 337

Date Due

1-6 70		
FE 14		
FE 02 '89		
FE 16 '89		

Demco 38-297